The Complete Basic Book of
HOME DECORATING

THE COMPLETE BASIC BOOK

OF

Home Decorating

EDITED BY
WILLIAM E. HAGUE

DOUBLEDAY & COMPANY, INC.

Garden City, New York

CONTENTS

Part Three: IDEAS FOR EVERY AREA OF THE HOME

The "Living" Look • Bathroom Lighting •
Easy Decorating Ideas

Part Four: SPECIAL DECORATION

PREFACE

THERE HAS probably been more written on decorating than any other subject of homemaking. Much of it is mumbo jumbo. Books and magazine articles usually take one of two roads: they stress the lofty, aesthetic approach with words like "flair," "taste" and "ambiance" bandied about carelessly or they take the lower "nuts-and-bolts" tack, namely, that decoration is simply a matter of putting ingredients together, like baking a cake. As in most endeavors, the successful, sensible approach lies somewhere between these extremes. There is no doubt that in the hands of a few, truly gifted designers decoration can be an art form. For the rest of us, it remains a craft, and a craft can be learned. It will be the aim of this book to explore, with you, all the ramifications of this craft with the hope that, once its principles are understood, you can bring your own personality into play and arrive at an environment that expresses you and your family, if you have one, in a distinctive, attractive and comfortable way.

And let's be candid: In today's fast and often bewildering pace, personal environment is perhaps more important than at any other previous time. Every person, every family longs for a refuge, a place to feel really "at home," a place for solace and also for enjoyment with friends. And for most of us, it isn't enough to say that appearances don't count. Whether we like it or not, we live in a sophisticated age that demands that we be aware of the homemaking amenities. We *do* care what our friends and neighbors think of the way we live and not in a superficial, status-conscious sort of way. It is simply a matter of wanting others to know that we are aware of our culture, part of the scene, as it were. We also know that a compatible environment helps to make us better, more understanding, more fulfilled and fulfilling human beings. An interesting-looking house or apartment sparks our imagination. It makes a growing child brighter, more alert. It makes for more rewarding family relationships. It makes entertaining more stimulating to hosts and guests. Whether we like it or not, our home, partially at least, expresses us to the world. And that is a large and important order.

THE STUMBLING BLOCKS TO DECORATING

Fancied ignorance is a stumbling block. Women and men about to embark on the adventure of amateur decorating feel that they know absolutely nothing about the subject when, in fact, they may know a great deal. For example, a woman who dresses in perfect taste and who instinctively knows what is right for her husband to wear on any given occasion often goes to pieces when confronted with "doing over" the living room. If she would call on the same instincts in choice of color and pattern, fabrics and rugs a lot of her fears would evaporate.

Still another stumbling block to a wholesome approach to decorating is the ever-present budget. Here, a sense of balance is helpful. A woman who may spend two hundred dollars for a dress may balk at spending the same amount for a chair. Now, the chair will be expected to last indefinitely, while the dress will be useful for only a season or two. There is no logic here. What is the answer? Simply that when you are embarking on a decorating project, you must change your thinking, set up a whole different kind of budget. You must prepare yourself and your family to spend in a different way, to spend more and for long-term quality and comfort rather than short-term pleasure. If you analyze your budget fearlessly and find that you can't afford to do the room or the whole house right, then you must wait until you have accumulated enough. That immediately removes the money nightmare that may ensue otherwise.

At any given period in time when you contemplate a decorating project there will be current styles, fads, so-called "in" colors and patterns, new materials and an array of choice in the market place that is absolutely staggering. When walking into the home-furnishings department of a store, many just throw up their hands when faced with this array. How, they ask themselves, can they ever choose anything that is the best buy, that is right now and will be right five or ten years from now? If there are twenty or thirty major choices for their living room, will they be able to live with all or most of them in a month or a year or five years, or will they berate themselves every time they look at that wall of expensive draperies that were the wrong choice? We all know that living with self-inflicted mistakes eats away at our self-esteem to a degree that is harmful to us and our associates. How can we avoid all or most of such bad choices?

How to Overcome the Stumbling Blocks

A good question and the answer to this and the other stumbling blocks we have discussed is the same: with study and careful planning. And that is exactly where this book comes into play. When you choose that yardage of drapery fabric, you will *know*, after studying the decorating principles explained in these pages, that your choice was right. You will know something about the correct fiber, what color will blend with a predetermined scheme, what pattern will balance others in that room, what style of drapery treatment is correct with your room plan. You will be able not only to live with your choice, but also to take pride in it. You will know how to call on your own personal reservoir of knowledge gleaned from observation and to add this to certain rules and come up with a highly personal expression in a room. You will have a better idea of how to spend money wisely, because each step in the decorating process is planned. For example, if you decide to splurge on an Oriental rug, you will be able to live with a lower priced upholstery fabric. Knowledge, in short, will take the fear out of your project and free you for the enjoyment of the adventure.

And, believe us, it is an exciting adventure. There is nothing more satisfying in homemaking than watching a room or a house blossom from drab to colorful. Armed with information, the market place becomes a treasure trove rather than a fright. Deciding which of a hundred lamps is the one for your need is suddenly a joyful challenge. And when it comes to mistakes—and, mind you, even the most talented professional designers make them—they won't get you down. Remember, the same style factors that work for automobiles and mechanical equipment are rapidly coming into play in home furnishings. You don't have to be "stuck" with anything in your home. Unlike the couples who went to housekeeping thirty years ago expecting to end up with the same furniture for their sunset years, today's homemakers want and expect to change the look of their homes, as their needs grow, as their tastes change, as their wish for a new environmental image develops. You will want to keep some things, since they were chosen with knowledge and care and because they are familiar friends, but you will be able to build on them for your new look. You will plan all over again and with the same relish.

How to Use This Book as a Permanent Reference

This decorating book, unlike many others, was planned to serve as a timeless compendium, a digest of basic information on every decorating subject. For the rank amateur, a study of all its pages would serve, in a sense, as a course in decoration. For the more experienced, it can serve as a source on a given subject. For example, if you need draperies in the master bedroom, you can turn to the sections on window treatment and bedrooms and find help. Use it much as you would use, say, a cookbook or a guide to etiquette. Turn to the index and go with your immediate problem from there. We hope that each page will be an adventure into the fascinating subject of decoration and also a way to a more enriching life. So remember, the more imagination you exert on your home, the more interesting you and your life style will be.

W.E.H.

PART ONE

The Basics

CHAPTER ONE

PLANNING

THE FIRST STEP in any successful venture is a plan. Otherwise you just flounder and end up with a mess or, when you finally get onto the track, you find you've spent time and money far beyond what was required. Now, you may say, that's all well and good, but when you know little or nothing about decorating how can you possibly plan anything? The answer is that you may know more than you think. When you plan your wardrobe for a given season, when you plan a picnic or a dinner party, you follow certain procedures in a logical fashion. The same principle applies in decoration. First think the matter through, then start a list. It is amazing how thoughts crystallize when something is written down. Such a list should include a bit of philosophy: Namely, what do you want this room, or house or apartment to express? What life style, what pattern of living do you hope to follow in the space that confronts you? What are the practical requirements involved? For example, who will use the space, how many and how old? What kind of entertaining will the room or rooms have to serve? And, importantly, how much money can you afford to spend on the project? Get all this down on paper as a starter.

ONE ROOM OR A WHOLE HOUSE?

Obviously, the planning process becomes more complicated as the scope of your project increases. It is simpler to co-ordinate one room than a whole house or apartment. If you are decorating one room in an otherwise finished home, you must make a choice. Either this room must blend in some way with what is already decorated or else it will stand out like a sore thumb. You cannot go off on a completely different tangent without running the risk of visual chaos. There is one exception, perhaps—the bedroom which is a private sanctum and off limits to guests, so if disparity doesn't offend you, it is permissible. However, remember, most of us do not have the luxury of great space today so that if you create a totally different effect in a bedroom from that in the other rooms of a house or apartment, there is a loss in serenity. It will be jarring, for example, to move from a French country living room to a Victorian bedroom. So rather than find solace in your bedroom, you may experience a bit of shock each time. So the rule is: Continue in the vein you have already established. Refine the style, of course, but stick with the underlying idea. That is, if it still appeals to you.

If it doesn't, then you may have decided that the new room is to be the beginning of a whole new look which will be applied to other rooms as you can afford to do them over in the future. That way, you have a completely different ball game. Say, you are planning a new living room that is to be the beginning of an English eighteenth-century look for the whole house, then you study that style thoroughly and proceed without too much regard for what exists in the rest of the house. For the sake of economy, however, if you have just painted the walls and woodwork throughout the house, it is practical to develop a color scheme for the new living room with a thought to eventual co-ordination. The same goes for a fixed investment in a new carpet. Chances are, you liked the color of the paint or carpet, so work your new room with them. Of course, if you have always been uncomfortable with wall paint or carpet installed sometime ago, and you can afford to make a totally fresh beginning, then plan from scratch.

WORKING WITH WHAT YOU HAVE

As in most projects, you build on something that exists rather than have a room emerge full-blown, like Eve from Adam's rib. Even the most confirmed bachelor has a few treasured possessions he wants to keep and display as part of the decor of a new home. So whether we're talking about a few paintings and a lamp or fifteen pieces of furniture for that new room, the rule is the same: Be as realistic with your possessions as your budget and your emotions can afford. In other words, use this decorating project as an opportunity to shed burdensome and unwanted objects. Throw them out after making an honest decision as to their monetary and sentimental values. Remember, one of the great pluses of decorating or redecorating is that it is a cleansing and purifying process. It is as atavistic as making a new nest, with all the hope and excitement that come from a new beginning. So don't get bogged down with the remnants of the past because of a bit of Scots blood. Get rid of the junk. You'll feel so much better.

What objects remain after your fearless evaluation go onto your list as items to build on for your new room. In later chapters you'll understand what to do to bring these into line with a new decorating scheme—a new frame for a picture, an upholstery or slipcover job for that sofa or chair, a fresh paint finish for a chest of drawers. If you have a collection of brown and white Staffordshire or Rose Medallion you will find a way of making it a focal point of the room through an inventive display technique. What you retain is precious to you and it is just this kind of treasured belonging that gives a room character. Favorite objects personalize a room more effectively than anything else you can add. One collection, one fine piece of furniture, one good painting can literally "make" a successful room.

THE RELATIONSHIP OF ARCHITECTURE AND DECORATION

Another matter your plan will have to include bears on the architecture of the space you're dealing with. If you have built a new house or bought an older one in French Provincial style, you have already made a choice. The same for contemporary or Early American or whatever. Whether you like it or not, and hopefully you do, you're more or less involved for the duration. So be careful as you buy or build: Make sure you understand and like the architectural style in question. Because, for a successful over-all result, you must decorate the interior in a compatible way. You can create an Early American setting inside a contemporary structure, but it will be discordant. Better to plan a basically contemporary scheme, leavened with a few Early American pieces of furniture as accents. With Early American farmhouse, or Federal or Colonial architecture, you can mix traditional styles fairly easily with a few exceptions. High Victorian or Mission will look strange in a Colonial house; Oriental will look odd in Federal, while it will blend well in contemporary. Eighteenth-century English decor is fine in Colonial or Federal, but looks a bit curious in a Victorian gingerbread or a steamboat Gothic house.

When it comes to apartment decoration, you need not be so bound. Older apartments with small-paned windows, heavy moldings, and ornate mantels can be interesting foils for contemporary furniture, provided that these architectural details are erased with paint. Much of success in decorating depends on what a person is conditioned to accept visually. There is something impermanent about an apartment, so one can accept a greater degree of difference in furnishings and background. In fact, many striking contemporary apartments are arranged in older houses turned into apartments and in older apartment buildings, with the Victorian architectural details painted in white, against which bold colors are dramatically played.

Another aspect of the relationship of decoration and architecture is the dichotomy stressed by contemporary-minded architects who are openly against efforts to "decorate" their structures. They feel that the architecture should be paramount, that decor is essentially nonfunctional frills that detract from the effect of the structural detailing. Granted that too much surface decoration can be meaningless and even harmful, the same can be said for too little. To an architect a house may be a "machine for living," as Le Corbusier termed it, but to the homemaker it must be much more. It must be a refuge and a comfort, and this includes the familiarity that personal possessions can bring. In short, architectural design and interior design must be worked hand-in-glove for the truly satisfying home. If one is spared, the other is spoiled.

COST AND DESIGN: ARRIVING AT A BALANCE

What is it worth to have a given room or a whole house look the way you want it? That's really the crux of the matter here. It's not difficult to spend a great deal of money on one room, or even one piece of fine furniture or one painting. Luckily, there is a broad choice in all the components of decoration in all price ranges—low, medium, and high. So the important thing is to set a budget for each project and search the market for the items that fit your over-all plan in the price range you've chosen. If you want to splurge on one thing, go ahead. A special accessory like a more expensive lamp, painting, or an Oriental rug will add extra excitement to your room and can be an investment for the future. However, sticking to your budget and choosing fabrics, rugs, and furniture in your set price range will give a more even look over-all and will give you the satisfaction of knowing that you haven't gone overboard.

We are fortunate today that top design doesn't necessarily mean top price. For example, classics like the Parsons table can be found in the dime store; excellent reproductions of Early American are abundant in stores that sell relatively inexpensive furniture. Posters that reproduce the great masterpieces of the world's art can be found in almost every shopping area and, framed inexpensively, can bring great distinction to a room. If your budget is on the high side your decorative cup runneth over, so to speak. You'll have to use even more discipline than if it were low or medium, because the wealth of choice is so great. There's one word of caution if money happens to be no object: Be sure that you invest wisely. And we use the word "invest" advisedly. Because if your over-all plan is low budget, you can easily get rid of your belongings when you move up in the monetary ladder. If you're already up, you're more apt to cling to things because they were costly in the beginning, even though they may have been mistakes. So if you're spending heavily, make as certain as you can that you are investing. Buy good paintings, well-made upholstered furniture, classic contemporary or antique pieces, the best-designed lamps. Make yourself something of an expert about each element in your scheme and get sound advice—from professional designers, art galleries, antiques dealers—before you buy. Buy slowly and from a pre-established plan.

How to Develop a Foolproof Plan for Each Room

Every part of the decorating process seems to come back to planning; there's no way around it. For the beginner, suffice it to say that this discussion of a plan will become more meaningful after having progressed through the book further. However, for now, it will be helpful to study the work sheet shown here. You may want to add to it or subtract from it, but the rudiments of a successful plan are here and, primarily, it is of enormous benefit just to get something down on paper as a starter; the work sheet will help to marshal your thoughts. If you're doing a whole house or apartment, simply set a color scheme that is to run throughout and be sure the work sheet for each room implements it. Set an over-all budget and be certain the sum total of all the separate work sheets adds up to it. The work sheets for each room will then constitute your entire home plan.

Sample Work Sheet

Type of Room (living, dining, etc.):
Function (who will use, when, how?):
Size:
Light or Dark (north, south, etc. exposure):
Basic Color Scheme (main colors plus accents, number of windows):
Backgrounds: Walls (color)
               Floor (type of material—carpet, tile, etc. and color)
               Windows (type of treatment—drapery, Venetian
                     blinds, shades, etc. and color)
               Ceiling (color, light fixture, etc.)
Period of Decor (contemporary, traditional, a mix):
Pattern (in rug, carpet, drapery and upholstery fabric):
Pieces of Furniture: List each piece required for room function
Room Focal Point (such as fireplace, windows, a piece of furniture, built in):
Furniture Arrangement: Attach plan worked on graph paper
Lighting (built-in, portable lamps):
Accessories (types, colors, location):
Budget:
Breakdown (from items above): Paint or wallpaper .... $oo.oo
                                  Furniture ....
                                  Area rugs or carpet ....
                                  Lamps ....
                                  Accessories ....
                                  Drapery and other fabric ..
                                  Total .... $oo.oo

CHAPTER TWO

THE BACKGROUND

IN A CERTAIN SENSE, a home is like a stage set. It is the background against which family living with all its fun, its real life drama, its trials and tribulations are played. So just as the stage designer creates backgrounds to extend certain moods, to enhance the message of the playwright, the home decorator must create a backdrop for living. And make no mistake—the background is vital to a successfully designed room. It is the beginning, the first step in the decorating process and it can make or break whatever follows. To convince yourself of this, imagine a room with only painted ceiling, papered walls, carpet, and draperied window wall. It has no furniture, no lamps, no personal objects, and yet the room already "speaks." It says something. You know already, for example, whether it is in the traditional or contemporary style; you know whether it is in a light, airy mood or a somber, serious one; you know whether the color scheme is pleasing or jarring. In short, it is already on the way toward being a place for living rather than just four bare walls, floor and ceiling.

As an example of the importance of a background, professional interior designers are often called on to do only the backgrounds of model apartments. It is amazing how a skillfully planned background, without a stick of furniture, can stimulate the prospective tenant's imagination, whereas a series of plastered walls summon up little response. In fact, the lack of furniture and accessories stimulates the imagination on what kind of pieces would complete the mood the designer has set. As a house or apartment hunter browses through the rooms, he or she becomes intrigued with the thought of finishing what the designer began. The background has "sold" the house or apartment.

One dominant painting can establish the background of a whole room, as seen in this contemporary setting where elongated flower forms in the painting restate the design of gooseneck lamps.

How to Set the Stage

To start off on the right foot, you must decide on the basic style of the room. This is true because certain treatments are prescribed for certain styles; they are sure-fire ways of arriving at a correct scheme. For example, if you want an Early American living room, you have these choices, among others: for walls—white plaster or paint, pine paneling or a documentary wallpaper (which is, of course, a copy of a paper found in an antique house of the period); for floors—wood planks, pegged or plain, braided rugs, Oriental rugs for a more formal effect, old brick or any of the new vinyls that simulate brick or wood; for windows—a documentary fabric, either matching the wallpaper or blending with it, or simple, natural linen or other homespun-looking fabric; for the ceiling—white plaster, with or without exposed wood beams; and for the small room you want to look larger, paper in the same documentary pattern as the walls.

Let's see how this works for a different period style. For example, contemporary. A sound scheme can be done this way: for walls—white paint, either flat or the glossy "wet" look or supergraphics with swirls of primary colors painted over the basic white background, or silver mylar paper for a shimmering, sophisticated look; for floors—quarry tile, dark or very light-stained wood, vinyl tile in a solid expanse of light or dark color, or wall-to-wall carpet, preferably textured; for windows—an architectural solution with vertical Venetian-type shades, shutters or the simplest traverse drapery in a light, neutral tone; for the ceiling—white paint.

For ideas on the various kinds of correct backgrounds, study model rooms in department stores, magazine photographs of room settings. For special effects with traditional styles like French country, eighteenth-century English, Mediterranean, or American Colonial, books found in the public library, period rooms in museums, or historic houses open to the public can be of enormous help. They'll have authentic details that can be scaled down and adapted to today's materials. For example, an antique paneled wall can be approximated with plywood and moldings; old brick flooring can be simulated with vinyl brick.

Since the background areas—walls, floor, ceiling—are the largest expanses in a room, the color and pattern applied to them are especially important in setting the mood. In the following chapters you'll learn how to use color and pattern to set a mood, how color works with orientation—how a room relates to natural light and the path of the sun—and what tricks can be played with color to make backgrounds seemingly recede or approach and make space appear larger or smaller. For visual drama, contrast becomes necessary. For example, if walls are light, a dark floor with a brilliantly patterned rug will make a room vibrate, or, conversely, if the floor is wall-to-wall carpet in a light neutral color, drama will come with walls in a vivid color or in a highly figured paper. When it comes to orientation, be mindful that north light is cold, south and west light, hot, east light is morning light and cool. Therefore, walls are better in a warm color in rooms facing north and east, and better in a cool color if they face south and west. That is unless you are deliberately seeking a somber mood. Then simply reverse the rule. There will be more detail on this in Chapter Three, but it is necessary to think of it with reference to background.

THE PRACTICAL ASPECTS

Stylistic considerations are not the only ones when it comes to setting a background. Your walls and especially your floors must be practical as well. Walls that are soil resistant are important in all rooms, but vital in baths, kitchens, family rooms, and children's quarters. We'll take up the various kinds of surfacing when we come to a discussion of decoration for individual rooms. For now, we'll just say that wipeable, washable surfaces are the watchword. However, even for formal rooms like the living and dining rooms, there are vinyl wallpapers, prefinished paneling, and other surfaces that can give the most elegant appearance without any sacrifice of practicality. When it comes to painted walls, the acrylic and rubber-base paints can literally be scrubbed clean over and over again. For rooms where fabric-covered walls are desired, be sure the fabric is Scotchgarded or otherwise factory-treated for stain resistance. To sum up, the background is the decorative "skin" of the room and it must be as functional as it is aesthetic. It must "do" certain predetermined things in your overall scheme and it must do them in a practical way. Now, let's take up the three main elements of background—ceilings, floors, walls—in detail.

CEILINGS

For years the ceiling was the stepchild of decoration. It was usually surfaced in an inexpensive calcimine paint in an off-white tone, given a nondescript light fixture and that was that. Today, eyes are looking up, as it were, and with ceilings at a standard eight-foot height in most new construction, it has become important to handle the ceiling carefully. Treated much lighter than side walls, it seems to look more lofty; treated in dark color or patterned paper, it can make a tiny room seem more an entity and therefore larger. The eight-foot ceiling, given a lighted cove around its perimeter, seems infinitely airier at night.

Tenting is a clever way of covering a multitude of sins overhead. In this old French house, cracked ceilings were simply erased with a striped floral cotton which continues down over some walls. Woven rattan chair seats pick up the same pattern for background unity.

The open-beamed, or cathedral, ceiling also used extensively in new houses permits a much roomier feeling and can go either contemporary or traditional in style. For a true Early American, French country, rural English, or other provincial traditional styles, the open-beamed ceiling is a must, and this can be attained with actual supporting ceiling joists or with applied, false beams—either stained wood or the new styrofoam plastic that simulates antique wood so well that it is hard to tell the difference without lifting one. Between these real or false beams, white painted plaster or provincially patterned wallpaper will underscore the period look.

And don't forget what a chandelier can do to dramatize a ceiling. The ceiling fixture is a sure-fire way to underscore period style; for example, a black iron design for a provincial room, a crystal chandelier for a dazzling addition to a formal, traditional dining or living room, an eight-branch brass-ball-type chandelier for a Colonial Williamsburg look. In the contemporary room, a good way to add importance and greater ceiling height to the standard eight-foot apartment is to mirror the ceiling. In the traditional room, change of pattern and scale of wallpaper can give an interesting effect; for example, in a garden room, use a strong floral for walls and a trellis design for ceiling, or in a bedroom, use a plaid paper for the ceiling with a stripe for walls. If a room has painted walls, add verve with a bold paper for the ceiling. Available now, too, are a number of textured plastic designs which permit you to simulate a coffered ceiling, an anaglyph design and other treatments that set a formal traditional theme.

FLOORS

The various types of floor coverings will be taken up in a subsequent chapter. Here, it is important to study the floor in a general way as a contributor to background. And make no mistake: The floor that we take for granted as something merely to walk on, something that must be first and foremost practical, can also add enormously to the mood of a room. The eye instinctively goes to the floor first on entering a room; it is a reflex action for the security of the step. Therefore, what is on the floor can make or break the decorative scheme at the outset.

Given the basic wood floor—usually oak strip or oak block—you can treat it to establish your traditional, contemporary, or transitional theme. If you stain the floor dark, it adds to one feeling; if light, to another. If you leave the bare wood, you arrive at an almost monastic scheme and have to rely heavily on pattern and color in other areas of the room to offset the bareness. If you want a rug or rugs over the wood, they can help stamp room style. An Oriental will automatically give a traditional effect; if used with strongly contemporary furniture, it will give an eclectic "mix." Moroccan, Indian, and other rugs in a "today" pattern will help achieve a contemporary look. A boldly patterned rug must necessarily minimize the use of pattern in other parts of the background; otherwise you end up with a jarring effect. Breaking up a floor expanse with a lot of rugs tends to make

One end of a formal, transitional dining room is a forest panorama, thanks to a highly patterned cotton fabric which covers walls and hinged doors of a storage closet. The adjacent mirrored wall doubles the effect. Table is an interesting combination of marquetry top on chrome steel sawhorses. Venetian chairs are velvet-covered.

the space seem smaller, while a solid color room-size rug makes it look larger. Oval, free-form, polygonal, and other odd shapes of rugs jog the balance decoratively and must be handled skillfully or they detract from other furnishings. Deep-piled and heavily sculptured rugs give an immediate sense of luxurious envelopment and should be reserved for the drawing room or other formal room with an opulent look.

If you bypass the wood floor entirely, you can go the wall-to-wall carpet route. This can help to set a contemporary theme, especially in a light, solid color. If the carpet is patterned, a period motif will reinforce a traditionally decorated room, a modern geometric design will add to a contemporary effect. Either way, a wall-to-wall carpet will help to make a room look larger. It also adds a rich, plushy feeling underfoot if the pile is deep and this is especially comforting in a bedroom. Thick carpet is also sound deadening because it absorbs sound, voice noises as well as footsteps. All this adds to background effect.

There are still other ways with floors as a contributor to background. For example, masonry in the form of brick, ceramic tile, slate or marble gives very definite effects to different areas of a home. Antique brick for a country house living room or kitchen gives mellow, old-fashioned warmth; marble tile adds elegance to a foyer or bath; quarry or other ceramic tile is practical for a family room, kitchen or bath. For the most part, these masonry solutions are used with a traditional room plan, but not necessarily so. Depending on the color, texture and pattern of the marble or tile, they can be just as successfully employed in a contemporary scheme. And, of course, area rugs can be used over them to underscore any desired decorative effect.

Walls

Most important to the background of a room are the walls. They cover the largest area of all rooms and so make a major contribution as background for furniture, accessories and other decorating components. In considering your walls, be guided by your decoration plan, your budget, the condition of the walls (a prime element in an older home), and the care and maintenance that they will require.

Today the most commonly used wall coverings are paint, paneling, wallpaper and masonry. Increasing in popularity are laminated and vinyl wall coverings. Interior walls can also be of structural materials, the stone, wood, brick, and various kinds of masonry that with glass are usually associated with exterior walls. These materials are especially favored for informal rooms or homes in contemporary designs because architects like to relate the outdoors to the interior. One way to do this is by using "earthy" materials.

Paint

The old stand-by paint continues to be a relatively inexpensive wall treatment that usually can be handled by budget-conscious householders on a do-it-yourself basis. It is quick and easy to apply, and many types, including rubber bases and alkyds, are easy to wash. Be sure to check a reliable paint dealer for the type of finish most suited to your purpose. This will be determined by variables such as the location of the room, the structural material and condition of the walls, etc. A flat finish is generally recommended for walls and ceilings of the family room and study, with semigloss suggested for the woodwork.

Among the latest developments in paint is a product particularly suited to the family room, a flat paint which is guaranteed washable for eight years. Painted walls, incidentally, should be dusted frequently and occasionally washed with a mild detergent solution. When choosing your paint colors, remember that dark colors tend to advance and make a room look smaller, while light ones, which tend to recede, make it look larger. A big area of wall color will appear quite different from a color chip, and, as walls reflect each other, the color will be intensified. Ceilings are generally neglected areas, although usually painted. They are expected to reflect light, and in most modern homes it has become common to paint them white or a light tint of the wall color. However, in a room with an annoying high ceiling, a dark color will "lower" the effect. Instead of paint, it might be wise to consider acoustical tiles for the family room, which will be filled with music, conversation, etc.

Paneling

A step up financially, but widely acclaimed for the family room or den, is wood paneling. This durable, rich, and warm treatment is suitable for almost any area that is not exposed to excessive moisture. The color, texture, and pattern of the woods used for paneling, including, most familiarly, pine, maple, walnut, oak and birch, answer a need for beauty in a natural form. Sometimes a study may have the walls covered in wood. The same treatment in the usually larger family room means greater expense, of course, so here paneling may be limited to one wall, as an accent, and paint used for the others. Paneling can be of solid wood planks (the most expensive), plywood (medium range), or hardboard paneling of wood chips (relatively low). Paneling makes an effective foil for furnishings of nonwood materials, i.e., plastics, fabrics, or metals. If price is no object, you might like to cover your walls with exotic patterns of rosewood, teak, or zebrawood plywood. These cost more than, say, pine or cherry, because these woods are not readily available.

In the long run, in spite of the initial expense, you probably will be extremely satisfied with the intimate room that is sheathed in this natural form, not only because of its psychological and visual appeal but because the maintenance is reduced to a very occasional waxing. Relatively low-priced surfaces can be painted or stained to almost any color if your choice of wall covering has been dictated not so much by aesthetic considerations but as a practical cover-up for poor structural walls.

Wallpaper

The wide range of finishes, textures, colors, patterns, and special effects in wallpapers almost defies classification. Although papers come at many price levels and wallpaper has a long and romantic history, until quite recently it was out of favor, decoratively speaking. Now, once again, it is beginning to be appreciated for its many advantageous qualities. Among them are the warmth and interest it gives to walls as well as the camouflage it offers irregular architectural room features or wall defects. The strippable paper, a new development, has removed a former disadvantage which, aside from its minor place in home fashion trends, had made householders reluctant to use paper. Previously, when three or four layers of covering had been put on the walls, they had to be removed before repapering. Although an amateur could do this, it was an annoyingly slow and messy process, so that professionals with steam equipment were hired and another expense added to the family's budget. Now with the strippables, papers are chemically formulated so that wall covering can be released from its adhesive. This means an entire strip can be zipped off the wall without any wetting.

Wallpaper can be divided into three general types: nonwashable, washable, and scrubbable. Forget about the first for the family room or study. It is too fragile and impractical for consideration. Concentrate on the washables and scrubbables. Washables can be subdivided into two further categories. There are those which have a protective coating so that a damp cloth will remove dust. Even more practical are those which can be washed with a mild soap and water.

And, finally, there are the scrubbables. These are papers with a highly protective finish, usually plastic, that makes them quite resistant to scrubbing and the removal of spots and stains. They are good

An excellent example of how fabric can create almost the entire backdrop in a room: An intricate, yet subdued floral covers walls, serves as drapery and lines the platform and backrest of the low, built-in seating arrangement. Small-figured print for foam rubber sofa base is a strong foil, as in the animal hide rug.

for rooms frequented by the youngsters, rooms where there is grease in the air from cooking, etc. Even more durable are fabrics, such as lightweight canvas, impregnated with a coating that lets them withstand repeated washings. In choosing any of these wallpaper types, be sure to read the hanging instructions provided by the manufacturer and use the proper adhesive. There are papers available with a chemical paste on the back that require no adhesive. You merely dip them into water before applying to the wall. In addition to wallpapers per se, there are vinyls, both nonwoven and vinyl-treated fabrics. Vinyls are a fairly recent development which offer a wall covering that is durable and easy to maintain, resistant to stains, fading, and peeling, and kept clean with a mild detergent. Lightweight vinyls, steadily gaining in popularity, are as easy to hang as real papers, if you use the correct adhesive. Check, too, on potential strippability. This may involve a lining paper. Properly hung vinyls can be stripped off in a single sheet if a corner is loosened, giving them another plus for the renter or temporary house occupant. A word of caution on vinyls is in order here. Be sure you use a strippable vinyl in the first place, because another wallpaper of whatever kind will not adhere to a vinyl surface, except with very special and hard-to-find mastic which is used to adhere metal surfaces.

As a general rule of thumb when choosing a wall covering, select a design according to the size of the room. Small-scaled patterns are best for small rooms; large bold patterns are most suitable for big rooms, as they call attention to the walls. The theme of the design and color tones must blend with the decoration of the room. But in a small room, for example, you might want to create a dramatic effect by using a mural or a large-scaled pattern on one wall.

In addition to obvious patterns there are subtle textured-surface effects that imitate bamboo, grass, brick, or fabric. These slightly textured patterns provide a good background for furnishings and form a family room. Another "quiet" effect comes from the selection of subtle tone-on-tone colors or medium-colored solids. Remember that if your wall is in poor shape and you cover it with a rough surface it will collect dust and grime and will need frequent care. A slightly textured paper is easier to keep clean, but if it doesn't give you the camouflage needed to conceal irregularities, perhaps wallpaper isn't the best choice for you.

Other Wall Coverings

If you are remodeling, for really poor walls consider a laminated sheath. You are no doubt familiar with this material, so often used for countertops in kitchens. Laminates, made of bonded layers of various materials with resins and other plastics, result in substances extremely useful too for wall surfaces.

These materials are still quite expensive for walls, when compared to paint and wallpaper. However, their permanence and easy-care features can make them most desirable, especially for children's rooms, kitchens, and family rooms. Laminated surfaces are durable and resist stains. A wipe with a damp cloth is all that is needed to keep up their attractive appearance. New techniques in the process can produce almost any desired effect. There are wood grains and marbleized patterns and styles and finishes that resemble leather, linen, even driftwood. In addition, there are novelty textures and treatments that make no effort to copycat natural materials but highlight the unusual.

And remember, fabrics are not limited to draperies and upholstery. They can climb the walls, too. Long popular for this application have been burlap, canvas, felt, and grass cloth, and now there is a pile fabric made especially for this purpose. Some of these fabrics come with adhesive backings so that the amateur can easily install them; the new synthetic must be cemented to the wall. Rusticity and textural interest make all of them appropriate for informal rooms. An attractive scheme is to upholster a sofa or a pair of chairs with a printed fabric and then repeat it on one wall. This adds warmth and interest to the room. Aside from the adhesive-backed fabrics, methods of installation include stretching the fabric by tacking to the wall, top, and bottom, pasting it directly to the wall, or tacking it on frames. It is best to use a closely woven material, as fabric-covered walls tend to sag. Although these jobs can be handled by the do-it-yourselfer, because of the cost of the materials and the fact that installation can be a tricky business, the fabric-covered wall is most satisfactory when it is the work of a professional. Somewhat surprisingly, it is often done by an upholsterer, rather than a paper hanger. Other wall choices include ceramic tile, excellent for bathrooms, laundries, and kitchens; carpet in rooms where sound conditioning is important, and mirrors where seeming space enlargement is desired.

The Glass Wall

When an emphasis on the indoor-outdoor relationship of rooms became important in the early 1950s, the glass wall came into prominence. First, it was associated with the contemporary-designed room, but later as large panels became available with traditional mullions, the period room partook of the glass expanse too. Where there is a view—of a skyline, of a garden, of a forest—the glass wall creates an automatic panorama that can be breathtaking and give a room an aliveness that can be achieved in no other way. At a stroke, it adds all the background pattern that a room may need; it provides an intimacy with nature, and it is a sure-fire way to make any space seem larger. The disadvantages that may occur to you can be overcome: insulating glass makes the wall as thermal as any other; the black void that comes at night can be alleviated with clever outdoor lighting that gives a soft glow, dramatizes a piece of sculpture or highlights the pattern of a tree.

CHAPTER THREE

COLOR

TRY TO IMAGINE A CITY, a house, a room without color and you begin to realize its importance in our lives. In a sense, there is no home planning without color; it is the cornerstone of decoration. We are fortunate to live in a day when color for our homes is abundant and inexpensive, because there was a time when, aside from the beauties of nature, color was possible only for the wealthy. Dyes were costly and rare; the world of color was centered in the panoply of the court or the temple. In the Middle Ages, interior color to millions of people was limited to the stained-glass windows of their cathedral. Today, of course, natural dyes have given way to chemicals and there is no nuance of the color spectrum that cannot be simulated in a fabulous array of objects. In the last ten years, marvelous colors in almost every mutation have appeared in every element of decoration, from the smallest accessory to the largest expanse of window drapery or carpet.

In fact, color in itself has become our most plentiful and inexpensive decorating tool. What, for example, can give a room the immediate lift of a budget coat of paint? A few sofa pillows, new lamp shades, well-placed bouquets—any of these if chosen as part of a preplanned color scheme can provide an immediate and refreshing change of pace. A visit to a department store surrounds us with a tantalizing array of color. Where towels, tablecloths, and bed linens were once white, they are now found in the most exotic shades—plain, striped, or patterned. The salesman of upholstered furniture presents binder after binder of colorful fabrics from which to choose. In the drapery department you are engulfed in a sea of fabrics, one more colorfully appealing than the next, while at the paint counter you can leaf through stacks of color chip books. It is an embarrass-

ment of riches that serves to emphasize the fact that we live in a be-
wilderingly colorful world.

It is perhaps because color has become so ubiquitous and important
in our lives that it is approached by so many women with fear and
trepidation. Everyone feels the need to belong, intimately, to this
world of color, and because the range of choice is so wide, the amateur decorator is understandably confused and uncertain. She knows
that a color scheme is basic and will underlie all future decoration
planning. Much of the investment in upholstered furniture, carpets,
and draperies will impinge on color and therefore it is realized that a
serious mistake in color can be costly. Then, too, everyone knows
that colors stimulate emotional reactions, that living indefinitely with
the wrong color or combination of colors can be disastrous to family
harmony.

Taking the Fear Out of Color

Because of this concern of making the wrong color choice, many
women settle for a "safe" color scheme rather than an interesting one.
They accept blandness when they could surround themselves with
drama and excitement, and this is as unfortunate as it is needless. For,
like all fears, the fear of color disappears with understanding, and
there are many means to this end.

The first is what we might call educated instinct. It is amazing how
many women who instinctively choose the right hat or suit go completely to pieces when it comes to deciding on colors for the living
room. It may help them to remember that everyone is naturally
drawn to certain colors that are flattering. Usually there is a harmony
in these tones: They go well together. For example, blondes often
prefer pastel blues and pinks; brunettes, rich greens and reds; red-
heads gravitate to spice tones like beiges and oranges. Rely on the
same instinct that gives emotional comfort in clothes. It can also allow
you to choose acceptable colors for the home with which you can
live happily.

Analyzing these color preferences and then studying the mutations
that are possible in each is a first, sure step to success. As we go along,
you will see how color values diametrically opposed to the basic
scheme can be used on accents. And so from instinct a complete interplay of colors evolves.

As a corollary to this approach, it helps to ask yourself what color or colors you positively dislike. Usually there is at least one you can't abide and two or three you can take or leave. Again, this helps to center attention on the area of possible choice and gives confidence.

Another way to overcome fear is to remember the old adage, in unity there is strength. Sound out the members of your family; discover their color preferences. Often a blend of family favorites will help you to arrive at a harmonious scheme. This approach is especially important for rooms which the whole family will use—the living and dining rooms and the family room, or informal living area. Of course, when it comes to decorating a study for your husband or rooms for your children, it is axiomatic that their color preferences be taken into account. Children, even quite small ones, have an intuitive sense about color that many a parent can learn from. They have not yet known fear and their color attitude is bold and bright.

SELECTING A COLOR SCHEME

In the drama of decorating, the basic color scheme might be compared to the main actors in a play, the accent colors to the bit players who serve as foils to the principals. As with the successful play, there are no rules about how many principals there must be. You may have a one-man show, a monochrome, in which the room is made up of many shades of one basic color. However, a monochromatic scheme is usually best left to the professional designer; essentially a tour de force, it is difficult to bring off and often more difficult to live with. And, incidentally, it is well to point out here that anything can be done with color in the home, providing the designer, amateur or professional knows what he or she is about. It is undisciplined lack of knowledge and training that spells trouble.

The most successful color scheme usually consists of two to four colors and one or two unrelated hues that play the vitalizing role of accent. The principal colors should be among those usually regarded as being compatible. Often one color is chosen as a neutral—beige or gray or white—for use as a background in expanses of walls or carpet. At other times with equal success the background color can be a lighter shade, a pastel, of one of the three main tones.

How are these all-important basic colors selected? Well, there are many sources of inspiration. There may be groups of colors to which you have always been drawn. For example, there are many women who have always wanted a blue and green living room or a pink and gray bedroom which represent color combinations they have seen and felt comfortable with. Then there are trend colors, combinations that are in current vogue, usually set by leading interior designers. While this is not the best approach, mainly because such color fads are apt to go out as quickly as they came in, it is at least a means of experiencing what certain colors look like together.

For a more enduringly pleasurable scheme, nature is a reservoir of ideas. Flowers, fruit, vegetables, the plumage of birds all reveal the unfailing hand of nature in creating color harmony. There is not a better way to see firsthand the blending of colors than in a flower shop or in a food store. A dollar's worth of fresh fruit and vegetables can be taken home and arranged in endless combinations until the right one is found. Or go to your florist and buy random blooms you are drawn to. Then create groupings at home. Many a lovely room has been built around the delicate shades of a single iris or the brilliance of a bowl of anemones. In your nature studies, don't overlook the leaves and stems which are part of nature's faultless palette. One woman we know created a strikingly fresh scheme for a sitting room from the plumage of her parakeet, building the effect around a brilliant blue, green, and yellow chintz with the identical hues of the bird's feathers.

As another source of a scheme, we all have favorite paintings, either ones we own or the work of masters we have admired. The painter is perhaps the greatest of all color specialists; he has an instinctive flair for putting colors together. Most often the painter combines a few main colors in his composition, and these can form the basis of a successfully decorated room. You may not particularly like the subject matter of the painting; it may not be anything with which you would want to live, even as a framed print, but as a source of color it may serve you in excellent stead. If you are drawn to a painting, buy a reproduction, take it home, and study the relationship of the colors. If you already own an oil painting or a water color or a print, it can form the basis of your scheme and at the same time hang on the wall of the room as a talisman.

Still another approach to a color scheme is to use a fabric, wallpaper, or a rug as the basis of your room plan. This is a method used by most professional designers. They will take a printed fabric which has several colors and draw from it for their effect. An Oriental rug is an excellent starting point, especially for a traditional room, while for a contemporary effect, one of the new woven rugs from Spain, India, or Morocco forms an ideal springboard. Like the painting on the wall, the rug itself remains as the decorative focal point of the room, around which its colors are assembled in draperies, walls, upholstered furniture, and accessories. Often the accent colors as well as the main tones of your scheme can be drawn from the fabric or rug. Some of the most beautiful rooms in the world have been built around the print or prints used for draperies and upholstery. For the contemporary room especially, the fabric need not be a print. New rough-textured fabrics come in magnificent color combinations and the tweedy tones can be distributed around a modern setting with great success.

One foolproof way of arriving at a color scheme—and in this case a traditional decoration plan—is to copy the colors of a known decorative style of the past. Certain periods were renowned for colors which became the earmarks of their style. French Provincial, for example, is built around white walls, fruitwood brown for furniture and woodwork, and muted reds and greens. The style of Colonial Williamsburg, one of the most graceful in the history of American design, comprises a group of blues and greens for painted walls and woodwork. These documented colors can be found at your paint store and, properly used, will automatically guarantee a correct color scheme. The pale, cool blues and yellows of eighteenth-century English decoration combined with pure white and the richness of mahogany conjure up still another handsome period. Nearer to us in time, if not in favor at the moment, are the vivid schemes of the Victorian era: shocking pink, cabbage green, shades of mauve, brown, and eggplant that can provide heady combinations. In each period, the leading decorators set certain colors that have come to symbolize the era. By studying examples of these rooms you can arrive at an authentic scheme.

How Mood Affects Choice of Color

Our discussion of period style merely hinted at the vastly important subject of mood which underlies the whole subject of color selection. We all know the emotional effect that color commands. It is both universal and individual: Certain colors have much the same effect on everyone, others affect each of us in special ways. In the former category, red universally arouses the senses as the color of excitement; blue has a restraining influence; green is the color of cool serenity; white and black, the "noncolors," give respectively the impression of freshness and purity, the somberness of formality. Yellow, to most people, is a lilting color; orange, the color of vivacity; earth tones, browns and beiges, are usually found to be restful. In addition, each of these tones or mutations has special effects due to personal association. To some, green may not be at all conducive to serenity, but rather provoke restlessness; orange may be a depressant, while shades of blue may bring out a feeling of recklessness.

Before formulating a color scheme, it is important to "color-analyze" yourself and your family, as it were, to find out what your real feelings are about each hue. Once you feel sure about your true feelings, then you are ready to face the corollary problem: What mood do you want to evoke in your home, as a whole and room by room? In this light, it is not enough to tell yourself that you want to create a pleasant, comfortable feeling. You can have these qualities and others, too. A room can be pleasant and also stimulating; it can be comfortable and either formal or informal. It can be sophisticated or cozy, provincial or urbane, vibrant or retiring—all are possible in the context of attractive living. But you must know yourself what you want, and then plan your colors for that effect.

Let us take two examples. As a hypothetical case, a family has a city apartment and a country house. They have chosen to evoke distinctly different moods for each. For the sake of argument, let us assume that they choose to turn the tables and have a relaxed, provincial flavor in town where they spend most of their time and a sophisticated flavor for the country place where they spend weekends and vacations. For the apartment, a basic scheme of golden beige, moss green, and brown wood tones is settled on, with accents of red and black. The entrance foyer sets the scheme at once with golden-beige walls, a natural quarry tile floor in terra cotta color, a black iron chandelier, and an antique Spanish console in rich, dark oak, flanked by a pair of French fruitwood side chairs upholstered in a black and white houndstooth tweed. A mirror in an antiqued green-and-gold frame is flanked with small oil paintings matted in green velvet and in antique gold frames.

The living-dining area, leading from the foyer, has the same golden wall tone; artificial box beams are stained a deep walnut against the white painted plaster ceiling. Green takes its place as a luxuriously comfortable, tufted club sofa in velvet; tomato red and black tweed pillows are accents. Armchairs are covered in a tweedy fabric the gold color of the walls. Oriental rugs with creamy beige backgrounds combine greens and reds, set against gleaming walnut parquet flooring which repeats the patina of a large, antique Welsh cupboard and occasional wood furniture. One bedroom is papered in a damask design in shades of green, with gold carpet and hangings; the other has charcoal walls, a red room-size rug, and lounge beds in moss-green corduroy, designed in the manner of a sitting room-study.

In the country the mood changes. The house is white clapboard with black shutters. The foyer is papered in a fresh black and white stripe; over gleaming black painted floors a strip of carpet is peppermint pink; the staircase has black treads and a similar carpet runner; the banister is black, spindles and newel post are white. The living room has its original board floors painted the same gleaming black as the foyer with a zebra skin as a striking accent. Walls are white, draperies, pink. The sofa is covered in a white-on-white cotton damask with pink and raspberry pillows; a contemporary storage system covers one wall, presenting along with music-making equipment a collection of small contemporary paintings, ceramics, and books. A pair of Barcelona chairs are in raspberry leather, while the black marble Victorian mantel is enhanced with an abstract painting in all the shades of the room. The effect is bright, witty, eminently urbane. In town and country the mood is comfortable, pleasant, stimulating, but in each location the effect is quite different. Color has worked its subtle magic.

DEVELOPING THE COLOR SCHEME—A HOUSE-WIDE OR ROOM-BY-ROOM PLAN?

Deciding on a basic color scheme is only the beginning of your decorating adventure, although a most important beginning. Now comes the vital task of interpreting the basic scheme, of embroidering the framework of your carefully built plan. Developing the scheme ranges broadly from the distribution of colors to the selection and placement of the most minute accessory. It impinges on the interacting roles of pattern and color; on orientation or the relationship of exposure and color allocation; and on the many special considerations for the various rooms of a house or apartment. Interpreting your scheme is intimately wrapped up with a period style: Are you planning traditional decor, contemporary, or a transitional blend of the two?

The first decision is whether to undertake a house-wide color theme or to approach the matter one room at a time with each as a separate entity unrelated to the others. Here and now, let us make a plea for the house-wide theme. In today's living, space is the most expensive commodity. Whether you are leasing an apartment or building a new home, economics boil down to cost per room or cost per square foot, respectively. Your main concern, then, is to exact as much living potential as you possibly can from each square foot. In this task, color can help you greatly if you will let it.

There is nothing which seemingly stretches walls and gives an expansive feeling more than color continuity. Setting a house-wide scheme and interpreting it from the front door to the smallest closet will do more to make your house or apartment seem larger than anything you can do. It gives the small house or apartment an air far beyond actual room dimensions, and it provides larger quarters an extra measure of importance and drama that make them look even more costly.

Taking the opposite tack, a room-by-room plan makes the place seem cut up, episodic, and unresolved, no matter how large actual space may be. In a house where the scheme changes at the entrance to each room, you feel as though you are being put through color paces as you travel from one space to another. The large house seems far smaller than it is and the small house seems infinitesimal.

You may ask, isn't a house-wide scheme apt to be monotonous? The answer is no, provided that it is cleverly carried out. The successfully arranged over-all plan is so subtle that its effect is subconscious. As you walk through the rooms, you are dimly aware of certain colors reappearing, but your main impression is one of a most agreeable harmony. It is like listening to a superb symphony: You are suffused with pleasant emotions, while not concerning yourself with the mechanics of composition.

The most difficult part of developing the house-wide theme is sticking to it unswervingly. You would do well to establish a basic scheme of, say, three colors and use them throughout, emphasizing one and then the other, using them in different combinations and proportions, using different shades for different effects—all in a subtle point and counterpoint relationship. Accent colors can be your spice and these in small doses can vary from room to room; in fact, they should. It is well to announce your scheme straightaway in the entrance foyer, gently but firmly. After all, the foyer is the most public room of your home, so it is not the place for the most personal interpretation of your scheme. Let your color plan unfold in an ever more intimate way as you go from living and dining areas, to bedrooms and baths, intensifying intimacy through the handling of colors.

As you work on the various rooms, you will undoubtedly be tempted to depart from your scheme. You will find a fabric or rug, far from your beaten path, that you think you just can't live without. However, resist it you must in the knowledge that eventually you will find other elements just as enchanting in the range you have chosen. One of the greatest features of the house-wide scheme is that it permits you to decorate a room at a time, as you can afford, and still adhere to an over-all plan. The set scheme is just like money in the bank on which you draw as you need. With your scheme in the back of your mind, or as swatches in your purse, each shopping trip becomes an opportunity to study and compare what is possible for the next phase of your project. You do not waste time in aimless browsing; the eye, now selective according to a basic plan, sorts over an immense amount of merchandise and accepts or rejects elements as future possibilities. It permits you to buy upholstery fabric now for a pair of side chairs you may not be able to afford for several years, in the security that the fabric will be right when the time comes. Conversely, it enables you to buy the smaller, less costly elements like accessories—pillows, lamps, accent rugs—now and enjoy them in the certainty that they will blend harmoniously in an eventual whole. The house-wide scheme has numerous advantages over the other approach, attested by the fact that the most skillful professional interior designers all follow this plan, developing an over-all scheme for their clients at the outset and then helping them execute it over the years as budgets permit.

Of course, if your house is largely decorated and you are reading this book for help on a single room you will find in subsequent discussions ideas for color planning every room in the house. Here are a few points to consider at this juncture. The chances are that, regardless of the degree of success you feel you have achieved in your decorating up to now, there is probably a thread of color unity in what has been done. It is not too late to take the essence of the scheme and translate it into a well-co-ordinated plan for the room now confronting you. You may be able to tighten up the effect of your previously done rooms if you are dissatisfied with them. This can be done without major reinvestment through a few well-chosen accessories or by simply retiring an element or two temporarily—a picture that does not add to the color plan, an upholstered chair in the wrong color, etc. Or it may be time to have a few things re-covered, in which case you are presented with a golden opportunity to reintegrate your over-all plan.

If you have an established plan, by all means continue it. You may feel that you are tired of it or that it was not quite right from the beginning and want to discard it for something fresher in the room you propose to redecorate. You will do well to restate your basic theme, however, and you will find many ways of reinvigorating it. Consider a change of emphasis by using a color for walls or floor covering not previously employed for this purpose. If the rest of your rooms are, say, painted beige with blue as a secondary color, consider having blue walls and picking up the beige in another part of the room. In this manner you are keeping continuity and only changing the proportions of the colors. Then, too, accents can be changed to give your scheme a whole new lease on life. Here the sky is almost the limit and you can introduce some new favorites without impairing the old. All in all, there is much more to be said for improving and continuing an established color plan than in striking out wildly in some new direction, unless the upcoming room is the beginning of a whole new over-all approach.

NATURAL LIGHT AND COLOR

At this point, before you enter the mechanics of color distribution in a room or a house, you should take into account the exposure of your rooms to natural light. For color cannot stand alone; without illumination, either natural or artificial, color does not exist. The two must work together and time spent in critically studying the light in your house or apartment will pay dividends later. Quite often people take natural light for granted. When you ask which way a room faces, many women are not certain. Neither are they sure of the variation in sun intensity in winter and summer or of the different point of entrance of the lower winter sun into rooms, which also directly affects decoration.

A sun-drenched bedroom restates the golden and azure scheme of the outdoors, setting the colors in a rich floral print. The design is stated on the chaise longue and restated, interestingly, in the tapes and laminated slats of Venetian blinds. Filmy overcurtains are the only other window treatment, topped with the suggestion of a valance—both held within the refined carving of the window frame. Other pleasant touches: a collection of porcelain urns on the marble mantel, files bound in the same pale blue to fill the niche behind the tiny desk. As befits a bedroom, this is a very personal color signature for the home's most personal room.

A family room was planned in the colors most admired by all family members, tones of green and white. The scheme is set in window shades of citrus green with white binding. The window frame is chartreuse, the baseboard continuing this bright stripe around the room. Sofa upholstery repeats the basic scheme, while the rug —aqua and off-white—is a subtle accent, chosen in the same value as other colors in the room. Accessories are informal: a wicker basket as a telephone table, an idle hour wall shelf of books. Colors in the bouquet were carefully arranged to give dash and verve to the rest of the color scheme.

INTERIOR DESIGNER: PAUL KRAUSS.
WINDOW SHADE MANUFACTURERS ASSOCIATION

A man's study is appropriately decorated in restful earth tones, making it a favorite and comfortable retreat. Paneled walls and heavy ceiling beams are in mellow walnut tones; the French Provincial mantel and English coffee table are in different but compatible wood finishes. A neatly patterned stripe combines brown, orange and white, the three principal colors, in the upholstery of wood-framed armchair and sofa. Blue is the accent.

INTERIOR DESIGNER: DAVID EUGENE BELL, BLOOMINGDALE'S, NEW YORK

A living room dons its summer garb in a cool, strikingly effective scheme of blue, beige and shades of red, colors drawn from a collection of paintings. Turquoise blue is found in pillows, chair upholstery and accessories. Commodes at either end of the sofa are banded in the same hue; their fronts are painted in a delicate floral design in shades of red on off-white. The least used color in the scheme, beige, is reserved for the largest piece—the sofa—and for light cane chairs, picture mats and frames. White shines forth as an ideal summer accent, in materials associated with coolth—a milk glass lamp, marble coffee table.

A master bedroom has style and warmth even though its colors are cool. Blue and white are suitable for one reason because the room has a bank of windows facing south and is sunny and bright all day long. At night the canopy gives a pleasant sense of envelopment, while the wood tones and fireplace add coziness, too. Here is a good example of the use of single chintz for many areas—tester and side hangings, spread, bed wall and chair.

The wood-toned kitchen is a current favorite. In this case it blends beautifully with a family room in open proximity. Copper-colored equipment is unobtrusively built-in and harmonizes with fruitwood cabinets in a provincial paneled design. Plaid curtains in orange, brown and beige sum up the scheme. Yellow is the accent.

Taking color direction from an unusually rendered abstraction, neutral *black*, *off-white*, and *wood tones* are brought to life with splashes of strong color and pattern in this small dual-purpose room. Metal-framed chair and day bed add their own sparkle to the total scheme without introducing another definite color.

Monochromatic *scheme in varying tones of green—yellowish, leafy, grassy. A cool summery mood is established through use of large area of white, the see-through glass table heightens the effect. Pattern interplay of carved carpeting, awning-striped upholstery, and small-scale documentary wallpaper is pleasing.*

Neutral *black, white, brown accented by vivid red compose the sleek background to a collection of accessories whose origins are widely separated. African zebra rugs, a brass-bound campaign chest lacquered Far-East red, Middle-East copper bowls and pitchers; an intriguing three-way spot-light lamp that highlights all.*

Warm *colors in a dining area are inviting colors. A small detail like keying the color of demi-tasse cups to the mat surrounding a featured print shows an awareness of how color can lead the eye to any desired destination. Here, it was the picture arrangement to which we have been unconsciously guided.*

Harmonious *colors for a cheerful kitchen environment to lighten heavy chores. Warm, appetizing yellow, orange, and rust tones serve as a backdrop to appliances and cupboards in a "frosty oak" finish. Especially attractive is the plain vinyl floor—a shiny reflective surface to mirror ceiling light fixtures.*

A pleasing scheme derived from a fabric—yellow, yellow-green, and yellow-orange. The result, a room that's sunny-bright in evening lamplight or rainy-day gray. Spread, headboard, and Roman shade distribute the print in lively contrast to the large amount of solid color. Antique satin, cotton, and linen combine textures and surfaces.

Once certain of these facts, you will proceed with greater certainty. Assuming that you want a warm, friendly, inviting effect in your home, there are rules of orientation which can be helpful. North light is cold light. It is also constant light, which is the reason artists prefer a northern exposure for their studios. A room with exclusively northern light can be greatly enhanced by using a warm color, such as the earth tones of red, yellow, orange, and conversely by avoiding the cold colors—gray, shades of blue, and some tones of green. That is not to say that you must depart from a house-wide theme in a room with northern light. Not at all. One of your three or four colors will most likely be a warm one and that color, in an appropriate shade, will serve well for the largest expanses, holding the cooler colors for subordinate roles. By following this tack, the north room can be as appealing as any in the house.

East light is strong in the early morning, gentle the balance of the day. If your bedroom or bedrooms face east, you will do well to consider cooler tones that will be warmed in the early hours when most time is spent in this room under natural light. For the evening hours artificial illumination can be planned and manipulated for emotional comfort. Southern exposure is, of course, the one which receives the major share of daylight; unless you have tremendous areas of glass which are unprotected by shading devices on the exterior of the house, you are free to use almost any color you wish. If there is a sun intensity problem, both winter and summer, it is well to add a trellis or overhang outside, calculated to both the high summer and low winter sun. Failing such an installation, you can temper the sun's effect somewhat by avoiding the extremely hot colors and using a balanced scheme of cool and warm tones. Rooms that face west should almost always have cooler tones; otherwise you are subject to discomfort, especially in the summer months in the late afternoons.

In all these instances of orientation, we are talking about color in major expanses—walls, ceiling, floor, and unusually large pieces of furniture like sofas and beds. The large, white sofa, for instance, in a living room with large windows facing south or west can be a devastating source of glare. So can white or very light-toned walls and flooring. Wine-colored carpet in a living room facing west may be passable in winter, but can be an active depressant in summer. Pale blue walls in a north-facing bedroom can make it almost unendurable, especially in winter months. Keeping to colors that absorb rather than reflect light for large expanses in south- and west-facing rooms and in east bedrooms will help to solve orientation problems as will the use of warm, light-giving colors for north areas.

ARTIFICIAL LIGHT AND COLOR

In its many subtleties, artificial illumination and its relation to color can comprise a volume in itself. Suffice it to review here a few elementary considerations. Decoratively speaking, the aim with artificial lighting is to create an atmosphere as much as possible like that which prevails with natural light. There are two kinds of artificial illumination, general, or background, lighting and specific lighting for certain functional uses. The former is best accomplished by simulating the source and direction of natural sunlight. Soft illumination at the windows playing down over an expanse of drapery is an ideal device, called "valance lighting." Other general illumination is cove lighting which bathes the ceiling in a soft, diffused glow, a luminous ceiling consisting of fluorescent or incandescent light concealed by a dropped surface of diffused glass or plastic or a luminous wall made of plastic panels behind which are concealed lighting sources in the manner of a Japanese shoji screen. Ceilings and walls so designed add a pervasive glow to the whole room, creating shadow-free light which is especially desirable in kitchens and over a mirror in the bath. To supplement the general glow and for efficient reading, games, sewing, the enjoyment of paintings and sculpture, specific lights are added in the form of lamps, concealed spotlights, and other stationary or portable devices.

With a balanced lighting plan including both general and specific illumination, color can be used much as it is in natural sunlight. There are a few exceptions. As every shopper knows, colors look different under fluorescent lighting and as a result the wise shopper takes a fabric or other colorful object to an outside store window before buying it. Tinted incandescent bulbs—pink, yellow, blue, etc.—also change room colors. Pink bulbs, while flattering to the skin are not always flattering to wall, drapery, and upholstery colors. For that reason, if such bulbs are to be used, color planning must take these effects into account beforehand. Fluorescent lighting must be anticipated similarly.

For its dramatic impact, artificial lighting can be a powerful ally of color. A wall painted in a special tone can be bathed in light to create a remarkable color accent in a room, while specific lighting played over pieces of sculpture, oil paintings, shelves of collections, and other focal points of decorative interest add immeasurably to the enjoyment of color in a room. Artificial lighting is perhaps the least understood of all the decorative aids at our command, an unfortunate circumstance since its dramatic potential is so great. While incorporating the most effective lighting techniques into an existing room or whole house can be extremely expensive, planning them into a new house before it is built is surprisingly inexpensive. For that reason, those who are pondering the decoration of a house yet to be built would do well to put themselves into the hands of a special lighting consultant.

The Mechanics of Color—Its Distribution and Proportion

Once you have settled on your color scheme, decided on the style of your room or rooms, studied the orientation of your home, and fitted your current project into an over-all plan, you are ready to face the most difficult part of decorating—the distribution of the colors in your scheme. It is a mammoth leap from a few color chips or fabric swatches in your hand to a completely decorated room, but it is a leap you are qualified to take if your groundwork up to now has been thorough. It helps to remember at this point that for the first time you must visualize your project in the round. Until this phase, you have been thinking most likely in terms of flat planes—walls, floors, ceilings. Now you must begin to think in terms of volume.

As you have settled on the three or four major colors of your scheme, you probably have had certain areas in mind. This is all to the good, but you must also keep an open mind and be ready to reassign colors if you find better places for them. First, tackle your largest areas—floors, walls, ceilings. These are your backgrounds, and in most cases you will be wise to employ the most neutral color in your scheme and in a fairly light value. For example, if your colors are gray, blue, and yellow, a warm shade of gray would be a good choice for walls, with the ceiling, if fairly high (nine feet or over), in the same hue. If eight feet or lower, the ceiling would be better in a much lighter shade of gray or in white. A very satisfactory scheme can be formed by using a floor covering the same color as the walls but perhaps in a different shade, especially in a rather small room, since this will make space seem larger. For greater impact, the floor should be decorated in a different color of the scheme, a rich blue or a gold.

There are obviously certain practical considerations. In most cases you will want a color for carpet, rugs, or hard-surface flooring that does not show dirt excessively. A neutral color—beige, gray, or rust —or a medium shade of almost any color is preferable to a very light or a very dark tone. For walls, practicality is less important, though desirable. Today most paints and wallpapers are washable; vinyl-surfaced wall coverings are actually scrubbable. As we shall see later, certain functional rooms like kitchen, bath, and foyer require specific, easily maintained materials.

With the major expanses color-set, you can turn to the distribution of color in furniture, drapery, and accessories. Probably the most helpful factor to remember is contrast. Just as a dark necktie looks better against a lighter shirt or a diamond pin is more dazzling against a black dress than a light one, so will a sofa stand out against a wall or a floor if it is in a color value lighter than its background. In the gray-blue-yellow scheme, for example, a soft yellow for sofa and upholstered chairs would be highly effective against either a gray or blue carpet. If your room is on the small side, however, you may want the sofa to blend with walls and floor, in which case a cover of the same or almost the same color would be desirable.

Continuing your study in contrasts, sofa pillows should be color accents, with a decided change in tone or value. As you look at your room, thus far, you see light against dark, dark against light, one element playing on the other, for decorative vitality. In the same way wood pieces can be played against painted walls and the texture and color of rugs and upholstered pieces. Either lighter or darker wood finishes will be contrastive depending on what the piece stands against. It is important to point out here that several different wood finishes can be successfully combined in a room. There is no reason in the world why everything should be fruitwood, walnut, or mahogany. The only thing to guard against is using too many sharply different finishes in a room, as with three or four Biedermeier chairs, a dark oak console, antique fruitwood tables, and picture frames in light pine.

The window is an important area of color interest. Since it is the source of natural (and often artificial) light, it becomes one of the dominant architectural features of a room. The windows are often a sound point of departure in color planning with printed drapery fabric providing the color scheme. From the print, its various colors are distributed to other decorative elements. Restating the fabric in a pair of chairs or a sofa can help visual unity, while often it is a pleasant change to repeat the fabric in a reverse pattern. For example, where a two-toned fabric is patterned white on brown for drapery, the same design in brown on white is an effective foil for upholstery. Where for one reason or another—awkward proportions, too large an opening for the size of the room, or where a view is undesirable—one wishes to minimize a window, it is helpful to use solid color drapery that blends with the walls or use the same design in fabric at the windows if the walls are papered in a pattern. Besides overcoming window problems, this treatment helps to make space seem larger.

Not all the color load is carried by the major expanses. The smallest accessories can help to distribute color. In fact, as your eye travels around the well-decorated room, it is often the accessories that are most noticeable. Accessories, like jewelry in costuming, are what add the touch of individuality. A grouping of prints, a collection of fine china, a tapestry, paintings, lamps—all must be considered sources of color and chosen accordingly. As part of your basic scheme or as accents, they should be strategically located to punctuate the color rhythm. This rhythm is what makes a room come alive: As the various hues vibrate one against the other, your room takes on personality and verve.

In distributing the colors of your scheme, remember that color can be used effectively for emphasis. If you wish to delineate distinct seating groups in the same room color can do it nicely, interpreting one group in certain tones, a second in different tones or a variation of the first. A wall for a collection of paintings or sculpture can be set apart by a change of color. In the open planning of contemporary decoration where large space is separated only by function, color can provide a token barrier. For example, a dining area in an ell of the living space can be set apart by a change of rug color or by painting the ell walls a different color from the others in the combination room.

As an exercise in color planning, let us analyze for a moment the ell arrangement prevalent in today's apartments. In a period scheme where the ell should not be emphasized (it is not a feature of traditional architectural style), the color scheme should be implemented to negate it, to make it seem an integral part of the whole area. In this treatment, the room appears as a large, single space. However, for a contemporary treatment, the ell can be handled in different ways. It can be dramatized by painting it a color used as an accent in another part of the room, thus setting it apart. The furniture would follow in color that used in the other area. Another way would be to continue the wall color, using accent colors for dining chairs and a different colored rug to give importance to the ell and a change of decorative pace.

COLOR AND THE PROBLEM ROOM

It has been said that there are no problem rooms, only faulty solutions in decoration which create problems. Perhaps this is an oversimplification, but it is true that imaginative design can cover a multitude of sins. In this endeavor color is a valuable ally. It can seemingly correct bad proportions in a number of ways. As we have seen, the too high ceiling can be "brought down" by painting it the same or darker than the walls, while, conversely, the too low ceiling can be "raised" by painting it white or a lighter shade of the walls. A long narrow room can be seemingly shortened by painting end walls a darker tone than the longer side walls. The minuscule room can be visually enlarged by treating walls and ceiling in the same color. And it need not be white, contrary to much popular belief. It is surprising what patterned wallpaper can do to make such a room seem infinitely larger, provided it is used over all the surfaces.

New apartment buildings and some older ones, too, are riddled with architectural flaws: exposed beams, posts that seem to come from nowhere, off-center windows, obtrusive radiators and air conditioners, doors located without regard to symmetry, etc. Once again, color comes to the rescue. By painting the entire wall—door frames, beams, radiator—the same color, all the elements blend into a whole. A dark tone in a flat finish is usually the most effective camouflage in this case. Colored drapery can help with difficult windows. By treating the whole window as a single element, disparate features can be obscured without interfering with either the control of light or air. It is well to point out here that the window is architectural and that anything which interferes with its proper functioning is not good decorating. Too often there is a tendency to create elaborate windows in front of windows for a dramatic effect. This is not what we meant in referring to camouflage treatment. We mean, rather, a simple, colorful expanse of drapery that fills the total wall, but can be partially or fully opened for air and light or can be made of a loosely textured, light, translucent fabric that will admit both light and air while obscuring all the architectural flaws.

Often older homes present difficulties with too many doors and windows. In this case, it helps to paint everything the color of the walls, blending woodwork, trim, and walls into one unified backdrop. Odd bays and room extensions, arbitrary divisions between areas of the same room, and overpowering stairways are often the earmarks of the late Victorian house. With these, color works its same magic, underplaying one element, emphasizing another to bring everything into harmony.

The Importance of the Color Accent

Just as the clever cook departs from a recipe to add her own inimitable seasoning to a dish, so does the decorator give piquancy and verve to an established color scheme with a few accents. Of course, an herb is chosen for specific reasons—as a subtle catalyst or as a pungent contrast, diametrically opposed to the basic flavor and texture. And the accent color must be chosen. It must "do" something to the scheme; it cannot just sit there, looking like an out-of-place member of the color family. It must be so vital that if withdrawn from the room you are conscious that something is lacking. It spells the difference between rooms that come alive and those that never get off the ground.

How is the color accent chosen? In an understated scheme it need not be a bold tone; in fact, it would look odd as such. However, for example, in a room done in soft shades of green and lilac, accents in melon or saffron would be dramatic, the contrast coming in counterpoint of lighter and darker tones of colors in the same intensity. Conversely, in a strong room in white, orange, and gold, accents in crimson or Kelly green would vibrate. Here again you are using equals which are strong, with the accent dominating. One of the most useful and overlooked color accents is black. Leading decorators swear by it and there are certain rooms that "cry" for it. In rooms done in earth colors, black is an amazing catalyst, pulling the whole scheme together. Where you might have walls in a rich, burnished gold hue, chairs in light green damask, and walnut wood tones in furniture and trim, black in picture frames, lamp shades, fireplace equipment, and perhaps a footstool would give great drama in the quiet way suitable to that room. There is, in fact, almost no room in which a touch or two of black is not an improvement.

By the same token, a room in pastel shades can use white effectively as an accent. Syrie Maugham, one of the first women to practice interior design as a profession, was a devotee of white, using it with great style both as an accent and as a monochrome. The accent is often an unexpected color in a given setting. In a traditional room with mellow wood pieces, patterned fabrics, and Oriental rugs, a pair of French armchairs with frames painted white or black or green would be stunning accents, simply by not being what is usually seen in that kind of scheme.

It is the degree of difference you wish to create that helps in the choice of the color accent. If you want a few touches to make the decorative pot boil, as it were, small areas of a color completely out of the range of the room's concept can be effective. Say, in a room of blues and greens, a bit of orange or red, while in a room of royal blue and beige, a hint of bitter green can be striking. These add powerful bites to a scheme if used sparingly. Diametrically opposed colors—red and green, blue and orange—are usually best left to the professional for use as proper accents. However, in small quantities and with experimentation, they offer no serious threat.

It is often asked how large the color accent should be. There is no rule about this; it is a matter of gauging by eye and instinct. In a large room all in green and brown, a huge sofa in white is an acceptable accent. In the same room, a small ashtray in white on a dark walnut table can be strong, too, but not as strong as in a small room in these colors. A room-size rug can be an accent if it is unrelated to the family of colors used everywhere else. Four walls cannot be a color accent, but one wall in red can be a striking accent surrounded by three white ones in a room with white upholstery and drapery. A piece of painted furniture of any size (from a small cigarette table to a breakfront) can be an accent if there are no other painted wood pieces, especially if it is in a color not part of an interwoven scheme.

Special objects of themselves can be brilliant accents: a crystal chandelier in a room with dark walls and ceiling; a single magnificent oil painting; an expanse of natural brick in an otherwise formal room; a bizarre piece of furniture in very dark or light wood; a brightly colored door in a room with all other woodwork in white; a Louis XV fruitwood fauteuil in an otherwise contemporary room with metal furniture; a collection of English willowware in a contemporary dining room; or a collection of abstract bronze sculpture in a traditional setting.

As you see, the acceptable accent varies in almost every way. Its only common denominator is that it is an unrelated color that plays at times the role of a pungent gadfly, at other times the role of subtle foil. Always, it adds stress by being different and the degree of difference is the clue to its power.

COLOR AIDS AT YOUR DISPOSAL

There are many sources of firsthand color assistance available to you. First of all, remember that every room you visit can be regarded as an opportunity to test your skill as an interior colorist. From what you have studied in this book, quietly analyze what your friends and acquaintances have done with their homes. Seeing their successes and mistakes objectively can be of great help. Discreet questioning about why they did certain things will give you a better understanding of the psychology of color. You will find that people with very little or no knowledge can often do remarkable things with color from sheer instinct. This plus a few rules and a bit of experience can often make an excellent amateur decorator.

Seminars or round-table discussions on color planning will also give you many ideas. Pooling knowledge and experience, while it can never dictate your own individual solution, can familiarize you with the mechanics of putting a room together. In such a seminar, it would be helpful to invite or hire a qualified professional decorator to serve as moderator. Guiding the discussion and interpreting individual color problems and solutions, he or she can provide further insight into the planning process.

In addition, every shopping trip affords a chance to see color and pattern in action. Model rooms in department stores, decorated by professional designers, offer many ideas. As you study the way colors are assembled in these rooms, you must be mindful, however, that they serve a twofold purpose for the store. Besides being designed as examples of decoration, they are also a promotional vehicle to show merchandise. As such they are often far too theatrical to serve in the home exactly as they are. If you like a certain effect you see, remember that it can be interpreted in a toned-down version for success in your room. Usually a shopper takes an idea here and one there, building a color and pattern scheme from many sources.

Store decorators are another source of help. Their advice usually costs you nothing but the price of the decorative components you buy. If you are in doubt about the widsom of adding an important piece of furniture to a room don't be hesitant about asking the opinion of a staff decorator. Don't let the salesman influence you on a color choice; you already have one amateur—yourself—and don't need the advice of another. The decorator, on the other hand, once he or she knows the ingredients of your room, may see the perfect color choice right on the floor, a piece you overlooked.

The fabric department of a store is another gold mine of help. Most often a printed fabric dictates the color scheme of a room. As your eye goes over the display tables, you will be attracted to two or three fabrics, any one of which could provide your colors. Also there will be solid fabrics—cottons, felts, corduroys, silks, and all the rest— and viewing the complete color range in any of these will give you ideas about compatible colors. By all means take cuttings of a few patterns and a group of co-ordinated solids with you and study them at home. Remember that any solid color can be matched at the paint store. Remember that you need not be slavish about interpreting all of the colors in a printed fabric.

Don't forget the rug department in your travels. A patterned rug can suggest a scheme, too. Building from the floor up can also be a good way of developing a plan. There are many beautiful Orientals or simulated Orientals which present fabulous color combinations, and whole collections of new textured and patterned rugs that can be striking, especially in a contemporary scheme. And while we are speaking of rugs, don't sell or discard an Oriental you have because the colors are dark and unfashionable. Such rugs can now be bleached to give spectacular effects that are in perfect harmony with today's color scheming. Call your local dyer and find out if the rug is a kind that bleaches well. Not all do, but some can be bleached to give a faded, antique look that is beautiful and impossible to get in any other way.

Your best place for color ideas is likely the paint store. There you can take any number of color chips from a rack and can see various tones of the same basic color, side by side, comparing the most subtle shades. Your paint dealer is also an oracle for color information—the effect of various kinds of light on walls; how colors look together, their interacting effects; the kinds of paint for different surfaces. He can give the same kind of information on stain. It helps to know, for example, that the best and largest paint stores can match any color in wood stain, not only those in the wood family. Paint cards and chips are yours for the asking and become helpful additions to your kit.

A good way to compare all your swatches and color samples is to use an 8½-inch by 11-inch sheet of heavy paper or cardboard and attach samples with a notation as to where the various colors go. Use one card for each room or each area. In this way you can see at a glance the relationship of the two or three main members of your color family and how the accents work with them. Once you have finished juggling the various swatches and have reached a final effect, staple them to the card and stick to your scheme. You cannot change color horses in the middle of the stream except for minor accents. And don't listen to your maid, your friends, or your aunt Tillie once you've made up your mind. They are no more decorators than you are, in fact, less so after you have completed your studies.

Trends and Fads—The Long-Range Color Viewpoint

Two of the dreariest questions one is apt to hear about color are: "What colors are they using this year?" and "What colors are new?" As has been emphasized by savants far beyond the talent of this author, "they" do not exist. Color is a personal and individualistic response; what someone else finds suitable and enriching will not necessarily be so for you. Also, there is no such thing as a new color; all are taken from the rainbow which has been with us since time began.

For these reasons the questions have no validity. They merely register a desperate attempt to arrive at social prestige by following an accepted status symbol in home decoration. A color scheme to be sound must be elicited from those who are to occupy the rooms: colors they like, are comfortable with, and sparkle to. If handled well these colors can provide a meaningful effect. Colors may be handled in many ways. From historical study we can attribute definite color use to the homes of the wealthy as far back as classical times. There are different color treatments for interiors during Colonial American, eighteenth-century English or French, or seventeenth-century Italian, etc. Similarly, there is a way of handling color to arrive at the modern or contemporary style of decoration prevalent in the last twenty or so years. Whatever the period, color handling includes the intensity of tones, the combination of shades of various colors, and their distribution to the components of a setting.

All the foregoing, we feel, helps to formulate a long-range viewpoint about the use of color. It is a guide to understanding and may help eliminate the fear-begotten faddist approach. By knowing what is taking place in a broad scope, we can pinpoint our own color attitudes and responses, trying to settle on a scheme that will offer a good many years of pleasant living before the need for change is felt. Color planning, if it entails all the components of decoration, is an expensive matter and since the successful scheme is part of a jigsaw puzzle which cannot be separated without the whole thing coming apart, large changes are difficult. So it is well to think ahead as you color-plan now.

The Fifty Most Common Color Mistakes

1. Putting one color on one wall, another on a second, etc. Instead, distribute color and use accents.
2. Using neutral colors to be "safe."
3. Thinking everything has to match. It makes a dull room.
4. Using too many colors in one room or a small apartment.
5. Trying to combine true color opposites if you are an amateur; it is a tricky job for the professional.
6. Mixing blue and green together, willy-nilly. You'll end up in an aquarium.
7. Making a man suffer in a pink bedroom or, worse, pink living room. Think of others when you plan a scheme.
8. Using bold colors for draperies if windows are off center or awkward architecturally.
9. Using cold colors if your room faces north.
10. Using pale colors if the room gets hot sun.
11. Jumping from one color to another in the rooms of a small home or apartment. Keep color continuity.
12. Using bizarre or offbeat colors in ceramic tile, laminate counters, or other fixed architectural elements in a bath or kitchen.
13. Using colored lights in valance or cove illumination.
14. Using colored patterns that are too different in the same room.

15. Locating large paintings in the same room which conflict in color.

16. Worrying about the colors "they" are using this year; find colors you like that suit you.

17. Using bouquets of flowers that conflict with the colors of your decor.

18. Using plants to cover up decorating mistakes.

19. Using pastel colors with furniture that is less than superb.

20. Copying exactly the color schemes of model rooms in stores and houses. They usually don't come off at home.

21. Buying pink dinnerware for a green dining room or brown for a room done in purple. Co-ordinate tableware and room decor.

22. Using a conflicting color in the same room with a brilliant collection of china.

23. Planning a monochromatic scheme unless you are a skilled professional.

24. Having everything so matched that it looks as if a decorator just left.

25. Throwing in an off color after the scheme has been set.

26. Letting a decorator talk you out of a color you like for one you dislike or are lukewarm about.

27. Using bold color and pattern in a large expanse.

28. Using colored silk lamp shades; they throw off a bad light.

29. Painting a piece of furniture any color rather than one which blends with an established scheme.

30. Doing the house in colors you like but the rest of the family dislikes.

31. Painting every ceiling a different color.

32. Using too many different colored Oriental rugs in one room.

33. Being afraid to cover everything in a living room in a bright chintz. It can be charming.

34. Using different colors and patterns of a laminate in a kitchen or bath.

35. Using stiff, formal colors in children's rooms.

36. Using too much painted furniture.

37. Thinking that what is right in color by day is necessarily right by night.

38. Thinking white or light colors are too pallid; white on white if used properly can be as bold as red.

39. Using too much stained wood in a room.

40. Thinking that because a room has large windows facing a garden that it must be decorated in outdoor colors. Contrast can be more effective.

41. Having the idea that because a house is old, it cannot be color-treated in a contemporary way. A Victorian house responds brilliantly to modern color scheming.

42. Using color to emphasize too many different parts of a room. Color cannot be dissipated without losing its effect.

43. Relying on color to do the whole job; it must work with the other elements of decoration.

44. Permitting one dominant element—say, an old-fashioned red brick fireplace—to spoil a color scheme. There can be no sacred cows in good decorating.

45. Overpowering a room with too much vibrant color. Subtlety in color planning is found in contrast of the bold with the subdued.

46. Trying to please everybody with the living-room scheme. Strike a balance between what you and most family members like.

47. Going wild with accessories on the theory that once the basic scheme is set you can do anything with accents. Overaccenting spoils an otherwise good room.

48. Hoping that color will offset badly designed furniture. Color camouflage can go only so far.

49. Trying to be "different" with bizarre or inappropriate colors. You and your friends will soon tire of a shock treatment.

50. Starting to put a room together before your color scheme is established. You'll end up with a hodgepodge. The color scheme must come first.

CHAPTER FOUR

PATTERN

EQUALLY IMPORTANT in the lexicon of decoration is color's sister, pattern. And pattern, in whatever of its many roles it is used, is intimately bound up with color. This is not to say that a stunning domino effect cannot be created simply with black and white, but rather that for the most part pattern presupposes color. After all, it is the delineation of shapes in different contrasting hues that creates the design of a fabric, a wallpaper, or an over-all room. People too often overlook the fact that pattern is also created by texture and form, that it is found in the shape of a chair, in the groupings of furniture, in the arrangement of a wall of paintings, in parquet flooring, or in the sum total of all the decorative accessories in a room. Pattern can stem from the play of light and shadow, from architectural detail. Pattern is also contributed by the human beings in a room, a fact too often forgotten in the overpatterned room that can be a disaster when entertaining large groups. People feel uncomfortable when overwhelmed with pattern. Bold pattern can be especially jarring when viewed behind women's patterned clothing.

That is the scope of pattern in decoration and it is enormous. Thinking of it in this full sense rather than in terms of a single fabric or wallpaper helps you to manipulate it successfully. And make no mistake—it is in the distribution as well as the choice of pattern that decorating success lies. Pattern is essentially contrast and it must be worked as a relationship of recessive and protruding visual elements in a given space—areas must seem to move to and from you for maximum effect. The degree that they do can be controlled by the boldness of the color and shape of the various objects. For example, in a muted eighteenth-century Colonial room, there will seem to be very little movement; the elements were manipulated for serenity. In a strident contemporary room, loud blocks of color can cry out in a decorative blast, if that is the effect desired. It is all done with pattern, in combination with its ally, color.

WHAT GOES WITH WHAT?

The answer lies basically in pattern and its role. Perhaps that is why it is so tricky. Many amateur decorators find that the easiest way to handle pattern is to avoid it in favor of solid-color fabrics and other decorating components. There is no denying that beautiful rooms can be developed in solids, but it is begging the question, because if pattern is not understood in a fabric, it can never be brought off in the broad sweep of an entire expanse where solid blocks of color become in effect the elements of pattern. The better way is to face pattern squarely and manipulate it with its ally, color, to bring off a successful scheme.

Pattern and color work together in three principal ways. They join forces as an accent; they act together for harmony, as a blender; and they can establish a background. The accent works as a focalizer, or contrived eye catcher, either vivid in tone or sharp in line. Most often the patterned accent is at its best against a background in a lower color key. For example, a brilliant Oriental rug will attract far more attention in a neutral setting than in a multicolored room filled with furniture and collections. The patterned accent would be exemplified by crewel pillows for a plain white sofa; a tapestry against a pale wall; a large framed print in colors not found elsewhere in the room; a pair of armchairs upholstered in a printed fabric in black and white where the basic scheme was yellow and green. The boldness or scale of the pattern is usually proportionate to the area of the object. However, this is not necessarily so. Large, bright-patterned dinner plates can be marvelous accents against a different colored cloth, while an outsize chintz can be charming on a small slipper chair. Again, it depends on the skill in handling.

Pattern for harmony is epitomized by the use of one colorful chintz for everything—all upholstered pieces, drapery, accessory pillows, even lamp shades. This is an easy way to achieve unity and the effect can be as charming as it is certain. By the same token, the surest way to total chaos is to inflict several patterns in different colors and of competitive strength on the same room. This is the quick way to kill

Strong pattern is a favorite of children. Here, a bold stripe provides a multi-colored backdrop for a bunk room, with spreads and bolsters adding further verve with the design at right angles to the wall pattern. Cube ottoman also reinforces the scene, relieved by white accents in low table, vase and cornice molding.

a room. Choosing not to use the same pattern over-all, there are ways to achieve a perfect or near-perfect patterned balance.

It is not only possible but interesting to play one black-and-white print against a different black-and-white print in more or less the same style and design scale. The effect of a patterned toile in one color against the same toile in another can be interesting. Co-ordinated wallpaper and fabric ensembles are great harmonizers, as are designs in the same colors and style used in different parts of a room. For example, a fleur-de-lis design for draperies, in shades of beige, is picked up in a fleur-de-lis carpet design in blue, one of the other colors in the scheme.

As we have seen, continuity is one of the main considerations in the best-planned color scheme; pattern, working with your colors, can be of invaluable help in achieving it. In this pursuit, avoid the very bold pattern except in very special kinds of rooms—family rooms and children's rooms—relying on subdued designs that permit the eye to appreciate a sense of unity without being engulfed by it.

MIXING PATTERNS

What kinds of patterns can be mixed? A good question and one with few rules to answer it. There was a time when a well-decorated room had no conflicting designs in it and a very pleasant and serene period room can still be designed in this fashion. However, the transitional room is in vogue and an eclectic mix is what most people prefer. This means that diverse patterns must be mixed and to mix them successfully you must bring color and scale into play. For example, if you want to use a geometric and a floral, keep at least one of the colors in each of them the same, then underscore the effect by using that color in a solid area. A third pattern could be introduced following the same rule, but it must be used sparingly. The eye simply will not accept too many dominant patterns and, remember, no two patterns should get the same amount of exposure in a given area. Use one dominantly and the other as an accent. French country chairs and sofas almost always had the backs upholstered in a plaid, the seats and arms, if any, in a brocade or some floral, but, of course, the back was a smaller area and as such an accent.

Much the same principle applies to the size of pattern. If you're working in a fairly large area with a large-scale print, keep the surrounding pattern smaller scale and less complicated in design. That way, you offer the eye some relief from all the pattern activity. Too much activity will be dizzying and will turn the room into an unpleasant place to relax and converse. Large areas of solid color and texture will lend refreshing counterpoint to a patterned room. A favorite color, preferably subdued, taken from the surrounding prints is a good choice for walls or, if in doubt, use white or a light neutral. Small over-all pattern, used lavishly, can seemingly increase the size of a small room, just as large-scaled pattern can make a too-large area seem more comfortable to human scale.

Pattern can be the sum total of room elements, not the usually thought of fabric or accessory design. Here in an almost wildly eclectic mixture of patterns, textures and furniture styles, unity is attained with the use of one tone—white. Long area rug, chandelier, upholstery, lamp shades combine in their effect to hold the melange together.

However, it is usually best to restrict pattern to one large area of a room. If the floor is covered with an Oriental or other highly figured carpet, then keep walls in a solid and use pictures and other wall decor carefully. Conversely, if the floor is plain, then you can use pattern more liberally on furniture, for drapery, etc. Pattern must be balanced and that is perhaps its first and foremost rule.

Proving that pattern need not be of the same design style to be effective, this contemporary sitting room juxtaposes a whimsical floral fabric with the rigid geometry of a built-in wall. One pattern is linear, the other an over-all design, yet they work together because they include colors strongly set in other elements of decoration.

PATTERN AS BACKGROUND

There are two aspects of pattern as background. Patterned walls or floor or ceiling can set the dominant background, or pattern can be considered the sum total of all the background objects. Since over-all pattern is pretty much the province of the traditional room with its paper or paneled walls, its figured rugs and elaborate ceilings, the contemporary room gains its background pattern from the sum total of all the many blocks of color and shapes of furniture. The background becomes the composite of all the other decorative elements. In a way, the room is its own backdrop. The contemporary room can provide great serenity if the blocks of color are not too strong, or the walls are painted liberally in white or a light color. The transitional setting, on the other hand, is by its nature a somewhat restless one, a

*An authentic pattern, in this case a paisley print, is a sure-fire way of set-
ting period style. In this French country kitchen, walls, drapery and chair
seats stamp the basic style, underscored by flooring and window millwork.
Sleek louverlike cabinets and checked backsplash become effective elements
of counterpoint.*

stimulating and often heady mix, if you like. But here again, if all
the patterned elements—the fabric, the displayed collections, the rug—
are kept in one subdued color, there can be great repose. In some
ways the more somber hues—browns and earth tones—seem to work
best in this kind of a pattern mix for a background. The easiest of the
three decorating styles, when it comes to pattern, is the traditional
style. It relies heavily on pattern and has definite patterned motifs
associated with definite periods. By using fabrics, rugs, and accessories
in such a related pattern, the desired style is automatically set. For
example, the toile de Jouy pastoral patterns are a definite part of
French country or Provincial style. Using a wallpaper or fabric with
such a pattern sets an authentic background at the start.

CHAPTER FIVE

LIGHTING

LIGHT IS A FACTOR in our daily lives that we take for granted. As with the air we breathe, we are seldom conscious of it until something goes wrong, like an evening power failure that plunges everything into darkness. And we certainly seldom think of it as a decorating tool and yet it is one of the most important. When you begin a decorating project, you are suddenly aware of the light around you. You wonder how it can be used to minimize structural defects in a room, how it can create special effects. However, before you start any decorating project, it is first necessary to understand the nature of light itself, what it can do for you, some of the requirements for visual comfort, and the various ways you can actually build light into your home.

In its broadest sense light can be divided into two kinds—natural light or daylight and man-made or artificial light. Although it is desirable to have as much natural light as possible in a home, few homeowners are in the fortunate position of dictating or even changing the amount of daylight. The architect is usually responsible for regulating the natural light in a house, and he does it through designing window walls, an atrium, skylights, or other means that make the daylight hours a force to be reckoned with. A person building a new home or redesigning an apartment should consult with his architect on what plans have been made to use natural light, how much of it will be available and how it will be controlled.

Although we have come a long way since Thomas Edison successfully bottled that "hot hairpin" ninety years ago, the basic function of good lighting has never changed. It is designed to let us see better. In fact, in the beginning that was the sole purpose of lighting. It has only been within the last twenty-five years that the whole environmental aspect of lighting has been explored.

INTERIOR DESIGN BY DAVID MOLL/CHARLES BERRISFORD

The successful chandelier has a definite relation in scale to the dining table it overhangs. An antique billiard fixture is perfectly sized to this Parsons-style dining table. An Oriental screen, applied flat to the wall, becomes a dominant element of background consonant with the windowed view.

What Proper Lighting Can Do

Just as a gloomy, dark day can depress our spirits, so can a poorly illuminated room. On the other hand, a well-lighted room can ease tensions, help to create harmony, make reading and TV watching a greater pleasure and heighten the enjoyment of furniture, paintings, and rugs. Poor lighting can spoil the over-all effect of the most expensively decorated room, while proper illumination can make a simply decorated room seem far more exciting than its budget might suggest. Just as the theatrical lighting designer uses light to excite emotional responses in audiences, so can home lighting evoke moods of gaiety, romance, and excitement.

On the practical side, lighting's main functions in decoration are to visually increase the sense of space and to physically change the use of space. Illumination can be manipulated to seemingly widen or lengthen a room, give it added height, draw people to certain areas, obscure others, and direct traffic circulation through a home. It can emphasize or play down certain features. It can add importance to a painting, a collection of china in a dining room, call attention to a magnificent rug or a beautifully sculptured ceiling. The whole quality and effect of color are largely influenced by light. At low light levels, color is almost nonexistent to our eyes; at bright levels, it is intensified. Texture is also greatly enhanced by lighting: Nubby upholstery fabrics and shag rugs come to life with correct illumination. With all the things that light can do, it obviously can never be an afterthought in decorating. Rather it should be considered as part of the original design scheme.

You Need Two Kinds of Lighting

The first step in developing a decorative lighting plan is to understand that there are two principal forms of interior illumination—general or background lighting and specific lighting. The successfully decorated room requires both, planned in tandem. The former sets a general "wash" of light over most of a space, while the latter is pinpoint light for various special activities—reading and sewing, for example—or for accenting room features such as paintings and art objects. The most common form, but not necessarily the most effective form of background lighting, is the chandelier type of ceiling fixture. However, the best background lighting is engineered, that is, it is built into the room.

General, background illumination is practically synonymous with structural lighting. One of the major functions of structural lighting is to make walls and ceilings appear lighter and more attractive. Since they occupy three quarters or more of a room's space, their treatment is especially important. With proper lighting and colors, walls can be made to recede and the sense of space increased. Lighting a wall's surface improves visual comfort by providing soft, shadow-free light.

Structural lighting certainly does not provide all the answers to your decorative light problems, but it should be one of the key considerations in any decorating plan. In many situations you will need added fixtures for specific tasks or as decorative accents. In the main living areas, structural lighting can be accomplished with valances, cornices or wall brackets. An electrical contractor can figure out how much structural lighting you will need. As an example, for a room size over 250 square feet (i.e., 15 feet by 20 feet), one foot of structural lighting is generally recommended for every 15 square feet of floor space. In a room 15 feet by 20 feet (300 square feet), you would need 20 feet of structural lighting.

Installing structural lighting can be a do-it-yourself project, though any wiring job should be handled by a licensed expert. Faceboards for valances and cornices are most commonly made of white pine or plywood, sometimes of beveled cedar siding. Several manufacturers make packaged valance units and most of the large electrical manufacturers offer construction tips on installation.

Here are a few hints to improve your structural lighting.

1. With a valance the spacing between the fluorescent lamp and the front of the drapery material is critical. At least a two-inch space will light the draperies more evenly from top to bottom.

2. Valances should not be less than four feet in length and should be extended beyond the window to accommodate the draperies when they are pulled back during the day. Tying two small windows together with a single valance is effective.

3. Drapery fabrics beneath a valance should be light or at least have a light background if they are patterned in clear, bright colors. Stiff fabrics should be avoided.

4. When installing luminous ceiling panels be sure the cavity holding the fluorescent units is lined with fireproof material and that the units are mounted on fireproof materials (never on fiberboard, for instance).

5. It is important that cove lighting, which is rather flat and lacking in character, be supplemented with other lamps and fixtures to supply highlights and shadows.

6. Use luminous wall panels to emphasize soaring ceilings, to act as a room divider (it should be luminous on both sides), or to make a room seem brighter or larger. They are installed in the same fashion as ceiling panels, with the inside of the cavity being painted flat white. The cavity opening is usually covered with patterned plastic diffusers or an overlay of grillwork on the diffuser.

Recessed downlights effectively emphasize the dining table, especially when lighting levels are controlled. The planter-chandelier is well shielded to prevent glare in the eyes of those seated at the table. Note the garden lighted at night—a pleasing view through the picture window.

7. Shop for decorative plastics, grilles, and screens at lumber dealers, builder supply houses, decorator supply shops, glass and plastic supply outlets. Grilles with large openings (at least one inch) light up more effectively than do very fine mesh patterns. Open grilles need a lightweight diffuser behind them.

Specific lighting supplements general, background lighting and usually takes the form of portable lamps located in places and at heights efficient for the light requirements of the task at hand. There are, however, certain kinds of specific lighting that are built in: suspended fixtures, wall washers, ceiling spots to highlight paintings or table centerpieces in dining rooms. Lamps, of course, serve decoratively as well as functionally and so must be carefully chosen for their effect as accessories. There are table lamps to blend, stylewise, with every period of decor from Early American butter churns into lamps to the most sleek, goosenecked contemporary floor lamps in shiny chrome steel. Again, you can learn what type of lamp goes with what by observation. And remember that lamp bases and shades are important sources of color and pattern and like other accessories must be artfully distributed around the room.

LIGHTING TERMS

Cornice Lighting

The light source, usually fluorescent lamps, is placed behind a cornice built at the junction of ceiling and wall. The cornice, which is easy to construct, should be at least six inches in depth and the inside of its faceboard should be painted flat white for the best light reflection. Since cornice lighting is directed downward on a wall's surface, it is most effective for dramatizing a mural, pictures, wall textures and wall hangings. A cornice helps to give the impression of greater ceiling height, so it is particularly desirable in low-ceilinged rooms.

Cove Lighting

The light source, usually fluorescent lamps, is placed in the trough of a wooden "cove" built at least one foot (or more) below the ceiling. Since the light is directed upward and then reflected from the ceiling back into the room, the ceiling should be white or off white. Although the illumination thus provided is soft and uniform, it should be supplemented by portable lamps or other light sources for activity areas or tasks like sewing, reading, etc. Cove lighting adds drama to rooms with slant- or cathedral-type ceilings or ceilings with two levels, and makes a high ceiling seem lower.

Luminous Panels

This refers to panels in a surface, usually a wall or ceiling, that emit or reflect light. The light source, fluorescent units or tubular incandescent bulbs, is concealed under the panel. Luminous ceiling panels are frequently used in entryways, kitchens, dining areas.

A family room, designed for practicality and good looks, features this play area that can be concealed behind folding doors when not in use. A pair of swing-arm lamps light the drop-down table, and a fluorescent lamp concealed beneath the second shelf illuminates the toys.

bathrooms, and recreation rooms—wherever comfortable, glare-free illumination is desirable. Such ceiling panels contribute to a feeling of spaciousness. They are most adaptable to high-ceilinged rooms, since the plastic diffusing panels must be dropped ten to twelve inches. The interior cavity is painted flat white.

Soffit

A type of structural or built-in lighting using at least two rows of lamps in recessed air spaces over kitchen sinks and work areas, over dressing-room or bathroom mirrors, and on the undersides of pass-throughs, niches, and beams. Lighted soffits direct light down onto a horizontal plane or outward to a vertical surface (as when you are facing a mirror). Polished aluminum reflectors are recommended with fluorescent units when lighting work surfaces, since they more than double the light output.

Valence

Another structural or built-in lighting term most commonly used for lighting above a window is a valance. Fluorescent tubes are installed behind simple or decorative frames, and the light is directed

Bathrooms are becoming very luxurious, and this custom-made countertop with a generous expanse of mirror illustrates the trend. For proper grooming by night or day the soffit holds both de luxe warm white fluorescents and de luxe cool white, which can be mixed when desired.

In spite of dark wooden cabinets this kitchen has a light effect from the excellent use of structural lighting. Fluorescent wall brackets are mounted between the cabinets and ceiling and are shielded by decorative plastic panels, giving a luminous over-all light. Counter surfaces are lighted by fluorescent lamps concealed beneath cabinets.

upward over the ceiling and downward over the window. The valance frame or faceboard should be painted white inside to reflect the light. It will conceal both the light sources (fixtures) and the top of draperies. Since it is usually made of wood it can be painted, papered, or upholstered and trimmed, if desired, with moldings or scallops. At least a ten-inch space between the top of the valance and the ceiling is recommended. The amount of light on the ceiling or below on window or draperies may be increased by tilting the faceboard out at the top or bottom. Valance units can be custom made or prefabricated.

Wall Bracket

A high wall bracket is very similar to a valance, and provides the same type of lighting for a wall and ceiling that a valance does for a window and ceiling. It is installed like a valance and is sometimes used on a wall opposite a window with a valance to balance the illumination and make the room appear larger. A low wall bracket is used for lighting specific areas such as a countertop desk in a kitchen or over the headboard of a bed. This type of structural lighting has many uses in the home.

MINIMUM STANDARDS FOR VISUAL COMFORT

The size of a room or any living area determines its lighting requirements. It is perfectly possible to light a room by several different methods, no matter what its size. A very small room is usually described as up to 125 square feet (i.e., 12 feet by 10 feet); an average room, 125 to 225 square feet (i.e., 12 feet by 18 feet); and a large room, over 225 square feet (i.e., 12 feet by 20 feet). Often it is desirable to combine general with local or accent lighting.

Among the recommendations from the American Home Lighting Institute are the following:

1. All the incandescent bulbs—except the low-wattage decorative types—must be shielded by diffusing materials such as opal or ceramic-enameled glass or plastic.

   The fluorescent tubes that produce a lower brightness require less diffuse shielding such as frosted or lightly etched glass or plastic; they may be louvered or even unshielded when seen against very light surfaces in utility rooms.

2. A minimum of one permanent lighting unit per room must be on switch control at room entrance—or entrances when they are ten or more feet apart. This is an important safety precaution.

By proper positioning of light sources you can eliminate the problem of adequate task lighting that can cause headaches, nervousness, mistakes, and even accidents. Good task lighting is particularly needed when studying, reading, cooking, cleaning, sewing, carpentering, and playing indoor games.

Types of Bulbs

There have been so many changes in household bulbs during the past few years that it's difficult to keep up to date with developments. In general, bulbs are smaller and more efficient, both incandescent and fluorescent types, and come in a variety of shapes and colors to fill your needs and create interesting decorative effects.

Now let's look at some of these bulbs more closely. First come the incandescent bulbs, the most common of which is the familiar standard we've known for years. Recently its inside frost finish has been replaced with soft white (a milky inside coating) that is more attractive and conceals blackening. This standard type also comes in color with an enamel coating of pink, blue, gold, or green. It can be used to change the appearance of a room.

Three-way bulbs offer great flexibility, since a single lamp can provide a subdued general light, a brighter light for conversation, and a bright light for reading, sewing, or putting on make-up.

Among the more recent innovations are the long or extended life bulbs. They are supposed to give satisfactory light for twenty-five hundred hours. They are generally more expensive and use more electricity.

The most interesting changes involve the strictly decorative bulbs —those that are designed to be seen in or around the home and to present an attractive appearance whether lighted or unlighted. Some of these actually do double duty as both light source and fixture. They include:

Chimney light—This gives the effect of an old-fashioned kerosene lamp light. It's appropriate for Early American decor in Colonial-type fixtures, either standard or candelabra.

Crackle frosted—These bulbs, reminiscent of cut glass, come in several shapes and sizes and are often effective in crystal chandeliers and wall sconces.

Flame shape—These are designed to give varying effects.

The "flickering flame" flutters like candlelight, giving a mood effect in conversation corners, dining areas, or other places where an intimate, romantic atmosphere is desired.

The "gas-flame" creates the soft glow of gas lamps. It's effective in entranceways, foyers, hallways, wall sconces or chandeliers. It's weatherproof for outdoor use.

An important rule of artificial light is to have it in the same location as the source of natural light. In this small bath, a perimeter of incandescent bulbs is at the base of a tray ceiling which is capped with a skylight. Note custom marble lavatory counter which gives a luxe look to compact space.

The "torch" is slim and tapers to a fine point. It's useful in lampposts, chandeliers, and wall sconces. A smaller version in clear or white blends well with contemporary or traditional decor in chandeliers and wall brackets. The same size in a wavy-textured finish comes in clear, white, ivory, and two shades of rose, and is popular in traditional chandeliers and wall sconces.

Globular—These bulbs range in size from very small to very large. The small or "bubble" size (15, 25, 40 watts) give softly diffused or tinted light in sconces, multiple-socket ceiling fixtures, and chandeliers. Inspired by the light in theatrical dressing rooms, they also can be found rimming make-up mirrors in bedrooms and dressing rooms. The large size (150 watts and five inches in diameter) spreads light without glare in hallways, terraces, and outside entries. A tear-drop shape directs light both upward and diffuses it downward through a bowl tinted ivory or pink. It's particularly useful in closets.

Low voltage—Twelve-volt lights are ideal for outdoor lighting, particularly along pathways and steps, in entryways, patios, and gardens. To use 1-v lights it is necessary to transform standard 120-volt household current to 12-volt current, but this can be easily done with weatherproof transformers designed to plug into any regular outlet; 12-volt cables can be buried about six inches deep in the ground, and the wiring strung along walls or run up trees.

Reflector type—These bulbs have several uses and come in three different types. Reflectorized bulbs have silver or aluminum reflector coatings either inside or outside and direct their light where needed.

Useful in home work areas (laundry, workshop), silvered-bowl bulbs are shaped like regular household bulbs, but their round, silvered end eliminates glare when hung above a work area.

Reflector bulbs resemble small floodlights and give brilliant spotlighting to decorative objects by directing their light in a narrow beam. Their silver coating is applied inside. They are also popular in recessed ceiling fixtures for directing light to art objects, a piano, or a conversation area.

PAR bulbs are molded out of heavy, heat-resistant glass and are commonly used outdoors, since they are weatherproof. They offer floodlight protection at night and lend decorative touches to gardens and Christmas displays.

Some floodlights come in a variety of tints for both indoor and outdoor use. Pink and blue white are flattering to both people and furnishings. Yellow and amber are used to create warm sunshine effects. If pink, blue-white, and yellow reflector bulbs are mixed together equally in the ceiling of a living area, they produce a pleasing and interesting "whitish" light. A garden can be washed in moonlight by floodlighting the branches of a tree with a blue-white PAR bulb. Since red, blue, and green are strong colors, they are usually reserved for holiday decorations or other special effects.

An entrance hall should, ideally, give a warm welcome to visitors. In this home, light is provided by adjustable ceiling-mounted "bullets" or recessed "eyeballs." Some are directed down near the door, while others are used to highlight the painting and the interesting and uneven texture of the stone walls. The result is pleasing and without glare.

Tubular shape—These slender bulbs are 1 inch in diameter and about twelve or eighteen inches long. Resembling fluorescent tubes, they come clear, frosted, or in colors. Showcase bulbs are similar, though they are only about six to twelve inches in length. This type of bulb is good for slender ceiling-hung fixtures or to highlight certain areas (in a range ventilating hood, over an aquarium, in niches, over pictures, or music racks).

Fluorescent tubes, though long familiar in commercial establishments, are now gaining popularity for household use, primarily because of their versatility and efficiency. A fluorescent tube is not a light source in itself but must be coupled with the necessary electrical accessories in special fixtures. They come in two shapes, straight and circular, and several shades. The cooler colors (those frequently found in offices and stores) are unflattering to complexions and furnishings. For home use de luxe warm white is recommended in either straight or circular tubes. Its light is flattering and it harmonizes well with incandescent bulbs. The four basic types for home use are eighteen inches long (15 watts), two feet (20 watts), three feet (30 watts), and four feet (40 watts).

TYPES OF FIXTURES

Fixtures can be divided roughly into three categories—those that are essentially functional (for kitchen, laundry, and activity areas), those that are both functional and decorative (lanterns, sconces, chandeliers), and those that are purely decorative (luminous or opaque pendants, glittering chandeliers, graceful candelabra, and glittering cluster effects).

Before you select any fixtures, you must draw up a complete plan for every room or area you wish to decorate with light. Even if you're working with a contractor on a major project, you'll get better results if, in the beginning, you can give him a clear idea of what you have in mind. He'll handle all details of specifications, but he can also tell you whether your daydreams are impractical and have to be modified.

First, you'll indicate how much structural or built-in lighting you'd like. Incidentally, structural lighting is best for a home or apartment that you own (co-operative or condominium). Landlords take a very dim view of any major wiring changes—to say nothing of the fact

This living room contains large-scale table lamps used for over-all lighting, while a tree lamp behind the wing chair spotlights the arrangement of branches in the corner, casting interesting shadows on the wall. A trio of tiny recessed downlights, wall washers, are available to flood fireplace wall with light when it seems desirable.

that in most city apartments you are expected to tear out any structural improvements you have made when you move out. However, if you are lucky enough to rent an apartment with plenty of electrical outlets you should be able to add a valance or install wall brackets without too much sweat and tears.

With your structural lighting plans on paper, you'll be in a better position to decide where you will locate such fixtures as sconces, chandeliers, ceiling fixtures, hanging lamps with a pulley or on a ceiling track, decorative spotlights or pendants.

Your final step will be to arrange mentally the placement of any portable lights, whether floor or table lamps. The greatest virtue of portable lamps is their flexibility, and ideally they should be both functional and decorative. In many cases, however, their ability to shed light has been all but eliminated. Like portable lamps, fixtures must be chosen to extend the decorative theme of the room in question. Again, manufacturers' catalogues will have fixtures to blend with every period style. Size is especially important when it comes to fixtures: The fixture must be in proportion to the size of the room. A small fixture in a big room stands out like the proverbial sore thumb. A large fixture can provide the same quantity of illumination and goes better with the scale of the room. That is the general rule. There are exceptions, such as the outsize chandelier in a narrow stair hall that is chosen out of scale for its drama. The fixture then becomes a means of making an area look more important. Here your eye will be the judge of correct size.

LIGHTING AND INTERIOR COLORS

In planning your lighting system the color and texture of the walls must be carefully considered. For economy in lighting, paint your walls and ceilings light colors. White and other high-value colors reflect a high percentage of light. (White actually reflects 82 per cent, as opposed to coconut brown, which reflects 15 per cent, and black, which reflects a mere 2 per cent.) Other light colors that have high reflectance values for walls are ivory, canary yellow, cream, palest green, and palest pink.

It's possible to light dark walls satisfactorily, but it's more difficult and expensive. A dull finish is usually recommended for walls, since it is more comfortable on the eyes than a shiny surface which can cause reflected light or glare.

A cold, white room can be warmed with the orange-color quality of incandescent light, yet this same quality is a distinct disadvantage if, for instance, you are trying to bring out the colors of an oil painting. Incandescent lamps are useful for highlighting texture (like a wall of brick or natural stone), contrasting with fluorescent lamps which offer better color rendition. One New York museum, hoping to achieve both excellent color and textural quality in its paintings, combined incandescent and fluorescent lighting. Unfortunately, it's been rumored that the high number of foot candles on the canvases is causing them to deteriorate at an abnormal rate.

You can change the color of your walls simply by changing the color of the bulbs lighting them. Tinted bulbs reflect subtle tones of the bulb color, and if you wish to emphasize a certain color in your room, such as rose, select pink bulbs. Since tinted bulbs absorb some light, you will need to use a higher wattage than with white bulbs to get the same amount of light (150 watts instead of 100 watts, for instance).

Do you want your room to have a cool, spacious look? Try incandescent bulbs in cool shades (blue and green) or cool white fluorescent lights.

Do you want to create a warm, cozy, and intimate atmosphere? Then choose warm shades (pink and yellow) of incandescent bulbs and warm white fluorescent lights such as the de luxe warm white.

CHAPTER SIX

STYLES OF DECOR

THE CHOICE of a decor style for your home is perhaps the most personal choice you make in your project. For when you choose, you identify with a given period in time. This is not to say that any of us slavishly copies the way anyone lived in the past or lives in the present. The plan you evolve for your home is a distinctive one that fits your own unique pattern of living. However, there is an underlying choice that we build around, and so we must decide at the outset which of the three basic decorating styles we want to live with. These are *traditional*, *contemporary*, and *transitional*.

Let's define what we mean by each of these. Traditional refers to all the styles of the historical past. We could go back as far as the Egyptian civilization if we chose to, because there are enough wall paintings and furniture to reconstruct pretty much the way they lived. That would be a tour de force that few if any could find as a comfortable backdrop for living. Our heritage usually begins with the sixteenth and seventeenth centuries and in the Western world. So for us, traditional decoration refers to one of the many styles that flourished in western Europe and in America from, say, 1600 to 1900. To a much lesser extent, it also refers to the styles of the Orient—of China and Japan. These are a very special matter and are usually contributors to blend with another style, but in the lexicon of decoration, they belong in the traditional category.

Contemporary obviously means those things that are current in time. In decoration, it means this and a bit more. There was a gradual break with the past styles in the early 1900s, and then in the 1920s a very sharp break which resulted in a quite special and different form of decor which was called at the time "modern," but this is a matter of semantics. It seems, to this author, to make more sense to refer to the entire movement from the early 1900s to the present as contemporary design and to refer to modern as a style within that broad category.

Transitional (or eclectic), the third style, is a mixture of the two others. Very few people want either a strict interpretation of the past or the stark simplicity of the contemporary idiom. They prefer a mixture of the two. It becomes a highly personal style, difficult to bring off successfully but very rewarding when it is attained. Now let's go into detail with the three main styles.

TRADITIONAL

The traditional style of decorating refers to any of the historical design movements of the past, from Jacobean English (about 1600) up to and including Victorian, which predominated in the entire Western world until about 1910. We'll first take a look at each traditional style from a historical point of view, pointing out the characteristics of the furniture, the predominant colors, and accessories that characterize the particular period. You can then refer to these as you build a decorating plan in one of the styles.

Early Influences

As we noted earlier, our decorating history really begins in the early seventeenth century. Before that only kings and the very wealthy nobility lived in anything that might faintly resemble a conscious approach to interior design. The adjectives used to describe what existed in England, France, Spain, and Italy are "massive," "heavy," and "somber." Room backgrounds were either rude plaster, stone or brick; wall ornamentation consisted of tapestries (they helped keep out the cold), wood paneling and/or oil paintings. Furniture consisted of rough-hewn, heavy tables and chairs, chests and massive cupboards. The wood was dark walnut or oak and in the finest furniture might be fancifully carved or done in chipwork, with some turnings for additional ornamentation. Beds were simply heavy corner posts supporting a canopy overhead and side curtains to keep in as much body warmth as possible. These effects were pretty much standard in the western European countries in what was the last of the Middle Ages or Gothic period. There were differences, country

LEES CARPETS

The combination living-dining room must be carefully integrated style-wise. Here, the traditional effect is complete from sofas to the smallest accessory. The predominant mood is eighteenth century with a combination of French, English and Italian furniture styles of that period. The oriental influence, common to the era, is seen in sculptured figures atop luminous cubes and in the over-mantel bird and flower painting. Pale carpet, blending with upholstery and wall color, is a strongly unifying element.

by country: In France, the interpretation was lighter, less robust; in Spain, there might be Moorish influences with more carving, more ornamental metalwork. The same might be said for Italy.

In the New World, what habitation there was (the Pilgrims didn't land until 1620 and the earlier Virginia settlement soon expired) was meager and held belongings brought from England. The Jacobean furniture that the first settlers brought with them were ruder versions of what was current in the mother country. Carved wood furniture—banister-back chairs, massive cupboards with half-round spindles,

BURLINGTON HOUSE CARPETS

A sitting room in traditional guise was more or less dictated by the hand-some eighteenth-century mantel. Pair of armchairs in quilted chintz, tufted love seat and English armchair in striped and flowered silk form an effective conversation grouping for the small room. Louis XV chest, with marble top and ormolu corners, holds down its side of the room.

painted dower chests, and chairs and stools were among the first few prized possessions brought by the earliest settlers. Pine and oak were the most available materials, although walnut was also used. As the Pilgrims began making their own pieces in the New World, forms were simplified and changes made. Among the first items of furniture were settles, tavern tables and plain, open cupboards for dish storage and slat-back chairs with rush seats. In the more refined homes, there might be a braided rug on the floor and simple linen curtains at the small windows with their tiny glass panes.

As English and other European styles gradually changed, the New World furniture reflected the changes. Close ties with the Dutch court and the resultant reign of William and Mary from 1689 to 1702 introduced baroque design to England. Completely upholstered sofas and chairs brought greater comfort; wood pieces had intricate floral marquetries and stylized ball and trumpet turnings; there were more paintings and other decorative objects. Contact with the Orient prompted experimentation with the cabriole leg (derived from the hind leg of a crouching animal) and with lacquered surfaces. Furniture making, with the many new woods of America, notably mahogany and walnut, flourished. Veneering was employed extensively.

The Neoclassic Revival—the Eighteenth Century

All this coincided with the Renaissance and its awakened interest in the designs of Rome and Greece, which greatly influenced interior decoration. The refinement of the *Queen Anne* (1702–55) style replaced the dark heaviness of the previous Jacobean and William and Mary periods. The design pendulum swung to more graceful, simpler lines. Marquetry was less used; new designs included unusual small pieces of furniture.

This led to the *Georgian* era with its elegant proportions and classical details. Many of the great houses of England were being built or extended at this time. Marble mantels in the Ionic or Corinthian orders and with delicate fluting were works of art; floors were installed with the most intricate parquetry. Colors in English decoration during the early Georgian period (1725–60) were green in all its ranges, blue, gray, white, and gold. During the later Georgian period (1770–1820) the Wedgwood colors—lilac, blue, dusty green, and off black—were favored, as were Bristol blue (a vivid turquoise), pale shades of pink and blue, light olive, gold and white with gold. These tones carried over into the later Regency period.

The eighteenth century was an extraordinarily rich period in England and America, not only in terms of furniture design but of life generally. There was a gracious, elegantly formal or informal way of living among the well to do and their homes and belongings reflected it. This was the age of *Chippendale, Adam, Hepplewhite* and *Sheraton*, among the greatest names in the history of furniture design. The style known as Chippendale came as a relief from the massive, ornate furniture designed during the Queen Anne period for the great houses of the English nobility. Thomas Chippendale published a com-

CHIPPENDALE DESIGNS

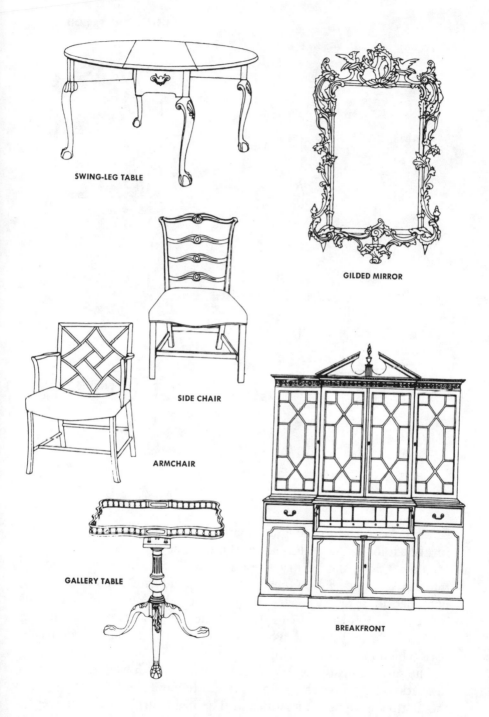

SWING-LEG TABLE

GILDED MIRROR

SIDE CHAIR

ARMCHAIR

GALLERY TABLE

BREAKFRONT

QUEEN ANNE PERIOD

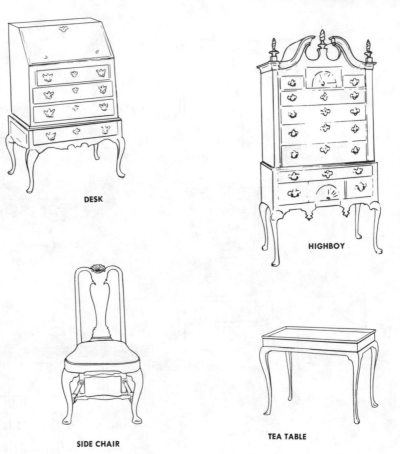

DESK

HIGHBOY

SIDE CHAIR

TEA TABLE

pendium of furniture designs suitable to every kind of house being furnished in his day. Research shows that two of his assistants, Matthias Locke and Henry Copeland, were actually responsible for this book, titled *The Gentleman and Cabinet Maker's Director*, published in 1754. Whoever its author, the book had a tremendous influence in England and in the Colonies. It established the flowing rococo style in England which wiped out the trend to ponderous mass which had been flourishing.

The so-called Chippendale style showed three distinguishing design derivations: the French rococo, the Gothic and the Chinese oriental, the first being the most significant. The main furniture forms were a continuation of those in the previous Queen Anne period: highboys, lowboys, secretaries, cabriole leg tables and chairs. Breakfronts and library desks were familiar large-scaled pieces. Mahogany was king and it permitted a delicacy of carved decoration as skillful as any ever done anywhere in the world. Chairs were typified by cabriole legs and claw and ball feet. Chairs with square block legs were often decorated with fretwork designs in the Chinese fashion. Gothic details included the pointed arch and tracery designs.

The most interesting aspect of Chippendale style was its ubiquity. It was to be found in the greatest houses in England in the form of massive breakfronts or library desks as well as in the guise of a simple maple chest in Pennsylvania or an ornate mahogany highboy in Boston. The block front chest with its convex and concave shell carving is a purely American design contribution to Chippendale. Lacquer work, often called japanning, was used on chests and cabinets, and some of the finest and most ornate carving was actually done in Philadelphia.

The same neoclassicism which flourished in France after the sensation caused by the Pompeii findings was also felt in England and the Colonies. In England, Robert Adam, one of several architect brothers, led the reaction in favor of it. It was he who designed the furniture which went into the great houses his brothers planned for the English wealthy. The new furniture was light in scale compared with Chippendale and exceedingly elegant in line. These lines were straight, enhanced with classical motifs and ornamentation. Chairs and tables had straight, delicately tapering legs; simple, oval-backed chairs and semicircular consoles were popular. Adam reigned from 1765 to about 1790.

Hepplewhite (1780–1800) continued the classic purity and became a style much copied in America. Mahogany was the main wood, with satinwood inlays as accompaniment. Pieces were gracefully scaled with tapered legs and delicate carving. Popular pieces were bow-front chests with bracket feet, armchairs with shield backs, cabinets and breakfronts with arched, fan-carved pediments, and Pembroke tables. The image of Hepplewhite as a style is based largely on a posthumous publication of the man's designs, called *The Cabinet Maker and Upholsterer's Guide.*

Thomas Sheraton also gained fame from books of his furniture sketches and these, along with Hepplewhite's, circulated in America and captured the imagination of American cabinetmakers. Sheraton

HEPPLEWHITE DESIGNS

SHIELD-BACK CHAIR

POUDREUSE

SIDEBOARD

TABLE

BOW-FRONT CHEST

SOFA

continued the interest in neoclassicism and, in fact, it is often difficult
to distinguish his work from that of Hepplewhite. In later years
Sheraton's work became awkward and heavy; square tapering legs
often ended in spade feet. At its best, Sheraton is characterized by
slim, tapered legs, inlays, drop-leaf tables, elegantly carved desks, and
scrolled sofas and day beds.

In Colonial America, as the great houses of Virginia, Philadelphia,
and Boston attest, there was great comfort, beauty, even luxury, and
a lively interest in beautifully detailed interiors. Expensive hand-
painted wallpapers were imported, magnificent fabrics came from
abroad and ships that plied the Orient and the Middle East brought

SHERATON DESIGNS

DESK

ARMCHAIR

CHEST

SECRETARY-BOOKCASE

COLONIAL AMERICAN PERIOD

SECRETARY-CABINET

LOWBOY

SLANT-FRONT DESK

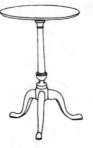

CANDLE TABLE

BRACE-BACK
WINDSOR ARMCHAIR

back rugs and exquisite porcelains. The simpler Colonial homes were apt to eschew the soft tones copied from the stately homes of England for the more robust primary colors which combined well with pine, maple, or cherry furniture, and natural wood paneling.

In Spain and the Mediterranean countries, bright, clear, even wild undisciplined colors predominated—marine blue, pimento red, deep sunburned peach, bougainvillea purple, brick and baked clay tones, sea green, cypress green, metallic gold, all accented with black wrought iron.

In France, concurrently, an extraordinary heritage of furniture design was developing. The luxury of the French court and the magnificence of the homes of the nobility brought about an immense effort in furniture design and production. The Renaissance in its first manifestations during the rule of Louis XIII in the early part of the seventeenth century was not too unlike the heavily carved oak and walnut designs found in Holland or England. Scale was massive; heft was pronounced. Louis XIV (1643–1715) style, which followed, was far more sophisticated. Pieces were still massive and heavily carved. Designs were, however, symmetrically balanced; bold curves and florid motifs were used in counterpoint. Furniture was extremely elegant with gilding, intricate inlays and painted decoration; proportions were excellent even in the most massive pieces. Ebony was much used. When Louis XIV died, a regency was set up until his successor, Louis XV, reached his majority. This period, known in furniture design as *Régence,* is among the most interesting. Designs began to show a softening and grace; formality and grandeur gave way to gentler lines. Curves flourished; cabriole legs, crossed stretchers, carving, and painting held sway.

Under Louis XV the court furniture factories were organized into an immense establishment directly under regal control, and production for the palaces of the Bourbons and other nobility assured a steady flow of furniture. Fortunately it was a period of some of the world's loveliest designs. The "rocaille" or shell design predominated, a classic motif, but one which pleased the French love of curves and movement more than the straight fluting and the geometric look of neoclassic design. Except for the uprights of cabinets, practically no straight line was used in any piece. The term "rococo" stemmed from the rocaille which took the form of elaborately carved mirrors, carving on the backs and fronts of chair frames, on the ormolu or brass mounts used on court furniture, on armoires, cabinets, and desks. Ma-

LOUIS XV PERIOD

BERGÈRE

SMALL SETTEE

SMALL SLANT-FRONT DESK

COMMODE (BOMBÉ)

TOILETTE TABLE

hogany and fruitwoods were used extensively. Much of the court furniture was gilded or painted. Carving was still used, but it became a leitmotif to enhance linear quality rather than the dominant design element. Carving was delicate and fanciful to the point of daintiness. Inlays were intricate; tortoise shell was a popular form. Richly figured marble and veneering were widely used as were gilded bronze mounts called bronze doré ormolu which served a secondary purpose of protecting the corners of delicately veneered pieces. Caning was extensively used for chairs. Upholstery fabrics and Savonnerie carpets designed in lush floral patterns were rich and elegant, as were velvets and cut velvets, damasks, brocades, and tapestries. Many lively pastels were used in design, some like Du Barry rose and Pompadour pink were named in honor of reigning court favorites. The most popular tints were salmon, light Pompeiian red, powder blue, citron, pale yellow, chamois, pale apple green, all varieties of pink and turquoise, often combined with pure white, narrowly striped, sprigged, or dotted.

LOUIS XVI PERIOD

FLAT-TOP DESK

FAUTEUIL

SETTEE

The reign of Louis XVI, known for its political turbulence, is also famous for a style of furniture that expressed the neoclassicism of the era. The design pendulum, swinging away from the curves of the rococo, went to the other extreme: the straight line. Curves were kept only where fluidity of design dictated. Legs were straight and decorated with fluting or reeding. Cabinets were more architectural in feeling, perhaps a result of the excavations of classical ruins at Pompeii and Herculaneum which caused great excitement at the time. Plain surfaces were found as often as inlaid or painted ones. Fabrics, still rich, were more delicate.

French Provincial

Side by side with the brilliant formality of court furniture, French Provincial, a simpler style, was developing in the smaller cities and in the countryside of France. Native woods were used—oak, walnut, pine, beech, elm, and wild cherry. Pieces were almost always in natural wood, without gilding or elaborate ormolu. The principal decoration was carving and it was especially beautiful and unusual. Armoires, chests of drawers, armchairs with rustic stretchers and exposed back slats and rush seats; fanciful clock cases, open cupboards and china cabinets with whimsical curves and carving were among the most common pieces. Provincial furniture was solid, sometimes even crude, but its design was imaginative and its charm was and still is enormous. In fact, French Provincial has influenced current decoration and design more than perhaps any other past style. The country look so popular today usually means French Provincial.

Nineteenth-century Styles

In France the neoclassicism, begun in the reign of Louis XVI, grew apace in the swaggering *Directoire* and *Empire* periods. Identification with the emblems of Roman and Greek times became a passion with the leaders of the Revolution who desperately needed to associate with something of substance and grandeur. In the Directoire period (1789–1803), efforts were made to keep the French cabinetmaking industry alive, but any motifs that identified with former court luxury were scrupulously ruled out. Geometric lines, moldings and brass trim, arrows and other warlike design motifs were accepted. Under

Napoleon, the classic features were continued and after his exploits in Africa, Egyptian motifs were added to them. Furniture took a massive, assertive look; marble was widely used; ormolu mounts took the form of classical creatures on a wide array of flat surfaces. Mahogany was much used. Since Napoleon's life was spent to a large extent in war camps, craftsmen often took camp furniture as design inspiration. Empire style long outlived Napoleon's reign and lasted until about 1830.

In England, the same period (roughly 1795–1820) was called *Regency* and showed the same interest in neoclassicism. There was a combined interest in Gothic and oriental motifs as well as Greek, Roman, and Egyptian. English Regency was elegant and, above all, formal. Canopy beds were elaborately draped; chaise longues, benches, and day beds were widely used as elements of decoration

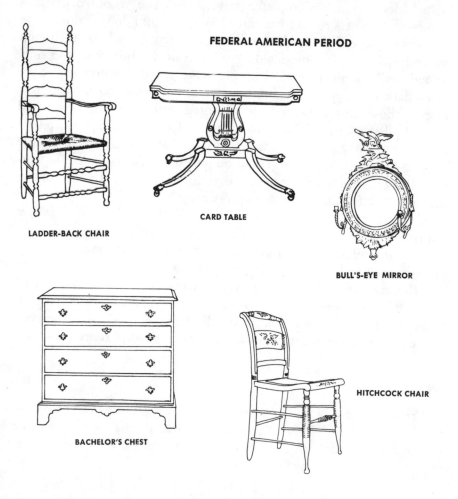

FEDERAL AMERICAN PERIOD

CARD TABLE

LADDER-BACK CHAIR

BULL'S-EYE MIRROR

BACHELOR'S CHEST

HITCHCOCK CHAIR

and their wood frames were elaborately scrolled and carved. Chairs were graceful with bamboo turnings and interesting caning patterns. Satins were popular for upholstery, in stripes and dark, rich colors. In time the style degenerated into awkward fussiness, foreshadowing the romanticism of the Victorian age.

The concurrent *Federal* period in the United States was typified by the work of the Scottish-born American Duncan Phyfe. Eagles and other patriotic emblems started to reflect the new national consciousness. Phyfe, who originated no new designs, incorporated motifs from the styles of Sheraton and Hepplewhite and left behind a great body of beautiful work. Sofas and chairs, gracefully curving, were designed in dark, highly varnished veneers of mahogany or rosewood. From 1820–1840, Phyfe turned to French Empire style, and the designs (in desks and chairs, for example) became heavy and massive.

In Federal room design, ceilings were high and woodwork was a dominant part of a room's backdrop. Window and door frames were often in the so-called Greek key design, ears that jutted out at the top on each side, in the same molding pattern as the frames at the side. Wood and marble mantels had the same motif. Wallpapers were often dark olive or grayed blue in stripes or simple classic patterns. Deep yellow was a favorite for painted walls. Rooms often had applied pilasters, fluted, and with Ionic or Corinthian capitals; pillars in the same orders were used as token barriers between double parlors; heavy, sliding doors could be pulled out for complete separation. White remained the usual background color and, as a foil for the massive, dark furniture, it was impressive.

In Central Europe, an interesting style called *Biedermeier* flourished about this time. Named from a fictitious character epitomizing the middle-class German, the style was at its best pleasantly proportioned and elegant in line, copying to a great extent Directoire and Empire designs. Light fruitwoods were accented with areas of black paint; surfaces were plain and few moldings were employed; brass ornamentation was sparse. Small chests with columns, carved frame settees and chairs with square, tapered legs were representative.

Victorian

The influence of England at the summit of her power and prestige was so great from about 1840 to 1910 that almost throughout the world the age took the name of the British monarch—*Victorian*.

SIDEBOARD

HALL CHAIR

SOFA

ARMCHAIR

There was a strong reaction against the formality and pomposity of the past classic styles. Victoria, as monarch and wife, emphasized a cozy family approach to everything, including decoration. As a result homes were highly eclectic. Gothic motifs—spires and ogee curves— were put with wild floral patterns; elaborate rickrack and other gingerbread woodwork were widely used as the fascination with the possibilities of the machine invaded every aspect of interior design; prints and paintings covered every inch of walls and what could be seen was also pattern in lushly flowered wallpaper. Widely used colors were sharp apple green, chartreuse, cabbage rose, eggplant, mauve, and all shades of brown. Furniture was often a highly exaggerated, overly carved version of Louis XV with the cabriole leg.

One exception in High Victorian was the work of an American, John Henry Belter, whose individual pieces showed great grace and have become prized collector's items. The pieces are heavily carved, often in rosewood, but with a fluid grace that gives an appearance of lightness. His was for the most part, however, a voice in the wilderness. Other furniture was heavy, using marble extensively; it was swagged, draped, and fringed; individual pieces were often massive. Some of the few small pieces had charm and these are today valuable antiques.

Just as the machine was influencing woodworking, so did it bring about a new range of woven fabrics—cut velvets, plushes, tapestries, and all of these took their place on upholstered furniture. As one can imagine, the result was often a rather wild melange with too much of everything—too much pattern, too much furniture, too much carved woodwork. At its best, Victorian was a highly romantic and sentimental style of great charm.

When we talk of Victorian, the Far Eastern, or oriental, idiom must be included. We have already seen that the eighteenth-century Chippendale style borrowed some designs from the Chinese. With the nineteenth-century creation of spheres of influence in China and the opening up of Japan, the effect of Asia began to be felt strongly throughout western Europe and America. There had been commerce for over a hundred years, of course, and certain elements of decor—rugs, porcelains, silks—had been brought from the Orient, but in the middle to late nineteenth century, oriental as a positive design influence began to be felt. It became another element to add to the heady mix of Victorian. From the salon of the Goncourt brothers in Paris to the Crystal Palace exhibition in England to the Chinese corner of a house in Boston or San Francisco the influence was felt. Along with the Far Eastern look came all the gorgeous colors so strongly associated with oriental design—lacquer red, kumquat orange, peony pink, deep turquoise, jade green, black. Accents included real gold thread, mother-of-pearl, and highly worked brass. Against these colors were to be found ornate ebony or other dark wood pieces of furniture from China, or the rattan, peel cane, and bamboo designs of India and Malaysia. Exotic peacock chairs and intricate cane and wicker pieces were standard fare on Victorian porches and garden gazebos. These designs came as a few of the light touches to what was usually a heavily overblown style of decoration.

CONTEMPORARY

The pendulum of taste finally swung away from the extreme romanticism of Victorian times. One important corrective influence was the British Arts and Crafts movement, headed by William Morris, designer of the famous chair that bears his name. Here the attempt was to return to the basic honesty and simplicity of handmade furniture. In Austria, clean-cut, flowing forms were manufactured by the me-

Contemporary decoration plan for a ski cabin relies heavily on plain white walls, textured shag carpet and the natural look of wood-encased leather seating pieces. Tables, lamps and all accessories except the Victorian clock are contemporary classics.

INTERIOR DESIGN BY DAVID MOLL/CHARLES BERRISFORD

Chrome steel dining table and chairs, lush fur cover for a divan and animal hides for accent rug and pillows are sure-fire ways to strike the contemporary decorative note. Zebra hide, a permissible import from Africa, is a strong foil for folding screens covered in a Moorish-patterned cotton fabric. Accessories are a mix of old and new.

chanical process of steam bending wood, and the Thonet furniture so popular today was born. Still another reaction to Victoriana was the Art Nouveau movement in France, England, and the United States which drew on the forms of nature for design inspiration. These fanciful designs grew so bold that the style became as romantic and ex-

BOUSSAC OF FRANCE, INC.

Attic workroom is a contemporary, functional unit in the shell of an old house. The geometric cotton fabric used to cover walls establishes the style quite positively and simple built-in wood storage pieces and sawhorse writing table underscore it. Pull-down light fixture and table lamp are sound, present-day additions to the scheme. Note how the interplay of dark and white restates the feeling of the wall covering.

cessive as Victorian and the movement died rather quickly. In the United States, the British Arts and Crafts style became the Spanish mission furniture which was so well known in the premodern period (1910–20), the massive oak, four-square desks, tables, and sofas that crowded many a bungalow in California and Pennsylvania.

ART NOUVEAU

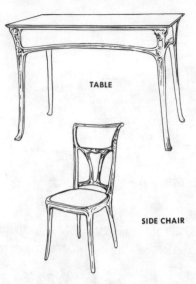

TABLE

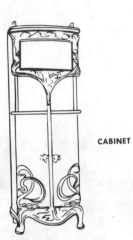

CABINET

SIDE CHAIR

BAUHAUS DESIGNS

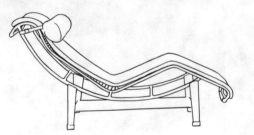

LE CORBUSIER CHAIR

CESCA CHAIR

BREUER CHAIR

BARCELONA TABLE

BARCELONA CHAIR

DANISH MODERN

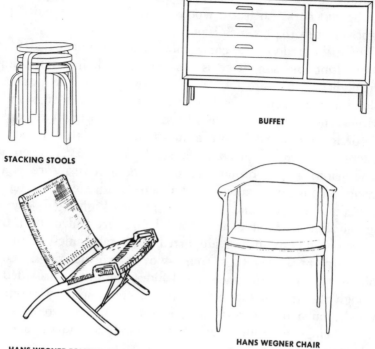

STACKING STOOLS

BUFFET

HANS WEGNER FOLDING CHAIR

HANS WEGNER CHAIR

Meanwhile, certain influences were at work paving the way for a completely new design idiom—modern, or contemporary, as you choose to call it, which was and is today a fresh approach to furniture styling, different from anything in the past. The Bauhaus school in Germany, founded in 1919, taught designers to free themselves completely from the past and try new ways of construction; in Sweden, designs for mass production brought experimentation with new and pleasant forms; and later, other Scandinavian designers brought forth a style of sculptured shapes which emphasized the beauty of wood, really an outgrowth of the ancient handcraft traditions of the Danes and the understated designs of Swedish furniture. The greatest contribution of Bauhaus was in furniture engineering, and the style is based on a frank revelation of machine-made attributes. The Barcelona chair of Mies van der Rohe was designed in 1929. The tubular steel, one-piece design for a chair by Marcel Breuer was first introduced in 1928. Laminated wood with its light, natural finish, first used successfully in Finland in 1934, was in reaction against dark, varnished woods. This led to the molded plywood Eames chair in 1946, which is now a classic.

The main credo of the contemporary movement is that form must follow function; simplicity is the watchword, hair-shirt simplicity. The light, airy, white look in home design became popular, with color introduced in abstract paintings, hand-woven rugs and simple artifacts such as sculptures and handworks of primitive peoples. The best designed modern furniture shows clean lines that reveal the basic structural system of a piece. Great strides in the development of man-made materials have brought much to modern furniture as a style—plastic, reconstituted and shaped wood, synthetic upholstery fibers, steel, aluminum, chrome, and other metals. Lighting is engineered—the old kinds of table and floor lamps are ruled out; beds are mattresses and box springs supported by metal frames; texture is used as pattern—in shaggy rugs, rough-woven wall hangings, bedspreads, upholstery, and in fur and animal hides. Pattern is provided largely through the architecture itself. In the contemporary room, people provide much of the pattern; it is a style which attempts to make human beings more important than bric-a-brac and to focus interest on human interchange rather than possessions.

TRANSITIONAL OR ECLECTIC

Of all the styles of decoration, transitional is the freest and, as we've said, the most difficult to bring off successfully. It is, in fact, the most common kind of decor, simply because most people don't care to live either with a literal translation of a past style or with the contemporary. It would be encouraging to be able to say that, with transitional, anything goes, but it is not quite that easy. As with the other styles, there are rules as to what can be mixed with what. Granted that the style is an eclectic mix, it takes great skill to mix without chaos. The first thing to remember is that any transitional room is based primarily on one of the two other styles: It is either mostly traditional with contemporary touches or mostly contemporary with traditional touches. One or the other predominates. For example, it is quite possible to do a living room with eighteenth-century antique desk, lamp tables, paneled walls, and Williamsburg-style brass chandelier, and include contemporary sofa and lounge chairs and abstract paintings. The secret of success would be in a color scheme that ties

This transitional-room setting is basically traditional—a country look. The decorative balance is jogged by a contemporary abstract canvas, a glass and metal coffee table and the shag area rug. Lavish fur throw for the tuxedo sofa is also a "now" touch. Other furniture and most accessories are period inspired.

everything together—perhaps colors for upholstery and carpet taken from a painting. The carpet would have to be neutral; a colorful Oriental rug would throw the whole scheme out of kilter.

Or an opposite solution might be a basically contemporary room with white walls, light-colored nubby upholstery for sofa and lounge

*Here is a brilliant example of the mix in current vogue. A Jacobean arm-
chair on one side of a free-form U-desk, and a pair of elkhorn chairs on
the other are about as eclectic an arrangement as one could imagine. Extreme? Yes, but it works, largely because of the clever manipulation of
white, and the built-in backdrop which becomes one single element of pattern, simply because it is so busy.*

chairs, light, neutral shag rug, and one magnificent antique piece—a
dominant armoire or chest-on-chest—and all traditional paintings and
accessories. Here the simplicity of the upholstered furniture, walls,
and floor would permit the pattern of the traditional elements. A balance of color and pattern would hold the scheme together.

How to Create the Three Styles

If you choose one of the traditional styles, a sure way to re-create it is
to use furniture—either antique or reproduction—that is authentic to
the period. You can use, for backgrounds, walls painted in the colors

typical of a particular period or papered in the given style. If you feel that a series of rooms or even a single room would be monotonous with all one type of traditional furniture, then mix periods. But carefully. An eighteenth-century country French piece in fruitwood will blend with an English eighteenth-century piece, but not happily with a highly Victorian or an oriental piece. A successful room can combine the many periods of English eighteenth-century furniture— Queen Anne and all the Georgian schools. French Louis XIV, XV, and XVI will blend, provided that they are either all elaborate court furniture or country furniture, preferably the latter, as the gold finishes and formal look of court furniture seem quite out of place in the home of today. The secret of blending is to keep some over-all relationship in scale, wood tone, and line. Then set against an authentic background—paneled, painted, or papered—the whole scheme settles into the traditional mood you have chosen. Last but not least, you should then accessorize the scheme with paintings, lamps, and other objects compatible with the period.

Where do you get the ideas for an authentic scheme? There are any number of places to find correct period style. Colonial Williamsburg is a gold mine of information on eighteenth-century American style at its best. There you can note the background colors and textures, the furniture, the flooring, rugs, accessories, and all the rest. Museums in the large cities have rooms decorated to a period—for example, the miniature Thorne rooms in the Chicago Art Museum, the various galleries of rooms in the Metropolitan Museum in New York. More and more, whole antique houses are being restored and decorated to period and are open to the public. Natchez, New Orleans, Key West, and many other cities have house tours annually where much information can be found. And, of course, the library will have a plethora of magazines and books with pictures of houses and rooms.

To create the contemporary room, you are in a sense breaking fresh ground. Again, however, the first rule is the same as with traditional: Choose furniture and accessories that are sold as good examples of contemporary and you can't go wrong. Keep backgrounds light toned and simple; don't crowd the space; keep air around everything. Use color in blocks rather than dabbling it here and there and use strong, preferably primary, colors. Use texture as pattern. Design your lighting carefully. Remember, one of the basics of contemporary is the use of engineering, the evidence of the machine in everything. This can get gimmicky and gadgety, so restraint must be used for a successful room or else the effect will be jarring and not comfortable. To find examples of good contemporary rooms, the furniture departments of some of the leading stores usually have display rooms with ideas. Keep in mind, however, that these designs are promotional and usually a bit too extreme to be copied as is in the average home. The quality home magazines regularly feature rooms in this style by top interior designers and these can be of great help.

When it comes to the transitional scheme, as we said earlier, it is the most difficult to bring off successfully. Choose one basic style—either a traditional or contemporary style—and mix a bit of the other with it. Equal parts of each will not work; one must predominate. Basically, you are balancing pattern in this style: Traditional relies heavily on pattern, contemporary, very little. So you must strike a balance, and distribute pattern carefully. When it comes to color, remember that, for the most part, traditional styles employ subdued color and also show very definite color preferences. Certain colors epitomize certain periods. Use some contemporary furniture and objects against these and you begin to get a pleasant mix. Conversely, contemporary relies on strong color, so a period chair upholstered in a vivid red fabric gives you a mix to start with. Accessories go a long way toward creating the transitional room. A highly personal mix with reliance on displayed collections—of paintings, china, paperweights, or what have you—can be a strong foil in an eclectic room.

As will be emphasized time and again in these pages, for success in decorating, move slowly and with knowledge. Study before you buy. Build all the elements of your plan carefully—the background, the color scheme, the pattern balance, the furniture and its arrangement, the accessories. That way you have a better chance to arrive at something you can be proud of.

PART TWO

The Main Ingredients
of Decoration

CHAPTER SEVEN

FURNITURE

WE ARE LIVING in a golden age of furniture making. Never before has there been such an abundance of beautiful, well-made furniture available to so many in such an immense range of style and price. New approaches to wood, new glues, new veneering processes, new finishes, new synthetic materials have been combined to produce a dazzling array of furniture for all tasks. This section should help you find the best possible furniture at the price you can afford and hopefully make shopping a rewarding experience.

CONSTRUCTION AND FINISHES OF WOOD

Since the first rude tables and benches that man fashioned for his use, furniture has been almost synonymous with wood. Exacting as much beauty, variety, and utility from wood as possible has been the goal of furniture design and engineering for centuries. Broadly speaking, there are two classifications of trees and their woods—hardwoods and softwoods. The former come from those trees with leaves that they shed in winter; softwoods come from trees with needles that are retained. Both are widely used in the furniture industry, pine being the most commonly used softwood and walnut, pecan, oak, maple, cherry, and mahogany being important hardwoods.

Hardwoods have richer grains and are more often found in expensive furniture where the beauty of wood is emphasized. Each hardwood has its natural basic color, grain, and texture, but different sections of a tree yield different grain and pattern.

The patterns, or figures, produced in cutting are often photographically or mechanically copied and applied to nonwood sur-

Contemporary designs are characterized by streamlined simplicity, with pattern stemming from the materials themselves used in direct way. In this setting, oak—in a light, bleached finish for the cabinet, dark patina for the octagonal table—blends handsomely with glass and with the leather and chrome of the chair and ottoman. The inside of cabinet comes in a brilliantly painted finish.

faces or to wood of less value. This kind of imitation is often referred to as "walnut finish" or "oak-grained." When these terms are used, it is wise for the consumer to ask the salesman just what the actual hardwood is or what process the surface of a furniture piece represents. The Federal Trade Commission has established strict rules against mislabeling simulated hardwoods, but the consumer is well advised to ask just what she is getting. Fine hardwood surfaces command premium prices beyond the simulated finishes, which are suitable and much in demand, however, for certain kinds of furniture.

The Nature of Wood

Whether wood is soft or hard, crotch, burl, quarter sawn or ribbon sliced, it has certain peculiarities around which the woodworking craft has been built for centuries. Its most significant peculiarity and one which affects furniture construction most importantly is its reaction to moisture. Wood is hygroscopic, that is, when exposed to damp air it will pick up moisture; when exposed to dry air, it will give off moisture. Contrary to much popular belief, high or low weather temperatures themselves seldom affect furniture, but weather temperature affects humidity, and humidity changes do require attention not only in the treatment of lumber before its use in furniture making but in construction techniques, too.

The moisture content of wood also affects its strength and so manufacturers give the closest attention to the control of moisture from the time they receive the rough logs to the finished piece of furniture. In most cases a certain amount of yard drying is given and then the lumber goes into kilns where it remains from one week to three months, depending on the nature of the species. However, as long as the piece of wood lasts, it will shrink or swell somewhat whenever its moisture content changes. Sealers and finishes will delay this process at the beginning, but in time, as humidity changes occur, moisture changes will take place in the wood. There is a theory that as time goes on the amount of change is somewhat less than at first. Some antiques seem to confirm this, but there is no solid proof of it. The safe procedure which manufacturers use in working out furniture construction is to assume that the amount of shrink or swell will always be the same as at first.

Veneered Wood Construction

One wood technique designed to control dimensional changes is veneering or plywood construction. Two hundred years ago veneered pieces were made simply by gluing a thin layer or veneer of fine wood over a panel of a common species. Over the years antiques so made often deteriorated because glues were inferior and the expansion and contraction of the two wood components occurred, causing swelling and peeling. More recently sandwich panels were developed in which layers of wood were glued on either side of a core, placed cross grain to hold the unit in tension as expansion or contraction took place. Fifty years ago this method of veneering was only as successful as the animal glues which were used. These were not strong and as a result veneered furniture got a bad reputation when peeling occurred in humid climates.

Today, veneered furniture, or plywood, as it is called in the industry, has completely overcome all its former disadvantages and the consumer should not regard it with the slightest suspicion. New urea resin glues are used between layers of wood to create a bonded whole of immense strength and great resistance to shrinkage and swelling. Plywood panels are made by pressure-bonding three, five, or seven sheets together. The most usual construction is five ply, with a core of poplar, basswood, chestnut, or some uniform wood, in narrow pieces cut with the grain and edge-glued to the desired width. Often a reconstituted wood product of wood chips in plastic is used as a core, a product that has no grain direction and as a result does not expand or contract. The veneer cross bandings on each side of the core have their grains running opposite to the core grain. They are usually $\frac{1}{20}$th of an inch in thickness. The face and back veneers whose grains run in the same direction with the core are usually about $\frac{1}{28}$th of an inch thick.

The advantages of this kind of construction, in addition to its strength and dimensional stability, are numerous. First, there is said to be less chance of inferior work in plywood construction. Second, much more beautiful wood patterns are possible with veneers; great grain interest results in the finish where selected and matched face veneers cut from either simple or exotic woods are used. Beautifully figured wood can be made more widely available at a price, since the veneer sheets are thin and many can be cut from one tree; different patterns are possible, too, when cut from different sections of that tree. Beautiful inlay or marquetry effects are possible with veneer. The veneers are taken from a given log with a sharp knife in a continuous sheet, the segments of which when cut apart are assembled successively in "flitches" or bundles, simplifying matching for magnificent effects, since the grain formation tends to be similar in given sections of a log.

Today a great percentage of all of the larger, flat, visible surfaces of furniture—tops, cabinet doors, sides, etc.—are made of plywood. This is also true of visible surfaces which are curved such as the fronts of cabinets or the rim of a grand piano. Legs and other parts which are carved or shaped by turning on a lathe are made from solid wood, or lumber, as the furniture industry refers to it.

Solid Wood Construction

Solid construction, of course, is as old as furniture itself. Actually, it is somewhat of a misnomer today, since veneered panels are also solid construction. What is generally designated as solid furniture is that with cabinet and table tops, drawer fronts and panels, bed panels, etc. made of one piece of wood. There is a substantial production of solid wood furniture in the same price brackets as veneered, since there is little difference in over-all production and marketing costs. In solid construction, the wood is milled to the proper thickness, length, and width and is kept at a proper temperature and humidity level in the plant and generally handled to minimize dimensional changes, warping, or splitting. In construction, the manufacturer must allow for more expansion of solid woods than is required of veneered panels. Solid wood, incidentally, expands across the grain rather than with the grain.

The advantages of solid construction are many. It can be carved with a greater degree of artistry than plywood. Worn down by use, it may be refinished by planing or heavy sanding. It cannot peel off and if it becomes scratched, dented, or chipped, there is no danger of a different wood showing through. Solid wood need not have an entirely plain effect, for it can be cut to bring out a variety of figurations in the grain, such as the swirling designs in mahogany. And it is obviously more adaptable to massive designs with intricate carving.

In order for a piece of furniture to be legitimately represented as "solid" walnut, for example, all exposed surfaces must be lumber, not veneer. This means that walnut-faced plywood cannot be used on any exposed surface if the furniture is to be sold as "solid walnut." If the piece has all exposed surfaces made of walnut, it can be sold as "genuine walnut" even though some of the surfaces are walnut veneer. One exception is Philippine mahogany and if the exposed surfaces are made of this wood in either lumber or veneer, the furniture cannot be sold as either "solid" or "genuine" mahogany. This is because, botanically, Philippine mahogany is not mahogany at all, but something else.

Finishes

It is the finishing that provides the final beauty of a piece of furniture. This step, which brings out the grain and adds the lustrous, deep

Instead of a conventional desk, a handsome Parsons table was chosen for writing chores in this den. The clean-lined piece, finished in tortoise shell lacquer, matches a little table next to the lounge chair and ottoman. In another setting, the Parsons table could be used for dining.

patina of the wood, is done by a series of careful hand operations conducted by highly skilled craftsmen. When the piece arrives in the finishing room, it must have been thoroughly sanded, polished with fine sandpaper, and given a final release to finishing. Defects are exaggerated by finishing, never hidden by them, and a satin smooth surface is mandatory not only for tabletops and cabinet fronts but for such areas as carvings and moldings.

Then as many as twenty-five hand operations are required to attain the finish you see on the furniture in the store. From bleaching the wood to its basic surface to the final rub, a piece may go through staining, toning, wash coating, sanding, filling, shading, sealing, sanding again, glazing, hand padding, spattering, and lacquering. Most finishing rooms are vast affairs with ovens to speed drying of the various coats.

The first step, sap staining, brings the lighter shaded sapwood to the tone of the heart wood with stains especially suited to a species of wood. A synthetic toner along with a toner reducer is the next step, followed by a pigmented toner. These accent the pattern of the grain. Often, hand sanding is done between the various sprays, including a pigmented filler, which is followed by shading lacquer. Glazing, the furniture maker's oldest finish, is a light oil-pigmented stain applied and brushed on to bring out the depth and tone of the grain. Light rubbing with fine steel wool further highlights the figure of the wood.

Distressing usually follows this step. It has taken a long time to convince the consumer that distressing has been deliberately done for an antique effect and was not a mistake in the finishing process. The attempt is to simulate the patina of age which has, in the case of antiques, come about through besmirching by insects, inadvertent scarring, age darkening, etc. The distressed surface is sprayed with a special ink to give the effect of spotting; age marks are applied with a special crayon. Distressing is a craft requiring the greatest skill. It is an excellent way of comparing superior and inferior furniture; the latter will be heavily and obviously executed, the former, lightly and sparingly, so as not to dominate the delicate patina of the basic finish.

Two coats of lacquer follow, sprayed on, and then hand or machine rubbing follows. Rubbing is a long operation during which half of the second coat of lacquer may be removed. It is the step when the effect of the finish begins to emerge, which may range from dull satin to high gloss. The last step before inspection and packing is hand waxing, which protects and enriches the finish. Painted finishes, which are so popular today, are created in much the same way as a natural wood finish. Paint as we know it is not used, but rather an opaque pigmented stain. This is put on first over the smoothly prepared surface and when dry, it is covered with a light sealer. Then a glaze is added for an antique finish. A clear lacquer is the final coating, just as it is with a conventional wood finish. Hand rubbing is done between coats and as a final step. The heavy brush marks which are often seen in an antique painted finish are added during the glazing process.

As you have gathered, furniture making from raw lumber to final finish is a thorough, scientifically controlled, and hand-administered process, with each step engineered and supervised to afford the most durable and beautiful wood effects possible. It is a unique operation which combines machine and hand in a manner different from any other industry. Both are necessary in the making of fine furniture; the day of the small cabinetmaker is past. For success today, furniture making requires a factory approach, but one that is always mindful that there are certain effects only the human hand can attain with wood.

How to Judge the Quality of Furniture—What Questions to Ask

Wood Furniture The foregoing should give you a considerable background of knowledge with which to approach the furniture salesman. Quiz him carefully on the nature of the piece in question; you will be able to tell quickly whether he knows his subject or is merely an order taker. Most salesmen on the floor of major department or furniture stores are trained and knowledgeable. However, in addition to questioning, there is much you can do and observe. Examine the piece carefully. The top should match the front for a uniform look; with veneered construction, a wild, swirly piece should not be placed next to a subdued grain. If it is solid construction there should be grain and figure uniformity. The finish should present a sheen rather than a shine; there should be a soft glow rather than a harsh gloss. Run your hand over the surface; it should feel perfectly smooth. Bend down and look over the surface against the light. Does it look flat and smooth or are there little bumps that shine like an orange-peel texture over the surface? If there are it is a sure sign that the piece has not been hand rubbed. The end panels and the inside of a cabinet or case piece should hold to the same examination of hand and eye.

Notice the edges, especially the edge banding on mitered pieces; this area should be done in a neat, workmanlike manner. Turn a chest or dresser around and look at its back: the back panel should be recessed into the upright posts, not just nailed or stapled flush. The inside of cabinet doors should be as pleasant to the touch as the outside. Doors should not stick or grab; if they do there was no hand fitting, which is always given to quality pieces. If you are buying a dining table examine the leaves; their grain should match that of the top. On a small piece and if possible on a large one, examine the joints to see if they appear to be made in a neat, strong manner. Try to force a fingernail into the joint. Hand sanding at the factory should have removed any excess. Notice whether joints were also corner blocked and screwed where major stress will occur. Look for the glue joint on the back leg of a chair; there, it should be especially solid.

Remember that while some modern glues are stronger than wood, glue alone is not enough for success. In some cases, glue has a forty-five-second set and there is no adhering quality at all if the surfaces were not joined immediately. Glue lines in lengths of a furniture surface—a back chair leg or a solid top of a chest—are not in themselves bad construction, but you must be aware that while a solid piece can be foolproof, edge-glued segments can embody human and machine failure to some degree.

Work the drawers in a chest. All drawers on quality furniture should be hand fitted. Inexpensive furniture tries to get around hand fitting with drawers that are too loose. You will see a large dark opening around the drawer which detracts from the quality of the piece. When you open the drawer, it should track in and out easily on a center wood or metal track. Drawers should be dovetailed with lock joints holding the sides to the front and back. This keeps the drawer from warping. Notice whether there is a dust panel between drawers; this should be on all quality furniture to keep anything which might protrude in a drawer from being drawn into the one above when it is opened or closed. This panel also keeps things from falling through. Some furniture also has a stop arrangement so that the drawer cannot be pulled out completely, causing spillage.

Test a small piece and, as much as you can, a large one for stability. As it is lifted or weight put against a side, it shouldn't rock or twist, a distortion due to too light construction. Does the piece have the heft that is required for its design? A large cabinet or armoire should give the feel and impression of mass and solidity.

Hardware is very important for the successful over-all appearance and function of furniture. There has been great attention to hardware detailing in recent years and some of it is magnificent. Generally speaking, hardware should be in proportion to and consistent with the design in scale and size. An overscaled, ornate piece of hardware is not suitable to a small simple piece and vice versa. The hardware should blend with the over-all design and not dominate it. Generally, as lines of furniture go up in price, the quality of the hardware goes up both in design and quality.

Feel the hardware. On bail pulls—those with handles held in two positions to a decorative back plate—the bail should have a solid feel. It should be a casting rather than a stamping—solid rather than hollow. The back plate should have thickness. Finishes should look antiqued or oxidized on a reproduction or an adaption of an old piece; they shouldn't appear painted or sprayed to look like brass. The best hardware is, of course, solid brass. There is also hardware that is cast metal, brass plated, which is lacquered to prevent further oxidation. Pewter is another variety of hardware finish. On pieces of certain styles—French Empire, Directoire and Louis XV—there has been lately a return to the use of decorative hardware called ormolu or trim, which takes the forms of rosettes, the anthemion, classic heads, figures, etc. It should be solid brass.

Hinges, whether concealed or decorative, should do the job they are designed for, namely to keep the doors from sagging and hold them in position. On some French Provincial and other pieces in country style, large brass and pewter hinges are exposed as part of the decor and offer an authentic charm when they are properly scaled. Notice, too, the less obvious details like the small ribbon of brass on the leg of a chair or table, called a shoe. Notice whether it is flush and appears to be attached firmly. The ferrule or metal foot on a table or chair leg, another so-called reticent detail, should also be neatly attached.

Upholstered Furniture When buying upholstered pieces, the home-maker is in great measure buying hidden assets. There are, of course, many things that can be appraised by the eye and the hand, and these we will study first before going into an examination of construction features and other elements under the upholstery covering. First of all, feel the chair or sofa. Does it seem rounded to the touch, with no wood or metal noticeable? This is important, because if you can feel an edge now, it won't be long before it comes through. Push on the upholstery with your finger along the outside arms and the back. Well-constructed pieces never have these areas left hollow; they are webbed or covered with cloth and a layer of cotton is used to soften the frame.

Run your eye over the welt line. It should go around straight and be neatly sewn. A welt covers a seam and the smaller the welt, the smaller the seam and usually the higher the quality. Double welting often means that the seams are too big to be covered with single; this does not bespeak top quality. Notice exposed seams; quality manufacturers recommended seven, nine and eleven stitches to the inch ac-

Hallmarks of traditional English design appear in this formal yet inviting setting. The camel-back sofa is an adaptation of which we think Chippendale
would approve; the print-covered wing chair looks back to the Queen Anne era
for its inspiration. The parquet-topped cocktail table, a modern innovation, is
supported by graceful cabriole legs.

That sleep-sofas have come into their own is seen in this handsome example. Tufted in vinyl upholstery, it is constructed of comfortable and durable latex foam rubber. The cocktail square and chair are both easy to move at night when the sofa becomes a bed. Another practical note in this family room is the two-drawer chest which doubles as a lamp table.

A tranquil, relaxing room offers the same winsome floral stripe on the sofa and wing chair. The gold, tangerine and oyster palette makes a fine foil for the warm walnut tones of the English-adapted occasional pieces. The lamp table is an unusual wedge-shaped design while the cabriole-legged cocktail table with its scalloped apron is a more classic example.

WALLCOVERINGS COUNCIL, LATEX FOAM RUBBER COUNCIL

The comfortable seating in this den includes a sofa which is sufficiently deep and well-proportioned and a roomy club chair upholstered in a stylized print. There is also a capacious cocktail table
sized to hold an ash tray, books and decorative objects yet still leave
space to put down glasses.

Furniture designs can draw from many geographical inspirations and blend many motifs. These two dining room settings are decorated with pieces reminiscent of ancient oriental designs from several Far Eastern lands. Yet in each instance, the effect is overwhelmingly Western and contemporary.

The collected look has replaced the old concept of furniture "suites." Many new collections of furniture are available which draw on many sources for design inspiration, but which form groupings that look compatible. Here a hunt table-desk (it includes a removable center section which converts it to a large dining table) of English derivation combines with chairs that have a French Country flavor. All are from the same group of pieces suggested by designs of foreign influence that flourished in yesteryear America.

French-inspired cabinet is another example of furniture which draws on the heritage of America for its inspiration. The painted and striped maple piece has paneled sides and front; ladderback maple chairs have a fruitwood-like finish.

HENREDON FURNITURE INDUSTRIES, INC.

ETHAN ALLEN, INC.

*A corner of a room in true French boudoir
style is an example of how pieces not authentic
in handling can give the flavor of authenticity.
The serpentine front dresser and mirror are
Louis XV in flavor but in a painted finish and
a scale probably not found in that eighteenth-
century period; the low armchair suggests the
country Régence look. Note again how finishes
can be mixed without any hint of effort.*

*Wood pieces, painted and decorated in authen-
tic Early American designs, provide colorful
and decorative accents in a room. Skilled artists, using the techniques of Colonial times,
stencil and stripe the pieces entirely by hand.
Lady's desk and rush-seated bench are examples of the best of today's offerings, with a
delicacy of coloring and a nostalgic charm ideal
for traditionally styled rooms.*

In a contemporary study, furniture and accessories that are traditional in design and inspiration mix pleasantly. The catalyst is color, handled in a contemporary way.

WALL-HUNG FURNITURE BY ROYAL SYSTEM, INC.

Systems of wall-hung furniture are especially popular for contemporary rooms in houses or apartments. Such modular wall systems appear as an architectural solution to decoration, permit attachment of shelves and cabinets in a variety of arrangements to suit individual needs. Special fittings secure wood or metal rails or supports to the wall. Here hi-fi record playing equipment with twin stereo speakers plus bookshelves, bar cabinet and magazine rack form a striking family room wall.

A Japanese tansui chest makes a good choice for the home where something old but not outrageously expensive is desired. The bright lacquer orange wood with its black metal trim inspired both a color scheme and a design theme for this foyer. Note how the accessories, down to the paisley-patterned fabric frames, continue the Oriental aura.

CELANESE

The small room which is kept light in feeling is most likely to succeed, decoratively speaking. Here the elements are a convertible loveseat, (smaller than a standard sofa), a see-through glass and chrome table and a space-expanding wall mirror. The wrought iron grill against the the white brick wall also underscores a bright and airy quality.

SIMMONS HIDE-A-BED SOFA

Several contemporary furnishing ideas meet in this room corner. First, there is a molded plastic upholstered armchair with a tilt-and-swivel mechanism that comes with a matching ottoman which swivels too. Then there are Plexiglas-framed dining chairs, a glass-topped table and a wall-hung storage system: all examples of up-to-the-minute design.

cording to the type of fabric and seam usage. On the top of a long sofa back, count the number of seams; the less there are the higher the quality, because it means that to minimize seams the manufacturer has suffered considerable waste material. Remember, neatly hidden seams tend to show up later after the piece is in use. Also helpful are the "contents" or bedding tags which many states require by law to be in evidence on the bottom of an upholstered piece and with mattresses. These show filling materials used and in what proportions.

Look at the side of an armchair; is it one piece of fabric or is it pieced? If the latter, has the piecing been neatly done with the fabric pattern matched for continuity? Study the symmetry of the design. With a patterned fabric for a sofa, the design elements are aligned. For example, a sofa covered in a fabric which repeats a bouquet of flowers should center a bouquet in each sofa bay. If there are three bays with three seat cushions the bouquet should fall in the center of each and correspondingly in the back panel above. The bouquet should also be skillfully placed on the arms and on the front all the way to the floor. Obviously this kind of careful matching is expensive in terms of the amount of fabric used, and it is a sign of quality.

Besides padding on the arms over the wood frame, there should be a soft edge along the front under the seat cushions, with a layer of rubber or cotton. In tufted pieces, the comfort wrinkles should spray outward from the tuftings. Learn to distinguish between hand tufting and machine, pretufted construction. Hand tufting will have a more casual look to the folds. Certain fabrics should not be tufted, so be sure to ask the salesman's advice. He should be able to tell you the kinds of fabric that lend themselves best to this design. Remember that climate has an effect on fabric, especially wool and silk. If a silk-covered sofa tends to sag a little in damp weather don't worry; it will contract again when the weather dries. It is much like a silk suit in its behavior.

Get an all-around view of a chair or sofa. The back should be as well finished as the front. In fact, a freely placed piece has no back or front. If legs are exposed the wood detail should carry around from the front so that all legs match. Be sure to ask whether a sofa or chair is covered completely in muslin under the upholstery; higher priced pieces often are. Notice that zippers on seat cushions are concealed neatly; look for straps or other fasteners that hold seat cushions in place.

Then sit down in the piece. Does it feel comfortable to you? Upholstery is one of the most individual areas of furniture buying: Some people like to be enveloped by a chair or sofa and luxuriate in downy softness. Others prefer softness with rigidity. If you and your family are rather short legged be certain that the piece is not too deep. Arm height is an important factor in comfort. Are the arms placed at a level right for your body? Do all the upholstered areas seem resilient and firm?

The Hidden Assets Now is the time to ask pertinent questions about what goes on underneath the covers and to evaluate what the salesman may tell you about construction. Ask the furniture salesman if

Assorted furniture styles work together because of two unifying elements: the tweedy wall-to-wall carpet in the same tone as the built-in wall, designed around a narrow, oddly placed window. Furniture includes a Parsons writing table covered in an oriental print, a metal-framed chair and matching ottoman in camp style, a graceful Sheraton-like settee and two English armchairs in different eighteenth-century styles.

there is a piece on which the dust guard has been partially removed for inspection. The following is information that may help equip you for this step. Let us start where the manufacturer does—with the frame. Fully concealed frames or frame parts are made of hardwood, the best for this purpose being hackberry, elm, oak, maple, birch, or ash. Kiln drying is usually done to reduce moisture content, but it is not as vital with unfinished frames as for surfaces which have to be finished. Air drying alone is sometimes used, reducing moisture content to about 16 per cent. Good frames do not vary too much, simply because they are not expensive. For example, the frame for a one-thousand-dollar sofa might cost only fifty dollars.

However, a good frame must be well joined. Frames should be doweled and corner blocked with the blocks glued and screwed for durability and greater strength. Screws act as clamps, helping to secure the parts as they dry. Foot and leg construction is heavily glued. Back posts are made of a single piece of wood and are doweled, screwed, and glued into place. An aliphatic (fattylike) resin emulsion glue is now more widely used than hot animal glue. Any exposed wood parts will be of a finer appearing wood than the frame and should be kiln dried. Hand sanding and rubbing will give it the smoothness required before the finish is applied.

Seat construction varies. Unquestionably the best method when practiced by master craftsmen is what is called eight-way hand tied. The highest quality upholstered furniture is so made, with springs tied eight ways over a fully webbed bottom. And don't be misled: Hand looping is not the same and is, in fact, an inferior way of attachment. Eight-way hand tying over a webbed bottom includes closely interlaced strips of jute or rubber webbing which are stapled to the frame. Jute strips are double-folded at each end before attachment. For additional strength, steel bands are sometimes attached to the frame under the webbing. Then double-cone upholstery springs are evenly spaced over this webbing base and each coil is coil stapled through the webbing and the tops tied in eight ways, by hand, with jute twine—front to back, side to side and across two diagonals.

This construction, while the top quality when properly done, is not the only good one. More frequently used is the solid burlap base since it is faster to assemble. Double-cone upholstery springs are then clipped or tied to the burlap. The springs are hand tied or clipped at the top both horizontally and vertically to form a level and stable platform for the seat cushions. One successful machine-made variation is a coil construction over a welded steel grid in which the springs are machine attached with strong wire. This unit is then dropped into the frame and secured with metal fittings. This spring-base construction is called "drop-in" and is prefabricated to fit a specific piece of furniture. A variation of this method is the use of spring units, muslined, pocketed coil springs, attached to a sagless solid piece of burlap with wire supports or suspension rods, with both joined to the frame. The advantages of these drop-in methods are said to include no frame strain, no twine breakage, and no spring bulge. The units may be either tailored or have a spring edge. Drop-in construction also permits a three-seat sofa to include three individual bays so that the sitter has in effect his or her own springs.

Tight-seat construction where no cushion is used often employs zigzag springs stretched from the front to the rear of the frame and attached with metal clips. These springs can then be joined laterally with link, extension, or helical springs and attached to the side rails.

Springless construction consists of a thick slab of urethane foam or latex foam rubber supported by a heavy-duty sheet support laid over a base of rubber strip webbing, closely crisscrossed to prevent sagging. Steel bands may be used under the webbing, to provide extra support. Most of these constructions can be examined by looking through the cambric or denim dust guard tacked to the bottom of the upholstered piece.

Edging comes next in the process. A hard edge roll of burlap or cellulose or a soft one of foam rubber is tacked along the top of the front rail of a sofa or front and side rails of a chair. Most heavy sofas and large club chairs are made with a soft edge, while those with a narrow base line have hard-edge construction. At this point, the base is ready to be finished.

To hold the springs steady, a sheet of burlap (sometimes with steel wires running through it) is placed on top of the base construction and tacked to the side rails. With hand-tied springs, the tops are also tied to the burlap. This step prevents the filling, which follows in the operation, from slipping through to the springs. The layers of filling material, placed atop the burlap, can be of a number of natural or synthetic products. Cotton provides good support, is odorless and doesn't disintegrate; interlaced hair, natural or rubberized, is moth and vermin resistant and gives a smooth surface. Feathers and down, once widely used, are today less common fillers. Foam rubber is crushproof and lightweight; urethane foam won't slip or tear, is crushproof and virtually odorless. Fiber fill approaches the comfort of down. The salesman should be able to tell you what kind of filling is used. The manufacturer readily provides this kind of information.

After a layer of cotton is added over the filling, a final fabric cover is sewn on with welts. Often this cover is the same fabric as the upholstery used on the outer areas and this is called self-decking. Once the dust guard is attached to the bottom, as noted earlier, the base or deck unit is ready for the upholsterer.

Back construction somewhat approximates that of the seat or base. It may be strip-webbed with hand-tied coil and edge-wired, using springs that are lighter than those for a base. As with the base, a prefabricated spring unit may be set in and fastened to the frame. The back may be simply strip-webbed, without springs, covered on the inside with heavy sheet webbing and then filled. Some spring back construction uses a layer of urethane foam and one or two layers of cotton.

After an outer muslin cover is added, the back is ready for the upholsterer. Arms are shaped to the frame and covered with a predetermined amount of filler—rubber, hair, roll cotton, or whatever. This material is tacked or sewn over webbing attached to the inside of the frame. Covered in muslin or denim, the arms are ready for the upholsterer.

Today, seat cushions are seldom found with springs. This type of construction does not hold up as well as the following types which account for the great preponderance of seat cushions. Down, once almost universally used in top-quality pieces, is still the choice in expensive furniture where a loose, fluffy cushion is desired. It consists of the soft under feathers of water fowl, wrapped in downproof ticking which is sewn in channels to maintain an even distribution. Luxury in a firmer, more fully bodied cushion can be obtained from polyurethane foam wrapped in Dacron. Polyurethane is one of the lightest weight cushioning materials, is resilient, soft and porous, and with great tensile strength.

Latex foam rubber also makes an excellent cushion. Made from the latex of rubber trees combined with synthetic latex, it can be individually molded into cushions or cut from slabs. Often there are pin cores extending from top to bottom. It boasts quick spring back, resiliency, and durability. It can be wrapped or used in conjunction with other materials. Such a wrapping material is polyester, a fiber with an even consistency and resistance to damage from alcohol or acids and with low water absorbency. It has a soft feel and offers a downlike comfort in the form of a new variation which has a denser denier and longer staple. Acetate fiber is another wrap-around material commonly used with a cushion core of foam rubber or urethane.

UPHOLSTERY FABRICS

Since style, decoration, and personal taste enter the upholstery picture, there are few guideposts that apply universally. Suffice it to say generally that where an upholstered piece will get a great deal of use and wear, a close-woven, heavy fabric is more suitable than a light silk or cotton. Where a piece is lightly used and serves more as a decoration than for seating—a hall bench or a bedroom sofa—less concern for wearability can be justified. Wherever you intend to use a piece of furniture, it is wise to invest the slightly extra cost in a Scotchgard or Zepel finish that makes it resistant to stains. Make as certain as you can that fabrics are color fast and shrinkage resistant just as you would in buying drapery or dress fabric. If spot cleaning is apt to be necessary, choose a covering and type of under construction, too, that will not be harmed by solvents.

REPRODUCTIONS OF PERIOD FURNITURE

It is important to remember if you are looking for newly made furniture that unless you are told a piece is an authentic reproduction, it is likely an adaptation. There are, of course, exact reproductions available today in quite a wide range of prices, but usually you are choosing from among pieces which have been rescaled to today's rooms. Fidelity to detail will vary in the translation and this is an area where a reference is useful in comparing, say, the treatment of an arm or a leg, the design of a chair back, etc.

We tend to forget that reproductions are nothing new. For example, the market abounds with copies of Louis XV and Chippendale pieces made barely a hundred years ago. True, their age makes them antiques, but it is important to remember that they are not of the period and will have variations in detail from the original concept of the style. Here again, comparison will be useful. When it comes to authentic antiques, there will also be variation. No two craftsmen interpreted the then current designs exactly the same way: The cabinetmaker of the eighteenth century who was a master of his craft was usually far too individualistic for that.

Authenticity is often difficult to recognize. Very little signed furniture remains and what does is not apt to be found readily. Age will often be revealed only in the condition and patina of the wood, in hardware, and in construction details such as joinings. And all of these can be simulated by the clever faker. Perhaps the important thing for the average collector to seek are examples of a favorite style which possess many of the details unique to the period and hope that his find is authentic.

SPECIAL FURNITURE

Besides wood and upholstered pieces, there is furniture in metal, rattan, plastic, cane, canvas. and many other materials. There are also wood pieces that are painted and decorated, and there are special systems of modular components that require a separate discussion. For want of a better term, we have included these under the heading of special furniture and will analyze the most important ones.

To lead off, consider the variety of metal that is used in furniture today. Besides brass and pewter for decorative hardware, which we have already noted, chrome, stainless steel, aluminum, and wrought iron are all widely used as part of furniture design. In contemporary or modern pieces—whichever term you prefer—designers use metal as a functional material which becomes a basic part of style.

Metal, once considered a crude structural necessity, is now regarded as a thing of beauty in itself and is handled with great attention to detail. So as you examine a piece of metal, give it the same appraisal as with wood. Feel it: Are the surfaces and edges smooth or are there jagged corners, clumsily welded seams, snagging rough edges? When you look at the metal surface against the light, does it have a smooth sheen or are there ridges, bumps, and scratches? Does the piece have the stability—whether it be a heavy or lightweight design—that the use of metal connotes? If it is combined with other materials are the joinings neat and workmanlike?

Wrought Iron

Perhaps the most common metal furniture is wrought iron. First designed for outdoor use because of its obvious weather-resistant properties, this kind of furniture has become a style idiom that is equally at home indoors. Wrought iron lends itself to contemporary design as well as traditional. Combined with glass, marble, wood, and any upholstery for seat cushions, it provides handsome groupings for any room in the home.

Wrought iron is really a type of mild steel which is formed by dies to create the details of legs, arms, etc. In manufacturing the basic frame, the welds which come into contact with clothing or hands are longer and more carefully made than others. Care is taken to eliminate little pockets which catch and hold water. Joints are ground down for smoothness. Equal attention is given to finishing.

Several types of metal furniture and accessories blend in a garden room with an entire window wall overlooking trees and lawn. Whimsical French baker's rack becomes a plant and accessory stand, an antique coal scuttle is now a coffee table to serve the sofa made from a metal camp bed. The armchair is in an ornate wrought-iron design. Plants reinforce the garden look.

For example, by one quality line, pure molten zinc is applied to the metal frame under pressure, becoming an integral part of the iron. This completely eliminates oxidation which is the cause of rusting.

The best wrought-iron furniture comes in colors that make it adaptable to any decorating plan. Seat pads and cushions can be covered as formally or informally as you like, either for indoors or out. For outdoor use, plastic materials should be mildew resistant and water repellent and as sun-fade resistant as possible. There are plastic seats resembling rush which is an integral part of chair design and construction. Outdoor cushions of a woven plastic-thread material provide ventilation with a construction that makes it unnecessary to lug them indoors at the first sign of rain or dew. Such cushions can be hosed down or scrubbed and will dry throughout the construction quickly and thoroughly.

Besides feeling the metal surfaces of a piece, inspect it to be sure it includes glides encased in rubber at the ends of legs to eliminate rattle and protect floors, indoors or out. If a table has a glass top, for full safety it should be tempered glass which, under strong concussion, does not shatter but rather turns into harmless particles like auto safety glass. Look also for rubber pads set into table corners to help eliminate rattling and breakage. Test a seating piece for comfort and mobility, remembering that backs can be lacy and light-looking and still support your back without digging into it.

Rattan

A jungle growth called calamus which stretches vinelike over the jungle floor has come to be a household word in furniture, namely, rattan. Found from Borneo to the Philippines, it is cut into twelve- to thirty-foot lengths and after being dried in sun and air is shorn of most of its bark and all its thorns. Later the material is sulphured to bleach its color and prevent infection by insects. For its use in furniture, certain varieties are stripped of the outer bark by scraping and the inner bark is carefully sanded to keep the quality of the joints or nodes, which add to the distinctive look of the wood. Rattan poles are seasoned, straightened, and inspected.

In the factory the poles are steam bent into various desired shapes and properly dried, and will retain their shape indefinitely. Machining creates the required joints; most successfully for load-bearing areas, a chucked and bored joint is used, comparable to mortise and tenon in regular wood construction. Joints are then glued and fastened with nails or screws. For decorative effects and greater strength, rattan straps and cane winding are glued at the joints, applied wet so that they will shrink and tighten as they dry. Seat frames and other parts of the rattan piece are, of course, hardwood, like any other fine furniture. Frames are finished for a natural or painted appearance and in the best finish. A final coat of synthetic varnish is applied for stain and alcohol resistance.

All of these features are items to look for and ask about. Rattan, once almost entirely a porch or sunroom variety of furniture, has now moved to many other areas of the home as the finishes and accompanying fabrics plus the approach to the design of the pieces have made it a highly sophisticated material. The current interest in Far Eastern designs—Japanese in particular—has brought the material into forms which look handsome in any room of a house decorated in this persuasion. For family and recreation rooms, it is sturdy, comfortable, and attractive.

Plastic

With each passing month, plastic becomes more and more a part of our lives, from the handle of our morning toothbrush to the cup from which we take our dinner coffee. The versatility and usefulness of the material in all its ramifications have not been lost on furniture designers. Plastic, being an inert material, is unaffected by humidity: It does not shrink or swell. It can be integrally colored to any hue in the spectrum; it will accept almost any patterned simulation, such as wood grain, marble, or tortoise shell. It can be molded into almost any shape. It is resistant to most stains, and while not immune from scratching, it will take considerable punishment and retain its appearance. For tabletops, it is resistant to dry heat up to about 275°.

For all these reasons, plastics have a great and growing place in furniture. The most widely accepted use is for the tops of tables and cabinets, areas which receive the greatest abrasion, and, of course, for upholstery in the form of flexible vinyl. Laminated plastic panels have been developed which simulate the pattern and even the texture of almost any species of wood to an amazing degree. Furniture manufacturers send samples of wood with the desired finish to plastic companies who can match them in a laminate with great fidelity. For the design purist, of course, something is missing and to the most sensitive eye and hand there is a false note. However, laminates, at their best, are undeniably handsome and practical. Perhaps they are most successful when used on their own merits rather than as a simulation of something else, and for that reason solid colors and black and white are the most successful in appearance. For example, black can be a stunning accompaniment to natural wood as the top of a mobile server or the lining of an open cabinet. White and brilliant colors are ex-

The modern-contemporary idiom is conveyed in a room where new furniture shapes and materials predominate. A pair of body-hugging, but different chair silhouettes, brightly upholstered, offer two types of contours with variations of metal bases. Bands of chrome outline the sofa sides while Plexiglas tables appear to float in the setting.

cellent for certain contemporary designs—simple-lined, modern chests and desks where the entire unit is surfaced in the material.

Like all other materials, laminated plastics vary widely in quality. They are not all the same. First of all, the finished look can only be as smooth as the plywood to which it is pressure bonded: if the under surface is not perfectly level and smooth, the plastic surface cannot possibly be so. Look across a table or desk top toward the light just as with a wood piece; if there are peaks and valleys, small bumps or scratches, you would do well to inspect another brand of merchandise. With the highest quality, you may be amazed at the degree of surface smoothness. Some manufacturers give almost as great care to a plastic surface as to a wood one: The laminated panel is hand rubbed with pumice to a soft sheen that can have the quality of fine ebony or slate.

Other successful uses of plastic are molded chairs, drawers, and decorative accessories like wall plaques where the pourability of the material makes it well suited to the design. Quite whimsical contemporary designs for bucketlike chairs and small sofas are to be found and here the only tests are eye appeal and comfort. Sit in the piece. Test it for resiliency. Feel it for smoothness, especially around the edges. Notice how it is attached to its base. Does the contoured form look flimsy or has it the stable look of something that is well designed and well made?

Stenciled and Striped Furniture

In the first half of the nineteenth century, American-decorated furniture reached a peak of perfection. Boston rockers, Hitchcock, thumb-back, and Windsor chairs and settees were elaborately stenciled and striped in gold and other colors, on black surfaces mostly, but also in colors and on natural wood finishes. Feathery designs were used for narrow posts and the other supports; gold striping became heavier and bolder on legs and chair rails. The new interest in Early American designs has made this kind of furniture available as volume-produced reproductions and adaptations.

For example, a chair or rocker is prepared for decoration by applying many coats of lacquer and stain to bring it to an almost finished state. An authentic design is selected and from it a stencil is made, an intricate design often requiring as many as fifteen stencils to record the detail of the original. Artists make the conversion from sketch to stencil by designing each stencil separately on architect's linen; these outlines are then cut by hand with scissors and sharp knife. A thin coat of varnish is applied to the surface; the first stencil is placed and the succeeding ones carefully follow in the same position. The varnish holds stencils in place and serves to hold the bronze powders to the wood surfaces. The artist with chamois around index finger gently rubs a few grains of bronze powder through the open areas of the stencil. By going back and forth to the palette box, he adds and shades colors which form the built-up effect of the decoration.

Striping which accents the basic line of a chair also is used as pattern along the arms or sides of a rocker or to frame the seat design. It is a technique which requires a high degree of professionalism. There has never been a tool to equal the sword striping brush in the hands of an artist who uses the middle finger as a guide where possible, holding the brush between thumb and index finger. Black is usually striped in gold; white in dark brown or black.

In selecting a piece of decorated furniture, the degree of the artist's skill will be easily recognizable. The designs themselves may be simple, even primitive, but the execution should be workmanlike, with straight lines of consistent thickness, subtle shading, and authentically muted colorations. The design should not look "stuck on," but should appear as an effortless part of over-all pattern and color. The final lacquer finish should give uniformity to the whole piece.

Modular Wall Systems

One of the basic tenets of contemporary decoration is that furniture and other elements should appear as part of an architectural design solution. This concept led to modular furniture which could be grouped into wall compositions, whether standing pieces of furniture, side by side, or units attached to the wall in various combinations. The bareness of most present-day apartments and houses has made this kind of wood and metal furniture especially appealing to the lovers of contemporary design. For example, bunched cabinets, flush-sided along a wall, can go to ceiling height, if desired, to form an entire built-in look. Wall-hung components can fill awkward corners, go around doors and windows, or can be adapted to serve as area dividers.

The wall-hung system includes a group of shelves, cabinets, and chest units of similar width with specially designed fittings to secure each separate element to wood or metal rails or supports fastened to the wall. Units can be arranged to any desired composition. Quality items to note include the basic rules of sight and touch plus a close inspection of the attachment system to be sure that fittings are foolproof and that wall supports are compatible with the type of construction in your building. Be certain, too, that the basic module is not overscaled for the area you have in mind. For example, if each modular bay is thirty inches and you have a fifty-inch space to fill, you cannot achieve a fully built-in, architectural look.

THE PROBLEM OF SCALE

Even to professional interior designers the choice of furniture scaled properly to a room, to a given wall, or even to a person can be extremely difficult. Rooms today are smaller and people larger; ceiling heights are customarily about eight feet; windows are apt to take up large wall areas. All of these factors add up to the importance of scale. While contemporary furniture is inclined to be long and low, antique pieces are apt to be proportioned to the large rooms of bygone days. The most successful adaptations of traditional pieces are those which have been rescaled to present-day situations. This is one of the most interesting contributions of furniture design in the last ten years: So many past styles have been beautifully interpreted in sizes that fit our rooms. For example, French Provincial furniture—enormous armoires, cabinets, and chests of drawers—has been translated in smaller scale while retaining much of the original flavor and charm in the carvings, paneling, and design motifs, to say nothing of the fruitwood finishes, complete with distressing marks and simulated worm holes.

Much of the success of French country style, so-called Italian Provincial, and Spanish has been due to successful rescaling. And so, for the most part, you can be sure that a newly designed adaptation will be compatible with the average-sized room. However, as you shop for furniture, it is important to have a specific location in mind and to know its dimensions. In the following pages will be a discussion of the finer points of floor planning. This is a linear aid, but you must also consider volume, the amount of cubic footage a given piece of furniture displaces in room volume. It is more difficult to think "in the round," as it were, but it is important. In certain cases a large piece can be interesting in a small room, but usually it proves only to be awkward. This does not mean that as the eye travels around a room everything should be at the same height. Not at all; variation is desirable, but some relationship in the depth of pieces on various walls is necessary or the room will look like a furniture store.

Considerable thought should also be given to the individual sizes and shapes of those who will be using the furniture. Too-tall cabinets can frustrate a short woman and too-low occasional tables a tall one. Nothing is as unhappy-looking as a large man in a small armchair or a short-legged woman sitting on a deep sofa. Today there is so much variety possible in size and shape of furniture that there is no excuse for the inhabitants of a home not being comfortable. Even if you do a great deal of entertaining, at least in your private quarters have pieces scaled properly for you.

The factor of apparent scale as affected by painted finishes and upholstery patterns and colors should also be studied. For example, in a room with dark walls a light sofa will look much larger than the same sofa in dark upholstery. Large fabric patterns for chairs can make them seem enormous, too, while small prints on large pieces can seem out of place. As you choose upholstery, you must once again think in the round. Close your eyes and try to visualize the given piece or pieces in the room you are decorating and then choose a design that will balance the background color, the other furniture, etc.

Standard Furniture Sizes

There are so many different pieces of furniture available that it is difficult to systematize more than a few sizes. Dining tables and desks are 29″, 29½″, or 30″ high. Width and length vary greatly and dining tables almost always come with extension leaves (be sure they are "aproned" to blend with the table). Table desks are very popular now and some are 72″ and longer. The rather new continental, or party-height, dining table is 26″. Chair seats, usually 18″ from the floor, are lower for this table. Cocktail tables are 12″, 14″, and 18″ high. Lamp and arm tables vary. Tall chairs can be 44″ to the top of the back and higher. Chest depth is usually 16″ to 18″; heights are 30″, 32″, and 34″. Wardrobes and tall cabinets can run as high as 84″. There are no standard sofa sizes. All one can say is that to qualify as a sofa there must be at least 72″ between arms.

Most upholstery manufacturers have sofa increment programs which permit an almost custom scale. Some of these are referred to as "sofas by the inch." However, it is important to know that if the size you request does not correspond with the manufacturer's standard spring width, it may not give the strength and durability you need. Bedding sizes are given in another section. One word of warning when ordering furniture: If you live in an apartment be sure you know the maximum size of sofa or cabinet your service elevator will accommodate. In a house, be careful of narrow stairways and small doors. Plan your dimensions in advance and your purchases will present no problems.

FURNITURE ARRANGEMENT—RULES AND TIPS

In many ways furniture arrangement is a key to both a good-looking room and one that is comfortable. In the previous section, we

One of the greatest contributions of present-day furniture designers has been the adaptation of traditional forms to the scale and use required for today's homes. Here are two excellent examples. The china cabinet with three long drawers was rescaled from an antique Venetian piece without any loss of authentic feeling. Its dimensions—65 inches wide, 14 inches deep, and 85½ inches high—make it appear comfortable in a new house or apartment. The bedroom wardrobe was adapted from a Louis XV French country armoire which had a single, solid door. In the adaptation, the door opening was created in two sections, so that the upper portion could accommodate bedroom television.

Lots of room for sitting in comparatively small space is offered by a novel furniture arrangement in which a one-cushion sofa is flanked by a pair of day beds. An oversized leather ottoman and a nest of table sturdy enough to act as stools further expand seating space.

discussed scale; here we must proceed on the assumption that scale has been taken into account and that the pieces chosen for a room are consonant in size and shape. With all the pieces assembled for a given room, where does one begin? The answer is with paper and pencil. On the theory that it is easier to push a pencil than a piano, we recommend that you buy graph paper at the stationery store (quarter-inch scale is good) and draw your room, one foot to the square, marking all the jogs, windows, and door openings. Then on another piece of graph paper make cutouts of your pieces, having measured them carefully. Now you are ready to proceed.

First rule: Analyze your room. Every room has a strong focal point of interest—a fireplace, a large window, a niche, or, in the plainest of today's new houses and apartments, at least a long wall that presents possibilities for creating a dramatic focus with furniture, an arrangement of pictures, a brilliant tapestry, or some other dominant decorative detail. Whatever kind of room it is, this area will form your springboard.

Second rule: Study the traffic pattern of the room; make sure you keep passageways free of furniture and that the most traveled route between doors permits an easy flow. Remember, too, that you can deliberately create lanes of traffic by furniture placement. For example, in a living room with little wall space, it may be desirable to force traffic around the perimeter.

Third rule: Distribution of the various pieces and groups should be even. The largest piece should be on the largest wall. Opposite walls should have groupings similar in area. That is, if you have a breakfront on one wall, for visual balance create a similarly sized grouping of pictures on the opposite wall. On the wall across from a dominant mantel, locate a bookcase or cabinet of about the same size.

Fourth rule: Balance is best achieved by distributing large pieces around the room. A cluster of small pieces in one corner and a grouping of heavy ones in another does not look well.

Fifth rule: Large units like sofas and cabinets should be kept parallel to walls; catercorner arrangements not only waste space, they look odd and amazingly old-fashioned. If you are determined to fill a certain corner find a corner cupboard, a small, crescent-shaped sofa, or some other piece designed especially for this purpose.

Sixth rule: It is important to achieve a balance of high and low. As we noted before, nothing jars quite as much visually as a room whose furniture height line resembles an electrocardiogram. You cannot successfully combine, say, a high-backed sofa and wing chair with a low contemporary armless chair or love seat. It is interesting, often, to have one tall piece as an accent, but it should take the form of a cupboard along a wall. Remember, however, that it is quite possible to decorate an interesting and functional room with all low seating pieces, relieving the scheme with tall window treatments, high mirrors, and large picture groupings.

Seventh rule: Plan a room in groupings. For example, in a large living room, a primary grouping could include seating pieces at either side of a fireplace, with a secondary seating group of lighter scaled pieces in a window bay. Or you might prefer a sofa and chair grouping at one end of the room and a game table and chairs as auxiliary furniture at the other end. There are as many variations as there are family in-

A cozy country look for a living room is set with tufted sofa and chair grouping. Tall chest and desk in the same wood tone hold down the far end of the room, while a pair of country French armchairs in a flowered chintz play against an unusual wall treatment which employs a flamestitch fabric, knife-edge pleated and held in place by moldings top and bottom. Wall-to-wall textured carpet is in a color common to other elements.

terests: music groupings with a large piano, television arrangements, informal dining areas, etc.

Eighth rule: It is better to have too little than too much furniture in a room. While a balance is the ideal arrangement, your rooms will look and function more satisfactorily if they are underfurnished. Clutter, once the order of the day especially in Victorian times, is no longer fashionable. Today the goal in most homes is visual serenity and this can usually be best obtained by having open areas where the eye can come to rest as it moves about a room. Today, too, space is at a premium, so it is important to be able to serve and entertain easily in many small areas. None of the foregoing is meant to say that a stark room is desirable. There is, however, a way to keep furniture to a functional minimum and embroider your walls and floor with texture and pattern that will make the room warm and enveloping.

Ninth rule: It is most important, as you take stock of the furniture you have, to be just as critical and unsentimental as you can. Weed out bulky chairs of indeterminate design origin, tables of awkward heights, and cabinets that don't look right. These can be catastrophic in an otherwise well-arranged room. In Part Three, where we discuss the aspects of decorating every area of the house, we will go into furniture arrangement pointers for each particular room.

How to Take Care of Your Furniture

Since good furniture represents a considerable investment, the homemaker is well advised to care for it as she would any valuable possession. It is a common mistake to believe that because manufactures are better able to get a durable finish on furniture today, less care is required. Fine furniture is like a fine car: Routine maintenance is necessary. It is also well to know what various finishes require and, equally important, what not to use in your maintenance program.

Wood Furniture

First of all, it is the kind of finish rather than the kind of wood which should guide you in cleaning. Also important is the degree of gloss you want. Present-day furniture is categorized as high, low, or satin gloss. All three finishes are provided by the lacquer sealer applied in the manufacturing finish, which you are protecting. In this protection process, the degree of gloss can be changed. In other words, if you want to change a low-luster finish you can switch to a polish that will provide a shine.

Dusting is the basic maintenance task. For this there are specially treated dust cloths or you can use a soft, lint-free cloth (knit underwear from which buttons and seams have been cut off is good). Cheesecloth is not recommended because it contains a starch sizing ingredient. Always dust with the grain of the wood. For cleaning fingerprints or an accumulation of dirt, a leading manufacturer recommends using a solution of one teaspoon of detergent powder in a quart of lukewarm water. Wring out a soft clean cloth with this mixture and apply to a small area at a time, stroking with the grain of the wood. Follow with a cloth wrung out in lukewarm water and then dry with a clean cloth. Never, under any circumstances, wash wood furniture with a quantity of water. Water is wood's enemy and manufacturers spend fortunes kiln-drying wood to remove the water. Don't complicate matters by putting it back.

For polishing, you can choose from an array of products for various requirements. There are spray containers with which you can dust and wax in one quick operation to give a high shine. There is a liquid polish that dries to a haze, then wipes off, providing a high luster without rubbing. Cleaning agents remove dirt and oily film. Cream polish is good for dull-finished furniture (such as Danish oiled walnut) and for oil-rubbed, open-grain wood like teak. Paste wax is recommended where protection is important. It is recommended for antiques or for worn, damaged or porous wood and will give the furniture a new lease on life with a rich polish. In this case, the more rubbing you do with a soft cloth, the more interesting the patina will be.

Here are a few hints for special maintenance problems on wood. Water rings from the bottoms of glasses will make white blemishes. Wipe water immediately. If rings occur, they can be removed or minimized by sprinkling a small amount of rottenstone from the hardware store and rubbing lightly. Another method consists of cigarette ashes and butter. Put some soft butter on the end of a finger, dip into ashes lightly, and rub lightly in a circular motion. Then wipe off the residue. On certain kinds of wood finishes this works almost miraculously with either water or alcohol rings. Speaking of alcohol, it is important to remember that no lacquer is alcohol-proof. If alcohol is spilled wipe off and wax right away. From a well-known manufacturer of household cleaning products come these handy tips: Never let a damp cloth—whether of water, dry cleaner, or any liquid including furniture polish—lie on a wood surface. It could damage the finish because the moisture will be trapped under the cloth and cannot evaporate. Avoid extremes of temperature and humidity and exposure to direct sunlight; checking and cracking may result. Paste wax will improve appearance if checking is not severe, however.

Scratches on dark wood can sometimes be hidden with an application of brown shoe polish rubbed in lightly. Don't cry over spilled milk; just remove it promptly and completely. Otherwise, white spots will appear the next time you wax. Should this happen, rub briskly with a damp cloth and rewax.

On cabinet and table surfaces, lamps and other objects can cause marring and scratching before you are aware that their bottoms are doing the damage. If such bases are not perfectly smooth make a felt pad of the same shape and place it underneath. Don't use rubber pads; some contain sulphur which will cause staining on a light surface.

Marble and Other Special Surfaces

Marble should be treated like any other fine furniture surface: coasters should be used under glasses and foods should be wiped up immediately, as with wood. Moisture rings may result from sweating glasses; beverages containing acid fruit juices or carbonation may etch the marble finish. Marble will also, merely through normal use, lose some of its lovely polish and acquire an occasional scratch. Fine scratches may be buffed away and the entire surface repolished when necessary with putty powder (from the hardware store) applied on a damp cloth. This polishing may be done by hand or with an electric polisher. Waxing is never necessary for marble, but if you prefer to wax yours, use a colorless, light paste wax. White marble, however, shouldn't be waxed, as in time it may take on a yellowish tone.

Routine cleansing should be done with clean cloths and fresh, luke-warm water. Twice a year it is well to wash the marble surface with a mild detergent to remove any residue dirt which might become ingrained. All stains must be drawn from the marble by poulticing with white blotting paper, paper napkin, or cleansing tissue soaked in the required solution for the kind of stain. This process may take from one to forty-eight hours depending on the age of the stain. To learn the proper solution for various kinds of stains, call a local marble dealer or worker. Some materials both stain and etch and two operations are required: poulticing to remove the stain and buffing to restore the glaze.

Laminates and other plastic surfaces can become dull-looking from wear and abrasion. Renewed beauty and color can be obtained by polishing with a low-luster cream polish or a silicone wax polish. Badly worn areas can be partially remedied by using a one-step au-

*Representing the currently favored eclectic look in decorating is a
dining room in which traditional elements such as that hallmark of
the eighteenth century, the oriental carpet, are teamed with a dining
set that is very much in the modern mode with its tubular steel and
glass composition.*

tomobile cleaner polish. Use a soft clean cloth and rub in long even strokes in the direction of the grain or pattern until an even gloss appears.

Metal and glass, if waxed, will permit finger marks, rings from glasses, smudges and other spills to be removed easily. Any type of furniture wax can be used to polish these surfaces. Tables and desks with leather tops are usually sealed in the same manner as wood surfaces by the manufacturer and the same procedure as with wood can be followed. If the leather becomes worn or the surface is slightly porous, paste wax will give good surface protection.

Upholstered Pieces

Upholstery fabrics may be of man-made or natural fibers or blends of both. Each fiber brings special qualities of wear and maintenance. Each possesses individual cleanability characteristics. Because of the variety of fiber blends, many fabrics are difficult to classify. Knowing general fabric make-up is an important guide. Here are thumbnail sketches of several popular fiber groups.

Acetate: Good cleanability and spot removal properties. Holds color well, has fair wear resistance and shrinkage resistance.

Acrylics and modacrylics: Excellent soil and spot resistance, resilient and fast drying.

Cotton: Strong fiber, with fair to good cleaning and spot removal properties. May be cleaned successfully if not excessively soil stained.

Nylon: Good cleanability and spot removal properties. Very durable, resilient, with good resistance to shrinkage.

Rayon: Good cleanability. Generally good durability and excellent color fastness, when solution dyed (dye added before fiber is produced).

Wool: Responds quickly to cleaning; strong and resilient; fair spot removal qualities.

As you can see, basically all furniture fabrics are cleanable, if not allowed to become too soiled. Occasionally, through no fault of the fiber or furniture, a fabric may shrink. This problem is traced back to the loom, when too much tension, perhaps, was placed on fibers during construction. Later, when exposed to cleaning solutions, the fibers "relax" to normal tension. Special caution should be exercised in cleaning foam-upholstered cushions, since the soft foam offers little resistance to shrinkage. In answer to the frequently asked question

"Will colors run?," it must be pointed out that while many fabrics are color fast, always be sure to guard against bleeding or running of colors by pretesting the fabric with your cleaning solution. There may be a single migratory member woven in with color-fast fibers.

Here are a few tips on how to care for upholstered fabrics. Fabric furniture can and should be cleaned regularly to keep fibers fresh and alive. Brush and vacuum upholstered pieces at least once a week just as you do rugs and carpets. Vacuuming will remove simple surface dirt, loose dirt, and crumbs. But a second type of dirt—the oily film of atmospheric soil from auto exhaust, cooking, heating, etc.—calls for extra measure. Don't delay when your sofa shows symptoms of needing attention—loss of color, darkening around the arms and headrest. Putting off cleaning merely gives this dirt an opportunity to penetrate deeper into the pile.

For effective home cleaning, start in the professional manner by pretesting the fabric's natural characteristics. To test for color fastness, moisten a white tissue or paper towel with the cleaner you plan to use and then hold it tightly for at least two minutes against an obscure fabric corner where all colors are present. Check for color transfer to the tissue. For shrinkage testing, sponge the underside of a cushion or fabric skirt with your cleaner. Allow to dry for about ten minutes, then compare the cleaned area with others for size. If your furniture passes the precleaning test safely, "damp-dust" fabrics whenever necessary.

Follow this simple formula. After vacuuming, spread suds of a synthetic solution you use on carpets over a small, one-foot area of fabric. Use a circular motion on loop fabrics, flat on normal cut-pile fabrics. (Velvet requires a special technique to prevent excessive shading. For the safest way, use a soft towel and a dry cleaning solvent.) Keep to a small area and be sure to rinse dirt from the sponge by squeezing several times in the cleaning solution before starting a new section. Work suds well into the fabric, but do not overwet. Then wipe with a clean white cloth and prop cushions on white paper toweling. Never lean them against a cushion liner of a different color since this could cause color transfer. Of course, if colors run or shrinkage occurs, a dry cleaning solvent should be used. While dry cleaning is the answer to both of these problems, it is not so effective in removing soil as the "wet method" and is always best left to professionals.

While spots are a secondary problem in furniture cleaning, they can become a nuisance if not treated immediately. Keep calm and act fast in case of spot emergency. About 90 per cent of all stains can be removed with just two products: A neutral or slightly acidic, nonre-soiling detergent will be effective on spots caused by food or food products. A dry solvent such as carbon tetrachloride will remove substances with a petroleum or vegetable base. (But use it only on natural materials; it may dissolve synthetics.) The prescribed formula for removal is: Scrape or blot up the excess; sponge with solution; blot and sponge again as necessary. No one cleaner, however, can solve all spotting problems. Get a first-aid kit with solutions for every type of spot cleaning.

Plastic and Leather Upholstery

Vinyl or plastic upholstery requires minimum but routine care. Sponge the surface with a household detergent whenever signs of soil appear—at least once every three months on light, less often on dark materials. Leather requires more devoted care to preserve its natural oils. For example, in addition to periodic cleaning with an approved detergent, leather should be treated to a special dressing to replace oils that are dissipated by the atmosphere. This treatment will also restore much of the original texture and flexibility of material.

Scratches, chips, or other damage to plastic and leather may be repaired through a unique recoloring process in which color is sprayed on and becomes an integral part of the fabric. This specialty service is available through professional experts.

Checklist for Proper Care

These tips will eliminate many cleaning problems before they occur.

1. When cleaning multicolored fabrics, pretest each color in turn for fastness.

2. Do not remove zippered covers when cleaning foam upholstered cushions. In case fabric shrinks, it will be difficult to replace covers.

3. Use foam of solution when damp-dusting to avoid overwetting fabric.

4. Protect fabrics from spot accidents by having a professional service apply an invisible, stain-resistant finish if furniture does not al-

ready have such protection (Scotchgard or Zepel finish).

5. Do not use strong acids or alkalis on metallic yarns in fabrics.

6. Avoid exposure to direct sunlight which causes fabrics to color fade and change.

7. "Browning" or discoloration caused by water-based spillage or some cleaners can be removed by a professional technique which draws stain material from the fabric.

8. Use only approved synthetic cleaners on plastic fabrics. Harsh solvents or paint remover will damage plastic upholstery.

BUYING ADVICE

At the outset, may we point out that all the foregoing design and construction details should help you to distinguish quality and value. What follows are suggestions on shopping procedures and attitudes. Here are a few don'ts:

1. Don't buy anything extreme just because it is on sale; a sofa with a bizarre fabric or an overscaled cabinet in an indeterminate period style will be hard to live with long after the sale is over.

2. When buying an upholstered piece, don't buy from the floor just because of the fabric. Later, if you want to co-ordinate drapery and other upholstered pieces you probably won't be able to find the fabric.

3. Don't be impatient and buy something just because you can get immediate delivery. You may have had that bare spot in the hall for ten years, even though you've decided to have a party next week. Most department and furniture stores don't stock enormous amounts of a given group; they have to order from the manufacturer and you must figure at least six to eight weeks for delivery.

4. Don't go on the assumption that furniture mark-ups are exorbitant and that there are always ways to wheel and deal around price. Mark-ups are higher than on some merchandise, it is true, but so are freight costs on items which are so heavy and bulky. The merchandising and distribution of furniture are a complex, time-taking business which requires the talents of many high-priced men and women. For the most part manufacturing quality is high, too, and you are getting real value at the standard price.

5. Don't be talked into anything by a pressure salesman. If the department or furniture store has a trained decorator seek his or her

advice if you are in doubt about a color or pattern in upholstery or the finish of a wood piece.

6. Don't gear your shopping just to the sale months of January–February and August. Shop the store a month before these sales and this will give you an idea of values.

7. Don't get carried away and spend heavily on an unimportant piece. True, it is desirable to have one big investment piece, but it should be the most important piece—the sofa for the living room rather than a curio cabinet for the bathroom. Almost every family can and should afford one or two really superb things: a magnificent sofa and an exquisite wood piece are good choices in most cases.

8. Don't be hidebound about what you feel you can afford. Many women who would buy several dresses a year at seventy-five or one hundred dollars blanch at the thought of buying an occasional table every ten years at seventy-five dollars. Set up a realistic, long-range furniture budget and keep your house alive with new pieces from time to time. It's a big lift for everyone's morale.

CHAPTER EIGHT

ANTIQUES

THIS CHAPTER is for the traditionalist or for the aficionado of the transitional mix. The contemporary purist can take a breather. First of all, let us say that for a period room there are few things that impart the special cachet of a fine antique. Forget about the fact—at least at this point—that it may be a good investment, forget that it belonged to your grandmother or your aunt Tillie. We are talking about decoration, and antique pieces will flavor it as nothing else can. Let's go through the main rooms of the house or apartment and see the possible role of antiques in each.

IN THE FOYER

What kind of foyer do you have? Not many of us are lucky enough to live in the kind of house that boasts one of those great entrance halls that the magazines love to show—the kind that go right through to the rear. These are found mostly in houses in Bucks County, Pennsylvania, and below the Mason and Dixon line. Although, as in everything, there may be exceptions. There are a few houses in New England that claim eminence with their spacious central halls. And, of course, the owners of these are avid prospective antiques buyers.

A long church bench, painted shiny black or a soft color to blend in with the wallpaper or paint, makes an attractive "filler" and a convenient place for a visitor to plop a coat and hat. (We are now talking about the large hall or the more generous type of hall, just in case you do have one and are wondering what to put in it.)

The walls of these central halls provide a fine spot for a grouping of heavily framed old paintings that are bringing a pretty good price today. But if you are lucky you can pick one up in some obscure place, without having to borrow from the bank.

A pier table or one of the old card tables with narrow flaps, perhaps one with a spread-eagle support, topped by an impressive mirror, would finish off this kind of hall. If you could manage to find an old jardiniere, one on a stand, and fill it with fernery, spiky cattails, or crisp rhododendron leaves, that's an idea.

But what about the small hall which confronts the majority of home and apartment dwellers? Is there room for an antique in the small hall? Yes. Many people decorate the outside of the front door with Indian corn, baskets of flowers, etc., but it is the inside that you see most of the time, so why not use this as a background for some interesting accessories?

Pick up an antique or a good reproduction of one of the familiar old sayings and put this toward the top of the door. It might say "Keep this house, Oh Lord, we pray. Make it safe by night or day," or "May this house to every guest be a place of peace and rest," or any similar sentiment. Then below that (on the door) put a basket (the antique ones have a lovely old mellow look) and fill it with a fern, plant, leaves, or live flowers, if you can afford them, or everlastings with fresh leaves. As the guest departs and the door opens for her exit, she has a pleasant indelible impression of a friendly house.

Fitting comfortably into a vest pocket-sized foyer is a small snake-legged candlestand—a nice resting place for an old-fashioned card salver used as an ashtray, a tiny vase, and a small converted kerosene lamp (perhaps in emerald green) with a pleated shade. A forgotten galvanized bucket that once served as a measure for oysters becomes a holder for umbrellas and the mixture of gay umbrella colors is a happy corner-of-the-hall note.

A ladder-back chair with a bright cushion takes up little space and usually even the tiniest of halls can accommodate it. Ancient keys are fun to collect. The old ones are extra large and are great as decorative accessories to be used anywhere. But three or four of them look especially interesting in the hall, perhaps over the ladder-back chair.

For something unusual for the wall (we'll have these in other places too), put up a pair of candle molds. But stick some candles in them to carry out your color scheme. Candle molds have become rather scarce, but they still are available if your candle mold spotting scope is in good working condition, and you don't mind snooping around in corners. Even the dented ones (if you have a handy do-it-yourself-type mate) can be made presentable with a little patience.

Remember seeing the lacy old iron picture frames? Bargain for one and paint it a color to complement your hall, then have a mirror set in it. Place this beside the door. Every woman loves to be able to glance at herself when she enters or leaves, for that matter.

Then there is the stairwell area. There should be something of interest all the way up. And here is where you can do the unusual with a collection of antiques. Don't be timid. Just because you haven't seen something used a certain way doesn't mean it can't be charming and original. Everybody loves to see ingenuity at work. For instance, a little black chair with arms and a carpet seat made for a very small child or a very large doll, when hung next to a clock is a good conversation piece. But when told this, most people exclaim, "A chair on the wall?" Well, why not?

A collection of local prints, taken from a brown-aged book or magazine, can be framed with two-inch wide, one-half-inch-thick pine. Used en masse they make a fascinating going-up-the-stairs decoration. Some charming old frames were made from the wooden pipes of an ancient church organ as was a lovely hanging shelf in the upper hall. The mellow patina of the old wood gave the little hallway great prestige.

An old cranberry globe hanging lamp with its rosy glow is a pleasant hall appendage, especially when it shines on some Civil War paintings and a shiny ancient bugle complete with knotted gay red cord. If you can collect embroidered flag pictures, these make a nice companion piece with the war paintings and the bugle. If your hall will take it, this is the place for the grandfather clock or the grandmother clock, which is a smaller edition of the grandfather clock and a worthy object to place at the foot of the stairs.

In the Living Room

Nothing can make a living room come alive better than the softening effect of antiques. No house should be a museum, however. Nothing could be more grim than a historical collection in each room with the lady of the house acting as custodian and putting up a mental rope across each chair. And nothing can be more trying than to see the wary hostess' sudden scowl of fright when a hefty visitor sits down on her antique needlepoint, or her sudden lurch to rescue her treas-

One authentic element, the roll-top secretary, gives an antique look to an eclectic setting when combined with good reproductions like the small Louis XV sofa and open arm fauteuil. Clever distribution of the bright floral print—in window shade, valance, pillow and chair seat—adds bite to the otherwise rather somber scheme. Room is an excellent example of transitional style so popular today.

Looking like a medieval throw, this modern bedspread with its fat fringe, complements the heavily fringed canopied top. The Franklin stove is a thought for you when you want to break up the ordinariness of a room with a warm idea. Another "copying" idea is the group of Staffordshire animals on brackets for a fascinating wall diversion.

A brilliant turquoise table cover and accessories used with black and white and olive green set off this cozy Victorian group to perfection. The crisp window shades bordered in the same ebony braid as the draperies give the scene just the brisk modern touch it needs. Lighting up the hung-nice-and-low picture, the Rochester lamp is a good choice.

A pair of Victorian rosewood open-arm chairs and an Empire round table with green marble top create a focal point in this room. The mellow old mahogany armoire is from New Orleans and challenges the modern mirrored screen on the opposite side of the room, creating a pleasant balance between the old and the new.

LOUIS TREGRE, F.A.S.I.D.

A rag rug and a Hitchcock chair (whether authentically old or a modern rendition) can set the mood of a room. Of course when these are aided by a mantel decor of pewter, brass andirons and a chintzy flowered curtain it helps along the "George Washington Slept Here" effect. The deep scalloped bed cover and pleated under ruffle are well worth remembering.

Here eighteenth-century formality is reproduced with the aid of a harmonious background of wall-papered mural with birds and boughs, and a lushly draped window treatment. Hurricane chimneys and Meissen bowl lend a charming dignity to the buffet. The filigreed chandelier looks down on a company-for-dinner table setting that employs fine china, crystal and silver to carry on the mood of this room setting.

Looking very "country kitchen," this room may give you some idea of the accessories you could have fun collecting on your next antique hunt—coffee grinder, mortar and pestle, pots, pans, grille, jugs, hanging drawers, baskets, cradle for firewood or magazines, wooden bowls. Just about everything goes!

INTERIOR BY JOHN E. WINTERS, A.S.I.D., AND FABRICS BY BRUNSCHWIG & FILS, INC.

ured bellflower goblet from inquisitive fingers. Just as a gathering is much more enjoyable where there is a mixture of young and old people, so a room always seems more charming when there is a combination of contrasting eras in furniture and accessories.

No matter what type house you may have or how your apartment is decorated, it would be the better for a sprinkling of some lovely things of the past. What kind of antiques go into the living room of today? Let's start with the fireplace. And don't think that these are relegated to the old Cape Cod or Georgian or Federal houses. Practically every split-level or ranch house is sporting an outside chimney rising skyward with the television aerial. There are still antique andirons to be found as they were used not only in what was known as the "common rooms" of the old taverns (of which there seems to have been one at every crossroad), but in every cottage and even in the great houses where often they were made of silver and bronze. They come in a variety of styles—keyhole, Hessian soldiers, cannonball, etc., and in short or tall slender designs. The more elegant the andiron or firedog, as they are sometimes called, the later the period in which they were produced. The real old ones are sort of primitive-looking and mostly all are black. The polished brass ones are dressier and give a room that added note of shine so desired today.

Of course fire screens are of later vintage, but those and a shiny brass fender have practical uses and do dress up the hearthside. If you can pick up a working bellows, this makes an engaging addition to the fireplace dressing. An elegant long, brass-handled spiked poker adds to the picture and is most efficient. A set of fireplace tools with tongs, broom, etc. isn't really necessary and at most times is just in the way. But if you have them use them.

While antiquing, by all means look for one of those handy copper boilers. It will make an excellent receptacle for wood and kindling, nestled up to the side of the fireplace. Or find a generous, round iron kettle, which was formerly used importantly, if not elegantly, in butchering pigs.

Many of the modern fireplaces subtract the mantel, but if you have a traditional fireplace, what to put on the mantel rates more questions in a question-and-answer column than practically anything else. The idea is not to have a row of small objects strung out all across the mantel. This offers nothing. You might get away with using these small objects, if they are dear to your heart, by grouping them together and placing something of a different ilk among them, like two candlesticks (used together), a beehive clock, or three antique strawberry baskets, used en masse (with their dainty strips) filled with philodendron. Placed in strategic spots (you may have to try several effects), this arrangement is simple enough to be most satisfactory. Or a simply designed pitcher or urn filled with rhododendron for either side of the mantel, while not very original, perhaps, is always very effective. With a ceramic dog or a Staffordshire cat in the center, it can produce quite an impressive air. Old sconces make wonderful dress-up aids when placed low, flanking the mantel. And hurricane lamps, set in pairs, contribute their bit to mantel glamour. The use of live plants in interesting antique containers always seems to bring life to the accompanying inanimate objects.

Let us move out into the room. If you can get hold of an antique desk, this makes a good mixer for the living room. The slant-top schoolmaster's desk or the shopkeeper's desk is a rare find but worth the hunting and the cash involved. The apothecary desk is practical as a small bookcase, a desk and a series of small drawers for negatives, cards, and the array of things you never know where to put. An old inkwell or a quill pen resting in its pellets of lead adds character to any desk.

The use of the cobbler's bench as a coffee table has moved to the family room. But all kinds of beautifully designed antique benches offer plenty of space for a tray and an assortment of magazines. If you go for the rough primitives (which many young marrieds seem to take to), an old water bench sets the stage for simple, but unusual effects in interior design. An old wooden mixing bowl, filled with a wild shade of yarn (even if you don't know a straight knit from a purl) or a bowl filled with bright red apples on your coffee-table bench will add a nice dollop of color to that section of the room.

Antique doorknobs are still available and can pretty up any door with a touch of individuality. These and the decorative old curtain or drapery tiebacks and the antique brasses are yesterday's legacy for embellishing a room and make it enchanting.

Old glass paperweights make interesting items to collect, and when used in a group, become decorative side table conversation pieces. They were called "paper holders" when they were originated and present an array of flowers, shells, butterflies, and other interesting phenomena found in Mother Nature's kingdom. Circling a lamp base, they give the effect of the base being buried in a garden of jewels.

On the subject of lamps, some of the kerosene lamp bases are real beauties and if you can find the colored glass ones, a rich ruby red, a luscious emerald green, or a glowing amber, grab it fast. The authentic ones are becoming scarce and their pleasant highlight of color on a stand or table is sure to be appreciated by even the most callous observer. You still can find at antique shows and in antique shops the large glass bases with their thumbprint or raised sausage-link designs, and these, used with a smart shade, make good "light" conversation.

The coffee grinder, the scale, the cranberry picker, etc., used as lamp bases, have disappeared into the family room or have been converted into other things, and the lamp bases, using antiques, have been simplified. Old milk cans have been attractively painted, beautifully designed bottles, some in the original aquamarine hue, and clean-cut glazed jugs have taken the place of the tricky household utensil rage of a few years ago, in the living room, that is. Elsewhere they may still be in evidence. Perhaps we are getting back to an age of simplicity.

The commode, a relic of antiquity, has found a new place in the living room. It is now transformed into a housing for the stereo and works very well. The small door at the bottom disguises the speaker. The other speaker is encased in a correct sound spot inside a low, old pine cabinet with a niche for oversized books. (This is an idea for those who like their stereo but want to keep it companionable with the rest of their furnishings.)

Perhaps if it is your lucky day you may find a tilt-top table. Everybody seems too practical minded today to leave it tilted as a corner decoration. It makes a good-looking living-room piece and serves as a lamp table, a place for favorite bibelots, and a book or two.

A music box, with its tinkling theme of "Gentle Annie," is a favorite collector's article and is becoming quite rare. Perhaps with a little oiling and prodding you may find one that will play without skipping a note. Some of the music boxes are most elaborate. Some are enclosed in the rear of a photograph album, which is almost as much fun to look at as the music is to listen to. The cover usually is of embossed ivory and the back a bushy plush, and they are about the size of the family Bible.

Barometers and clocks, pictures and portraits keep the walls from looking dull. A great find is a piece of venerable tapestry that displays a picture of an old house, a child, or other person. When this is framed, it lends a certain dignity and a touch of novelty to the spot to which it is assigned.

IN THE DINING ROOM

There is a wide choice here. All you have to find is a dealer who is there with the table you want and can afford. It might be a primitive sawbuck table with maple trestle and a pine top with supports in the familiar X with horizontal stretchers. Or it might be the extra long table with the pine top and birch trestles. With this you would use long benches. The harvest table, usually made of pine, with its hinged sides and straight legs has been copied so well it's hard to differentiate often between the old and the new, especially if the new is slightly beaten up with simulated age marks.

For the more formal, a Hepplewhite table with eagle inlays would be money invested. (It's a question whether roast beef would taste any better from this than the simple sawbuck, but it would be a beautiful show-off piece for the real antique lover, where patina, form, and perfection really count.) With this, if you could find them, you could use any of the formal-type chairs, the Queen Anne or Chippendale would do nicely.

For the small apartment, there is nothing like the graceful, old drop-leaf table. It can be folded back against a wall when not in use and brought out with both leaves extended for guests. For a larger dining room, used against a wall, with one leaf opened out, it serves as a good food center for a buffet party. If you choose a drop-leaf table with slim tapered legs it could be a partner to practically any other period furniture you might select.

Practically any of the Windsor variety of chairs, with or without arms, would be an asset to a dining room bearing the Early American stamp, although they are so adaptable that they may be used in rooms of almost any period. The chairs most familiar to everyone are the Hitchcock chairs, with their identifying pillow backs. It is said that three fourths of the original Hitchcock chairs are still around, some with their stencils faded and dim. The earliest ones show the Hitchcock name stenciled with this inscription: "L. Hitchcock, Hitchcocksville, Connecticut, Warranted." These are the most valuable to own. Then the next age is the one bearing the words "Hitchcock, Alford & Co. Warranted." (Evidently Mr. Hitchcock annexed a partner during this period.) A later crop bear the words "Lambert Hitchcock, Unionville, Connecticut." This information is mentioned so everybody can turn over his Hitchcock chair to see what vintage he has. It's always fun to learn that you may have something special that you picked up at a bargain. Incidentally, Hitchcock chairs still are being turned out at the Hitchcock Chair Company in Riverton, Connecticut. They claim to be using the same techniques as back in the early days and the details do defy even the closest comparison with yesterday's models. Any Hitchcock chair is welcome in any room of the house. Used around a table or singly, they have that "right" look teamed up with English, French Provincial furniture, or any of the contemporary expressions.

Another chair that looks especially well used with an early harvest or trestle table is the slat back. Or it may serve as an occasional chair. Usually with rush or reed seats, the original ones were quite primitive, with roughly carved out knobs on the top of the back of the chairs. Not all the early homemakers were expert craftsmen, remember. Of course, the style was copied and polished later on and they are quite presentable anywhere. The proof of this lies in the fact that modern designers have copied this type with streamlined simplicity.

If you have a small dining area and are buying things with your wedding-present check, why not collect the old ice-cream chairs to go with a round table? Drop a gaudy flowered cushion on each chair and watch that corner of the room blossom out in cheer. These chairs, with their wiry scroll or sentimental heart-designed backs, painted a chalk white or shiny black or even a sunflower yellow or cyclamen pink to go with your color scheme, lend a lighthearted young spirit to a dining spot. (We must admit it's hard to tell the old ones from the reproductions, but if you are an antique buff you'll enjoy the searching and collecting.)

If you are looking for one piece to really "set up" your dining room choose what was called in the old days "a cupboard." This consisted of top shelves and a lower cabinet with doors. If you are carrying your four-leaf clover someday you may run across one of the primitive ones made of pine. These are of the simplest design. One, picked up at an auction years ago, had heavy top doors. Some owner, with dreams of creation, had painted wild palm trees on these doors. They were removed and the lower doors inverted to show up a nicely raised design, and this piece, bought for thirty-four dollars at that auction is today worth fifteen hundred dollars, as shown in one of the large department stores that stock antiques.

But if your dining room has a more formal feeling you may be able to pick up a beautiful specimen with shell carvings and scroll-top panels in the door. (This would be *the* find of the century and would take many pieces of eight to buy. But sometimes, even the very wealthy move, die, or fall upon bad times, and suddenly decide to part with their ancestral pieces, or their heirs do.)

But to get on with decorating with antiques in the dining room, the white ironstone in platters, covered tureens, and open vegetable dishes can look as modern as a Picasso. The early ironstone often was decorated and embossed. And some of the ironstone produced in the 1800s could be recognized by its garish colors. But today we think of ironstone as white, perhaps with a wheat-entwined border. A shelf full of these pieces creates a startling white backdrop.

A collection of glassware, smartly displayed, can serve both a practical and a decorative purpose. If you have antiques use them. Letting a cup collection or a glass collection gather dust, for example, and never using them is unfortunate. With care, there's no reason why you can't use and enjoy your collection hobby. A hoard of glass sugar bowls (always with the cover missing) is a boon when serving sundaes as there is room for all those luscious sauces or, for the diet conscious, serve a fruit cup. Ruth Webb Lee's *Handbook of Early American Pressed Glass Patterns* gives you the names of practically every glass pattern, so you know what to look for when filling your cupboard or hanging shelf in the dining room.

Pictures of birds may be found in the old print shops. Put into antique frames with an intriguing mat and used in groups, these bird of America are a good dining-room wall suggestion. And any of the old mottoes that look as if they were embroidered but are really done on paper, such as "Eat, Drink, and Be Merry," offer a delightful invitation before sitting down to the table.

All sorts of antiques can be used for a buffet. A long thin sofa table, a dry sink, an old spice cupboard, a chest of drawers, any interesting piece that you find, with a bit of imagination, may be turned into use as a buffet. With a charming old mirror topping it, any dining room would thank you for the addition.

Candlelight belongs in a dining room and luckily a collector still can find a goodly selection of candlesticks in brass, glass, porcelain, and if he's lucky, pewter. Even if your room goes in for twentieth-century innovations, candles still hold their own, providing a soft and flattering light for dining. A variety of candlesticks (always with candles, of course) used en masse creates a smart centerpiece or side-table talk about. Several candlesticks make an individual top-of-a-piano group.

While we are in the dining room, don't forget to enhance your silver chest with some fine old pieces. A few graceful-handled serving spoons, a long-handled stuffing spoon, or a soup ladle mixed in with your own service add a bit of pleasant variety and are practical serving aids to boot. Documentary plates or scenic plates hung on the wall or displayed on open shelves in a cabinet, or, if you have an old house, marching around a plate rail, arrange their own private showing of plate art. This makes another thing to look for when you're searching for an excuse to go antiquing.

IN THE FAMILY ROOM

First, let's set up a game table in the corner. It could be one of the old pedestal-base circular variety or the familiar tapered leg type or even an oval tavern table with turned legs and box stretcher (four pieces of wood joining the legs together and used as a support). Small chairs with caned seats, which seem to be in evidence at practically all antique shops, make fine seats for games or study or viewing television or watching family movies.

This room is a collector's haven. Here is where the duck decoys are displayed on the table or on an around-the-room shelf built high over the door tops or are grouped together on a deep windowsill. Here is where that old toy bank collection is on exhibition on semicircular single shelves over the sofa. As a new one (an old new one, of course) is added, the wall design becomes more interesting. Tiny, but fierce antique lead soldiers may be fighting a losing battle on a deck shelf. If you are fortunate enough to have collected lead soldiers a few days before yesterday you have a valuable collection. A group of these in early regalia recently brought eleven hundred dollars in a private sale. So you see, antiques not only are fun to collect, but, as we stated at the beginning, they can prove a good investment. The only sad part is that people become very attached to their collections and hate to part with them. But a harsh necessity for one may prove a bonanza for somebody else.

The family room is an excellent place for one of those writing armchairs with a drawer for pens and paper. Your child can write his composition on "Living on the Moon" on a writing board that has been in service over one hundred years, back when the moon was just something to sing about around harvesttime. Strangely enough, this old and practical item doesn't seem one bit out of step in this room with its modern sofa and floor cushions. If you can find an old wall box (probably used to store salt in former days), this would make a great garage for keeping odds and ends such as playing cards, paper clips, elastic bands, etc., necessary details but unattractive to have scattered around loose.

A pair of wing chairs with their draft-protecting wings would be a comfortable twosome especially if they were accompanied by two old footstools, covered in the same happy print as the chairs. Some of the early wing chairs are still around, but they have become real collector's gems and appear mostly in museums. However, they have been copied so faithfully, that used with the old footstools you could keep a would-be connoisseur guessing for days.

The old Bible stand can be utilized as a recipient for the giant family dictionary or a large art book. And here is where you could use that cobbler's bench if you had one. It serves as an adequate coffee table or cocktail table or a place to put up your feet while relaxing on the sofa.

An old butter churn comes in handy as an end table and is fun, as hardly anybody can identify this rural necessity of bygone days when churning butter was an accepted part of every housewife's daily chores.

A schoolroom clock, octagonal shaped, with its melodious half hour and hourly bong, would be a helpful wall adornment, or the popular Banjo clock would find itself in good company with the age-old sporting prints for the walls. If you are going to collect old prints, find old frames to put them in or have frames made out of old, old wood. An old print in a brand-new frame stabs the eye with a something-is-wrong sensation, but half the time the viewer doesn't realize what the trouble is.

If you can't stand that blank stare of the television screen when the television isn't turned on, you might try one of the old-time pie cabinets. With its pierced tin sides (to let air in on the pies) a television fits in its interior, and when the door is closed you have an interesting antique piece. Top it with a bouquet of flowers in an old teapot and an early saucer for an ashtray, and it will earn its keep in space any day. If you can't find a pie cupboard, use the bottom half of a cabinet that has lower doors. It works the same way.

A chess set is not amiss sitting on the game table by itself on a small stand. Some of the early chessmen were quite primitive as the more aggressive country people often carved their own, after a visiting peruked city relative had described the game to them. There's always something fascinating about the forms on a chess set, so even if you can't tell a knight from a castle, if you can locate an old chess set, keep it in sight, just as if a player were going to sit down and ponder the next move. It's a decorative piece of strategy.

In the game department, an old checkerboard, faded, but with its squares intact makes a charming wall decoration for a change of pace from pictures. Along this line, what do you do with a collection of old playing cards? A good idea is to paste them onto a good-looking background and frame them in one of the old rococo frames. If the frame isn't in too good a condition paint it a bright color to bring new interest to your room.

In the Kitchen

The country kitchen, so-called, whether it's in an apartment or in a house on a village street or on a country lane, offers all kinds of possibilities for antiques. And used in a decorative way, these items of the past help to warm up the room and give it a character that serves to distract from the so-functional look of the very necessary refrigerator, stove, and sink. Let's begin with shutters, indoor shutters. Somehow these immediately set the stage with an individual accent. Use them at the window with a window shade in stripes or florals to go with your bench or chair cushions. Use them as doors and on the cabinets.

Old shutters are available at antique barns, home demolishers, and construction plants (where they tear down old houses and put up new ones), or barns where shutters have been removed from the house and stored in the barn to get rid of them. Or use the modern louvered doors and shutters of today. The effect is the same. A series of tiny shutters that can be folded and unfolded is a practical and terribly attractive way to "curtain" a window. Painted a matching or contrasting color, these shutters can do wonders for any kitchen. And if you're tired of the same old fluttery kitchen curtain, look at your window. Why not try shutters?

You can use the full-length shutters hinged into three or four sections, either to hide something—your sewing corner, perhaps—or to add an interesting new texture to your background, or just because you like shutters.

If your kitchen is the all-around type, you will have room for a dry sink. This is a sort of kitchen cupboard (no top shelves) with a sunken well that was usually lined with metal where dishes were washed in a dishpan. You had to be careful not to splash the water as there was no drain for a spillover. It was exactly what it sounds like, a "dry sink." This makes an excellent bar with plenty of room for glasses, bottles, and other accouterments that go with serving cocktails. Bottles of soft drinks, paper napkins, and coasters find plenty of houseroom in drawers and in the cabinets below. There is usually a shelflike unit on the left-hand side. This can hold a bouquet of flowers in a delightful old urn or some sleeping spring bulbs in a lovely Meissen bowl.

Look for a collection of old-fashioned kitchen implements—the chopping tool with its flat, wooden handle, a long-handled fork, a flapjack turner, an old sieve, an iron muffin tin. Group these together and you have a wall decoration. The black muffin tin makes a smart emphasis note and invites a search for other black objects such as an old bootjack made of iron.

Over the door in the kitchen is a good place for one of the favorite old "Home Sweet Home" signs or for any of the old tavern and taproom adages. Old newspaper items used on a red or lemon-yellow mat and framed in pine add interest to a wall, as do the old flower and bird prints.

A live bird in one of the lacy old bird cages adds a joyous note, especially if the bird happens to be in one of those heavenly colors of bluebird blue or canary yellow. You can also fill an old willow or tin cage with live plants that drip their freshness through the slender bars. The cages themselves are most decorative, and although they have become more in demand the last few years, if you have the heart of a hunter you will find one to your liking.

A jewel-like old Tiffany shade is just the thing over the table in the dining section of the kitchen. Of course, these have been reproduced and do-it-yourself Tiffany shade kits have been on the market, but there still are authentic Tiffany lamps hiding in some of the old houses and in the better antique shops.

Any nice old round table is a pleasant partner for the Tiffany shade to shine upon and when it is surrounded with the real McCoy of captain's chairs (or an absolute facsimile thereof), nothing gives the dining area a more inviting air. This is a happy breakfast spot and it's a just-right site for a family snack. A little atmosphere means so much.

A row of apothecary jars used as canisters—for flour in the father size, sugar in the mother size, and coffee (instant or otherwise) in the next size, tea in the next, with the baby size holding the salt—are the most practical of canisters, as the visibility is so good. You can tell when an item is getting low and it's time to order. Besides, they lend a nice clean look to your kitchen as they decorate your sink counter in their various sizes.

The old breadboards were often cut out in the shape of farm animals. For instance, in a recent visit to a roadside antique place, there was a wonderful, exceptionally large one in the shape of a pig. It had been painted a mellow barn red and would make a perfect wall decoration for a kitchen.

Any of the antique implements, such as a sugar scoop, any old measuring cup or spoon, lacy old trivets (used in groups), become ornamental aids when properly placed. Even an old vegetable shredder when hung on a wall takes on the guise of an imaginative prickly porcupine. When you go antiquing, look for these early utensils, usually found sticking out of a basket or box in semiretirement away from the glamour items. Think of something that no one else has. Be original and selective in your choice and have fun with the hanging.

If you are an herb lover, scrounge around for some of the dainty herb prints and use them, framed, as a border around the top of your painted wall. Or even start a small herb garden, parsley or basil, for instance, in an antique tin breadbox, top open. You will have the interest of watching something grow as well as the reaping of the harvest when you need it.

Baskets are fascinating and these are something you *can* come across anywhere there are antiques. The variety of shapes and uses make them a captivating collector's find. Reserve a space on your wall for a whole collection of baskets, the large ones for a tumbled pile of crisp French bread, the square ones for hot rolls, the smaller ones for nuts and other small food items such as potato chips and anything "dry" that you haven't the proper sized dish for. The large old flat baskets, meant to gather vegetables in the old days or used by ancestral storekeepers, are most practical when put into service to pass all of the hors d'oeuvres, arranged attractively, at one fell swoop. This saves having three or four separate dishes to pass.

A pot of geraniums, set in a plump basket, makes any windowsill a special place in any kitchen. And one of the old-fashioned covered baskets, closely woven, is a smart way to house those essential paper napkins. An old rectangular wooden box, used to keep salt dry in the old days, can be painted an antique dark blue (or any color to go with your kitchen hue) as a receptacle for facial tissues.

If you can, pick up a mortar and pestle on your travels. They lend a bit of atmosphere, and you either can use them to crush whatever you want to crush (its original use was to reduce a substance to powder) or drop a mug into the mortar's small cavern and fill the mug with short-stemmed flowers or just put in a small potted plant, using the mortar as a holder. The pestle can lie beside it for an interesting still-life effect. This could be used as a practical centerpiece for that round kitchen table.

As many kitchens today have a small home office space allotted to the lady of the house for making out checks, signing report cards, etc., the small shelf, built-in desk, or a nice old pine tabletop desk with an upper story for drawers and pigeonholes offers great service. Here is where the beer stein you collected can double as a conversation piece and a pencil holder, and where one of the molded hands (so popular in the 1800s) can act as a paperweight. Perhaps your mug collection could be above this desk. But no matter how valuable your collection, just once in a while, have a "mug" party and serve something in your mugs, each guest having a different one.

The great tin trays of the past, with their borders of fine artistic endeavors could be used in practically any room as a wall hanging (but don't just let them hang there, use them for your coffee service and then put them back). Antiques are to use, and the repetition of these words is for a purpose—so you'll do just that. Use your antiques or sell them to a museum where they will stand in static splendor for the rest of their lonesome lives.

In the Master Bedroom

There are still antique beds around, but it does take a bit of doing to locate one of these early bedsteads as they were called. Back in the old days the "bed" meant a feather mattress, and it must have been like jumping into the center of a cloud to get into those beds. There are still sleigh beds to be had, so called because the headboard and footboard resembled the graceful bellied-out form of a sleigh. But antique dealers still point with pride to the cannonball-type bedstead or the rolling pin footboard and, of course, the spool on spool bedstead, familiar to many. Spindle frames were popular too.

Any one of these would set the mood of your bedroom, especially if it had as its companion an heirloom spread or quilt with its quaint dust ruffle. Patchwork quilts may still be found with such favorite patterns as Wheel of Fortune, Star of Bethlehem, Rose of Sharon, or Whig Rose. Most often the quilts were called "crazy quilts" because they were made up of bits of this and that left over from a calico shirt or worn-out dress. The pattern was a hit-or-miss type, quite attractive in its own wandering way, especially when put together with the popular feather stitching. If you use one of these as your bedspread, better wait to paint or paper, then pick out a prominent quilt color for the walls.

A small pine washstand or a more ornate sewing table might substitute as your night table. These are still available in the antique shops. Topped with a student lamp or any good-looking converted oil lamp, your Colonial feeling has been captured.

In the old days bedrooms did not have closets. Everything was folded and kept in chests or hung in an armoire, which was a sort of movable wardrobe. (And it is in good use today. In fact, the reproductions are best sellers for additional storage in a bedroom, hall, or living room.)

If you can locate a highboy and can afford such a piece, you are really lucky. It might interest you to know that the highboy was called the tallboy in the eighteenth century. For some reason chests were known as "boys" in those days. The highboy adds that needed bit of height to a room. It is monotonous to have chairs and beds all on one level and a highboy furnishes a fine collection of drawers for storage. You might have a lowboy (which was really the lower half of the highboy) to balance this, although you would no doubt want to show that off in the dining room or living room. These "boys" come in various period styles, but all have the same distinguishing graceful long legs.

We can't talk about antiques without mentioning the Currier and Ives prints. With over seven thousand themes, there is bound to be something for everyone. The seasonal topics are familiar and the old favorite "Home to Thanksgiving" is perhaps the best loved. A pair of Currier and Ives would enhance any wall, but if you collect, try to find some of the scenes that haven't been publicized to any great extent. A simple pine frame best serves these old-timers. Prints taken from *Godey's Lady's Book*, hung in groups, add to the fun of collecting. And, of course, the Audubon bird prints go well for the man's section of a bedroom, over his dresser or near the door of his clothes closet, or out in the hall.

Silhouettes make an intriguing collection and their black and white emphasis in the bedroom (or living or family room or foyer) is a sharp designer touch. A real collector has fun identifying the artist who created a special silhouette and can spot a reproduction at twenty paces. Even if an artist of today cuts a silhouette of your child, it's a valuable piece because it means something personal to you, and, after all, that's what possessions are all about.

The master bedroom is a good place for one of the wing chairs, covered in leather or make-believe leather or in the same handsomely hued fabric as the draperies. They more than pay their way in style and comfort. A tilt-top table with a piecrust edge or a butterfly drop-leaf table would make a happy partner for these chairs.

With more and more bedrooms having to serve a dual purpose these days, a desk is certainly in order. An antique slant-top or a simple lady's desk would be convenient with some sort of a slat-back chair sitting at attention next to it.

An old sea chest or a painted dowry chest makes a fine foot-of-the-bed antique. It serves as a resting place while taking off or putting on shoes, assists as a permanent luggage rack, and gives a room an unforgettable personality all its own. If you have room, this piece, placed under a window and utilized as a window seat, may become a favorite spot, especially if it is well stocked with pillows that also serve as an added color-bearer for the room.

We haven't said anything about mirrors and what would a bedroom be without mirrors? The early mirrors were known as looking glasses (an apt term) and were all in small sizes, as it was difficult to obtain a sizable piece of glass in those days. Then when glass became a more common product, the tabernacle, often attributed to Chippendale, and the Sheraton-type mirrors came into being, those with a wooden fretwork or ornate and gilded borders with a scene at the top. There have been so many fine reproductions made of them that you have to be an expert or take a dealer's word for it to tell the difference. (Somebody has said, "If it's that hard to tell the difference, what difference does it make?" But it's the authentic antique that is the good investment. Remember that when you're wavering between the authentic article and its well-copied brother.)

Before we leave mirrors, if you can find and have the room for one of those full-length Victorian hall mirrors on a stand, acquire it at once and give it a smart new coat of paint, or if it's gilded, leave it as is. It's a practical see-to-the-bottom-of-your-skirt reflection (no matter what length the fashion dictates) and makes an interesting tall item in a room.

WALLPAPER AND ANTIQUES

The role wallpaper plays is an important one. What goes on the walls either makes or breaks what goes into a room. If you are going to "decorate with antiques" the background is important. Today there are wallpapers for every decor mood. This doesn't mean that you have to use only the reproduced designs of the old days, but it does mean that your choice of wallpaper is an important one. If you put a fine jewel in a cardboard box with nothing around it, half of its glamour is dispelled. But set it in a background of satin or velvet and its full beauty is revealed to even the most callow observer. That is how the wall treatment affects the antiques or other furniture used in a room.

With the choice of stripes, plaids, polka dots, checks, and florals, to say nothing of the simulated damask and moire textures, why settle for dull walls? Why not put your antiques in their proper setting? We may not all agree on what that is, but your own good taste should prompt you. And never forget that color on your walls plays a big part. Color can warm or cool a room and you must picture your scene with its complement of pine, cherry, and mahogany pieces. Of course, there's no reason in the world why you can't have a painted wall with your antiques, but there again, your choice of colors is most important. Contrast is fun, but some of the weird psychedelic combinations of colors with each of four walls painted a different hue hardly seem the right atmosphere for either the friendly old informal or the stately eighteenth-century antiques.

If you want a different-looking room and don't want to change your furniture, let wallpaper do its own thing for you. It's the fastest and most magic decorator in the business. There are authentic prints taken from the lining of old trunks and hatboxes or preserved from some houses as old as 1639. These have been reproduced and offer a pretty picture, with authentic antiques playing the part of perfected performers on the stage. There are the large swags and swirls of the Victorian era to suit the more formal antique lover, and the new flocked papers that, believe it or not, claim to be scrubbable. These are almost exact copies of the papers that appeared in the great entrance halls of the old mansions. With these the Sheraton and Hepplewhite pieces feel quite at home.

FLOORING AND ANTIQUES

Since walls, ceilings, and floors represent a living showcase for furnishings, it's worth-while to spend a little time on floors and how they can help to "background" antiques. What do you think of first in connection with what goes on a floor when you are furnishing a Colonial-type room? That's right, braided rugs and hooked rugs. And these do give a comfortable at-home coziness when used with mellow antiques. But these need not be confined to the Colonial look. Certain patterns look perfect with other periods of decor. So if you like a hooked or braided rug in your favorite colors, don't be afraid to use it with your contemporary scheme.

The rich, lush colors of an Oriental rug make good partners for the more formal periods of antiques. A piece of furniture with "bracket or ball and claw feet," a "web or drake," or a "squared or tapered spade footing" sinking lightly into a burgundy or creamy backgrounded Oriental rug would be a pretty sight in any room. The names are quite descriptive of the types of feet on the more formal chairs of 1790–1800 vintage. As you know, the Oriental rug is having a renaissance today. And everyone who tried but failed to get rid of an ancestral Oriental in the past is now proudly showing off its unusual design and coloring. A successful color chart can be made with the rug and color scheme cued to your proud Oriental possession.

There are some marvelous patterns in the cushioned vinyl class for entryways, kitchens, family rooms, or such informal spots. One called "Georgetown brick" with its white earthy texture would sing a pretty duet with any pine chest or black rocking chair. The Williamsburg brick or the type in squares with an eagle in full flight and a stylized flower is a natural to face a Franklin stove or an original wagon seat, painted black and covered in flaming red corduroy.

A beautifully polished floor of wide boards with a few carefully chosen area rugs cannot be beat as a "floor ground" to show off antiques. The naked floor (and with the new waxes the care is minimum) gives a cool effect in summer and as its luster catches the glow from a fireplace fire in winter it looks alive with its warm and inviting brown sheen. The early antiques feel at home on a bare floor, as this is the way they started out in life.

CHAPTER NINE

FLOOR COVERINGS

This chapter hopefully will do the following: Serve as a before-buying guide by listing facts about various types of floor-covering materials and make suggestions that will save you time, money, and possible disappointment. A mere decade ago choices were rather limited to what suited your needs and your purse. Today, beginning with your front door, you have unlimited flooring choices as you go all through the house, upstairs, downstairs, basement, patio, terrace, and even inside and outside the swimming pool. Your selection could come from one or more of three sources: soft-surface floorings, which are carpets and rugs in natural or man-made fibers, hard-surface materials in man-made resilient floorings, and the natural hard-surface products, among which are ceramic tiles and wood.

Carpets and Rugs

Everything is going on the floor. Carpets and rugs are showing up in never-before-used combinations of colors; new combinations of fibers; new textures and new sizes, and if anything dares to be old, it's given a fresh new concept. Also, new methods of making carpet have been introduced; needle punching, flocking, and new concepts in tufted carpets have exploded styling possibilities. In addition, there are recent innovations of printing, cross-dye techniques, and the development of new backing materials. All of these new performances have helped to bring carpeting out of the realm of the "for some only" into what can be moderate-priced products for more and more people.

In the three types of carpeting: wall-to-wall, room-size, and area rugs, there is so much available you can cope with almost any flooring situation. Wall-to-wall carpeting is just what the term implies; it covers everything; it can expand a small room and when necessary hide a bad floor. The terms carpet and rug are often used interchangeably. Rug usually means a floor covering that isn't fastened down. A room-fit rug gives the appearance of wall-to-wall carpeting, but isn't fastened down and can be moved. A room-size rug usually comes within a foot of covering the entire floor. Area rugs are smaller than room size and come in just about any color, size, or fiber.

The Area Rug

With individual designs, flashing colors and interesting textures, area rugs are an important part of today's interiors. Some are so artistically color co-ordinated that they, like a fine painting, can easily set the mood and the theme in a room. They range from 3 by 5 feet to rugs in the room-size category.

No longer just round or square, area rugs come in ovals, hexagonals, octagonals, and free-form shapes. All will go anywhere, meet any space requirements, and are not limited to any fiber or fabric, design or period.

Inspiration for many of the design motifs have been adapted from age-old designs taken from countries around the world. These intricate designs, combined with modern ingenuity, modern methods of dyeing, and the new fiber developments, have made available area rugs that are often spectacular as well as outstanding beauties. Many add practicality to their beauty, and some cost relatively little. The diverse handsomeness of these rugs is played up as they top wall-to-wall carpeting, resilient flooring, ceramic tile, or wood floors.

In open-plan homes or apartments where one end of a living room becomes a dining area, and where the kitchen is either a part of, or adjacent to, the dining nook, one beautiful showing of rug color in each area will set it apart with distinction.

Look for Some of These:

The vigorously textured multicolored shags.

Intricate patterns from the Portugese, woven in riotous sparks of flaming colors and carefully thought-out designs.

Fake furs with soft textures and the smooth, swift lines of the original animal. They frequently come in gay unnatural colors and can be the dramatic touch in your room to lift it out of the ordinary. Held in

Startling color and design in a floor covering steal the scene in this room of fresh, dramatic furnishings. The Scandinavian rya rug with its bold sunburst pattern in brilliant tones of red, orange, brown, and blue creates an inviting circle of warmth and cheer. It has the lush, deep pile surface so typical of this special type of rug.

shape with a sturdy backing, you use them in the same way you would a real fur rug, just by putting a fake where you might have placed a fox. And for very little money.

One-of-a-kind designer rugs, giving everyone a chance to be individual. Many of these present round-the-world ideas in magnificent designs and colors from such countries as Italy, Spain, Greece, Scandinavia, and the Orient.

Flokati rugs from Greece, hand woven of wool, the surface texture a soft bed of long fiber feelers of great density and depth. Some color combinations: red, black, and gray; others just one big splash of sunny yellow or white. All have sturdy wool backing. One reason given for the unusually fine colorings is that after the raw wool is dyed, it is washed in the cool, clear waters of a stream which brings out the colors.

Oriental Rugs

The aristocratic Oriental rug will go anywhere in the home, and few items will add more to that "anywhere." Young Americans are showing increased interest in this type of floor covering, and one of the first questions is "Just what is an Oriental rug?" Officially, the definition is a hand-knotted rug or carpet made in the Orient. This broad area includes rugs made in India, Pakistan, Turkey, China, and Japan, as well as those made in Persia (Iran) and other parts of the Near East and Central Asia. The important word in the definition is "hand-knotted." Machine-made floor coverings in Oriental patterns, although imported from the East are not true Oriental rugs. And machine-made domestic rugs (made in America) patterned after an Oriental rug design are not true Oriental rugs.

According to experts at the Oriental Rug Importers Association, "No one should feel self-conscious about not knowing all the types of Oriental rugs or about being unable to spot the different designs by name. This can be a life's work. It is important to buy an Oriental rug from a reputable dealer. Most dealers are extremely knowledgeable and will give you definite information regarding any rug in their store, and will stand behind their sales.

"Many interested purchasers of Orientals ask, 'Can I expect my rug to appreciate in value over the years?' The answer is . . . the demand for Oriental rugs, both old and new, in recent years has been running ahead of the supply. As in the case of all handcrafts, the number of rugs which can be turned out each year is limited by the number of craftsmen able to make them. Because of this, one can be reasonably sure that the value of good Oriental rugs being made today, having been bought at a fair price and kept in good condition, will appreciate in the future."

Where do you use an Oriental rug? Anywhere you wish, all through the house. For example, the entrance hall often has little furniture so the floor covering is very important. The design, color, and warmth of an Oriental will help furnish this passageway, in addition to giving a distinctive welcome to all who enter. You might use a runner on the stairs that will harmonize with the hall rug. Stair traffic

When mixing modern with antique, an oriental rug can accent both. A beautiful Kerman rug is used as an accent under one of today's steel and glass coffee tables. Rug in blues and greens against an ivory background also has tiny flecks of red and contrasts dramatically with the simplicity of the table, and with bold painting over antique velvet sofa.

is usually heavy, and a durable, long-lasting Oriental will be practical as well as colorful. When a large living room is used for watching television, for music or reading, two or even three area-sized rugs can be used to set apart each special-activity center. The designs may differ slightly, but reflect a family resemblance and similar coloring to tie them together in a related group.

Some of today's interior designers create exciting effects by using even the most sophisticated Oriental rugs in ultramodern interiors with furnishings of stainless steel, glass tables, and nonobjective art. Because Orientals come in so many sizes, are well made, and have tremendous wearing qualities, using a small rug over plain wall-to-wall carpeting in heavily trafficked areas, such as in front of a sofa, under a desk, or in a doorway, will protect the carpet and add liveliness to the room as well.

What about price? Well, even a small Oriental of good quality will cost several hundred dollars. However, it is an investment, and I am told a good Oriental can appreciate in value up to 15 per cent an-

Bright spot for a teen-ager's relaxation is this former attic storage room turned into a sleek hideaway. Focal point is an unusual, American-made, oriental-looking rug in fresh contemporary colors, framed by a great swath of scarlet carpeting. Rug design was inspired by hidden Arabic wordings in Persian rugs, and center leaf tracery spells "Peace."

nually. The more expensive rug has finer weaving, has more knots to the inch, is tied tighter. Within a special type of rug, for instance a Kerman, there are many grades. A medium grade may be made by less skillful workers. The finest are made by skilled, sophisticated craftsmen; have beautiful colorations that are never muddy-looking; the wool feels "alive," and the rug is free from any weaving faults. A good Oriental will last longer than one's lifetime, so, like a fine piece of art, price is a relative thing.

INDOOR-OUTDOOR CARPET

The new-generation carpets called indoor/outdoor are said to go anywhere and do anything. Indoors these hard-wearing, easily maintained carpets are apt to appear any place you want to enjoy the good qualities that all carpets offer, but do not wish to expose the floor covering to excessively heavy traffic or excessive soil. Such areas are, for example, the kitchen, laundry, bath, and nursery-playroom.

Indoor space can appear to be made larger by extending it outdoors with carpet and color. To give an integrated color scheme, many manufacturers provide matching colors for indoor/outdoor carpets.

Outdoors, the carpeting adds foot comfort plus beauty to dining and relaxing in the open on a porch, terrace, patio, boat deck, at poolside, or anywhere. It covers concrete walks, barbecue pits, active play areas for children, and even makes lush and colorful lawns that do not require mowing.

In shopping for indoor/outdoor carpets, the label of an established brand-name manufacturer is your best guide. Established brands are backed by knowledge, skill, and integrity of carpet manufacturers who are willing to stake their reputations on the merchandise they produce for the public.

A carpet label will always give you the exact fiber content, country of origin, and usually the manufacturer's name or brand name, pattern or color designation as well. In addition to reading the label carefully when you shop, when you buy floor coverings, save the label for future reference in cleaning or repairing your carpet.

Also, be certain you understand the manufacturer's recommendations for the intended use of the carpet. It is important to know whether the carpet is labeled "for use anywhere," or "for use indoors only," or "approved for outdoor use." When specifically designed for indoor use (and so labeled) the carpet usually comes with a foam-rubber backing that gives it cushioning and makes it cling to the floor. If this same carpet is placed outdoors, the backing is subject to mildew and rot. For carpet to be used outside, it must be completely of synthetic materials (including the backing), plus other properties that you would not, as a rule, need indoors. It must be specifically made so as not to rot, mildew, shrink, or buckle, whatever the weather. You can use this (outdoor) carpet indoors, too, but you will need to forgo a foam-rubber backing.

Before you buy, have in mind the areas in and around the home you wish to cover. A reputable flooring dealer will answer any questions on the choices in colors and textures; the ease of installation and ease of maintenance. The way a carpet will perform depends as much on its construction as on the fiber with which it is made. If a carpet is poorly constructed a fiber's built-in characteristics do not have a chance to perform properly.

Before carpeting any of your rooms, think about the various activities that take place in each: How much traffic is causing how much wear and tear? Ask yourself how much you entertain by giving large dinner parties in the dining room, or if the living room needs your attention, is it used only for formal entertaining, or is it used for watching television and family gatherings as well? Do your children entertain their friends and their various pets in the living room also? Jot down the answers to these questions, have them fixed in your mind before you finally go shopping.

While there are no longer any rigid rules about which type of carpeting you choose for a particular room, it does make good sense to pick the one that will give you the most for your decorating dollars. Your carpet dealer with his vast knowledge of carpet will help you in every way possible, but you will be able to help him if you have at your fingertips the function of each of the rooms you wish carpeted.

Your shopping venture will be much more enjoyable, and profitable for you, if you do your homework before you go.

What Carpet Fibers to Buy

I believe that the answer to such an important question should come from the collective knowledge of a large group of major carpet and rug manufacturers, the Carpet and Rug Institute, Inc., of Dalton, Georgia. Here's what they say:

"The answer is tough because there really is no single answer. First, there is no one carpet fiber that is best . . . superior to all of the others in every characteristic. Second, the performance of the finished carpet depends more on how the fiber is used.

"All of the major carpet fibers used today will give excellent performance when used in good, dense construction. The more fiber used and the denser it is packed in the pile, the better the carpet. On the other hand, any one of these fibers, if misused . . . put into a sparse, thin, carpet pile could produce an unsatisfactory carpet.

"It is important to remember that carpet manufacturers select the

The influence of India shows up in color blends of reds, golds, and blacks. Dramatic paisley carpet in rich gold tones looks light-colored and fragile, but is made of sturdy, easy-care olefin fiber. Handsome black leatherlike sleep sofa is easy-care too. Authentic Indian accessories add more reds, golds, and blacks to luxurious-looking living room.

different fibers to meet the varied demands of their carpet customers. If the demand comes in for abrasive resistance, outstanding wear . . . certain fibers will get the call. If the customers want top-notch resilience and soil resistance other fibers may be used.

"If the order is for extraordinary stain resistance and easy spot removal, then other fibers could be chosen. Still other fibers may be favored when the ladies ask for that luxurious look and opulent feel in a carpet.

"A possible cause for some of the confusion over carpet fibers that besets the homemakers today is the great number of different brand names under which the synthetic fibers are marketed. While there are many fiber trade names, there are only five basic fiber types used extensively in carpets today. They are nylon, acrylics, wool, polyester, and polypropylene.

"The variations within each fiber group are significant, as for example, the 'second-generation' nylons or the differences between continuous filament and staple forms of a fiber. There are also meaningful similarities between different fiber types. For example, wool, polyester, and acrylics have a number of properties in common.

"In abrasion resistance, nylon and polypropylene are outstanding. Though wool, acrylics, and polyesters rate somewhat lower in this regard, they will provide long-term durability when used in quality, dense constructions.

"In soil resistance, wool, acrylics, and polypropylenes score high points. The second generation nylons with new soil-concealing features rate high also.

"In stain resistance, particularly in resistance to water-soluble stains, polypropylene, nylon, acrylic, and polyester are all excellent. But remember, stains should be removed from all carpets before they have a chance to set. Most stains can be readily removed from wool carpets, also, when promptly attended to.

"In resilience, the ability of fibers to bounce back and resist crushing, wool, acrylics, and polyesters are exceptional. Polypropylenes rate lower on this score, but when used in low, dense pile surfaces and in flat needle-punch carpet, this factor is not so important.

"All carpet fibers today are mothproof. This includes wool which is permanently treated during carpet manufacturing. All man-made fibers are also resistant to mildew, which is a problem for wool only in unusually damp conditions.

"To avoid confusion when shopping, be sure to compare the carpets and not the fibers alone."

CARPET TEXTURES

You can get bored with a room that has too much of the same kinds of surfaces. Each texture has its own end use. It's very personal, this appeal of texture. You may not even know which ones you prefer until you see the various types displayed in stores. The descriptions that follow are merely to add to your before-shopping knowledge. You may like plush or velvet, with its luxuriant quality look for your more formal rooms; twists are happy in casual, rugged surroundings, and the shags will go anywhere, anywhere an informal look is desired.

Some of the terms you will hear are:

Single-cut pile. Because of its velvety appearance, is often called plush or velvet.

Looped pile. The opposite of cut pile. Loops may be single level, all one height, or multilevel loops arranged to form texture patterns such as geometric designs, swirls, or circular motifs.

Sculptured. The effect is that of "highs and lows." Often created by a combination of cut and looped surface yarns sheared at different levels. In some sculptured or embossed textures, one level of looped pile is pulled down tight, with a level of cut pile suggesting a pattern.

Shags. Some have long, loose surface yarns up to three inches long; others are shorter with a twist-yarn texture. Shags are easy to care for and come in a wide range of colors.

Twists. Because the loops are twisted, the surface has a pebbly look.

CARPET TERMS

Backing Yarns. The materials that form the carpet backing or foundation to which pile or face yarns are anchored. A second backing fabric may be laminated to the primary backing, and the backing coated with latex.

Broadloom. This is not a "kind" of carpet. It is a term of measurement and does not describe any special quality, style, or construction. The term refers to any carpet made in a seamless width of six feet or more, and applies to all designs and qualities.

Carved. This is the effect of a pattern in relief, creating shadowy effects by shearing the pile in high-low designs.

Density. A carpet factor which is the single best clue to quality. It refers to the closeness of construction of the surface yarns, and the best rule of thumb is "the deeper, the denser, the better." Or, the more fiber, the better quality of carpet.

Ply. This refers to individual fibers which are used to make up yarn. Three-ply yarn means each tuft is made up of three strands of yarn spun together. The number of plies used does not necessarily improve quality, it does affect texture and surface effects in a carpet.

Tufting. The construction process used for most carpets and rugs today. Pile yarns are attached to a preconstructed backing by wide multiple-needled machines.

Wilton, Axminster and Velvet. These are types of looms on which carpet is woven. Carpets made on these looms may be described also by these terms: a Wilton carpet, a velvet carpet, or an Axminster.

MEASURING FOR CARPET

Before shopping you may wish to know how much your carpet venture is going to cost. To get an idea of how much carpet you will need, and then determine the cost, it is necessary to measure the area to be carpeted. Some stores will do the measuring job for you even before you buy, but it is best to check to see if this service is provided. For your own information, here is how the measuring task is done. Multiply the length by width of the room in feet, then divide by nine to get the square yards; for that is the way most carpets are sold. That figure, multiplied by the price per square yard, will give the approximate cost.

For example, a room that measures 12 by 15 has 180 square feet. This number divided by nine gives twenty square yards. If your selection is a carpet that costs ten dollars per square yard, your carpet cost will be two hundred dollars.

Before your carpet is installed, your dealer will make professional measurements of your rooms, give you the exact price of the carpet, plus the cost of installation.

PADDING

An underpad of cushioning material will prolong your carpet's life by acting as a shock absorber for daily foot traffic. Also, it will add to your personal underfoot comfort. In addition, an underlay adds to the carpet's capacity to soak up noise and provides support for a taut carpet installation, that is, it prevents slipping or shifting of the carpet. There are several types, among which are felted hair, jute, foam rubber, or plastic-foam material. All are serviceable, and you can decide which is right for you with the help of your carpet salesman.

TIPS ON CARPETING STAIRS

Stairways show off so beautifully when well carpeted. While you want to pick a color you like, to help in disguising signs of constant use, it is best to select a medium shade with a tight-looped pile. Color in stair carpeting does not need to exactly match the adjoining areas if it is chosen in a harmonizing color, texture, and pattern.

Here is one place where it would be foolish to skimp on the quality of carpet, for in most homes the stairs get a lot of traffic. Also, it is important that carpet on stairways be installed securely. In addition, be certain the carpet is kept in good condition with no worn spots or loose edges to present hazards.

Use a good quality padding under the carpet to protect it. A firm, taut padding is essential. Heavier carpet padding over the (stair) edges protects the stairs better, too.

Another suggestion: When the carpet is laid it should have an extra foot of carpet length folded under the top riser. When edges look worn, simply shift the carpet an inch or two down the stairs, and fold any excess against the lowest riser.

CARPET CARE

A good carpet deserves good attention. A light sweeping daily will keep dust and dirt from becoming embedded in the carpet base. Vacuum once a week, give quick attention to removing spots, and use a professional carpet cleaner from time to time. A well-established professional firm has the knowledge, experience, and equipment to do a thoroughly good carpet- and rug-cleaning job. Professional cleaners are also trained and equipped to go into homes for on-location cleaning.

If you have wall-to-wall carpeting, on-the-floor cleaning is a great convenience and is economical since the floor covering does not have to be taken up and then relaid.

Just in case you do not know a reputable rug-cleaning company, ask the dealer who sold you your floor covering to recommend someone. If he has no recommendation, write to the National Institute of Rug Cleaning, Fort Myer Drive, Arlington, Virginia, for names of cleaning plants in your community.

To thoroughly enjoy your carpets and rugs, you cannot be continuously worrying about children dribbling ice cream or guests upsetting drinks on the carpeting. To ease your mind, have first-aid spot-removal directions in an accessible place.

You will be kinder to your carpet if you keep a record of its cleaning schedules. Even with regular vacuuming, the dirt and dust in the air can dull carpet colors and even cause an apparent color change. A good professional cleaning usually restores the original hue.

And, incidentally, to keep your carpet looking lovely longer, try placing small rugs over the areas that get the most use.

Also, turn your area rugs around from time to time to equalize the wear and tear on all sides.

How to Know a Reliable Dealer

Carpets are sold in department stores, furniture, and floor-covering specialty stores. Over the country there are thousands of reliable retailers selling carpets in each type of store. These merchants take as much pride in the store's reputation as the manufacturer takes in his product.

According to carpet and rug industry sources, the hallmarks of a reliable carpet retailer are these:

1. A reputable dealer will have an established place of business. Good stores offer a varied selection of carpet styles and qualities which you may examine. Many fine stores also offer an "in-home" shopping service, sending a salesman to your home with samples on request. However, a reliable carpet business will not operate on door-to-door or telephone selling alone.

2. A good store will not use "bait" or misleading advertising. Whatever is advertised will be offered for sale at the price terms quoted.

3. A good store will not offer vague "guarantees" or "guaranteed years of wear."

Reliable salesmen will be glad to discuss wear conditions in your home and your carpet requirements. Also, they will help you estimate the service you can expect from various qualities. If a guarantee is offered it should be specific and should be clearly read and understood.

4. A reliable dealer will be glad to explain store services.

Wise carpet shoppers will ask questions to make sure that they clearly understand terms of delivery, measurements for wall-to-wall installations, or other services offered by the store.

The best carpet dealers go beyond these minimum standards of reliability.

Most stores offer additional, helpful information on decorating, carpet care, and the style best suited to individual needs.

The floor of a family room can have all the elegance of a marble "look" because of new developments made in today's floor coverings. Shown here is a new type of flooring that combines the look of natural marble or homogeneous vinyl with the versatility of vinyl-asbestos tile.

The reputable carpet retailer will always offer value to his customers, more than just cut-rate bargains which have only a low price tag to recommend them.

RESILIENT FLOORING

Because of its durability and easy care, resilient flooring has grown immeasurably popular, and you will find almost anything you wish from an expensive product to a do-it-yourself installation.

All the fabulous textures, fresh colors, and exciting patterns are enough to make you plunge right into a spending spree. The purpose of the following is to give you some beforehand knowledge of how each type of resilient flooring performs. This information can serve as

The beautiful show-off decorating the stairway has a practical side. Carpet color was selected in a medium shade, a lush American beauty red, to help disguise soil from constant stairway traffic. Important in this attention-getting much-used area is good quality carpeting. The one shown here of sturdy olefin fiber is securely laid over taut padding.

Even the terrace gets wall-to-wall carpeting. Areas outside the home now can be completely covered with a new decorating concept, the easily maintained, easily installed solution-dyed acrylic carpet. Boasting excellent colorfastness under extreme weather conditions, carpeting marked "approved for outdoor use," is said not to shrink or buckle even when soaking wet.

This delightful many-use room, with its fresh indoor garden look, could serve as a writing room, study, or an extra guest sitting room. Vinyl flooring has all the cool elegance of exquisite marble in creamy white with amber and olive accents. Flooring colors are complemented by woodsy earth tones in furniture and accessories; while sharp touches of red add warmth and drama.

CABIN CRAFT, WESTPOINT PEPPERELL, CARPET & RUG DIVISION

The seldom used porch of a mountain cottage is now a pleasant extra sitting room. Oak block flooring in nine-inch squares was chosen to add to the rustic effect of stucco walls and dark, exposed woodwork. The clear blue area rug, a touch of texture with its sculptured medallion and border, is the room's most vivid accent. French country furniture is perfect for the scheme.

uch a pleasure-giving color scheme; reens, blues and white with touches of ronze and wood tones. Gay entrance o living room looks as if big squatty eaves had cascaded earthward to make p the elegant blue and green pattern in he vinyl flooring. Embossed, or textured, o help hide the soil, it's just right to how off a deeper green area rug in livng room.

Especially for him, this handsome, color oordinated bath-dressing room. Lavatory counters are higher to suit his height. Bath towels are over-sized in bold strokes of black, gold, pewter and shades of brown. Easy-care flooring of vinyl asbestos repeats masculine motif in squares of white, yellow, black and russet on mustard ground, outlined in black feature stripping.

a money-and-mistake-saving guide for you and make your shopping days easier, too.

Floorings based on man-made vinyl are truly resilient, strong, easy to maintain, and resistant to soil. They come in two basic forms: tiles, which are cemented in place to serve as a permanent floor, and sheet goods, which are also cemented in place for a permanent installation. However, some types of sheet goods may be cut from the roll to fit a room's size and can be put down without being cemented to the floor.

In general, resilient tiles come in nine- and twelve-inch squares. Most major companies can give you special custom-cut designs in special dimensions, but, of course, these cost more.

With few exceptions, sheet floor coverings come in rolls six to twelve feet wide and in continuous lengths, usually up to ninety feet.

Take a Good Look at Your Own Floors

Before spending any money, consider the condition of the floor you wish to cover. Your subfloor (which is what the floor under your new flooring is called) has a great deal to do with the eventual look of the new resilient floor. While the new one will bring color, beauty, and function to any room or area, it cannot cure defects that already exist such as roughness, springiness, unevenness, and dampness. Resilient floors have a tendency to take on any bulges or bad grooming of the floor beneath it. Make certain your subfloor is clean, even, smooth, and dry.

Discuss any special symptoms showing up in your floor with your flooring dealer. Let him advise you if you need a new underlayment (such as plywood or hardboard). Also, be certain to tell him just where the new floor is going, that is, on which grade level in your home.

Grade Levels. While shopping you will hear floors described as below grade, on grade, and above grade. This is what is meant:

Below grade. Below the level of the ground, such as a basement which is in direct contact with the ground.

On grade. This is at grade level; for example, a house built on a slab without a basement beneath it.

Above grade. Any floor that is over another area such as a basement, or is a second story that is never in contact with the ground.

Any solid vinyl may be installed on any grade level provided you use the proper adhesive. Conditions vary in different sections of the country, therefore it is always best to consult your dealer before making an installation.

About Moisture. If you live in an area where excessive ground moisture penetrates the slab and collects under certain parts of the resilient floor, a special type primer (or whichever product is recommended by the manufacturer) should be applied to the concrete before installation.

Foot Traffic. You are the only one who knows how much soil your new flooring will get from the daily tramping in and out of adults, teen-agers, energetic toddlers, and pets. Color, pattern, and durability in a specific type of flooring should be determined by the use a room gets. Mixed colors in floorings will show less soil and dirt than a solid color, and textured surfaces will help to hide heel and scuff marks.

Tips on Types

What you pay for your new resilient flooring will depend upon design, amount of vinyl, whether or not you install it yourself, and the condition of your subfloor. Here are some of the popular types of resilient flooring that make up most of today's market.

Vinyl-Asbestos Tile. One of the most popular for do-it-yourselfers. High stain resistance. Good durability. Easy to maintain. May be installed on all grade levels.

Solid Vinyl Tile. Excellent wearability and easy to maintain. Wide color selection. Available in special sizes. Can be installed on all grade levels. Check your dealer for special adhesive for on and below grade.

Asphalt Tile. An all-purpose flooring. Can be installed on all grade levels. While it has excellent resistance to alkali, it is low in resisting grease. Considered very serviceable as a flooring when the budget is an important item.

Cork Tile. Wears well. Extremely resilient and is great for cutting down on noise. Has a fair resistance to grease but a poor resistance to average soil. For easy maintenance, some cork tile is coated with a clear-plastic finish.

Rubber Tile. Excellent resiliency, hushes footsteps and is easy to maintain. Has a fair resistance to grease. Comes in a fine range of colors.

Linoleum Tile. Good selection of colors. Long wearing, economical, and easy to maintain. Comparatively resilient. Must be installed above grade.

Sheet Vinyl (Inlaid). Inlaid means the pattern goes all the way through the thickness of the wear layer. Makes for the greatest durability. Comes in a variety of backings and is resistant to stains and indentations. Known for keeping its good looks for years.

Sheet Vinyl (Printed) *Felt Backed.* Pattern is printed on the surface. Not all felt backs are for permanent installation, some are put down without being cemented to the floor.

Cushion-Back Sheet Vinyl. Has a thick backing of vinyl foam that gives when you step on it. Comfortable underfoot and muffles noises. Some cushion backs are available in sheet goods for permanent installation; and some can be simply cut from the roll to fit the approximate dimensions of the room and installed without being cemented to the floor.

Rotovinyls. Rotogravure-printed surface design topped with a coating of clear vinyl for protection. Felt or moistureproof asbestos backing. Usually less expensive than inlaid vinyl.

Linoleum. An old reliable that is durable, greaseproof, economical, and long wearing. Easy to maintain. One drawback is that it must be installed above grade.

Browse Before Buying

Browse around, make a tour of the stores, take note of color, pattern, and texture in resilient flooring before you make your own selection. Take time to visit the flooring showrooms where you can leisurely view the new designs and very often get ideas from special settings of flooring and other home furnishings. Also, you can get any information you need for your own special rooms, then go on to your favorite flooring dealer to make the actual purchase.

So much has been added in new designs and new ways to use these easy-care, hard-surface floors. In addition to the good decorating effects gained from simulated flagstone, slate, terrazzo, mosaics, beach pebbles, and marble, dealer showcases now include:

Bold geometrics, some are adaptions of the weathered tile of a Moroccan courtyard. Colors are flamboyant reds and clear tropical blues.

Wood patterns that range from the elegance of parquet, displaying simulated squares of bleached oak and light maple colors, to the random planks that depicted an early America.

Adhesive-backed tiles with the three-dimensional translucence and richness of marble; or in a stone-chip design that can widen optically with the use of accent strips.

The unified floor. An exciting new decorating idea presenting two types of flooring, vinyl and carpet, as a new floor team. For example, an area rug in a lovely hexagonal pattern can be used to top its vinyl teammate in the same hexagonal pattern and in the same color tones.

These are just a few of the hundreds of designs you will meet on your marketing trip.

Resilient floor tiles are a spur to your imagination. You can work out designs of your own with the regular nine-inch tiles by including among them, at selected locations in a room, some of the very unusual tiles on the market. There are border effects, centerpieces, and many other tile types to bring out your own creative ideas.

Ask your flooring dealer to show you how to create further flooring interest by combining plain or patterned flooring with feature strips. These come in various widths, some narrow, some wide, in a broad range of neutral colors or in deeper tones of green, turquoise, blue, red, and orange.

To evaluate all the many new materials in floorings is a big undertaking. When shopping, your best guide (as said before) is the good name and reputation for quality of an established brand-name manufacturer and the reputable name of your flooring dealer.

How to Measure for Resilient Floors

To give your flooring dealer some idea of the size of any room you wish to cover, measure it before you go shopping. For sheet goods: multiply the length of the room by the width to get the square footage. From the square footage, your dealer can give you an estimate of the cost, including the price of installation. Most manufacturers recommend that you have an expert put down sheet flooring for you. However, as mentioned under types of floorings, there are some types of sheet goods which can be cut from the roll to fit the room size and put down without being cemented to the floor. This is found, for example, in the cushion-back sheet vinyls or felt-backed printed vinyls. (Ideal for renters in apartments when the landlord does not permit cementing down a new flooring.)

If you are one of the handy homemakers, and so many of you are, it will save you money if you install your own tiles.

The size of a room, or other area, and the number of tiles needed determine the cost. For example, to get an approximate idea of the number of nine-inch-square tiles required, multiply the length of the room by the width to get the square footage, then multipy the square footage by two.

To get the cost, multiply the total number of tiles required by the cost of each tile. Ask your dealer to recheck your estimate to make certain you have enough. It is a good thing to have a few extra tiles, and it is also advisable to buy all that you need at one time.

Read About What You Intend to Use

In speaking with many of the tile manufacturers, whose products are known around the world, this sentence kept repeating itself: "If only the homemaker would read the information that comes with our products. We spend time and great effort in writing careful directions. The customer should read everything, and even read every single line that comes with a can of adhesive."

If you follow directions and take your time, you should be able to do a very good job of installing your own tile flooring.

Your dealer will be glad to give you a booklet on any of the do-it-yourself types of tile. Each will explain fully how to proceed step by step.

Be certain to tell him whether the tile is going over concrete, paint, wood, old floor coverings, or old terrazzo. He can tell you exactly how to prepare your subfloor for the new tile covering. Success depends very much on two things: the old floor underneath and your willingness to follow the manufacturer's advice for the specific tile you are using.

Tips on Resilient Floor Care

Your new resilient floor is made to take somewhat of a beating from traffic, whether it is sheet goods or tile. But do give it a bit of attention. Most manufacturers recommend that you do not wash a new floor until it has tightly adhered to the subfloor, possibly a week. Each manufacturer markets various kinds of cleaning materials and waxes to keep the floor in good condition, and it is a practical idea to use products from the firm whose brand of flooring you are using.

For beauty's sake, sweep your floor daily and damp mop with a nearly dry mop when necessary. Use lukewarm water or a very weak detergent solution. By keeping the floor soil free, you will cut down on the times you need to do a complete washing. When an over-all job is indicated, try to avoid flooding the floor.

Buffing can produce a lovely patina even without the use of wax. If you like a high sheen, use a good wax recommended by your flooring dealer. Experts recommend that you do not apply wax directly to embossed flooring, but suggest that you dip the applicator in the wax and then apply it. Since many coats of wax can build up, and possibly change the looks of your floor, use a wax remover once or twice a year.

For removing special stains and spills, ask your dealer for a booklet on floor care that pertains to the type of floor coverings in your home.

Natural Hard-Surface Flooring

For the flooring of your own home, if you are building one, your architect or contractor will give you advice on the good or impractical points (for your particular use) of flooring materials to be used in the various areas in and around your home.

Among the rigid floorings are ceramic tile, wood, marble, flagstone, slate, brick, and terrazzo.

Ceramic tile in recent years has had a rebirth of popularity. Now this hard-surface material with its ancient history is used all over the house.

Wood is still one of the most popular of all floorings and has had many new developments in design and surface finishes.

Marble, so much the usual thing among ancient cultures and the most luxurious of floor coverings, is elegant in private homes and apartments in entranceways, halls, and bathrooms.

Flagstone can be attractive in halls and vestibules and will go almost anywhere outside in areas such as the patio, terrace, and bypaths. Slate also has a practical outdoor use on the patio floor or on the terrace.

Brick has come up with a new rosy glow; some bricks present a lovely pinkish cast, a fine idea in country kitchens, dining, and living rooms, also fine in the hall, the patio, or for garden paths.

Terrazzo (which is poured concrete made with inset chips of marble) is rugged and durable, fine in any heavily trafficked area such as halls and bathrooms.

We will concentrate on the two most popular of these natural hard-surface floors, ceramic tiles and wood.

Ceramic Tile

Today ceramic tile comes in more than two hundred colors, among which are golds, greens, pinks, blues, and various shades of celadon. Because of its many new designs, colors, and patterns, ceramic tile is appearing inside, outside, and all around the home. It is lovely to look at, wears well, and is easy to keep clean.

What can ceramic tile do? It can be very elegant in your entranceway by opening it out with sparkling, light colors and a smooth, fresh look. Since this is usually a heavily trafficked area, cleaning is the simplest ever.

In a dining room, in any period from contemporary to Mediterranean, you will be able to find a ceramic tile design to complement the setting. Again, in this area where there is likely to be spills of food and liquids, nothing can be damaged for more than the time it takes to wipe it up.

When shopping for tile, you will find them in three general types:

Glazed wall tile, which can also be used on the floor, is most familiar in four-and-one-quarter-inch squares, but does come in other sizes and shapes. It is available in a wide range of colors, designs, and various glazes.

Ceramic mosaic tiles, made in a large assortment of colorful shapes, may be had with or without a glaze. The ceramic mosaics are often just called "floor tile," but they may by used on other surfaces. They are ideal for inside and outside the swimming pool. Since tile colors and designs are permanent, there isn't any need to worry about fading.

The unglazed ceramic mosaics come in a wide range of colors from clear, crisp tones of the porcelain variety to the warm earthy shades of the natural clays. Glazed ceramic mosaics add many additional colors. While standard design patterns are shown everywhere, if you wish a special pattern it will be provided on special order. For a handcrafted effect some manufacturers provide triangular shapes and tiles with irregular edges, in addition to the usual square and rectan-

Color scheme in this kitchen began with a floor of earthen-hued quarry tile. Countertops are covered with ceramic mosaic tiles in complementary earth tones, and an abstract ceramic mosaic mural decorates the backsplash behind the sink. Glazed wall tile sets off the mural in this "tile here, there, everywhere" kitchen.

gular types. Standard mosaics are 1 by 1, 1 by 2, and 2 by 2 inches.

Quarry tile, a heavy-duty floor tile, traditionally available in earthen-red color, is now marketed in dozens of delightful colors, in new shapes, new sizes, and new textures.

Quarries can add warmth and color to foyers, kitchens, dining and living rooms where you may wish to have an informal, country, or

Spanish look. Outdoors in the patio, quarry tiles will stand up under heavy foot traffic, scorching sun, or rain. Colors range from near white to bluegrass green in unglazed quarries, and many of these can be varied by "fire-flashing" with subtle rainbow-hued effects. Glazed quarries provide an additional color spectrum.

Added to squares and rectangles, quarries come in geometric and other shapes to create exciting and unusually delightful flooring designs. Patterned or textured surfaces are also available, and sizes range from 2 ¾ by 2 ¾ inches to 12 by 12 inches.

In major cities, distributors of ceramic tile have beautiful showrooms where you can see all the lovely colors, designs, and shapes of tile. Also, here you can get any information you need. If your city does not have this type of tile display and if you do not know a tile contractor where you are able to buy, look in the classified telephone directory under "Tile Contractor, Ceramic."

Before buying, go to several tile contractors to check on prices. You are buying a material that will last a lifetime, so you are making a long-range investment.

In case you are wondering if you can install ceramic tile yourself, it is not recommended. However, there is always someone among you who is especially handy with anything. If you are determined to do it yourself, note that there are three setting methods for installing ceramic tile: conventional cement mortar, dry-set mortar, and organic adhesive (mastic). The first two are usually recommended for wet areas such as shower enclosures. Your local tile contractor will give you detailed and explicit information.

Tips on Cleaning Tile. Use simple detergents for cleaning tile. Waxing is never needed. For routine cleaning, use a damp sponge, and twice a year scrub floor tile with a mild cleanser. Common household stains are easily removed.

A soapless detergent is recommended; experts say that it is never necessary to use soap. In fact, it should not be used.

If cleaning has been neglected to an extent where a heavy accumulation of dirty film is evident, use a stiff brush.

Rust marks can be removed by applying any good commercial rust remover such as those sold at your local hardware store.

Smudges from rubber-heel marks may be removed by using an abrasive-type cleanser or by rubbing with a soft-rubber pencil eraser.

When you spill something that may stain, wipe it up as soon as possible. Scrub with a light scouring powder. If there is discoloration of

To provide a bright new flooring idea, this modern library
features a handsome flooring
design in white oak. The large
squares of the design have been
banded in four-inch stainless
steel strips to provide newness.
Brass strips could also be used
to give a similar look.

the tile joints, caused by grease or oil, scrub with washing soda or caustic soda.

Paint spots in the tile joints may be removed with a knife or a razor blade without damage to the unglazed tile.

Wood Flooring

The gleam of a large expanse of well-polished wood flooring has held homemakers enthralled over the years. This high esteem for wood continues, largely due to its enduring quality, its infinite variety of color, texture, and grain.

If you are dreaming of a new home, your best information on types of wood flooring will come from your contractor or architect.

If you are in an older home, and the flooring shows imperfections you do not wish to live with, see your wood-flooring dealer on the new designs in flooring materials. One such flooring combines the beauty of real wood with the roughness and cleanability of vinyl. Oak, walnut, or cherry veneer is bonded between sheets of heavy, clear vinyl. It comes by the square foot in various patterns.

Also available are prefinished hardwood-flooring blocks, nine inches square, and with a thickness of three-eighths or one-half inch. Each block is bonded with modified waterproof glue to provide high-dimensional stability. On the opposite sides of the block are tongues and grooves, placed there to assure interlocking and easy installation. No sanding and finishing is required after installation, and the floor can be walked on as soon as the installation is made. These blocks come in many beautiful designs, some taken from old-world flooring

INTERIOR DESIGN BY LEONA KAHN OAK PLANK FLOORING BY WOOD MOSAIC

The talented designer of this entrance gallery, featuring Gothic oak colonial planking, purposefully contrasted the luxurious Louis XVI background with the planking to demonstrate the versatility of the flooring design. Many New England homes in the eighteenth and nineteenth centuries contrasted colonial planking with imported French furnishings.

designs, and some adapted from the handsome floorings of an early America.

As mentioned before, your best help will come from working with a qualified wood-flooring dealer, and it is important that you advise him regarding any special conditions of your subfloor. For the special type of wood blocks of prefinished hardwood just mentioned above, the floor should be on or above grade, and it should be smooth, dry, and structurally sound.

Among the many other types of flooring are some made especially for the handy homemakers who love do-it-yourself projects. Before putting down these wood blocks, installed in mastic, be sure to read carefully the manufacturer's directions for the type of wood blocks you are using. What is so wonderful about this is, it saves you money, and the variety of designs is especially good.

CHAPTER TEN

FABRICS

FABRICS ARE LIKE PAINTINGS in that they make a strong statement about the inhabitants of a home. They are an important ingredient in the hierarchy of decoration—furniture, floor coverings, wall coverings, accessories. Since they can combine color, pattern, and texture, they must be carefully considered in every room scheme. Their practical considerations must be weighed too; depending on their weave and content, fabrics can help control both natural light and air. A sheer fabric can admit pleasant breezes; a heavy one can keep out unwanted cold.

Other practical considerations center around such questions as: Is there a label or trade-mark on the fabric? If so does the label tell how the fabric can be cleaned? Will it shrink if washed? Is it crease resistant, permanent press, fade resistant, stain resistant? What types of stains will it resist? All these and other questions about performance must be answered to your satisfaction before you buy a fabric, because fabric function is important. A fabric is likely to be in your home for a long time. Bear in mind, as you shop, that the store and ultimately the fabric mill are responsible for the claims tagged onto the fabric. Any good store should be informed about everything it sells and should stand behind its merchandise. That is its obligation. Yours is to treat the fabric with the care it requires.

Deciding on the right fabric for a given element of your decorating plan takes a lot of thought and study. Before you get into the creative part dealing with color, pattern, and texture, you must think about where the particular fabric is to go, how much wear, if any, it will get in that location, its proximity to strong sunlight, whether the room or house is damp or humid. For example, in humid climates certain fabrics absorb considerable amounts of moisture and a drapery height measured when the fabric is dry will turn out wrong when the drapery, moisture sogged, laps over the floor. You must think in the round, as it were; you must *know* both your fabric and the area where it is to go.

When it comes to choosing a fabric on the basis of aesthetic appeal, it may take a lot of searching and shopping to find the right one to fit the decorating scheme you have in mind. However, the scheme must come before the search, of course, and this leads to the questions: What goes with what, what colors and patterns and textures go with what period styles? Choice really boils down in great measure to personal preference, but there are a few rules that will help to guide your preference. After all, the market abounds in fabrics in every conceivable color, pattern, and texture, and in almost every price range; the choice is so broad that you are bound to find something that is correct for the over-all style you have selected and that you really like.

For a traditional scheme, you can find documentary fabrics with colors and patterns that are authentic to a given period. Certain fabric manufacturers specialize in documentaries. There might be a Williamsburg collection that would have exact copies of eighteenth-century fabrics used in that town; there might be a French country collection, an Early American collection, or a Victorian collection. From these, you can choose with absolute certainty of being correct. Failing this, turn to the pages in this book dealing with the colors and motifs of given design periods and then look accordingly. For example, if you are doing an eighteenth-century English room, you find that many tones of green were popular at that time and that classic motifs were used—flutings, acanthus leaves, delicate garlands, architectural scenes. Armed with these ideas, you can look more knowledgeably. Other examples might be: flower-patterned chintz for a late Victorian room, a toile (see following fabric dictionary) for a French country room, a paisley print for an American Federal room.

Remember, too, that there are formal and informal kinds of fabrics. Texture comes into play here. A smooth silk, a gleaming satin are for the most formal areas of the home; a nubby tweed, loose woven linen, wool are for the informal living areas. Pattern enters into this matter: An ornate brocade is formal, a plaid is informal. Your eye and your touch will help to guide you here. Texture becomes especially important when choosing fabrics for contemporary decor: you may remember we saw that solid blocks of strong color and rough textures are earmarks of this design style. A handsome contemporary scheme can be built around primary colors against white, in an interplay of many different textural weaves for the fabrics used in drapery, upholstery, and bedspreads.

UNUSUAL WAYS TO USE FABRICS

Fabrics are by no means limited to the conventional uses as drapery, upholstery, spreads, and tablecloths. Striking and practical effects can be made by using fabric on walls, as wallpaper is used. Fabric can be glued to wood furniture to "upholster" it; it is eminently comfortable and practical for headboards, outer shower curtains (an inner liner that is waterproof would, of course, be necessary), as a decorative liner for glass-door china or other display cabinets, and for open hutch tops. And don't forget the fabric ceiling—either applied like wallpaper or tented for an Empire look. When it comes to bed decoration, besides the fabric spread, you can have a fabric canopy, side hangings, pillow shams, bolster covers, dust ruffles, and all the rest. The French *lit-clos*, or bed niche, has the walls lined in fabric for a snug feeling and drapery that pulls across the front. Fabric dividers can also be used to semipartition rooms into given areas, in the manner of old-fashioned portieres. Later in Part Three of this book we'll go into more detail as we go through the house, room by room, with a discussion of appropriate fabrics.

FABRIC DICTIONARY

ACETATE—man-made fiber consisting of cellulose acetate and used in many luxury fabrics. It's quick drying, needs a cool iron. Rayon acetate is often used in drapery fabric.

ACRYLIC—man-made fiber often used in knitted fabrics. Its characteristics are warmth and bulk without weight. It can give great shape retention and wrinkle resistance to fabrics.

ANIDEX—new fiber similar in use to elastic-type spandex yarns. It is, however, much more resistant to heat, sunlight, and chemicals, but has less elongation stretch.

ANTIQUE LACE—handmade bobbin lace made with heavy thread and square knotted mesh. Similar types of lace can be found in drapery fabrics.

Femininity rushes out from every angle of this bedroom—a do-it-yourself floral arrangement. Brightly patterned sheets can be used not only on the bed but as dressing-table skirt and cascading trim for a teen-ager's many accessories. Leftover fabric can serve as cutouts for additional trim and borders.

ANTIQUE TAFFETA—crisp, lustrous fabric with slubbed yarns resembling types made before silk was finely cultivated. Formal draperies and bedspreads are frequently made from antique taffeta.

APPENZELL—Swiss hand embroidery done with a buttonhole stitch.

APPLIQUÉ—separate design which is sewn or attached to a cloth. Appliqué may be used to decorate plain fabrics and then be used as pillow covers, for instance.

ARABESQUE—ornamental, geometrically balanced design in scrolled effects.

BAININ—handwoven Irish woolen cloth made in the Aran Islands.

BARK CLOTH—nonwoven material made in the tropics from the inner bark of trees, soaked and beaten out to the required thinness, then dyed or ornamented with printed patterns. Also, woven drapery fabric that imitates the rough appearance of bark cloth.

BASKET WEAVE—interlaced weave resembling a plaited basket. Cotton blended with synthetic makes a strong and good-looking basket weave for slipcovers and upholstery.

BATIK—Javanese process of wax-dyeing fabric. Parts of cloth are coated with wax which is then cut to shape the design. Only the uncovered parts of the cloth take the dye. Batik effects are also simulated in printing. The prints, tropical in nature, are good for summery rooms as slipcovers and laminated on shades.

BATISTE—sheer fabric, once cotton or silk and now constructed of man-made fibers as well. Named for Jean Baptiste, a French linen weaver.

BENARES—silk and metal tissue made in Benares, India.

BIAS TAPE—double or single fold of tape cut on the bias and used to bind edges.

BLENDS—mixed yarns that often combine natural fibers with synthetics.

BLOCK PRINT—ancient process of applying design by means of carved wooden blocks.

BOLT—entire length of cloth from a loom.

BONDING—uniting of two fabrics to make a stronger cloth. Fabrics can be bonded to a number of materials including knit and foam. A lightweight fabric can be bonded to knit for a heavier weight and then be used for upholstery.

BOTANY—generic word for fine wool used interchangeably with merino wool.

BOUCLÉ—tightly looped fabric that is very sturdy. It's particularly good for covered pieces that take a lot of wear and tear.

BRAID—round or tubular narrow fabric for binding or trimming.

BRETENNE LACE—net with embroidered designs of heavy thread.

BROADCLOTH—closely woven fabric with lustrous finish made of many different fibers and blends.

BROCADE—raised, figurative designs on lustrous fabric.

BROCATELLE—heavy furniture and drapery fabric similar to brocade but with figures in high relief.

BURLAP—jute fabric that is coarse and plainly woven. Its uses include both wall coverings and drapery.

BUTCHER LINEN—coarse, homespun linen. The texture is now simulated in synthetics.

CALICO—plain, closely woven printed cotton originating in East India.

CANVAS—cotton, linen, or man-made fiber in heavy weave.

CASEMENT CLOTH—airy, open weave fabric most often used as draperies or curtains.

CHALLIS—supple, plain weave fabric, often wool, and printed in small floral or paisley designs.

CHINOISERIE—Oriental-inspired designs.

CHINTZ—glazed cotton fabric often printed. Although it appears delicate, chintz is a rugged fabric. This makes it a good cloth for slipcovers, bedspreads, and wall upholstery.

CIRE—patent-leather glaze on surface of a fabric produced by application of wax, heat, and pressure. Nylon cire is popular in women's fashions and would also be applicable to home furnishings; for instance, in outdoor fabrics.

COLOR FAST—term used to describe fabrics that keep their shades without fading. Dyestuffs used in home furnishings have color-fast ratings in terms of hours.

CORDUROY—wide- or narrow-wale fabric usually woven of cotton. Corduroy is extremely durable and is therefore a good fabric to choose for a study or child's room.

COTTON—natural fiber from seed pod of cotton plant.

CRASH—coarse toweling weave.

CREASE RESISTANT—newest development is referred to as permanent press. A treated fabric that requires no ironing. Items treated

Here's a perfect way to achieve a balance of those masculine and feminine qualities in your master bedroom. Choose a handsome manly plaid fabric for your walls and then hang it in soft, feminine folds. This wall curtain can even be taken down easily for cleaning. The fully skirted breakfast or writing table makes this a versatile bed/sitting room.

with permanent press would be identified on a label bearing content and washing instructions, along with fiber company guarantee.

DAMASK—patterned glossy jacquard weave, flatter than brocade. Tablecloths are still the most popular damask design, but it is also used in bedspreads and draperies.

DENIM—usually blue or white cotton cloth, sometimes printed or striped. Made of inexpensive, strong cotton and washable.

DOCUMENTARY—authentic copy of an antique fabric, true to period in color, pattern, and texture.

DOTTED SWISS—sheer cotton ornamented with small dots. The original is still made in Switzerland. Dotted swiss makes lovely curtains.

DOUBLE-FACE SATIN—satin cloth constructed so that front and back have same lustrous finish. Used for formal draperies.

DRIP-DRY—phrase used to describe fabrics that can be hung after washing and require little or no ironing.

DUCHESSE SATIN—plain-backed satin with crisp texture and lustrous, smooth face.

ECRU—beige color of raw fabrics such as linen, silk, and lace.

EMBOSSED—figures or designs raised on surface of fabrics.

EMBROIDERY—ornamental needlework stitched by hand or machine.

EVERGLAZE—Joseph Bancroft & Sons' trade-mark, signifying fabric processed and tested according to the firm's standards.

EYELET—open punched patternings.

FAILLE—flat, horizontal ribbed fabric. Period furniture blends well with faille upholstery.

FELT—matted fabric usually made of wool or fur.

FIBERGLAS—trade-mark owned by Owens-Corning Fiberglas Corp. for fine filament glass fiber.

FLAME REPELLENT—chemical treatment that makes fabrics less susceptible to flash or sustained burning.

FLANNEL—napped surface fabric in plain or twill weave.

FLAX—used in manufacture of linen. Flax adds the rustic texture to linen or to whatever fiber it is blended with. It is a coarse, strong natural fiber.

FLOCKING—application of clipped fibers to surface of a fabric to form a pattern, often used in wallpaper as well as fabric.

GABARDINE—diagonal weave, lustrous fabric, good for tailored upholstery.

GAUZE—sheer open weave used as canopy drape for four-poster bed or cradle.

GINGHAM—cotton fabric most frequently woven in two-color checks.

GLASS—fiber-forming substance with good stability, resistance to mildew, chemicals, heat, moisture, sunlight, and electricity.

GROSGRAIN—ribbed trimming fabric with pronounced cords.

HEMP—lustrous, harsh, fast fiber and used mainly for twine and sailcloth.

HERRINGBONE—broken twill weave, zigzag effect, like the skeleton of a herring. A masculine fabric that is also good for mixing patterns.

HOPSACKING—coarse basket weave.

JACQUARD—intricate patterns made on special looms named for the inventor Jacquard. Geometric upholstery fabrics are often jacquards. Very durable.

JASPÉ—drapery or upholstery fabric that has a series of faint stripes formed by light, medium, and dark threads of the same color.

KEMP—coarse white hairs, sometimes used in carpets.

KNITTING—process of making fabric by interlocking series of loops of one or more yarns.

LAMÉ—silver or gold metal fabric.

LAMINATED—fabrics which have been joined together or bonded. Window shades, for example, can be laminated to a fabric so that they are actually one.

LAWN—sheer cotton made of fine-combed yarns.

LENO—open weave with mesh effect.

LINEN—natural flax fabric.

MADRAS—named for Indian city in which it is made; madras colors bleed when washed. Patterns are usually plaids on coarse cotton. A durable cloth, madras is a colorful type of fabric to use for bed covers and throw pillows.

METALLIC—metallic yarns, which can be effectively used for decorative purposes, are costly, but have great resistance to heat and corrosion.

MILDEW RESISTANT—treatment of fabric so that it resists growth of mildew or mold.

MODACRYLIC—fibers used for fire-resistant drapery and synthetic fur.

MOHAIR—fiber that comes from Angora goat. Its character is coarse, but silky and very lightweight. Mohair should be tightly woven for use in interior design; it does tend to shed and is best when woven with another fiber like wool.

MOIRÉ—an effect created on the surface of fabric—usually silk—

and resembling water ripples. A formal fabric, moiré is often used in period rooms as upholstery and drapery material.

MOTIF—dominant figure in pattern of a fabric.

NACRE VELVET—pearly-looking velvet achieved with back of one color and pile of another.

NEEDLEPOINT—simple stitch embroidery completely covering mesh or canvas cloth. Gros point (coarse) and petit point (fine) are variations. Both are popular for seat covers.

NINON—sheer, crisp fabric frequently used in curtains.

NUBBED—fabric woven with novelty yarn containing slubs, knots, or lumps.

NYLON—versatile fiber in terms of home furnishings—from carpet to drapery. In strength and abrasion-resistance it is said to be superior to all other fibers.

OLEFIN—synthetic fiber that consists mainly of petroleum by-products. Of the olefins, polyethylene comes in a variety of colors and has good chemical resistance. Polypropylene is the lightest commercial fiber and, in a certain form, has excellent strength, great chemical resistance, and a toughness and abrasion second only to nylon.

OMBRE—French word for shaded coloring ranging from light to dark.

ORGANDY—sheer, crisp cotton used in curtains.

ORGANZA—French for silk organdy, most frequently used in fashion.

ORLON—DuPont trade-mark for acrylic staple fiber.

OTTOMAN—heavy, ribbed fabric especially sturdy for upholstery.

PAISLEY—multicolored pattern with India palm or cone figure and elaborate detail. Paisley mixes well with other patterns in a room.

PANAMA—hopsacking of coarse, yarn basket weave producing effect similar to panama hat texture.

PANNE—velvet with pile pressed flat in one direction and very lustrous.

PASSEMENTERIE—heavy braid trimming used as edging on upholstery or draperies.

Peau de soie—French meaning "skin of silk."

Percale—cotton sheeting in various qualities.

Pile fabric—velvets, plushes, velveteens, and corduroys—fabrics that have dense surfaces. Also fur imitations. Very durable; many of the imitations look very authentic.

Pilling—formations of little fuzzy balls caused by the rubbing off of loose ends of fiber too long or strong to break away entirely.

Piping—cord covered with bias fabric and used as edging on upholstery or bedspreads; also on pillows.

Piqué—fabric with raised patterns such as honeycomb, waffle, or diamond.

Plissé—lightweight, puckered cotton.

Point d'esprit—dotted cotton net, very fragile, could be used as canopy drape.

Polyester—fiber-forming substance which gives resilience, durability, dimensional stability to fabrics, making them wrinkle resistant and sunlight resistant.

Quilting—layers of cloth stitched either by hand or machine in a variety of patterns and used for bedspreads as well as upholstery. Headboards, too, can be upholstered with quilted fabric to match the bedspread.

Ramie—fiber from the ramie plant used mainly for table linen. It is similar to flax but more brittle.

Raw silk—silk reeled from cocoons before natural gum is removed. Used in drapery and upholstery fabrics. Quite expensive due to rarity of fiber.

Rayon—first man-made fiber. It is the least expensive and most widely used. Considered superior to any other fiber, natural or synthetic, by many experts; it has superb strength and blends well with all other fibers.

Rickrack—decorative flat braid in wavy chevron. Used for trim.

Sailcloth—strong, heavy canvas weave made in several fibers. Particularly satisfactory in outdoor fabrics.

Sanforized—Cluett, Peaboby & Co. trade-mark for fabrics processed by machine so that residual shrinkage will be minimized to 1 per cent in either direction.

SATEEN—satin-finished cotton.

SATIN—lustrous, polished fabric. Often silk.

SCHIFFLI—embroidering machine capable of tracing a vast number of patterns on a fabric and for making Venice lace.

SCOTCHGARD—Minnesota Mining & Manufacturing Co. trade-mark for a fluoride-based stain-repellent and rain-repellent finish. A special formula is made for leather.

SEERSUCKER—crinkled, lightweight cotton fabric good for summer curtains.

SELVAGE—outside woven edges of cloth.

SHAG—stout, haircloth made of coarse wool in the Orkney Islands. Shag often is used in rugs and for throw blankets on bed or sofa.

SHANTUNG—slubbed silk, originally made in Shantung, China.

SHARKSKIN—plain weave fabric often with dull luster and made of acetate. Sporty cloth good for outdoor furniture.

SHETLAND—wool from sheep raised in Shetland Isles of Scotland. Shetland is often used in blankets for its warmth.

SILK—natural fiber from the silkworm.

SISAL—coarse fiber obtained from the leaves of the sisal (Agave sisalana) plant.

SOUTACHE—decorative braid.

SPANDEX—fiber-forming substance which resembles rubber in terms of stretch and recovery, but is superior in resistance to sunlight, abrasion, oxidation, oils, and chemicals.

STRIÉ—irregular streaks in a fabric of almost the same color as the background.

SUEDE CLOTH—surface-finished fabric resembling suede. Good for upholstery or slipcovers because of its easy-care qualities and its resemblance to the real skin.

SURAH—lustrous silk in twill weave; also woven in other fibers such as acetate or nylon.

TOILE—French term for all kinds of coarse, plain weave linen or cotton; toile de Jouy is a pictorial design printed on cotton. Toile is popular as a slipcover fabric and also for upholstering walls.

TRIACETATE—a variation of acetate that holds more heat and usually retains pleats, shape, and texture.

Pattern itself creates an inviting niche. And the trellis motif is one that provides eye interest as well as compatibility with another pattern. In this case, an abstract printed velvet works counterpoint with the upholstered sofa and bookshelf—all solidly covered in trellis pattern. White shag pillows add texture and relief from two definite schemes.

TRICOT—warp-knitted fabric with fine ribs on the surface. Tricot could be used where very sheer, airy curtains are desired. It's washable and dries quickly.

TUSSAH—wild silk.

TWEED—mixed color effect in rustic weaves in any number of fibers. Tweed upholstery is probably the most durable and it blends with many other patterns.

VELOURS—French word for velvet.

VELVET—close pile fabric with smooth, silky surface. Luxurious, but sturdy, velvet makes a very good upholstery fabric. Silk or cotton content.

VELVETEEN—cotton or rayon pile fabric with short pile. Unlike velvet, velveteen is singly woven.

VIRGIN WOOL—the term for new wool.

VOILE—sheer plain weave with crisp texture that can be used for curtains.

WALE—rib or ridge running in any direction as in corduroy.

WARP—set of lengthwise yarns in a loom through which the crosswise filling yarns or weft are run.

WARP PRINTS—blurred designs achieved by printing warp threads before fabric is woven.

WATERPROOFING—fabrics which are rendered waterproofed with coatings of rubber, resin, or plastic.

WOOL—fleece of sheep.

WORSTED—fabric from the tops of raw wool, usually smooth surfaced like flannel and men's suiting.

ZEPEL—DuPont trade-mark for spot-resistant finish.

CHAPTER ELEVEN

ACCESSORIES

Decorative accessories reflect not just the mood of your home but also your personality. It is this latter factor that makes the selection and arrangement of accessories so important. They're the things that express your sense of humor, interests, imagination, and taste more than any other furnishings.

Decorative accessories give character to a room. If you are decorating an entire room by yourself, plan the accessories, at least in general terms, right from the start. It has often been said that decorative accessories can spell the difference between a well-designed room and a poorly designed one. This is not true. No accessories in the world can save a poorly designed room. They merely enhance what the major furniture pieces, draperies, and floor coverings have achieved—a warm, comfortable atmosphere.

The selection of accessories also contributes to the tone of a room. They can make a room more or less formal, brighten up a dark room, or tone down a room that is ablaze with color. Keep this point in mind when you plan your accessories; you can find any number that are truly attractive and suitable for your decorating scheme. Accessories also can be used to change your room's personality. You can create a different atmosphere in a room with the same furnishings just by changing the accessories as you would slipcovers for your furniture. Let your accessories set a seasonal mood for your home. There is no reason why the same accessories must be used the year round. Plan them for a winter mood or a summer mood to be changed when you change your draperies and put on slipcovers to capture the feeling of a total environment.

Treat your selection of accessories carefully. They should not be regarded as small odds and ends to fill empty spaces. Poorly selected

In this highly eclectic mix, antique wall lantern and scrolled iron plant stand combine easily with X-base Parsons table and whimsical fruit and vegetable print. All backgrounds are wallpaper: strawberry pattern for the floor was varnished for protection; plaid pattern doubles on door panels and small X-table.

accessories will only detract from your room's appearance rather than add to its beauty. They should simply supply the indispensable finishing touches to your room in the same manner as dress accessories do for an ensemble. Choose them not for beauty alone but for what they can add to the mood of your room. Put your accessories in important places in your rooms to create focal centers. They become significant to the total decor when arranged this way rather than being scattered about in undisciplined fashion. Placement of accessories is also important in creating unity and balance in the design of the room. Misplaced, they tend to jar the flow and motion of your design; well placed, they contribute an important part to the elements of balance and rhythm.

Don't expect to assemble all the accessories for your home in one fell swoop. Finding and choosing what you want takes time, often years, and you frequently have more enjoyment in searching for just the right object for a special place. In all probability, you will find yourself changing your accessories every few years—not because they are out of place but because you have found a new object that better suits a special place.

Always keep in mind that accessories have a much more important role in decorating than most people realize, and should be chosen with this in mind. They should reflect the mood of the room while providing accent or unity. Use them to establish a variety in texture, color, and period that you could not accomplish with the other furnishings in your room. And, most of all, let your accessories express the interests of your entire family wherever they are used.

Wall Accessories

Wall decor can be the most dramatic and effective of all the accessories in your home. More important is that the combination of various types of accessories can create a wall of unusual interest and reflect your ingenuity. Your walls are the one place where mixing materials and design periods can be most impressively demonstrated. Depending on the size of each wall and the furniture against it, wall arrangements can run the gamut from elaborate to starkly simple. Each wall should be studied for its best potential, each should get individual treatment that will blend with the others in the same room but not necessarily have the same format or atmosphere. Contrast, in fact, if it is not too startling will create a strong impact of good design and form.

Pictures

Pictures are the basic element of any wall arrangement. Pictures provide a combination of color, motion, and form. They are highly personal choices. Whatever may be ideal for your tastes may be out of the question for your friends. If you plan a transitional room, don't be afraid to mix various styles and periods of pictures. Well done, this approach can be a most interesting technique for showing off your favorite pictures. And, most important, try to distribute pictures on the many walls throughout your house—don't just relegate them to the living-room walls. Use pictures along the walls of staircases where other types of accessories would hinder easy passage. They can create a museum gallery atmosphere where little else could be used. It's best in this case to focus on small and medium-sized pictures with clearly defined subjects since the vantage point will be close-up rather than the distance needed for the appreciation of abstract or impressionist paintings. Pictures in bedrooms and studies should be scaled to the size of the room and the mood that is being set by the rest of the decor. When you plan pictures for bedrooms, don't forget the guest room where a warm touch of pictures and color is always a welcome sight for any visitor. Family-room pictures should reflect the mood you are setting in the rest of the furnishings. A brashly modern painting would be out of place in a rustic den that would be better enhanced by deep, rich colors in strong, simple frames. Pictures can add a bright note to kitchen or bathroom decorating. Be certain, however, that they are glass-covered—the warmth and humidity in both rooms can distort and warp pictures without glass.

Picture frames should be planned for the decor of the room, but they don't have to be in the same period as the furniture and other furnishings. Large pictures, obviously, should be framed with wide border moldings—some baroque or rococo, others plain or fluted moldings. Proper framing will result in a picture that does not compete with its frame for the eye's attention. Carved frames are particularly impressive on oil paintings of most periods. The use of mats to enlarge the scope of a water color is perfectly acceptable, but avoid having the mat dominate the water color itself. Frames for water colors should be light and slim. Baroque or extremely wide frames are out of place. Glass should be used over all your pictures except oil paintings. When you plan frames for any type of picture, be certain that frame colors do not blend into the wall. Frames that are too close in color to the wall color will not only lose the eye's attention, but

When you feel that your collection of paintings, prints, and sculpture has achieved a meaningful quality—that may be the time to devote a full wall to its display. Here, an off-white background and a pale beige carpet are subdued enough in color to allow the art to dominate the setting. Note how each frame has been selected to complement the picture's style and subject.

will distort the total impact of the picture. Attempt, instead, to provide a contrast that will compete with the wall background colorings. Dark walls will show off picures in gilt frames better than soft pastels or silver. Light walls need the robust accent of fruitwood or dark gold frames to accent the painting. Painted frames in lacquer colors also can be used impressively against light-colored walls.

Prints of all types have become exceptionally popular art for today. Also, the work of contemporary print artists is often inexpensive—a good way to begin your art collection. There are many types of prints, not just etchings that many believe are the most important type. Experiment with wood blocks, lithographs, stencils, steel engravings, wood engravings, screen prints, and linoleum block prints for unusual and exceptionally attractive arrangements. It was believed at one time that only large prints were suitable for hanging and that small ones belonged in a collector's portfolio. This is not so; a grouping of well-framed small prints can be a most effective wall arrangement. As with anything else, the use of one print alone in too small a size will be meaningless.

Mirrors

Mirrors can be decorative and at the same time create a feeling of spaciousness and depth in your rooms. More than any other decorative accessory, mirrors can help you fool the eye and make a room seem larger or lighter. Mirrors should be hung where they reflect something or they lose part of their charm and their function. Whether it is hung to reflect a part of a nearby room, or an outdoor scene, or an important object across the room, reflection adds to a mirror's decorative qualities. Entire walls of mirror are most effective decorative elements, but should be used sparingly. Mirror frames should be regarded much in the same manner as those for pictures. A heavy baroque and shaped mirror frame will be an important accent in a traditional room while a wide chrome or steel frame will add a dramatic touch to a modern setting. They're natural brighteners or backgrounds for any room.

When hanging mirrors, it is essential that they be hung low enough to be used. This generally means at the eye level of an average-sized person, standing up. Avoid hanging mirrors or pictures that are wider than the piece of furniture beneath them. The result will be a wall

These seventeenth-century English engravings (each is hand-colored) are part of a notable collection of one subject: mushrooms. They are variously matted (Naugahyde, silk, velvet, burlap) to co-ordinate in their russet and earth tones with the natural mushroom colors. Each frame is different yet eminently suited to its subject; finishes are silver or gold on carved wood; simple or ornate. The wall in back is covered with dark brown Naugahyde, chosen especially to highlight the picture collection.

that is out of proportion. Instead, try hanging vertical mirrors over smaller pieces of horizontal furniture when a mirror is the only wall object.

Wall Hangings

The wall hanging is becoming increasingly popular. The new wall hangings are a far cry from the tapestries of old. Hand-screened prints on fabric in stark Scandinavian motifs, small rugs in bold, bright designs, and even Indian saris are finding their way onto more and more walls as the focal point for a room. There is perhaps nothing more impressive as a single wall hanging than a Chinese or Japanese folding screen on a wall behind a sofa. Although old originals are extremely expensive, there are fine reproductions and some new designs. Unless your wall is exceptionally large, use a screen no bigger than four feet high and six to eight feet wide. Most often, these screens are hung flat against a wall as you would hang a picture. Some people, however, prefer to hang a three- or four-part screen slightly folded to create the impression of movement. If you do this, take care not to let the screen project out too far or the people sitting on the sofa will brush against it.

When using a wall hanging, try placing it alone. Another object or picture would tend to become lost because of its size and tremendous impact. A 3-foot by 5-foot area rug is most impressive by itself as a colorful wall treatment over a sofa. Hang rugs of this type from brass poles or attach metal eyes to the corners and hang as you would a picture. Keep the rug pulled taut so that it does not sag while hanging.

VARIATIONS

Although pictures, mirrors, and wall hangings are the basic forms of wall decorations, there are many other ways that you can dress up your walls. For collectors of small objects, a wall of individual decorative shelf brackets is an impressive and colorful way to display your favorites. Put the shelves on the wall above the back of the furniture in either asymmetrical or symmetrical patterns; never line them up one next to another. Wall sconces, wired for electricity or in their original candlestick form, can be an effective part of any wall motif. Early American rooms, particularly, can be enhanced with the use of a pair of pewter or chrome sconces. Metal accessories, especially the pierced brass figures from the Orient or Middle East, are becoming more readily available in this country. In fact, some modern artists are adopting this form of art medium to their own techniques. The important thing about these accessories is that they tend to be suitable for any type of decor, whether Early American, Mediterranean, or ultramodern.

Planning a Wall Arrangement

The size of your room and the walls are important factors in planning any wall treatment. If your walls are large expanses, unbroken by doors and windows or recesses, you can plan massive and dramatic arrangements. A simpler wall treatment is called for when windows or doors break up the wall. Otherwise, you will have too many elements competing with each other for the eye's attention. The size of the objects, whether pictures or other accessories, also plays a significant role in determining what you should use on each wall. The most important thing to strive for is a sense of balance and unity. Don't let one object or wall dominate the room. There should be emphasis of an important wall but not domination. When planning a wall arrangement, use your floor as an experimental area. Put the accessories on the floor to get the best idea of how they will look on the wall. Lay the objects out so they will not be too high or too close together.

One of the most difficult factors in planning a wall of pictures is the balance and proportion necessary to create an effective impact. Pictures in groups that are too close together negate the decorative elements of each picture. On the other hand, pictures that are spaced too far apart tend to look disjointed and unplanned. Leave "breathing space" between pictures in a group—more for larger ones, less for smaller ones. When planning a wall arrangement, strive for rhythm and flow. Repetition of a line, form, or pattern will accomplish this. The progression of the same or similar objects in different sizes also will have a rhythmic effect on the wall treatment.

Space is always as important an element in effective wall arrangements as the objects themselves. An important piece should be hung to allow the full impact to be felt; hanging other objects close to it will only detract from the total effect. Space also allows you to create primary and secondary centers of interest on each wall. And the vari-

Twenty-five photographs—really family-style snapshots—have first been enlarged to 8-inch by 10-inch size. Matted in white and then arranged on a wallboard panel painted the wall color, they become the center of attraction in a country-house room. A neat way to assemble a motley group of subjects.

ation of space areas on each wall will serve to enhance the total effect of the decorative scheme. Try to avoid too many horizontal arrangements when planning a wall. This common habit tends to create a feeling of sameness in a room because furniture basically follows the same pattern. Don't hang a horizontal picture, for example, over a commode or table. Try to create a feeling of contrast instead by using a vertical arrangement.

In striving for balance and proportion, avoid too many small objects that have no emphasis. In any grouping there should always be one object that is slightly larger than all the others. It makes the grouping more interesting and important and combats the effect of sameness. Balance also is achieved through symmetrical or asymmetrical arrangements. The symmetrical treatment generally creates a more formal and dignified feeling and is much simpler to achieve. The basic elements are equal distribution of size, weight, and distribution of the objects on the wall. Asymmetrical balance, on the other hand, is more exciting and dramatic. Balance is achieved through a carefully planned placement of large and small objects.

Asymmetrical arrangements can use objects of the same type or a variety of different objects. The latter often is more exciting, but care should be taken to avoid a busy effect. Restraint in number of objects and placement is essential in asymmetrical arrangements. A mantel, for example, with a large vase at one side and a group of figurines in varied heights creates more interest than a pair of candlesticks flanking a cachepot of leaves. Another technique is using the same type of objects—figurines, pitchers, or vases, for instance—in a row and in varying heights. The easiest approach is to place the objects in a progression of height, but it is even more interesting to mix the sizes, using the tallest near the center of the arrangement.

Another common pitfall in planning wall arrangements is the use of diagonals. Unless controlled, they tend to lead the eye right up

Wall shelves prove their versatility in this teen-ager's room where they are scattered at random on the wall. Between them—pop flowers give added color.

through the ceiling. If you are planning a diagonal arrangement, use only a few pieces to keep this from happening. Also, diagonals are most effective when used in the center of the wall rather than at the sides. Control, too, is better with this placement; other objects to either side of the diagonal will prevent the eye from constantly traveling upward. If you are planning a grouping of pictures that will go up the wall in a slanting line, you might try a pair of wall sconces at either side to bring the eye level back into the room. Another technique for pictures used alone or with mirrors and wall plaques is to have the frames of the highest pictures either curved or rounded to eliminate the straight effect. This rounding of the normally straight line will keep the eye from moving up.

Excessive curves, however, in wall arrangements should be avoided —they produce a restless result. Unless you are particularly adept at wall arrangements, the use of curves in planning can destroy the effect of what you are trying to achieve. If you use curves in picture or mirror frames, be certain that straight lines have a strong place in the arrangement. If the curves seem too strong when you're planning this type of grouping, straighten out some of the edges to achieve the proper results. If, for example, you have frames that are ovals or circles, include a long rectangular picture or mirror in the grouping, placed at the top. A tall, slender wood carving also will break up a wall that tends to be too busy and goes around in circles. Squares, too, can become a negative rather than a positive element if overdone. Generally, squares create the feeling of solidity, but too many in a grouping or on an entire wall will be monotonous. Try, instead, for a combination of squares and horizontal and vertical rectangles for maximum impact.

Originals or Reproductions?

There is still considerable controversy in the decorating world over the value of a good reproduction compared with an inexpensive original. With today's art explosion throughout the world, good and inexpensive original art is widely available. You often can find good originals from unknown artists at prices that are less than some of the reproductions. Prints—lithographs or etchings, for example—are a relatively inexpensive way to begin a collection of original art. While those done by the famous old masters are quite expensive, contemporary artists' prints are often well executed and inexpensive. Prints generally are numbered so that you can always tell how many copies the artist has produced. The lower the number of your copy, the more expensive it will probably be. But it will also tend to be sharper in color and line. This is how you determine the number of prints: 15/82 means that the artist produced eighty-two copies of the print and the one you have was the fifteenth in the production line.

The technique of reproducing fine originals have been improved immeasurably in recent years to the point where it is difficult to determine without close inspection whether it is an original or not. Fine reproductions can be a part of your wall arrangements, but avoid the brown- or gray-cast reproductions of the same paintings. Check the reproduction carefully. Many will be so faithful to the original that even the brush strokes are evident. No matter what you buy, avoid the cliché of paintings or pictures that match your room. Buy a picture because you like it, not because the blue matches your sofa. Of course, any picture that is too sharply in contrast with your room's color and decor will overwhelm the rest of the room.

Lighting. Many of us forget about the importance of lighting when we plan a decorative wall arrangement. Too often the fine details of a painting go completely unnoticed because there is not enough light on the picture. Or a group of bibelots are arranged in a semidark corner where no one can see them. Spotlighting is an ideal way to bring your accessories into the foreground of your room. Backlighting of cabinets and wall shelves with fluorescent tubes also is an effective lighting system.

Paintings, in particular, create lighting problems. The museum approach of individual clip-on lights is generally not suitable for home arrangements. If you have one major picture, the clip-on can be used, but try to avoid long, dangling light cords. For groups of pictures, avoid the use of clip-on lights, which only detract from the pictures and create clutter. Instead, try the new high-intensity spotlights that are available. You can use them on a table as a decorative accessory and beam them at the picture wall for proper illumination. They can also be used on open wall shelves to create a variety in brilliance for the wall arrangement. Because of their small size, you can focus them on your walls if you put them in a corner on the floor or under a piece of furniture. They'll be virtually inconspicuous. Best way for a wall of paintings is a ceiling track of spots, engineered into the electrical system.

WALL SYSTEMS, DIVIDERS, SCREENS*

Wall systems serve an important role as decorative accessories and an even more important one as added storage space. Many wall systems can be planned to your own specifications. This will allow you to plan for a bar cabinet, a desk, or several storage pieces to be incorporated among the arrangement of the shelves. Not all rooms need this type of treatment, but if you find it desirable or even necessary, you can find wall systems in almost every type of period design—a marked departure from the past when most systems were severely modern in either teak or walnut woods. A French Provincial wall system, for example, could easily take the place of a breakfront in your living room. It would also achieve one other decorative goal: a feeling of expansiveness without the depth of traditional furniture. Wall systems also give you an open stage for your decorative accessories. The individual shelves can be lighted to highlight the objects on them. While custom-made wall systems offer the most versatility in design and styling, ready-made units can achieve a great deal of this effect if you plan the components with care. Whether custom- or ready-made, wall systems should have shelves that are adjustable to allow flexibility in arranging your accessories. Most custom units can be planned with shelves of varying lengths and a variety of spacing between each shelf. Some ready-made systems allow you the flexibility of shelf adjustment, but all shelves generally are the same length.

Wall shelves allow you to display your accessories without dominating an entire wall, as a complete system will do. You can use them over your furniture or alone on the wall for maximum versatility. Ready-made wall shelves today are available with concealed brackets and standard supports that give a finished furniture look. Finishes and styles often encompass every decorating period. You can create a dramatic wall treatment with shelves of this type if you avoid the monotony of shelves in the same length and side-by-side positioning. Plan the arrangement as a unit. Determine, before you buy, what books, accessories, and lighting you will use for the complete unit before you put the shelves on the wall.

It is not necessary to have a massive array of wall shelves for an effective wall treatment. Often, just six or seven properly arranged will make a more decorative wall than a completely covered one. Some wall shelves are available unfinished, ready for painting. These

---

* See also Chapter Seven, "Furniture," and Chapter Twenty-five, "People on the Move."

Clever arrangement of wall shelves can turn an unattractive window view into a decorative asset. The extensive book collection is broken up by random placement of favorite bibelots to avoid a heavy, overpowering effect.

generally should be painted the same color as the wall if you are using a complete wall group so that the contrast between the two colors will not be too startling. Or you can finish them in wood tones that complement the furniture finishes in your room. If you are using only a few shelves you can add a note of fun and excitement by painting the shelves a brighter shade of your wall color or pick up one of the secondary colors in your room. Ready-made shelves with wood finishes now are available in a variety of tones so that you should be able to find a finish suitable for your needs.

Dividers are among the most functional and decorative elements that you can find for establishing space areas, showing off accessories to best advantage, and creating an atmosphere of open spaciousness. Some rooms, particularly in new modern apartments, literally cry out for a decorative room divider to break up the "bowling alley" effect that most living rooms create. There are many ways to use dividers.

Ready-made units are available in most stores—either ceiling-to-floor poles with attached shelves or floor-standing dividers that come in many different heights. You can also use a pair of étagères for a more decorative effect in space definition. Avoid the styles that come with pole lamps and excessive brass trim. They tend to be gaudy and distract the eye from the accessories you put on the shelves.

The range and variety of decorative screens will enable you to find one suitable for your decorating scheme if space definition or semiprivacy is needed. You can also use decorative screens as an important accessory touch in a living room, standing behind a pair of chairs or at an angle in a corner. Screens should be at least six feet high to achieve a proper decorative or functional purpose. A fine Oriental screen can assume a role of decorative importance in a living room or a wicker screen could be brightly painted to serve as a colorful definition of space in a living/dining or kitchen/dining area.

When treated as a functional element, a plain wood or painted screen can be dressed up with a few decorative accessories. Restraint is the key here. The screen should be high enough so the accessories can be seen and the accessories themselves should be small enough to fit the proportion of the screen. If a screen is a vital part of your living-room scheme, and you want it to be unobtrusive, paint it the color of your walls. If you want a plain screen to stand out as a decorative accent, use a wallpaper covering in a pattern that fits the proportion of the screen and the decor of your room.

COLOR, PATTERN, AND ACCESSORIES

When planning accessories, it is important to remember that color and pattern are important factors. Wall arrangements, for example, will be completely different on a dark wall than they will on patterned or light-colored walls. Dark wall colors need sparkle and lightness of wall accessories to act as a catalyst. A chocolate brown or deep blue wall will be effectively highlighted by a regal crystal or bronze mirror or a pair of sconces. Pictures on dark walls should be framed in gold or brightly colored frames, or the pictures themselves will be lost on the walls. Dark finishes on bookshelves or wall units should not be used against dark-colored walls; their combined effect will overpower your room and negate any potential decorative impact.

Patterned walls also require considerable care in the planning of wall accessories. Wallpaper with bold pattern or mural designs should be simply treated, with the emphasis on understatement. The belief held by many that pictures are not used against a patterned wall has long been dispelled. However, pictures and paintings on busy patterned walls should be simple themes—a portrait or still life that is easily discernible against the patterned backdrop. Abstracts and delicate water colors should be avoided for these areas; their beauty will be lost against such a wall. For the painting collector, light or brightly colored walls act as a splendid stage for fine groupings, no matter what type of paintings are involved. Neutral walls are unnecessary; you can paint your walls any color as long as the tone is bright and clear. Your pictures will act as the co-ordinating balance for the wall color.

Decorative accessories in themselves can act as a color focalizer in your room. If, for example, you have a collection of Wedgwood accessories, they can dramatically enhance the blue in a rug or upholstery fabric if you show them together. A wall treatment of wood plaques and carvings, highlighted by a brightly colored picture, will set off a room that boasts beautiful parquet floors or furniture with elegant wood frames.

When using color as a focal point, it is important to gauge the impact that the color concentration will have on the room as a whole. Too much color or too heavy a concentration of color will dominate and detract from the rest of the room. Your accessories should try to pick up one of the secondary colors in your room if you are using many objects in one color. A room done in avocado and gold, for instance, should rely more on gold accessories and a scattering of avocado, if the latter is the predominant color in the room.

Intensity of the dominant color also is significant in planning your decorative accessories. A room designed around a brilliant orange or red area rug should merely suggest this color in accessories, but groupings of objects and colors of picture frames should never be planned to match. Try to plan color focal areas so that there is a blend rather than a concentration of bold, bright color. The same color tones should be scattered throughout the rest of your room to establish a feeling of unity and balance.

Color can also provide the spice in your decorating scheme. Use it for pungency to bring life and vitality to a neutral setting or to tone down an otherwise bold color scheme. But the use of color must do something to the point where, if it were not present, the room would

Just because the room is a kitchen doesn't mean that it needn't have color-ful and attractive accessories. Here prettily patterned plates and casserole, plants and whimsical wicker stools help create a look that not only offsets the bulk of cabinets and butterfly-shaped island, but also carries the theme of the outdoor room beyond.

Pictures, the most useful and important accessories, are here employed to underscore the effect of the flower-patterned sofa upholstery and the texture of the fringed accent rug over pale wall-to-wall carpet. Note the antique Chinese tea box, used as an arm table, which also carries out the floral motif of the room. Bouquets help, too.

be incomplete. Accessories in the total scheme offer a most effective use of color. They tell the main story and act out the supporting role. Today, bold colors are considered fashionable in room decorating schemes, but they need not all be brash. Often, a subtle touch of a pastel or half tone will accent as well as tone down the over-all impact of a too bright room. Imagine, for example, a room decorated in vivid shades of blue and green. For subtle accent, a clear sky blue in accessories such as lamps and bibelots would provide the necessary softening touch. The power of a brilliant colorful accent in a roomful of soft pastels will serve to heighten the total impact. A room decorated in soft beige and gold will be dramatically enhanced with the addition of jade green, peacock, or bright orange. Similarly, a pastel pink room will acquire added zest with a shocking pink or brilliant clear red accent in accessories. But don't overdo your accents. It's better to have too little than too much.

Accessory Balance

When planning the accessories for any room in your home, the first objective should be balance. Too many, few, or too large or too small should be avoided, but proper balance depends on the accessories themselves. Strive for unity in whatever you plan; try to avoid having conflicting materials next to each other. Variety in materials and color in your accessories is important to achieve another element of balance. Too many items in one feeling tend to make a room dull and uninteresting. In striving for balance in the accessories you use, keep in mind that one's materials should be used for emphasis, the rest for accent. But don't be afraid to use your imagination in the mix of materials you select. Pictures, as well as other accessories, are personal and emotional choices in your home. Hang them dramatically. Don't be timid about mixing picture types and frames. If they're well planned they will be an effective focal point in your room. Common sense and good taste should also tell you when you are using accessories improperly. Understatement is always more effective than clutter.

Collections

Most of us are avid collectors. It's human nature and fun. Collections, whether rare old porcelain or sea shells from your favorite beach, add a note of warmth and a bit of your personality to your home. Whether heirloom or strictly modern, collections should be shown to advantage rather than hidden away in a closet where no one can enjoy them. Even if you are a stanch modernist, don't be afraid to show off a collection of old items. Properly arranged, the old and new can be a most effective decorating scheme. In the same way, a collection of stark modern crystal, colorful ceramics, or sculpture will not be out of place in a traditional room. Certain materials, such as old Chinese porcelain or Eastern metal figures and hangings, are ideally suited for any decor. Make your collection an important part of your decorating plans. These objects provide a focal point in whatever room you use them. If, as happens to many of us, you think you have no space for them, make space. Design a shelf or cabinet arrangement to set them on their own stage. It's not necessary to limit the display of your collection to one room in your home. Scatter them around your house with a major grouping in one room. A collection of plates, for example, could be the focal point of a dining-room wall, but the balance of the collection could be mixed with a living-room wall arrangement of pictures. If you're moving or starting fresh in decorating your home, plan your collections as an important part of one room's scheme. Let it set the mood or the pace for the rest of the room as you would with an important furniture piece.

Collections deserve to be shown off in a dramatic presentation and with good lighting. If you can't see them there's no point in collecting anything. Open shelves, china cabinets, and tabletops are the most common ways to spotlight a collection. A group of plates or fine porcelain figurines can be shown to excellent advantage this way. With the plates, for instance, you might try framing them against a velvet or felt background and hang them on your wall. Or perhaps you have a wide doorway in your living or dining room. Arrange the plates above the door in asymmetrical patterns. Figurines should not be limited to traditional cabinet display. A small group on a mantel by itself will create a dramatic focal point. Or group them on a wall shelf arrangement as important accents to your books. Figurines also can be used as a wall arrangement on their own. Try individual shelf brackets in a random pattern on the wall. Keep the shelf brackets simple and undecorated, or they will detract from the figurines they hold.

Collections of old bottles can also be shown to advantage in the same manner as figurines. An interesting approach would be to arrange them along your windowsills. If your collection of old bottles is extensive, perhaps you might put glass shelves in front of your windows. The sunlight will add another dimension of sparkle and color to the bottles. A simple collection of unusual sea shells can brighten up a bathroom or bring a fresh, outdoor feeling to your living room. Use your windowsills for large shells or group a few together on a tabletop. Smaller shells can create an unusual centerpiece for your dining table in a simple clear glass bowl. Try this also on a sideboard or buffet as the focal point.

A collection of sculpture, both large and small pieces, deserves prominent display. Don't limit sculpture to just your living room; a

Pre-Columbian artifacts and small sculptures are effectively placed within a shallow recess but they would look just as well arranged on a plain flat wall.

fine collection can be distributed throughout your home. A long, low table against a wall sets a dramatic stage for any pieces of sculpture. Don't limit the table finish to a simple wood finish; marble or slate tops and a carved base will add another quality of dramatic impact and warmth to the clean lines of sculptured pieces. Large sculptures are effective just placed on the floor in a prominent spot. Try them in an open corner of your living room or on the floor next to a sofa or large chair. Medium-sized pieces can become a dominant talking point if placed on a pedestal.

Cut crystal, perhaps, is the most difficult collection to show off effectively. Lighting and background must be right to catch the sparkle and pattern of each piece. Try to avoid glass cabinets if you have a crystal collection; even with lighting there is no color contrast and background. Instead, an open breakfront with a dark wood finish will set your crystal off as it should be. Lighting should be inside the cabinet, preferably individual fluorescent lights for each shelf. It's important, too, when lighting a crystal collection that the light be understated rather than glaring. Don't overcrowd cabinets. It's better to have space beween each piece; crowding will give the effect of each piece reflecting its neighbor.

Tabletops also are effective for showing off crystal collections. A few small pieces against a dark tabletop will pick up dramatic luster from the table lamp. If you use your tables to display crystal or any other objects, avoid clutter. Too many of us overcrowd tables. The result is clutter and lack of impact of any of the pieces.

One of the most impressive collections is one of silver, old or new. Here, too, try to avoid showing many pieces in one area; the impact of silver in large groupings can be overpowering. An elaborate old English pitcher is a stunning accent for a living-room table; a silver coffee service is always effective on a buffet accented by a pair of regal candlesticks. Silver, more than other materials, should be grouped with one piece dominating the setting. Feature one piece as the focal point; let the others serve as a supporting cast. Silver, too, is one of the easiest collections to display. Pieces can be scattered among books on shelves, put on tabletops, or in cabinets as dramatic accents without worry about lighting or background. The natural luster and sheen of silver eliminates the need for special lighting effects. Pewter can be treated much like silver in displaying collections, but care should be taken that lighting is bright enough to show off the lines of each piece. Unlike silver, the dark satin finish of pewter does not reflect light. If you have an extensive pewter collection, try showing a few pieces in your kitchen. It will create a dramatic yet understated focal center if used sparingly.

Wood carvings and sculpture are most effective when displayed on anything except wood. The conflict of wood cabinets and the wood object tends to put the carving in a secondary position rather than focus attention on it. Widely spaced wall shelf systems with a light-colored wall background can be used for wood figures and carvings. The best way to show them off, however, is with glass. Glass curio cabinets for small pieces or glass-topped tables let the figures stand on their own without fighting the eye for attention. Marble tabletops also offer an effective contrast for wood pieces.

No matter what the material, if your collection tends to focus on massive pieces, you should group them sparingly. Heavy concentrations of large pieces—vases, bowls, and pitchers, for example—will tend to dominate the room. The impact of a collection of giant porcelain jars or heavy silver pieces will be destroyed if too many are shown together. Small objects should be clustered together to create importance without clutter. The number of pieces for each grouping is always determined by the size of the setting. A buffet or cupboard obviously will be able to support a grouping larger than a coffee table.

THE FINISHING TOUCHES

When planning decorative accessories for your home, remember it's the little things that count. Forgetting about little things can detract from the over-all look of your home and spoil all the efforts you make to create a warm and attractive atmosphere. Things like door and furniture pulls, shade pulls, and ashtrays all contribute to the final look. Too often, even the best furniture is fitted with ugly drawer and door pulls. Or perhaps you just don't like the way they look with the rest of your room, although you like the furniture itself. A simple solution is a visit to a hardware store that sells decorative hardware. Take a pull with you to make certain its replacement will fit. It's no trick to remove them, just unscrew from inside the drawer or door. They'll pull out easily.

When replacing pulls, make certain that proportions fit the size of the piece of furniture. A dainty painted porcelain pull doesn't belong with a massive carved chest. Replacement pulls are available in heavy brass, enamel, porcelain, glass, crystal, and wood. If you live in an old apartment building or house, you may have a decorative asset that's been hidden for years—your doorknobs. Most knobs in older buildings have been painted over and over through the years. But underneath, you often can find hand-wrought brass plates and knobs or crystal knobs that will add a decorative touch to plain doors. You can find out quickly if you have a hidden treasure. Soak the plates and knobs in paint remover for several days, then wipe clean and polish with brass polish. If you want to replace doorknobs and plates, you'll find a wide variety of designs and types in most hardware stores or decorating shops. New ones can add a note of color or elegance or complete the total scheme of your home.

Personal bric-a-brac is vital to the decor of the study. Books, held between inventive "ends" in the form of a sculptured head and a pencil holder, a letter box and large ashtray are also functional atop the table desk. The open cupboard holds a collection of contemporary china. Note interesting window treatment of shades, plaid lambrequins and floral cafe curtains.

Frequently, when buying window shades, many of us forget that the pulls don't have to be the plain crocheted strings of old. Instead, you might paint a giant wood ring the predominant color of the shade or use a decorative metal bar clip as a pull. Shade pulls also are available in enamel or glass, many in clip-on types.

There is nothing more frustrating to a heavy smoker than an ashtray that's too small. Great piles of ashes and butts in a small ashtray —plus the necessity for frequent emptying trips to the garbage pail— can try the most patient person's endurance. Be sure ashtrays are big enough, even if they are cut crystal or fine china. Ashtrays can be highly decorative accessories, but again make sure they are big enough. Of course, for a living room or bedroom, there should be several of the large economy size; dining room and bathroom ashtrays can be slightly smaller. But whatever the size, they should fit your room's decor and perhaps add a color or design accent of their own. If your room is elegant and formal, don't use heavy cast-iron types. Instead, use a crystal or porcelain design. For contrast, the ashtray might be of stark modern crystal design.

CARING FOR YOUR ACCESSORIES

Fine accessories deserve good treatment. Today, manufacturers of cleaning products have taken most of the drudgery out of caring for valuable accessories, and there's a cleaning preparation for almost every type of material.

Chrome or Steel. Just wipe with a hot, soapy cloth and polish dry. Chrome and steel really don't need polishing preparations; their gleaming surfaces can be brightened just with a dry cloth.

Crystal and Glass. Crystal and glass should always be kept sparkling clean to set them off to best advantage. Washing should be done with great care to avoid breakage. Some people prefer to line the sink basin with a rubber mat or terry towel to prevent the crystal from cracking against the sink. Wash large items singly. Small items should not be crowded into the sink—they may hit against each other and break. Use warm soapy water and a sponge or brush to reach any hard to get at recesses. Take care that the water is not too hot: It may break delicate crystal. Rinse well to remove all soapy traces and dry and shine well with a linen towel.

China, Earthenware, Porcelain. Soak, then wash well in a basin of warm, soapy water. The basin may be lined or unlined depending on your care in handling the items. Again, don't overcrowd the sink. Rinse well and dry with a linen or terry towel.

Ceramics. Hand-painted ceramics should not be soaked in water. Instead, use a warm, damp cloth to remove dirt or dust. Glazed ceramics can be put into a basin of warm, soapy water, but don't soak them for a long period. Rinse well and dry immediately.

Copper and Brass. The new cleaning preparations take most of the work out of cleaning these materials. Follow the directions on the preparation you buy. If black spots appear, use a soft toothbrush with the cleaning preparation to remove them.

Some new brass and copper pieces have a lacquer finish to resist tarnishing. These pieces just need wiping with a soft cloth to restore the shine. If tarnish spots appear, it means some of the lacquer has worn off. When this occurs, all the lacquer should be removed so that a new application can be made. Professional handling of both removal and new applications of lacquer is suggested.

Fabric. Wall hangings and pictures made of fabric should be vacuumed regularly to prevent dust and dirt from being absorbed. Take them off the wall and vacuum with the upholstery brush attachment.

Marble. Marble tabletops should be wiped frequently with a damp cloth or sponge to remove stains or rings from damp glasses. A soft brush or sponge and warm, soapy suds will remove stubborn stains. A damp cloth should be used to rinse the marble. Dry well.

Pewter. A good commercial cleaner is generally all that is needed to clean pewter. Remember, too, that old pewter often has a darker cast than the new. This doesn't mean that it is dirty; it's the natural appearance and it can be polished to create a rich, lustrous appearance. After cleaning, rinse pewter well and dry thoroughly with a soft cloth to highlight its natural shine.

Picture Glass and Mirrors. Use a window cleaning spray preparation to clean picture glass and mirrors. Spray carefully to avoid the frames. If the frame does get some overspray wipe it off immediately with a dry cloth. Wipe mirrors and pictures with a lint-free cloth or a newspaper to eliminate streaking. Make certain the glass is completely dry to avoid streaks.

Pictures and Paintings. Frequent dusting or vacuuming with the upholstery brush attachment should be done to keep grime from settling in and altering the colors.

Silver. In times gone by, fine silver always needed polishing. Now new cleaning preparations have long-lasting nontarnish ingredients. Silver that is used frequently tends to tarnish less than infrequently used pieces, but it should be wiped occasionally with a silver-polishing cloth. Silver that is not used often should be wrapped in plastic film or in special nontarnish silver cloths. When polishing, follow the instructions on the preparation. For difficult or hard to get at spots, use a soft toothbrush to remove stains. Dry well with a linen or a silver-polishing cloth.

CHAPTER TWELVE

WINDOW TREATMENTS

THE WINDOW IS in many ways one of the most important features of a room. It is an eye on the world, as it were; whether it boasts a view or not, a window helps to bring a room alive. We've all been in windowless rooms and know the instinctive aversion that arises and a basement room, with the merest suggestions of a high window, seems far more comfortable than a basement room without such a window. Few windows, however, can stand alone—either from the standpoint of a view or privacy. The window must be treated and, as such, its treatment becomes a main ingredient of every room. When planning any window treatment, you must remember that the main functions of the window are to admit light and air. Anything which totally obviates these functions is not a satisfactory solution. All too often the amateur decorator simply creates a false window in front of the existing one, making it difficult to get to the window itself for light, air, and a glimpse of the world beyond.

Whatever type of treatment you decide on—and there are many possibilities besides the standard columns of drapery at either side of an opening, as we shall see in this chapter—keep it simple. Overelaborate treatments can kill an otherwise acceptable decorating scheme more quickly than any other element. To the beholder there is something presumptuous about trying to obscure the window. On the other hand, you may be fortunate enough to have a house or apartment with quite handsome woodwork, interesting small-paned sash, and other details that can be exposed as decorative elements that add to the beauty of your decorating scheme. Study your windows closely; often their attributes will suggest something for the treatment. For example, if there are frames with lovely moldings, perhaps a roller shade or a simple pleated drapery within the reveal of the window will create a striking focal point in the room. Now let's take up the various types of treatment in detail.

DRAPERY IDEAS

How do you decide on a new drapery treatment? First, you make a decision on the style you think will do the most for the design and size of your windows. Choosing drapery style is actually easy since the number to choose from is so limited; color and texture of the material plus extra fringe and frills are the elements that make the fashion statements, that help define the mood for the entire room, and give a seemingly endless variety to a few basic line and design ideas. Basic drapery styles are either straight hanging or tied-back panels of fabric gathered or pleated onto rods. The length, another style factor, varies from overlong poufs on the floor, to the floor, to cover the frame beneath the window, and to the sill.

Let the style you set for your window's wardrobe enhance the beauty of room furnishings, along with correcting any architectural faults. If the room is out of proportion, use line to correct by illusion. For example, horizontal treatment tends to widen a long and narrow room, ceiling-to-floor lengths seem to stretch short walls upward. A good window design also maintains the same decorating period or design feeling expressed in the other furnishings. Color, period, size, and shape—these are the elements that make up the style of window treatment.

The ultimate in drapery treatments for elegant room settings is made up of these three parts—sash curtain, draw curtain, and overdrapery. First and closest to the windowpane is the sash curtain; also referred to as the undercurtain, it is made of a sheer fabric which filters light and view. The sash curtain should be very full—three to four times the width of the window and shirred onto a narrow, round, or flat rod. It should fall straight from the rod, and be windowsill or floor length. It may be hung within the window frame or over the frame. The undercurtain needs to hang far enough away from the window to permit it to fall straight without having to "belly" out over woodwork.

Next, the draw curtain, made of a heavier, more opaque material, is used instead of a window shade in a very formal treatment. It may either draw on a traverse rod system or hook onto decorative rings and

Formal, translucent drapery of Dacron dresses windows that flank a chrome steel table in an informal foyer. Valance sports rococo trim which restates the tone of the wormy chestnut plywood paneling.

rod. The rod should be mounted far enough away from the sash curtain to permit both to fall freely without any cling. A lining of sateen helps to eliminate this possibility. The overdraperies make their dramatic finale as the third set, and they are intended to frame and define the entire window decor. They do not draw; they are two panels which drape back on either side of the window. For a touch of luxury, make them overlong so that they "break" and lay in poufs of satin or velvet on the floor.

Fabrics for curtains and draperies may be solid or multicolored, plain or patterned, textured or smooth, transparent or opaque. They also may match or co-ordinate with upholstery, window shades, or wallpaper. Whatever you choose, remember to keep your window treatment an integral part of the room.

For a formal room, you may choose from among antique satin, silk or rayon satin, ottoman, faille, moiré or metallic, damask, and velvet. The solid hues are preferred for formal rooms; stripes are good secondary selections.

For an informal room, chintz and a printed linen tie for first choice here, both for their pleasing aspect in an informal room and for excellent wear. Crisp and glazed finishes make a summer room feel cool and clean; they are also able to take humid climates without wilting. Another feature about these particular prints is the subject matter and the way it appears on the cloth. Varieties of gaily drawn flora and fauna, scenes of the country and ocean, documentary designs of Early Americana add to the effectiveness.

For a casual room, if the use of the room calls for a homelike atmosphere, such as a family dining area, game and hobby section, consider these attractive, hard wearables: denim, burlap, corduroy, sailcloth, and muslin, all of which can be found in patterns and solid colors. It is at this time that you must make up your mind as to pattern or fabric design. How many times will you have changed your ideas? Here are several good reasons for choosing the solids. They can be restful and are a must where the window is on the same wall with a busy wallpaper or scenic mural. Solids, stately additions to formal settings, are open to the design suggestions of various trimmings. On the other hand, patterns and prints have some arguments in their favor. Contemporary rooms respond to their fresh new outlook. Pattern also performs the illusion of distracting the eye from uninteresting elements in the room or at the window. One pattern at the window can draw all the other colors in the room together by repeating them within its design.

Texture is important—feel the surface of different materials when shopping in a store or showroom. Do you like the texture; is it what you expected to feel? See the change in appearance from the direct light to shadow. Notice that textures range from rough to smooth, coarse to fine in weave—this in turn makes the fabric have a matte, flat, or extremely glossy finish. Highly reflective surfaces—vinyls, satins, polished cottons—are stimulating in a room. Mattes, velvets, corduroys, and thick linens are restful, absorb sound, and feel substantial. The coarseness of burlap or airiness of casement cloth offers a complete change of pace—a feeling of freedom and informality.

MAINTENANCE FOR FABRICS

How durable and how much maintenance (laundry, dry cleaning) window fabrics will require are factors in choosing one fiber, weave, and finish over another. Learn complete details about the materials you look at. Your final decision may be influenced by which is more durable—which requires the least maintenance. Fabrics are more colorfast when the fiber is dyed before being spun into yarn.

Closely woven fabrics wear better, do not sag or stretch, and are easier to handle if you make your own curtains. Fabrics are given special finishes to improve or change their appearance, to increase wear, to permit washing with no ironing required, to add body and crispness. These finishes also make materials resistant to many harmful elements such as moths, fire, stain, and soil. Read the labels to know what has been added. If you know that a fabric you wish to purchase has not been treated for stains, inquire where you may have it sent for treatment. Most firms and stores can supply names of local places offering this service at a nominal price. The very fact that certain finishes can be applied has meant new popularity for some of the more precious silks and more perishable pale hues.

LINED DRAPERIES

Lined draperies have a richer appearance because the light does not show through. A lining helps to protect fabric from sunlight and dust; it also adds body, so that the drapery falls in softer, more graceful folds; and the same-color lining gives a uniform appearance to windows from the street view. Cream-colored or white sateen is the favorite for linings. Unbleached muslin or similar weight material can be a substitute.

Bright colors and prints may, on occasion, become linings for curtains in rooms that don't face on the street. Possibilities include white moiré for the curtain and coral pink sateen for the lining, with the lining brought around to face the front as a border trim of great beauty. A fern- or forsythia-splattered chintz might be lined in a sunny yellow, or a solid, deep blue linen could be backed in a red-and-white ticking stripe. A chair or window-seat cushion could be covered in matching red-and-white ticking.

Finally, be sure that the lining is lighter in weight than the drapery material. The lining is sewn to the drapery with the right sides facing, and it should be cut to measure two inches narrower than the drapery on each side. This allows for necessary hems and facing.

UNLINED DRAPERIES

Choosing not to line a curtain or drapery is fine so long as certain attention is given to the sewing details. Almost any fabric can be used at the window without a lining if hems are put in by hand and if the curtain is made extra full in width to compensate and give the body needed to make it fall gracefully.

Make a daylight test of a cloth you're considering, to determine whether the light coming through will make a pattern or texture in the material look peculiar, as it could, if there is to be no lining. Sheer undercurtains are usually never lined, but to look more luxurious, figure on purchasing enough ninon or marquisette to measure about three times the width of the window. Heavier weight fabrics when too full look as uncomfortable as the too skimpy. For correct yardage, figure on twice what the window actually measures. The side hems on heavier unlined drapery panels should be narrow (about an inch) and sewn in by hand. The selvage edges, if attractively finished, can sometimes be used as is—without hemming. When cutting curtain fabric, lay it flat on a long table or the floor. Pull a thread across the width to straighten uneven ends. If stitching curtains on the machine, be sure to adjust the tension and the length of the stitch so that the finished seams won't pucker or pull. Try out the adjusted stitch first on a scrap of the actual material. The bottom hem is not sewn in until after the curtain has been tried on the rod. Measure and mark the hemline with pins while the curtain is hanging; final hemming can be sewn then, too, or done off the rod.

DRAPERY TIPS

Your window's wardrobe can look as if custom made with these suggestions:

Buy the best quality, best price fabrics you can afford. Your curtains will hang better, launder and dry clean more safely.

Eliminate the possibility of any unevenness by hanging draperies unhemmed on the rod, then pin the hemline into position as you would a dress.

Let sheer undercurtains stop at sill length for use at kitchen, bathroom, and nursery windows. But make sheers floor length in a more formal setting in living room or dining room.

Put casement cloth, because it's heavier, below the windowsill—to the apron.

Borrow an elegant idea from France! Put extra-deep hems on draperies. Floor-length styles can use a hem six to ten inches deep. For example, the lighter the fabric, the deeper the hem. A heavy velvet might carry a hem six to seven inches deep, while a printed linen or cotton chintz could take the full ten inches, and a sheer might be slightly more.

Generous hems make the idea of double hems unnecessary extra work and may also rule out the necessity for special "weights."

Careful installation is another detail that pays off in prettiness. Drapery rods must hang at the same height from the ceiling on both sides of the window and be parallel with the ceiling line.

Wide windows may need one or more extra rod supports to counteract sagging of heavyweight treatments.

Heavyweight drapery treatments need heavy-duty brackets and other hardware. Consult your supplier for the special screws and other devices needed to make attachments more secure.

Lacquer, not paint, goes on decorative wooden poles to provide an extra-slick surface, so that curtain rings will ride smoothly back and forth.

Good construction includes straight seams and hems, with patterns and repeats carefully matched.

Clip off selvage edges, turn a narrow hem along the sides to prevent puckering, and sew side hems in by hand. All this is done only if curtains are unlined.

Window Terms

If you say "cornice" when you mean a canopy or "valance" when what you want is a lambrequin—the sky won't fall, but your face may if you wind up with something you didn't order. Chances are most, if not all, of the following terms are known to you. But in the world of fashions and furnishings some everyday words have different, special meanings.

Appliqué: Cutout pieces of material attached by sewing or pasting to a background fabric. An embroidery stitch outlines the cutout; light underpadding defines the design.

Awning: A canvas covering for outdoor use, usually installed above a door or a window. Also a type of casement window where the glass panel protrudes at an awning angle.

Baton: A decorative rod with a handle attached to one end and used to push draperies apart in lieu of a traverse rod and pulley system.

Bay Windows: A projection. of three or more straight-sided glass panels. If panels are curved this becomes a bow window.

Box Pleating: Pressed folds across a drapery heading—sewn or clipped into place at regular intervals.

Bracket: Flat-topped underprop attached to the wall to support a cornice or other drapery hardware.

Braid: An interwoven strip of matching or contrasting colors used for binding and trimming. Might be in silk, cotton, or synthetic threads.

Buckram: Sturdy cloth stiffened with sizing and important for backing and interlining on valances and drapery headings.

Canopy: A fabric hood suspended over a door, bed, or window.

Casement Cloth: Light- to heavyweight cotton, linen, wool, or synthetic fibers woven into various open weaves that filter daylight in interesting shadow play. Used both as undercurtaining or the main feature on wide glass expanses.

Casement Window: Glass panels hinged at one side to swing in or out.

Clerestory: A series of windows placed high on the wall near the ceiling. Also known as strip windows.

Cornice: See below.

Dormer Window: A double-hung window built into a sloping roof of an attic room.

Double-hung Window: Most common type with two sections—one pushes up, the other pulls down.

Fan Light: Crescent-shaped glass panels over doors or windows. Crescents may have radiating lines (called mullions) of thin wood or lead separating the glass into individual pie-shaped panes.

Festoons: Silken ropes, wreaths, garlands of various fabrics to be looped over a valance, bed canopy.

Finial: Decorative endpiece for curtain rod shaped as a knob, pineapple, foliage, arrow. Might be made of either brass or wood and applied to each end of a rod.

Gauze: Extremely sheer fabric in man-made or natural fibers used for undercurtains.

Guimpe or Gimp: Narrow, flat braid to trim or finish edges on upholstered pieces and draperies.

Hardware: The fixtures—brackets, rods, rings, hooks, cranes, hinges —used to install window treaments. Materials vary in decorative finishes according to whether they will play supporting roles behind the curtains. Hardware may be specially ordered as part of custom-made drapery installations in brass, wood, or other metals; but most of the hardware needed is ready-made and available through drapery workrooms, or is to be found on display racks and counters at local department and specialty stores. And there are literally hundreds of items, from acanthus leaf holdbacks and pineapple finials to curtain rods in zebrawood.

Heading: The hem across the top of a curtain or drapery. The heading can be concealed under festoons, fringe, ribbon, or guimpe, and sometimes in a very formal treatment the heading may also carry a jabot down one or both sides.

Holdback: A decorative brass arm that holds drapery to one side of the window. Many holdbacks have a release so that draperies may close or hang as straight panels.

Jabot: Cloth loosely pleated or gathered to form an ornamental frill or short drapery fall.

Jamb: Interior sides of a door or window frame, often called a reveal.

Lambrequin: See below.

Pole Screen: A decorative adjustable panel mounted floor to ceiling on a tension rod. Useful in screening off portions of a room or curtaining parts or all of window walls with sliding doors to a terrace.

Sash Curtain: Any sheer material hung close to the window glass. It softens, filters daylight, covers the blackness of a nighttime window-pane. This type is also referred to as an undercurtain.

Sill: The horizontal strip at the base of a window. On a door this portion is called a saddle.

Skylight: Glass panel set flat into a sloping or flat roof.

Swag: A somewhat dated word you might replace with "festoon" in discussing drapery treatments.

Transom: A narrow window above a door.

Tester: The curtaining on a four-poster bed.

Valance: See below.

THE VALANCE

A valance decorates the top of a window in much the same way that a headboard decorates the top of a bed. A valance may be plain or pleated, tufted or trimmed, straight or scalloped, in satin or sailcloth, linen or leather.

Some of the design ideas are very old, some new, but each has been devised to accomplish these things:

Point up the period or style influence of the entire window treatment.

Conceal curtain rods, shade brackets, and other hardware.

Add fresh design interest to a dull room.

Improve the window's proportions; too narrow can be made to appear wider by extending the valance beyond the window frame on each side.

Extend a valance across the narrow wall space between two or more windows to unite them into one important focal point in the room.

A valance, aside from its practical purposes, is the decorative touch that lifts the expected ordinary to the unexpected spectacular. It does for your draperies what ribbon does for a gift box. A valance may be made entirely of fabric to hang straight or fall into soft pleats. It may be suspended from a decorative pole by short, matching fabric straps or threaded onto a curtain rod. If formal, the fabric may be satin, damask, taffeta, velvet; informal, may be linen, chintz, toile de Jouy, corduroy; casual could call for canvas, sailcloth, gingham, or colorful felt. Some of the less intricate valance designs can be made at home. Felt is an example of an easy material to work with since it does not require hemming.

A number of interesting cut and shaped borders can be accomplished with just a pair of scissors. Contrast trims that trace and outline the felt valance edges are pasted on with white household glue. Colors in felt are most effective in the dark hues: tobacco brown, avocado green, black, or maroon. White braids of various widths are smart, stunning ways to pick out various border details. Measurement for a valance can vary from thirteen to eighteen inches. This is based on the total length of the window treatment and works out to be about one and one-half inches of valance to every foot of drapery. If mathematics is not your best subject, use a paper stand-in for a valance in planning to avoid mistakes in judgment. Heavy kraft paper makes a sturdy model to test our various design ideas. Use tape to affix it lightly over the window frame or on the wall where you expect the finished object to be installed. Stand back from the window to observe the size and shape in relation to the room and the other furnishings in it. Then, if you've made a final decision on the style for the accompanying draperies and undercurtains, you're ready to proceed with your order.

THE CORNICE

A cornice is a shallow, boxlike structure made mainly of wood and fastened across the top of a window. It may be very plain or made extra-fancy with applied wood or metal trim. A cornice could be painted to match the walls or a part of the room; it may be given a dark wood stain to harmonize with paneling or floors. Some cornices are fabric covered in a print or solid hue to match the draperies, and perhaps a chair or table skirt elsewhere in the room. Fabric is stapled or tacked to the wood, which may have underpadding of foam rubber.

In Victorian-style houses where ceilings were richly adorned in ornamental plaster and carved oaken beams, the cornice was sometimes treated with mirror sections. Not a bad idea for today's use; some ceilings are still beamed or broken up with skylights and other unique

Fringe accents a lambrequin, white window shade, and circular tablecloth into one pretty picture for dining. The scalloped-edged lambrequin covered in fabric to match walls and cafe curtains seems to increase the size and add new importance to the former small window.

The beauty of the well balanced arrangement is shown off in this symmetrical treatment spotted at the end of a long entrance hall. A studied blending of colors serves to enhance the classic lines of the tie-back drapery and its accompanying brass hardware.

The air of casual comfort in this living room is due to the deeply grooved, driftwood gray plywood paneling and to the tripartite window treatment with shades hung reverse-roll to conceal the rollers. Decorative strength results from the sunny color of shades and sofa.

OWENS-CORNING FIBERGLAS

WINDOW SHADE MANUFACTURERS ASSOCIATION

Move a batch of no-iron cotton, Dacron sheets out of bed to blossom brightly as slipcovers on chairs, on a foam rubber sofa mat; use sheets, too, as window shades, and gather them into curtains for sliding window panel screens. Coordinate the wild and shocking hues with vari-colored bath towels —perfect for adorning throw pillows and such.

Unite two widely spaced uninteresting windows into one important eye-catcher! Use a black and white print defined in two ways— with ribbon for trim and tiebacks; with gleaming brass for curtain rods. Match the couch to the window's dress then let yellow, and yellow-green take over the walls and upholstered pieces.

OWENS-CORNING FIBERGLAS

Bring a breath of the country into a cramped city apartment by means of garden-like treillage and interior plantings. The treillage, done-up in a series of hinged panels, screens out neighboring window views, yet brings in full daylight. Rug and upholstery fabrics are easy-care polyester fibers; tabletop is spillproof plastic.

CARPETING OF KODEL POLYESTER

Turn a now room into a wow! room with the zip of zinnia yellow, gold, and bittersweet. Choose a slubbed-textured translucent in white as the under-curtaining, flank it with deeply contrasting, ceiling-high screens.

OWENS-CORNING FIBERGLAS

"Hard-Edge" painting at left, inspires an entire room setting and its color scheme. The bold linear mood starts with the oil-finish teak paneling; moves on to the window area where built-ins add their dramatic impact; continues in the see-through table and important functional chairs to the rug which is rectilinear!

designs. A cornice could hide the workings of an exhaust fan or air conditioner set in the top of the window. Special design plans would call for two hinged frames opening like small doors giving easy access to the equipment. Open-weave materials would cover the frames and allow the equipment to "breathe" in beauty. Some open-pattern materials: latticework, caning, wire mesh, or small louvers.

THE LAMBREQUIN

A lambrequin is a complete or partial wood frame around a window. It can literally remake old-fashioned windows because it obscures the old frame. Possible finishes for this unique treatment include painting or lacquering the wood, "papering" it with a washable vinyl, canvas, brass-studded leather, felt, or even a fuzzy fake fur. If you plan to cover your own lambrequin (made at home or in a carpenter's shop) cut the material large enough to cover all sides with an additional two-inch allowance so that it will extend over the edges and attach to the back. For a most professional look, use an undercover of thin foam rubber before fabric is applied, and tack material to the lambrequin with heavy-duty stapling.

TIEBACKS AND TRIMMINGS

Trimming outlines the main design of draperies. It adds a certain dressiness; and it emphasizes details and special shaping on the various parts of the window treatment. Clever use of trimming can make a window wall hung with solid color an exciting backdrop that could pull attention away from nondescript areas in the room. Can you picture panels of marigold yellow cotton hung full length from a brass rod and dripping in green fringe? The fringe in this case was six inches deep, done in two overlapping layers. And adding to the bold use of color was the carpeting which continued the emerald green where the fringe left off.

Ready-made, store-bought draperies beg to be personalized. Perhaps you have a certain color or ribbon that you like to use often as your special touch. For example, one decorator's favorite is the use of pinstriped satin ribbon as his way to add interesting detail. Tassels, the longer, the silkier, the more offbeat in color, are another means of trimming, and repeated so frequently they practically spell the name of their decorator user.

A luxuriant fall of fabric held back with thick silken roping is not only useful and beautiful for windows, but is a highly decorative and practical way to create a semiprivate feeling to doorways between traditional rooms.

Something, anything that can take curtains from the store's rods and make them at home on yours is not as difficult as it may seem. Braid, tape, etc. are all available in so many different shadings—it's unlikely you wouldn't find your room's color scheme among them.

The ready-mades you buy in a solid color are frequently easiest to liven merely by sewing on borders of leftovers you might have from patterned fabrics used elsewhere in the room. Or match up velvet or grosgrain ribbon to the rug and baste it along the sides of the curtains. Use an overdose of tassels, the tiny type, as another means to break up assembly-line monotony. Sew or pin on the tassels in a scatter effect. Tiebacks, strips of material that hold drapery to one side of the window, may have straight, scalloped, or other cutout edges and can be made from almost anything. As an example, a string of brass or glass beads, a wide pink satin sash, even a child's red-handled jump rope might skip to the windows of a game room to hold back lengths of fishnet employed for the casual treatment needed there.

You might sew a pair of tiebacks to match or contrast with ready-made or homemade curtains. Determine the length needed for a tieback by looping a piece of string around the curtains, allowing extra for attaching tieback ends to the wall or window frame. Then lay string flat on a ruler to get the exact measurement.

Make a paper cutout for the desired shape and size, remembering that hems will require more fabric. Pin paper pattern, tieback fabric, and lining material together and cut one or more pairs all at once. Stitch together on the wrong side leaving a small opening at one end for turning. Turn to right side and press. Sew trimming tape, ribbon, or rickrack around edges to outline or trace special details.

A successful solution to window dressing does not always mean soft folds. There's also the hard-edge treatment made up of shades, shutters, blinds, and screens. Any one of these might offer an excellent alternative to adorn windows where floor space is limited, where windows are sized differently, where there's no scenic view, where hot sun is a problem, or because you might like to try newer materials especially suited to contemporary architecture. In the decorating world, the latest design idea does not overthrow the older— that's part of what makes home furnishings so fascinating. Instead, each new concept is considered for its eye appeal and function and given a place in the decorating scheme of things as the need arises for its use.

SCREENS

Screens can be made of a metal or a wooden framework to hold a material. The material might be fabric, pierced wood, bamboo, leather, vinyl, or open grillwork. Used in panels twelve to fourteen inches wide, they are hinged at top and bottom to stand on the floor, or fastened in sections to the wall or window. Other screens glide along on metal tracks attached to the floor and to the ceiling. They operate in a similar way to shojis, but can have other translucent-type materials mounted in the framework. Screens can be treated with architectural details—columns, posts, arched tops—to appear as another wall. They are a clever means to conceal windows overburdened with heating and ventilating equipment, and they can serve to screen out the view from outside. Even on a high floor you may still need to block your activities from neighboring windows, yet let in air and sunlight. Screens may also be completely covered in fabric, wallpaper, and vinyl materials to match the wall where the windows are located. Covered screens are an effective means for widening a too narrow end wall or to beautify a wall bereft of wood moldings and other trims. Cover one wall, the window wall, with gleaming black vinyl, as an example, with more of the same vinyl stapled or tacked onto twelve-inch-wide hinged panels; figuring on two panels for each side of the window. Then for a smashing, braid-border trim against the black vinyl, use a two-inch-wide yellow/white Greek key design. Shiny black, brown, or maroon vinyl wall covering relieved with white and bright trimmings are dramatic pep ups for small spaces; a foyer, den, TV/study spot, or miniature library.

Screens may be partially open, partially closed, may mount to the ceiling, or stop at the windowsill; they may be covered in caning, rice paper, or translucent plastics; they may match the woodwork, the wall, or nothing else at all. And the framework can be elaborately carved, with curved or straight sides. Screens offer amazing variety in "built-in" looks that conceal not only the necessaries for light, air, and heat, but can fold back to reveal shelving for hi-fi, china, and other household needs that may have to revolve about the window areas.

LOUVERS

Louvers have been letting in a lot or little light since the ancient Egyptians hit on this slat device to control light and privacy. From this beginning has come a host of good design ideas offering variety in color and styling to the louver lover. Whole windows are sometimes louvered to become jalousies: frosted slats, set in aluminum framework to open and close with a crank.

SHUTTERS

Shutters are another important member of the louver class and are very popular because they adapt to both modern and traditional windows. Types include horizontally set wooden slats in neat little frames. Or the newer, dust-resistant vertical slats, important to good room design since the vertical slat adds height to the lower ceilinged room. Shutters may be finished in several ways—painted in a color to match the walls and woodwork, stained in light- or dark-tone varnishes, clear lacquered, or merely waxed. Shutters can work alone at a bank of windows in exciting floor-to-ceiling treatments, or the

Shutters are an effective, original way to give the privacy a bathroom requires. Reverse roll shade shuts out light but lets in fresh air. The shade becomes an integral part of the design scheme when laminated with fabric to match the vinyl-covered walls.

lower half of the window can be shuttered, with the upper treated to colorful cafe curtains.

Venetian Blinds

Venetian blinds, included in this class, are generally thought of as horizontal slats strung on a string. They may be window or wall wide, standard size, or the thin-line model. The latter type seems barely there because the narrower slats have nearly invisible wisplike control cords and are strung together with nylon cord instead of the bulky-looking tapes. This version is especially suited to the picture window with a view.

Another boon to decorating is the vertical louvered shade with flexible vinyl slats that have a fabric feel, yet perform their hard-edge role to perfection—obscuring the view but not the light.

WOVEN WOOD BLINDS

Woven wooden blinds, though familiar sights in dark green or natural wood on summer patios, carports, and breezeways, rate mention here for past good performance and present-style adaptability. Clever use of color and material has turned these former country cousins into smart city window dwellers. Imagine if you will, what enameled, black, wooden strips woven together with brilliant orange, red, and lime would do for a contemporary living room. These blinds are easy to install, easier still to clean, and roll up or down by pulling a cord. They shade the sun but do not offer complete shadow-proof privacy for nighttime. Construction: Wooden strips in natural tone or colors are simply woven together with strings, pretty pastel wool yarns, metallic threads, or heavy cords. The result: Some very handsome hangings to adorn large windows and other openings. And great indoors, in a room of whitewashed walls, wicker furniture, and rush floor matting.

SHADES

Roller Shade. A hard-edge candidate that seems to be getting nearly all the votes for versatility is the roller shade. Gone is the dull green pull-down of yesterday. New now is the pull-up—brilliant in an array of fresh colors, designs, textures, and degrees of opacity—from light filtering to room darkening. You may choose to decorate your own window shade with cutout appliqués from the room's wallpaper or upholstery; you can stencil on patterns; you can paste on fringe. Or you may prefer to order shades custom made with precut ornamental borders. You may have shades laminated with the fabric you're using in upholstery, slipcovers, or draperies. You may select solid colors that will repeat the colors you've chosen for wallpaper, rugs, or painted walls. Shades, of course, still do the strictly functional tasks too, of cutting glare on hard-to-curtain skylights, clerestories, and stair-well windows. In neutrals, white, gray, or beige, shades present a unified exterior to a house or apartment.

The mounting mechanisms needed to install window shades are probably the smallest, least complicated, and easiest to install of any drapery hardware. Shade hang-ups are nothing more than small brackets tacked to the inside frame; or to avoid light seepage around the edges, tack the bracket to the outside of the window frame.

*Tangerine and beige stripes define the "hard-edge" theme that domi-
nates this play-study spot. Reverse roll window shades hide the usual
up-front mechanism and floor-standing screens covered in matching
stripe serve to keep the eye concentrated on the straight and narrow
design. Black and white floor blocks and a white tabletop are stark
against the enameled tangerine director's chairs.*

There's a dual-purpose bracket, making it possible to hang both shade
and curtain rod in the same space. Another fixture attaches to the ceiling to accommodate longer shades. There is also a mechanism allowing a shade to be affixed in a horizontal position to use on skylights.
Then there's a bottom-up bracket which positions the shade upside
down on the windowsill, where it pulls up and down by a simple

Dress-up day for a dusty attic turned studio includes: beveled cedar siding on the walls, cowhide throw rug, strictly functional furniture for storage and seating. Skylights and glass jalousie floor-to-ceiling window get Roman shades of sheer cotton plisse to permit maximum painting light without afternoon glare.

cord and pulley system. These bottom-up installations work well to cover radiators, air conditioners, and offer privacy at the lower window while the upper can be open to light, air, and possibly a view of trees and clouds.

Roman Shade. A Roman shade is made of fabric that folds into pleats as it is raised. The mechanism, a series of rings and cords for raising and lowering the shade, is hidden on the reverse side. Installation is a simple matter of fastening the shade's heading inside the top of the window frame. A Roman shade is a very easy home-sewing project, too, now that ready-made tapes can be purchased with the necessary rings already in place. It then becomes a simple matter to stitch down the pleats and attach the tape, making a handsome brace-up for a tired room. Local upholstery-drapery shops are ready and willing to supply Roman shades custom made. If stuck for a style decision be guided by the shop's decorator.

Austrian Shade. This shade, which gives an elegant, formal feel, may be made of soft and sheer to semisheer materials. It is especially lovely in tissue taffeta. Appropriate colors are white, eggshell, beige, and palest celery green. It is shirred up the back in several vertical strips. The shirring, which should be very generous, causes the fabric to fall into delightful, rippling festoons. It may be made extra-wide to span and unify two windows set slightly apart, or it can "star" alone at the window without accompanying draperies. If used alone, without other drapery, a valance to match the shade is handsome. Trim both with contrasting color silk fringe.

WHICH TREATMENT FOR WHICH STYLE OF DECOR?

We have listed all the major types of window treatments available to you. Now comes the decision, which to use in a given situation. So far we have merely classified treatments as informal or formal, but that's not enough. We must decide those that are suitable to traditional, contemporary, and transitional styles of decoration.

For traditional, you should consider pleated drapery, preferably with valance above or lambrequin around. Valances can be swags, elaborately fringed, ruffled or braided according to the degree of detail called for by the particular period. The same for tiebacks. In the eighteenth-century English, Colonial, or French styles the treatment was simpler than, say, in Empire, Regency, or Victorian. The latter period saw the height of overelaborate treatments, with tassels, fringe, and all the rest. Often the Colonial or English rooms had a mere swagged valance at the top of the window, dramatizing the beauty of the window itself, its moldings, and other woodwork. Venetian blinds were used, which may come as a surprise. The houses of Colonial America often had wood blinds with wooden works. Another architectural solution in the eighteenth century was the use of paneled shutters which pulled out from the sides of the window reveal for privacy. By day there might be a high swag valance, at night, the opened shutter panels.

Roman shades, Austrian shades, and roller shades are also for the traditional styles. The roller shade, with hand-painted fabric or wallpaper applied to fabric, came into vogue in the mid-nineteenth century. Today the whole range of traditional fabric patterns can be laminated to roller shades to add great style to a room. Austrian shades became popular in the high Victorian period as an example of the elaborate window treatment. Roman shades are an ancient solution to window dress and can be interpreted in any traditionally inspired fabric design. We will see in a discussion of contemporary style that roller shades and Roman shades are also quite suitable and effective in streamlined rooms.

The above include solutions in the more formal manner. The more rustic or provincial treatments for eighteenth- and nineteenth-century styles would include cafe curtains and the simplest other types of curtains. These would be in printed cotton or natural homespun fabric, in contrast to the rich silks, brocades, and damasks of the more formal treatments.

Streamlined architectural simplicity is the watchword of contemporary style, and you have many interesting choices for the windows of contemporary rooms. Expanses of drapery, floor-to-ceiling, without valance, are suitable in plain, colored, textured fabric. If a patterned fabric is used, it must be one with a motif demonstrably in the modern idiom. However, it is better to include the drapery columns as an integral part of a room's background and keep them in the same tone as walls. Louvered panels—shutters you can find as stock ponderosa pine panels at your lumberyard—make excellent choices, especially where a tropical scheme is called for. Woven wood blinds are another good choice for the contemporary room, as are Venetian blinds and screens. Roman shades, again in plain fabrics or in contemporary motifs, are correct. In the contemporary room, avoid tiebacks, cornices, tassels, and all ornamentation in favor of an architectural solution which emphasizes the window opening itself and its relationship in scale and proportion to the rest of the room. Roller shades in plain colors or fabrics, hung reverse-roll or with the roller exposed at the top, give a neat, architectural look within the framework of a window. They are an easy, highly effective solution.

If the transitional room is basically traditional, then contemporary touches are used as accent. And vice versa. Since the window is a major element of background, it is well to include it as part of the dominant theme. A basically contemporary room, then, can have any of the above-mentioned window treatments that will accentuate the contemporary flavor. When it comes to the traditional room, you

This transitional living room overcomes the bare look of most present-day apartment buildings. Window wall, devoid of architectural interest, was unified by pleated drapery panels, tightly tied back and valance-swagged. Low-hung cafes conceal heating and air-conditioning outlets. Fabric panels add interest to long sofa wall; tapestry area rug adds strong pattern over dark-stained wood block floor.

should avoid extreme treatments; for example, Austrian shades are just too fussy for most transitional schemes, as are overly swagged, fringed, and tied-back drapery panels. The simpler traditional window styles should be considered. Remember, the well-done transitional room must come off as an effortless blend; if any one element is obtrusive—overscaled, overblown, or in any way overpowering—the effectiveness of the scheme is reduced. This is especially true of any element as dominant as the windows of a room. Keep them treated simply and casually and pick up the eclectic mix in furniture and accessories.

A good window treatment tells the purpose of the room, can set the mood, and on occasion help to identify the owner, as shown here in a young college man's bed-study room. The strictly masculine leopard print, laminated to a series of pull-up shades, adds dramatic decorating impact for one entire wall and provides maximum privacy, light control as desired.

WINDOWS WITH A VIEW

Windows that look out on scenic wonders—water, sky, snow, forest —are the decorator's delight. Here, because there's no need for the absolute, black-out privacy city living requires, the sight of more conventional and traditional curtaining may seem too much or too fussy to compete with the natural beauty afforded by a beach, suburban, or country house. Windows that are bared to the view need not look naked if imagination and taste are applied to their adornment in other ways. For example, you might drape the walls. Unorthodox to be sure, but it is a scheme designed to get the most from the scene, yet offer all the creature comforts that fabric can provide in making an interior feel cozy.

Here's another imaginative turn to take: Twist nylon cord into knots to separate large beads as they are threaded onto the nylon cord, made large enough to span the window. Attach bead lengths in a row along the top of the window frame. In this idea, the completely bare look is offset as the beads dangle without tangling, to reflect sunrays and rustle actively to incoming breezes.

Another bid for inexpensive and ingenious window decor calls for the use of bed sheets. Sheets can serve to cover the window when more privacy, less light are needed. Bed sheets can be found in some out-of-the-ordinary colors and prints. Some printed sheets show animals stalking in the fabric jungle; others are leopard spotted, zebra striped, bright florals, and fanciful stripes. Sheets are made in so many sizes that it's perfectly possible to have handsome curtains without cutting into the sheet, and doing little more than hemming top and bottom. To install, slip a rod through the top hem (heading), or suspend the sheet along the rod from clip-on hooks. Homemade tiebacks of extra-wide rickrack, thick knitting yarn, hair ribbons, etc. let in the daylight and untie at night for privacy.

A penthouse and a vacation house can have similar problems when it comes to the windows. Both have wide windows that are usually left uncovered to daytime views, yet at nighttime require a black-out means for privacy and sleeping. There's a solution for bedrooms, at least, by the way shades and blinds are installed. Shades should be mounted on the outside of the window frame, so that the entire glass area is covered. The other, more usual, method of mounting inside the window frame leaves a space all around which allows light to come in, and this light can be insistently irritating to the sleeper. Be sure, though, to order shades longer and wider, for mounting outside the frame will require a bigger shade.

Windows without a View

Apartment houses no longer have mere windows; instead, they are faced with what seems to be miles of glass running wall to wall, floor to ceiling. This design technique has some advantages. It can help to lift up too low ceilings and widen shrinking room dimensions. But all the benefits gained soon seem to disappear when the view is no more inspiring than the apartment house across the street. Perhaps a solution to this might be found in translucent materials that offer attractive dress for the windows, allow daylight to stream in, yet are translucent enough to partially screen out the actual view.

Bathing these large glass expanses with sheer fabric hung completely across them is another easy to achieve cover-up that also provides extra wall space for furniture groupings. But caution is the key word when selecting the color for sheer curtaining. Since some hues do not reflect light as pleasantly as others, plan to make a "daylight test" with fabric samples at least a foot square, even larger if possible. White, ivory, cream, pale yellow are neutrals considered to be first color choices because they filter the light in a natural way. The pastels, pink, blue, green, mauve, should be considered very carefully, since these colors tend to give an unnatural look to everyday objects. On the other hand, looking at objects through rose-colored curtains may be just what you need to start the day happily. The point is to be sure you've chosen the tints you and your family will most enjoy. Casement cloth offers another good-looking way to deal with unsights. It is semisheer, lets the light in, and gives a degree of daytime privacy. Here, the weight is heavier, the texture thick and crunchy, and there are many unusual, open-pattern weaves which look stunning at night or produce delightful daytime shadows when the light is reflected through the fabric. Casement cloth also aids in muffling street noises.

In working out a treatment for a viewless opening, don't overlook the hard-edge group, shades, shutters, louvers, and latticework, any or all of which might be employed to work their individual wonders on your windows, whether large or small. The hard-edge group may be used alone or may be combined with curtains and draperies.

PART THREE

Ideas For Every Area
of the Home

A handsome stairway is the focal point of the above Early American room. The cheery red and gold print upholstery combines well with the pin-striped wallpaper and antiqued pine furniture. Wood beams and parquet flooring underline the frontier flavor of this cosy setting.

The problem of too little space has been completely conquered in this Early American living room. A sofa separates the sitting and dining areas, while storage units make the most of a few feet of wall space around one corner.

A neutral color scheme, studded with a few bright accents, sets the pace for this contemporary living room. The rosewood chair, upholstered in deep purple, contrasts richly with a white table-bench. At the cathedral windows, beige "Colony" shades are hung from the dark wood crossbeams to create privacy.

Subtle contrasts of line and texture distinguish this sophisticated room. A brilliantly patterned area rug provides the single splash of color. The shine of the steel-based table and chrome chandelier accents the muted olive velvet sofa and shapely pedestal chairs.

A flowered area rug on top of carpeting gives the living room below an extra design dimension. The clean, modern lines of the furniture, wood paneling, and the beautiful view from the floor-to-ceiling windows make it a wonderful study of contrasts.

SELIG MANUFACTURING COMPANY

Brilliant green walls and a bright blue rug set the tone of this perpetually sunny room. The gay floral sofa actually opens to sleep two guests comfortably. The spring atmosphere is further accented by potted plants that bloom all-year-round for an indoor garden look.

Turn to the East for a dramatic decorating scheme. Oriental furnishings are beautifully contrasted with a classic tweed carpet. The complementary area rug ties the two rooms together, while the hard-surface flooring provides visual interest.

SLEEP-SOFA BY CHESAPEAKE-SIEGEL-LAND, LATEX FOAM RUBBER CUSHIONS

CARPETING OF CRESLAN ACRYLIC FIBER, ALEXANDER SMITH

CHAPTER THIRTEEN

THE FOYER

THE FOYER or entrance hall of the home has a triple function and must be decorated accordingly. On one hand it must say "welcome" to guests and family members and on the other, it must be a semipublic room that serves as a discreet barrier to delivery men and other strangers from the private parts of the house. Third, in the well-coordinated house or apartment, the foyer should establish the decorative theme that will unfold in the remainder of the home. It is a tall order, but not an impossible one. Let us go through all the facets of decor and interpret them in terms of this important area.

First, let's discuss color. Most foyers are small, so a light background color that seemingly expands the area is a help. It can be a lighter shade of one of the three main colors used throughout. For example, if blue, green, and yellow are the colors, a light shade of any of the three would be suitable for walls and ceiling, if you like. Or a wallpaper in a small pattern that incorporates the three colors on a light ground could be effective. If you want drama, remember that a large-scaled pattern in a dark background for wallpaper, if used everywhere, can also seemingly enlarge space. There again, introduce the three colors of the house-wide theme.

Flooring is especially important in this entry room, because it will get the greatest wear. An easily cleaned hard-surface material such as vinyl tile, quarry tile, or marble is ideal. If you want wood, surface it with liquid urethane or spar varnish so that the wood can be damp-mopped without raising the grain of the wood. (*Note:* Never wash down wood floors; manufacturers of flooring spend millions of dollars getting the moisture out of wood.) Better to keep the wood in a light finish, as it will show less dirt. If you use a small Oriental or some other type of area rug, be sure to put a rubber pad under it to prevent skidding. It's a good idea to have a small rug right at the door that will take the worst of the foot soil at the outset; have it of a size that can be cleaned frequently. If you want wall-to-wall carpet, choose a short-pile style that can be vacuumed and shampooed easily. Carpet should state one of the principal colors in your scheme, again preferably in a light, nonwear-showing tone. If you use an Oriental, choose one that has some relationship to your colors. Carpet that continues up the staircase, if any, should be the same color as the wall-to-wall carpet below. If you use stair carpet and another type of flooring, it is often effective to use a strong color for the carpet, a bold shade of one of your three colors.

When it comes to furniture, your problem is not difficult because there is so little space that not much is required. If space permits, a narrow console table, with a drawer if possible for gloves, pencil and paper, and last-minute needs, is useful. A mirror above, flanked with electric sconces, is helpful for grooming before going out. If space permits, two small-scaled side chairs flanking the console are useful for putting on overshoes, etc. Another attractive solution is a bench with mirror above. These few pieces should be in the over-all style of the home—traditional or contemporary. If space is sizable, it is important to make the foyer serve double-duty, as a party dining area, home office with desk and telephone, or secondary sitting area, to name a few possible functions.

Fabric on a hall bench or pair of chairs should relate to over-all color and period style. If you choose fabric for the walls, here are some ideas for the long hallway. This kind of space usually has a head-on view of at least one interior room. Therefore, it should be treated as a vantage point. One of two dramatic approaches could be taken. First, keep the area clean and just employ texture to set it apart. Nubby fabric in a natural tone might be applied to the two walls. The fabric can be treated for soil resistance to make life easier. Vinyl is a good material to use in areas like this and it has great eye appeal. New vinyls on the market have all sorts of textures including some that look amazingly like grained leather. Patent finishes offer another kind of atmosphere. They reflect light and even hazy images. One could achieve a mirrored effect by applying the vinyl patent to the entire wall area. This makes a good background for artwork, particularly if it's framed in metal. A mirror hung against this background immediately would enlarge the area in addition to making a striking accessory. Furthermore, vinyls can take all the wear and tear an entranceway has to sustain. Fingerprints and dirt marks can just be sponged off with soap and water. The entire area can be washed down if it gets spotted. Vinyl is also easy to install.

Most vinyls have some sort of backing. Frequently it's a cotton knit or some soft fabric. With a solid color, there's no problem of lining up the fabric. It's just a matter of getting even seams and applying all-purpose glue to a clean, smooth surface. A cloth can be used to smooth over the vinyl so that a minimum of finger marks results. Long, sweeping strokes will smooth out the air bubbles behind the fabric. Edges can be finished off with fine strips of paneling or with decorative tape. Here's where fabric remnants can come in handy. Strips of one pattern could be cut and applied as trim around the ceiling and floorboard.

ENTRANCE WITH STAIRWAY

This is a traditional type of entranceway in a two-story home. The stairway is in full view as the front door opens—good opportunity to be courageous with fabric. Since the stairway usually leads to a landing and then bedrooms, one fabric can lead the eye a long way. Variations of the same fabric might reappear upstairs. If the stairway is in an older home, it might tend to be narrow and dark. This is an immediate clue that the fabric should be light in color and uncomplicated in pattern. Widely spaced flowers would work well. When dealing with fabric for the walls, it is wise to choose random patterns that don't require too much lining up. Stripes, for instance, could be deadly. Particularly if your walls are not quite straight.

If the view from the door leads directly upstairs to a solid wall or window, make the most of the view. Think of it as a stage setting. In the case of a solid wall, use a large piece of dramatic fabric and upholster the wall with it. Or make a brilliant fabric hanging as previously described. Where there is a window, treat it and the wall as one unit. Drape the window in the same fabric as the wall and laminate the shade with more of the fabric. If the wall is just too large to upholster, paint it in one of the colors appearing in the fabric you've chosen to cover the window.

LIGHT IN THE FOYER

Since the foyer is sparsely furnished, its lighting should be inviting and hospitable, and if the living room is clearly visible from the hall-way, the lighting should blend with the decor of that area.

Usually one ceiling fixture and a pair of wall brackets, flanking a mirror or painting are sufficient to light the entrance hall. Occasion-ally the wall brackets may be replaced by a table lamp. If the house is modern and the hall is small, luminous ceiling panels may be used. The same type of panels are also effective in narrow hallways.

The hall is an ideal place to install a dimmer switch so you can adjust the intensity of your light as you desire it. You can leave a dim light on when you are away for the evening, turning it up to a warm glow as you greet visitors or hang up wraps. Incidentally, all closets should have separate lights, preferably attached to an automatic switch that operates whenever the closet door is opened.

A wall or ceiling fixture should be installed at the top and bottom of every staircase. In some large new homes you will find lighted glass "bricks" built into the staircase risers providing a subtle glow. They add both a decorative touch and a valuable safety measure. Long hall-ways need a light fixture every ten feet.

What sort of decorative themes do you find in an entrance hall? If it's light and airy, a crystal chandelier lends a complementary grace note. Any fixture dripping crystal gives an elegant and formal feeling. For more informal settings, there are brass lanterns with cut-crystal sides, wrought-iron lanterns, and tole chandeliers.

If there is some feature in the hall you wish to spotlight, a recessed ceiling light with a swivel frame can be focused on a planter, an heirloom like a grandfather clock, or a piece of art. It can also bathe a mural in light.

If your foyer ceiling is too low for a chandelier but you still want something elegant and glittery, you might try a small round fixture designed to fit snugly against the ceiling but aglow with crystal pen-dants. You can dramatize a high ceiling by hanging half a dozen con-temporary pendant lights in a multilevel cluster over a low planting area.

A high ceiling in the entryway of a Pennsylvania home got a com-pletely new look when the architect "lowered" the hallway visually by adding a wood trellislike lighting element. The "trellis," running the length of the hallway, consists of ten 4½-foot wood beams, each housing a 40-watt fluorescent lamp. Some of the light is diffused downward and some is allowed upward. The lighting is dimmer con-trolled, and cool fluorescent lamps are used instead of the usual de luxe warm white, to provide a transitional area from outdoors to the warmth of the living room. Since the hallway has only an airy divider to separate it from the living room, this lighting effect actually seems to lead the visitor to the intimacy of the living area.

Finally, it should be noted that home builders have discovered that the lighting of the entrance is important not only in establishing a mood but in the eventual sale of the house. Along with the kitchen and bathroom, it is the area where prospective buyers demand attractive lighting.

Hall Accessories

We have already touched on wall brackets and chandeliers which are perhaps the most important accessories in the foyer. These must blend with period style. For example, if you've always craved a crystal chandelier in the hall and your house-wide theme is French country, by all means have one, but have it in black iron with crystals. The same for wall sconces. The role of the mirror in the foyer has been touched on. Since space is narrow in this room, a wall of mirrors, either in traditional or contemporary decor, is a marvelous choice; it seemingly will double space. If you use a framed mirror, you have another opportunity to underscore period style. Flower bowls, ashtrays, small lamps—whatever you may use on a console table should conform to period style and color theme. Fresh flowers themselves make a marvelously inviting note in the entrance hall and they, too, can be chosen with an eye to color co-ordination. The same for a collection of framed prints on a stair wall or over a bench. Unless a hall is wide, it isn't advisable to use a large painting or print or a massive frame; it will overpower the area and inhibit the viewer at the outset.

CHAPTER FOURTEEN

THE LIVING ROOM

DESPITE THE FACT that today's formal living room is less used and enjoyed by most families than the family room, it remains the most important room from the standpoint of decorating effort. It is a status symbol, in the best sense of the term; it is the location of the best furniture and accessories; it is where the most money is spent. For these reasons, let's hereby make a plea for greater use of the living room. There is no reason why, even though it contains the best in the house, it should not be enjoyed by family members on a regular basis. By its very name, the room implies that it should be lived in. One way to take the no-no, hush-hush quality out of the living room is to personalize it, to warm it up with favorite objects—collections, paintings, and other accessories—with textured fabrics and comfortable-looking upholstered furniture.

FURNITURE ARRANGEMENT

In the living room, furniture arrangement is more important and also more difficult than in other rooms. The first step in arranging furniture is to set a focal point. In the bedroom, this is easy: The bed or beds are the focal point and usually there are only one or two walls that will accommodate the bed. In the dining room, the table is the focal point and it usually goes in the center of the room under a lighting fixture. In the living room, you must find a focus of interest around which to group your major seating group. If you're lucky, there will be a fireplace and that should be your first choice of location (Plan A). Failing that, there may be a window with some size and some drama, perhaps overlooking a view (Plan B). If the win-

dows are all small, oddly placed and difficult to build around, then
you must create a focal point yourself. A dominant piece of furniture
makes a good one: in the traditional room, a handsome antique cabinet
or a breakfront, a magnificent credenza with a large painting above it.
In the contemporary setting, one of the new modular wall groupings

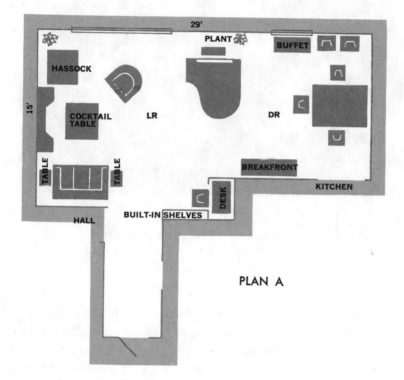

PLAN A

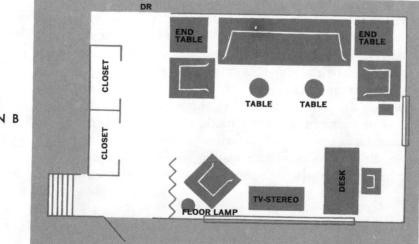

PLAN B

AMERICAN OF MARTINSVILLE

The fireplace is the focal point of this handsome living room. The straight, clean lines of the furniture and the zebra rug provide a good contrast with the stone chimney and beamed ceiling.

would be excellent, or a long, low wall-hung shelf with interesting objects of sizable scale arranged atop it, or perhaps a brilliant wall hanging with a low table below it.

Whatever type of object you choose for your focal point, it becomes the anchor for your sofa and chairs. The theory is that the attractive object of focus will draw people to that area and then an invitingly arranged grouping of seating pieces will do the rest. You can flank the fireplace, credenza, or breakfront with two long sofas or with love seats (Plan C) or one long sofa and a pair of lounge chairs (Plan D). The proportions of the room will dictate this. Here of all places in the house, it is important to draw a floor plan to scale on graph paper and make cutouts of furniture to scale. Move them around on the plan until you have the best solution. Remember, there is a lot of traffic in the living room, so you must keep lines of communication open for such activities as serving drinks, movement of guests. Be sure to keep your seating pieces close enough together so that people do not have to shout to converse, but far enough apart

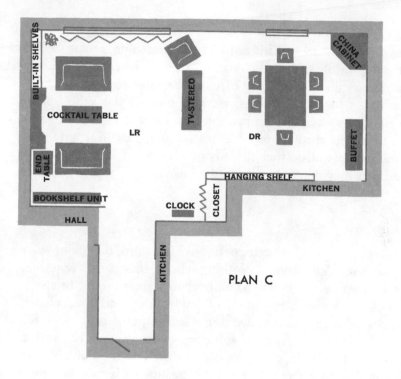

PLAN C

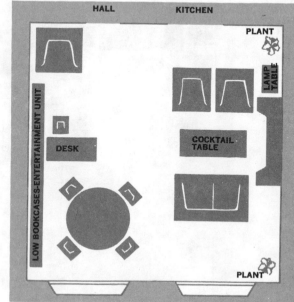

PLAN D

that knees *don't* touch. And instead of the monstrous, square coffee table that is impossible to circumnavigate, consider several small, portable tables. You must have plenty of tables or table space for the inevitable ashtrays, drinking glasses, purses, and all the other paraphernalia that guests require. Lamps must be carefully placed in this arrangement: Keep them if possible on lamp tables near sofa and chairs, close to the wall so that there is no danger of knocking them over and so that they don't obscure the line of vision of seated guests.

Other Furniture

In some very successful contemporary living rooms, the major seating group *is* the entire room. Nothing else seems to be required. However, in most rooms, you need more than seating pieces. In a separate area of the room, a grouping of game table and four chairs, located at a window, is attractive and useful as a permanent place for cards or snacks (Plan E). Another solution is a handsome desk with a small sofa or pair of light chairs nearby (Plan F). If your room is spacious, you'll want a secondary seating group—perhaps a love seat and two light chairs near an important window at the end of the

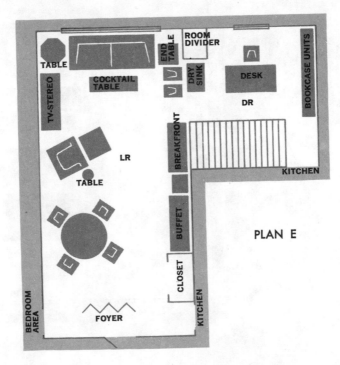

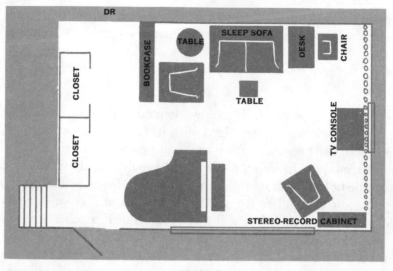

PLAN F

room opposite the main seating group. This is necessary for parties, but especially pleasant for two or three people to converse or take a cup of coffee or tea in the afternoon, when they might feel dwarfed if they sat in the big seating area. The secondary group should be intimate and, of course, comfortable (Plan G). And here and now, let us emphasize the importance of investing in well-made, enormously inviting and relaxing sofas and chairs in this room. Don't stint on this; it is the crux of the well-decorated living room.

If you want to include television and hi-fi equipment in this room (Plan H), by all means do so, but camouflage it. Make both a part of a wall system which permits you to close a door and mask the "evil eye" when it is not in use. Nothing kills a party more quickly and thoroughly than having television blasting away in the living room. In the traditional room, one workable solution for TV is a round table, with a floor-length skirt which can be lifted for viewing programs; a wall-mounted tube with a hinged painting or a hanging to cover it is also good. There are many ways to incorporate TV without letting it dominate or spoil your decoration plan.

Whatever furniture you choose, keep it in period style. If you choose to follow a particular period (for example, Early American or French Provincial), be sure of your background—furniture, fabrics, rugs, accessories. If it is contemporary, keep it clean and airy, with blocks of color and streamlined pieces. If you want a transitional mix, don't let it get cluttered; this is a room for serenity, where family and guests should always feel at ease. Remember, of all the rooms in the house or apartment, this is the one where you make a statement.

THE COLOR SCHEME

This room must be carefully color-schemed and color-co-ordinated with other rooms which may open onto it. Chances are a foyer and a dining room can be viewed from the living room. If so, there must be a color harmony. The living room must have drama, above all, so that you can be bolder with your colors than in the foyer or dining room, but you must manipulate the same three colors and color accents in all contiguous spaces. Color will help with drama in other ways. For example, if the living room has little natural light and is used mostly at night, perhaps dark walls are the answer. If it is a light, airy room with windows overlooking a small garden or a patio, capitalize on this attribute and consider light-toned backgrounds. If the room is badly proportioned or with awkward architectural features, use some of the color tricks suggested in a previous chapter. Along with color, balance your pattern. If you use a highly patterned chintz for sofa and chairs, avoid a figured wallpaper and a boldly pattered carpet or rug. Remember, too, the pattern that furniture and objects create: Keep the furniture around the room in some kind of a height rela-

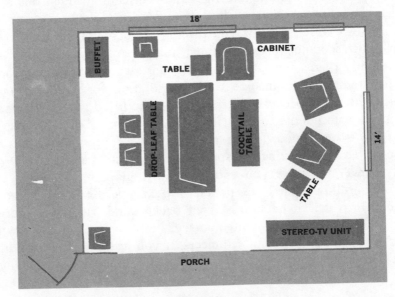

PLAN G

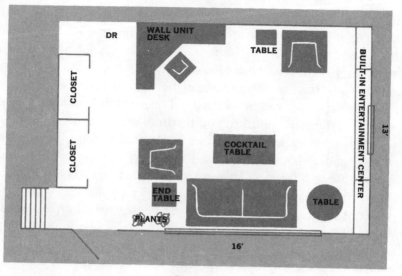

PLAN H

tionship; nothing is more jarring than a tall wing chair next to a low-slung sofa. Paintings and other wall decoration must be kept in an even height around the room or your eye will be jumping all over the place—which doesn't exactly make for serenity.

FABRICS FOR THE LIVING ROOM

The wear and tear on this area is usually intense. Not only does it sustain much traffic from just entering and exiting, but it is the main reception area for the entire house or apartment. Bearing this practical point in mind, it is necessary to "dress" the living room at least twice per year. Slipcovers are indispensable for this purpose. Just as one changes clothes in relationship to the season, so must this room be changed in order to freshen it up and preserve the fabrics in it. Also, from an aesthetic point of view, a change is welcome, particularly after a long, cold winter. Even in areas where the climate doesn't change too radically during the year, it is a good idea to have a change of fabrics in the living room. Slipcovers can be fitted and constructed so masterfully that they look like upholstery. Some women can achieve this on their own sewing machines; however, if there is any doubt, it is best to find a craftsman to do this work. The investment in fabric is worthy of the extra investment in getting covers that will fit well and last for several years. Consider that this fabric will be appearing in your home for at least three months each year, so it should be as presentable as the upholstery itself. A fabric change also allows for two different personalities during the year. If the living room has a formal ambience, it can be informalized come summer. That's the time rugs can be virtually eliminated, if you have area carpeting. Floors can get polished and textured mats used in areas. Homespun textures work beautifully in a summerized room. For instance, sisal rugs and slubbed fabrics used together. Colors can be splashed about with gay abandon. Take a tropical floral cotton and slipcover an armchair. Use the same floral on the other chair.

When it comes to the sofa, the fabric chosen has to go a long way. In other words, most standard sofas are about six feet long, and that's a lot of fabric. It might be a good idea to choose a textured fabric for the slipcover—one that is durable and treated, of course, to be stain resistant. All covers should, in fact, be treated against stains. Your Yellow Pages will inform you about cleaning establishments that offer the various types of treatments.

As for the most durable types of slipcover fabrics, here are a few suggestions. Tightly woven cloths are usually the most hearty. Glazed cotton or chintz is a good bet; its polished surface tends to wear quite well. Heavy cotton, plain or slubbed, is another strong fabric. Many cottons these days are blended with polyester or other synthetic fibers to render them washable and fast drying. If this is the claim, be sure to determine exactly what the washing and drying procedures are. Shrinkage should not occur with good fabric unless it is treated improperly.

Linen is also a good slipcover fabric, despite reports to the contrary. It must be tightly woven and of firm construction. If the linen is very heavily slubbed, it will not wear as evenly. Thick slubs that sit on top of the surface tend to pull away after heavy use. So if textured linen is your choice (and it makes up beautifully), just be sure to purchase a very good variety. Wool, by itself or blended with another fiber, can also make a good cover, depending on whether you like the sensation of wool. New developments in synthetics have produced a variety of leatherlike fabrics which not only wear beautifully but look terrific. Many of these are sold off the bolt just as regular fabrics. They can be purchased in yard goods stores or through decorators.

Plain slipcovers can be dressed up with contrasting piping on the pillows and skirt. This is a very attractive way to dramatize a good-looking, plain fabric. The contrasting trim can pick up a color in the corresponding patterns. Then, for the finishing touch, add an array of throw pillows (they're decorative and fun to toss about when curling up on the sofa). Cover them in the remnants left over from sofa and chairs.

You don't need another set of draperies in the summer. Try decorative shades instead. Fabric laminated shades are very good-looking and can finish off a room beautifully. Repeat one of the patterns on the window or add a plain, textured shade trimmed in the bright piping of the sofa. Lots of plants and fresh flowers will add the brighteners to your summerized living room. A room deserves air and light the same as its inhabitants. And it should complement the people in it with attractive color and ample amounts of light areas.

LIVING-ROOM FLOORING

For the traditional scheme, you can choose from wood floors with one or more area rugs or wall-to-wall carpet with, perhaps, an Oriental or two placed over it for accent. For the contemporary room, there is hard-surface flooring—vinyl tile in solid color or in a geometric pattern—or wall-to-wall textured carpet or a wood floor either bleached light or stained very dark. For the transitional room, a choice from either of the two other styles would be correct, depending on the other elements in the plan. Whatever type you choose, remember that this is another area of hard usage, so keep to colors that don't show wear and to textures and fibers that hold up under traffic. Since space is apt to be sizable in this room, area rugs can be useful in delineating various areas—conversation, games, fireside.

LIGHTING

The living room is likely to provide more lighting problems than any other room in the house for two simple reasons. It usually is the largest space to be lighted, and as the focal point of the house it sets the mood for other areas.

Here are a few questions you might ask yourself as you consider decorating your living room with light. Is this an all-purpose room or is there a separate family room or den? How much entertaining do you do? How many groupings of furniture do you have? Will certain areas involve conversation, reading, or playing the piano? Is a dining area included? What decorating styles blend best with the architecture of your home—Early American, contemporary, period? What decorative accessories do you wish to accent? Remember that to avoid the bland, unimaginative look of many living rooms you will need to highlight interesting textures, areas, or objects. Lighting is one of the tools you can use to stamp your individuality on your home.

Let's consider lighting rooms of three different sizes.

The small room needs to avoid clutter. That means eliminating as many small lamps as possible. A flexible, pull-down fixture can do double duty in a corner which may be devoted to conversation or reading or occasional sewing. A valance will dramatize a window, at the same time providing some general illumination. A collection of plants in a window can be accented with two or three swivel spotlights set in the ceiling, or a wall of bookshelves can be lighted with strip lights under the shelves, or incandescent spots to bring out the color of the book jackets, or a cornice between the ceiling and the top shelf.

When a room has several built-in units, as is apt to be the case in a small living room, the elimination of portable lamps is particularly desirable. However, if you do use lamps, perhaps on either side of a sofa, be sure they are scaled to the size of the room, and that their height from the floor to the center of the shade is the same throughout the room. This helps to create a unified effect. Dimmer switches are recommended for living rooms of any size.

The average room offers you a little more flexibility, since you will probably be dealing with 125 to 225 square feet of space—for example, a room 12 feet by 18 feet. A combination of fixtures and wall lighting is desirable here, and if you're using a valance, cornice, or wall bracket it should be at least 12 feet long.

One of the effective ways to light paintings, bookshelves, a collection of porcelain, or a stereo corner is to mount an electrified track on the ceiling about two feet from the wall you wish to illuminate. Since the track carries power along its full length, just clip on shielded spotlights evenly spaced at intervals (every three feet perhaps) and focus them on your treasures. If the spots are dimmer controlled, they will lend a greater enchantment.

Perhaps you feel that chandeliers belong only in the largest, most formal, or most elegant rooms. This is no longer true. An airy, graceful chandelier can be used in a low-ceilinged room. Two precautions must be taken—it must be placed so that no one will inadvertently hit his head, and if it is used over a cocktail table, the bulbs, even though small and flame-shaped, should not shine in the eyes of anyone. If possible, put it on a dimmer switch to give the soft glow of candlelight where desired. If you're using portable lamps to supplement your lighting, aim for balance in their positioning, and be sure they are in proportion to the tables they rest on. Many decorators prefer that all shades in a room be white and that the same material (linen, silk, parchment) be used for each shade. If there is a great deal of reflected light in the room, a dark shade lends contrast.

The large room, measuring over 225 square feet in area (that is, a room 12 feet by 20 feet), should definitely have built-in lighting. This should include at least 20 feet in cornices, valances, or wall brackets, plus whatever spotlights are needed. In a large room you will need to achieve some feeling of intimacy by grouping furniture and defining each area with light, either from table lamps or shafts of light directed downward from the ceiling. A large room also gives you the opportunity to do interesting things with wall washing from recessed fixtures. On a twenty-four-foot-long wall you could use eight fixtures three feet apart. Wall washing helps to give depth, warmth, and character to a room. Ceiling recessed downlights add still another dimension.

Frequently you can live with a room for a long time before realizing how poorly it is lighted. This happened to a New York family whose large living room was lighted by a blazing torchlike fixture on the fireplace wall at the far end of the room, and two table lamps, one beside a wing chair and the other beside a sofa. A handsome portrait of their daughter over the mantel was unlighted. In fact, the glaring fixture on the same wall actually prevented a clear view of the portrait.

The solution? Removal of the disfiguring wall fixture and installation of a dimmer-controlled valance to dramatize the attractive bay window. A ceiling track with three spotlights attached was installed near the fireplace wall. One spot was focused on the girl's portrait, another on built-in bookshelves, and the third on the wing chair near the fireplace, thus eliminating an awkward little table and its lamp. A pair of big matching table lamps was placed on either side of the sofa. As the owners themselves readily admitted, the results were spectacularly successful.

CHAPTER FIFTEEN

THE DINING ROOM

CURRENT SURVEYS tell us that every woman would like to have a separate dining room. What she usually looks for in a new house is the inclusion of a separate dining room as part of the floor plan, although in the decorating of her home she will try to include some facilities for informal dining in other rooms. But not all are this fortunate, especially those who live in modest city apartments. Although the original concept of the open dining area was in the interest of spaciousness, new apartments, on the other hand, of necessity make use of a dining alcove or ell or utilize part of the living area for dining. But even here we find a difference between the current dining area and that of twenty years ago. For while the two areas usually relate via color scheme and general mood, today more of an effort is being made to give each area its own distinct and individual look. All kinds of architectural and decorative devices are often employed to create this feeling of separation and intimacy. A change in floor treatment, for example, can provide a change of pace. The dining area off a carpeted living room can be left with a bare, stained, and waxed wood floor, or embellished with a striking vinyl or ceramic tile covering, or punctuated with a dynamic accent rug. A fascinating wallpaper used only on dining area walls will distinguish it from a living room with a plain or painted background. Or a dropped ceiling can be used to give the area a greater sense of identity, while dividers and screens can help mark off the separation of dining and living. Many professional designers will construct a partial kind of divider—a fretwork enclosure, draperies, or even a beaded curtain can make a great difference. Whether you live either in an apartment or in a house, your approach to the decoration of your dining room will be governed by the architectural floor plan, by its dimensions, size, shape,

Streamlined dining furniture available today can offer the great advantage of spectacular storage space as in handsome rosewood and cane designs in room shown here. Glass-topped table has interesting brass and rosewood base. Suedelike chairs are of a practical, easy-to-clean fabric.

and placement of windows, wall space, ceiling height, etc. Our purpose is to help you make the most of available space and plan a dining room tailored to your personal dining and entertainment needs.

Today there are many choices for you to consider when you decorate your dining room. For while the stereotyped and conventional dining room—table, six chairs, china cabinet and buffet, all matching —still exists in rooms of traditional purity, there is a new laissez-faire style to dining-room decor, and it is one that favors complete flexibility. A glass-topped metal table may be teamed with rosewood chairs and a painted Welsh cabinet. Sleek Parsons tables or bracketed shelves often replace the standard server; dining chair seats can boast a variety of covers—not only fabrics, but vinyls and furs. Sometimes each chair is in a different painted finish or in its own cover color. Conventional dining chairs can be replaced by stools, benches, director's chairs, or settles. Contemporary pieces are mixed freely with traditional designs. Wood finishes run the gamut from unpainted Mexican chairs to highly polished deep-toned mahogany. Tables are not only put in the center of the room; sometimes they sit under a window or jut out from a wall or back a sofa. They can be square, oval, rectangular, hexagonal, octagonal, or round. Or they can be a composite of several small tables. They can have skirted covers that match the wallpaper and/or draperies. There can be two or more separate dining table arrangements in a single room instead of the one large, formal table. In other words, dining is what you make it today. Charm and ingenuity can take the place of a bottomless purse. Invention and imagination can go a long way to create a dining room as personal as your fingerprint. A room can reflect the personality of the hostess and the menu of the moment.

PLANNING YOUR DINING ROOM

As we said a little earlier, dining-room decoration can and should be fun, but this will hardly be the case if you don't know how to start or where you're going. In the first place, certain general decisions have to be made before any specific choices such as style, color, background, etc. are exercised. Is the room to be formal or informal? Is the architecture imposing—does the room have carved paneling and tall, graceful windows or is it small and unsymmetrical in shape? Will your dining room be used only at dinnertime or for entertaining guests or will it be an area the family will enjoy at least three times a day? Do you serve sit-down dinners for twelve or do you prefer informal buffet suppers for a crowd? Is the living room an elegant parlor or a comfortable and relaxed interior? The answer to these questions and your own special feelings should determine the degree of informality or formality desired. No matter how small the room or informal the home is, one should try to strive for a gracious and charming atmosphere. For dining, at best, is a special event and should be treated as such. This can be accomplished in an almost unlimited number of ways and in any style you choose. As long as the over-all plan is suited to your particular room and is composed of a harmonious blending of elements and a balanced arrangement of furniture, the results are bound to be pleasing and hospitable.

The style of the dining area or dining room should complement the style of the adjacent living areas rather than conflict with them. If you're sitting in one room with a strongly established style, you'll find it quite jarring to walk into another nearby room furnished in a totally different style and look. It would be a rather strange feeling, for example, to go from a Jacobean living room into a severe, architecturally modern dining room, ablaze with vivid abstract canvases. Let your dining room follow the style, generally speaking, of the rest of your home, or choose a style for your dining room and carry it through your living areas.

THE FLOOR PLAN

Once upon a time dining-room arrangement followed a set formula: a dining-room table centered in the room, two armchairs at either end and two side chairs on either side, and a buffet and china cabinet and server (if wall space permitted). All the furniture was in the same style and in the same finish—the goal was symmetry and balance. This is the traditional solution and still a good one for the purist who prefers a consistency in design and loves a room that echoes the elegance and dignity of the past. There are others, however, who are searching for a more exciting and personal solution and who, perhaps, would like the room to serve the family in other ways than solely as a dining room. Also, many of us have rooms that lack the floor and wall space necessary to plan the traditional-style dining room. Sometimes a particular architectural facet will direct the furniture plan. A great view, for example, might suggest the placement of the table in front of the window. The shape of a long and narrow room might be modified by the choice of two separate round dining tables rather than one long one. Remember to allow for traffic patterns in your dining room. In doing so, it might make more sense to place the table at right angles to the wall. Or, if the dining room serves also as an informal sitting area, you would want to establish a dining arrangement in one part of the room and furnish the other area with comfortable upholstered pieces. To give balance to a room, large storage or serving pieces should be opposite a fireplace or window wall, rather than adjacent, if possible. This will prevent all the weight from being distributed on one side of the room. If there is little floor space for deep storage pieces in a small dining room, two corner cabinets and a shallow shelf or Parsons table would solve the problem. These might also be solutions for a room chopped up by many windows and openings. Chairs do not necessarily have to stay in position at the table.

Some can flank a storage piece or even be used around a game table in an adjoining room. It's wise, if you have a space problem, to select a pedestal style dining table that offers more knee room than a legged table of the same size.

After the floor plan has been completed, try to visualize the room in three dimensions. Evaluate each wall as you have laid it out in the plan and then give consideration to the relationship of one area to another. Is the total effect a cohesive and balanced one? Have you put too much furniture on one side of the room, leaving the other almost bare? Is the table too big for the space or too small? On entering the room, are you presented with an aesthetically pleasing and interesting composition? If a piece of furniture is to fit under a window, does it have adequate space and will it look well against the window treatment? An eyesore such as a pipe or an architectural mistake can be concealed by a screen and this, too, must be worked into the plan.

THE COLOR SCHEME

Certain basic factors must be considered in the working out of your dining-room color plan: the colors of the adjacent living room, the kind of wood finishes to be used, the size of the room, the amount of natural light, the degree of formality desired, and the over-all style of the room. Major living areas should relate in color, even if the link is only a subtle one. The primary tone played out in the dining room might appear as a minor accent in the living room. A color applied in a subdued value in the living room could come through much bolder and brighter in the dining area. In any case, avoid the shock that comes from walking from one color scheme into a room of a totally unrelated color family. This does not mean that the two rooms have to be rigidly color co-ordinated, but there shouldn't be a garish clash or unpleasant contrast between them, even when each scheme is a restrained one. One would hardly like to leave a green, white, and cyclamen living room for a blue and tiger-lily dining room, or enter a yellow, orange, and taupe living area after dining with red, white, and blue. The transition should be natural and easy—related colors in both rooms will accomplish this.

One should have already decided upon the wood finishes and/or colors to be used before settling on a color scheme. For quite obviously, cherry finishes would discourage the establishment of a predominantly red plan, while bleached oak would hardly be interesting against a beige and tan background. If you want to use at least one painted piece of furniture, keep this in mind when planning colors. Be sure to choose a color that will work out well in a painted finish or is easy to find in many of the commercial furniture designs.

Establish a Background

The dining room is unique, compared to other rooms of the house, in that it is frequently composed entirely of wood furniture—table, chairs, cabinets, servers, etc. And unlike other rooms there is no change of pace provided by upholstered pieces, as in living rooms and family rooms, or the large expanse of bed as in the bedroom. For this reason, dining-room background design must offer relief from the monotony of wood tones and serve to heighten their grain and luster. This can be done with pattern, texture, and color.

Where wallpaper is seldom used in the living room, it comes into its own in dining-room decoration. Providing generous expanses of pattern, wallpaper serves as a marvelous foil for wood pieces and is a quick and easy way to invest a dining room with personality and interest. And wallpaper covers a multitude of sins—unsightly and awkward jogs and protrusions are visually integrated by the allover sweep of pattern. An asymmetrical room is made to appear more balanced. Odd windows, if draped in a matching print, are camouflaged and made a pleasing part of the background scene. The choice of wallpaper for dining-room decor is endless—much depends upon the size of the room and its style. An elegant, grand-scale scenic paper would suit a large traditional room, while a houndstooth check would be a charming choice for a small, French country setting. Wallpaper comes in the most authentic period designs as well as in severely modern geometric and linear motifs, and many of the most handsome patterns around, especially florals, are whimsical contemporary interpretations of the traditional bouquet—often in outsized scale and in colors that irreverently disregard nature. Wallpaper can also provide a room with textural interest; so many papers successfully emulate or are surfaced with such textures as burlap, ticking, grass cloth, or raw silk. There are many architectural papers to choose from. These achieve the look and presence of molding, arches, carving, lattice-

work, columns, and add classic style to an architecturally characterless room. Wallpaper can be applied to all four walls, to a single
wall to focus interest, above a chair rail, or as panels framed by molding. Striped paper can cover the wall and then be mitered on the
ceiling to effect a tent. Papers can be used to upholster valances or
even to frame a window. The front of an old chest can be dressed up
with wallpaper; paper can be used to line the shelves of a storage piece
and the inside of its drawers or cover the entire open storage area in a
breakfront.

Achieving a similar but somewhat richer look is the application of
fabric, either plain, textured, or patterned, to dining-room walls. Fabric can be applied in the same manner as wallpaper or be put up with

*A mirrored wall can do wonders to any dining area—it doubles space and
adds light and sparkle. Formal setting is furnished with Empire and English
Regency designs. Walls continue the aqua, sand, and white damask fabric used
for the draperies. Floor has thick white carpeting.*

INTERIOR BY AUSBY E. LEE, F.N.S.I.D.

tacking strips and changed seasonally. Again, a single wall or an entire room can be fabric covered, and this decorating approach also applies to the addition of paneling and mirror to the dining room. Wood paneling can be very effective in a dining room where wood furniture is kept to a minimum—a room furnished perhaps with lacquered finishes or metal, glass, and molded plastic. Carved paneling creates a gracious formal look, although it is extremely expensive and therefore limited in use. Mirrors, also costly, can go a long way toward expanding the size and stature of a room—they also contribute a special elegance of their own and increase natural and artificial lighting.

For the inventive homemaker there are many superb forms of applied decoration on the market today. These include wood molding, decorative tapes and trimmings, anaglypta and free-standing fiber glass columns and arches. In planning wall treatment, however, one must first decide what kind of wall accessories, if any, are to be used. If the dining room is to display your collection of modern art, some rare Wedgwood plates, or an eclectic assortment of wall hangings, you would obviously paint your walls or choose a complementary wallpaper rather than use a conflicting pattern or texture, or one that takes the play away from your collection. Because of the dining room's special use, it is a wise consideration to treat wallpaper, wall covering, as well as fabric chair covers to a stain-repellent finish.

There are many other ways to achieve wall interest in addition to the treatments already described. A lot depends upon your own imagination and the amount of money you want to spend. For a country dining room, for example, you might strip away the plaster to reveal the natural brick behind it. Or you could invest in ceramic tile or an unusually patterned vinyl tile. If you are lucky enough to have a real fireplace in your dining room, make the most of it with the proper fire tools, a fire screen, some interesting andirons, plus a handsome painting over the mantelpiece and an intriguing collection of porcelains, candlesticks, or assorted bibelots on the top of the mantel. You can always invest in a false fireplace and get almost the same effect—a great idea for traditional dining rooms. Franklin stoves, porcelain stoves, and even pot-bellied stoves can add character to wall decoration, and if you can find an outlet for the flue, you can even put the stoves into use.

Before leaving the subject, may we hasten to add an important point: Do not choose your wall treatment independent of floor or rug

Existing space is turned to great advantage in a small dining area by the addition of open shelves and by framing the adjacent windows with fold-back screens. Small skirted table, covered with bold floral print, is accompanied by white bentwood chairs. See-through shades filter light.

selection. Make sure these two large areas of textures and/or pattern work well together. Think in terms of the entire room whenever you make a choice for a specific area.

WINDOW TREATMENTS

A glamorous window treatment can bring a dining room to life, a clever window design can disguise the banality of sterile architecture. As a matter of fact, the window treatment itself can more strongly establish the style and mood of the room than any other element. For these reasons, window decoration should be carefully planned and executed. Don't forget also that the window treatment must provide both light control and privacy. If you have no view, windows can conceal the lack of it or they can frame an exceptional view to its best advantage. Flexibility of light control is important too—you will want to let in daylight for breakfast, lunch, or tea, yet be able to cover the windows at night. The treatment should also camouflage any architectural liabilities such as undersized or awkwardly placed windows. Sometimes a whole wall can be treated as a window unit to disguise the poor window arrangement. The return on the drapery rod can be adjusted to allow the drapery to fall over and conceal radiator covers or air conditioners. The style of window that exists in your dining room will, of course, determine the choice of window treatment to a large extent; not every treatment is applicable to every shape or kind of window. There are all kinds of devices or combinations of devices one can use to reshape the window, to make it more dominant in the room.

FLOORING

As in the past, you're not necessarily stuck with the floor that comes with your dining room. If you have a wood floor, you can alter its appearance enormously by staining, bleaching, painting, or stenciling. Or you can add any number of completely new floors and change the surface completely. If you are fortunate enough to be building your own home and are in the planning stages, you can decide upon random-plank flooring, parquet, flagstone, terrazzo, travertine, marble, ceramic tile, brick, slate, or mosaic tile. Or you can put down a solid-color flooring or a gaily patterned one in the form of an easy-to-maintain, durable vinyl tile. And don't overlook the vast array of plastics that emulate the natural wood and stone materials described above. Often these vinyls so closely simulate the natural material that they can be distinguished from them only by touch.

Whether you leave your floor bare or punctuate it with a solid textured or delightfully patterned area rug will be determined by the style of the room as well as budget considerations. Today there are so many different kinds of area or accent rugs from which to choose in every style, price, and size. Your choice of rug also offers you a chance to introduce an exciting eclectic note into an otherwise conventional room. One example of this would be putting down an Oriental rug in a sleek modern setting. Another would be to blend a contemporary carpet texture with formal French furniture. While many prefer wall-to-wall carpet in the dining room, from the standpoint of even wear and cleanability, the area or accent rug idea is a more practical one. From an aesthetic standpoint, too, the area rug used on an attractive smooth flooring offers more interest than a blanket of carpeting. In considering cost, unless the rug is a quality product, it is not going to last or look very well for a healthy period of time. A good rug is a good investment.

FURNITURE SELECTION

It goes without saying that a dining table and chairs are prime prerequisites for the dining room. Here you equate your space with the number of people you have to serve. Tables come in every conceivable size and shape—in each of the different style categories. There are extension tables, pedestal tables, drop-leaf and harvest designs, trestle, butterfly, hunt, round, hexagonal, rectangular, square, and oval styles. There are also consoles and cabinets that open to become or to reveal various sized dining tables. For the inventive who are on a strict budget, a circle of plywood on an inexpensive metal pedestal can be covered with a gay cloth—a most effective solution. One delightful modern table, sometimes used for dining, is the glass slab supported by two steel sawhorses. Grandma's old claw-and-ball-footed table can be glamorized by stripping it down, waxing it, and giving it an elegant marble top. The ease of maintenance of plastic tops that emulate wood finishes or specially treated wood finishes, which are alcohol and heat proof, are worth considering if your table is to receive a great deal of use.

PHOTO BY ERNEST SILVA, INTERIOR DESIGNED BY BACHSTEIN & LAWRENCE ASSOCIATES

French Country dining room is executed in a serene blend of melon and blue. Chairs, painted a distressed off-white color, are teamed with fruitwood table while travertine-textured vinyl floor is terra cotta. Suspended cabinet displays dishes and serving pieces.

You may want to use all side chairs, two armchairs at either end or the added glamour and comfort of host and hostess chairs. Bear in mind that the extra cost of host and hostess chairs pays for itself when these chairs are pulled into the living room for extra seating. Two benches or settles can be placed at either side of a rectangular table, as can individual stools. Once again, if the room is to be fully enjoyed by the family, the main consideration of chair selection should be comfort, and if upholstery is involved, a practical cover such as any of the new vinyls that so closely resemble leather and other materials. Just as you would put a very small member of the family in a high chair, you may need a very large chair for an overlarge adult. Upholstered chair seats and chair backs, to make another point, are means of introducing color, texture, and pattern into your room.

A cabinet in the dining room can serve three major purposes: storage space, serving surface area, and display space. If there is enough room and wall space, it's wise to choose both a tall storage piece with a windowed top or an open hutch, plus a long piece that performs as a server. You will discover on your shopping tours that there is an enormous selection of cabinetry designed especially for dining-room use. However, it is often fun and more interesting to choose a piece of furniture that is not a typical or conventional dining-room style such as a handsome armoire or a cluster of library storage and shelf units. Instead of the conventional server, try a long and narrow Parsons table or support a marble shelf on decorative brackets. Such solutions could make the most of an otherwise unusable space underneath a window. The hostess who intends to personally serve sit-down dinners should give special attention to her serving-space needs. She might want to include a teacart in her room arrangements. The budget-minded young married who plans to wait several years before investing in quality cabinetry can buy attractive modular storage units, which come in both traditional and contemporary styles and are offered in a range of bold- and subtle-colored finishes. Eventually these storage pieces can go into a den, family room, or bedroom, when they are replaced by fine storage cabinets.

DINING-ROOM LIGHTING

There is never much question about what activity occurs in the dining room. It centers, of course, on eating, and this immediately raises two concerns. First, the lighting must make the food look appetizing, bringing out its varying colors and textures, and second, the mood of the room must be relaxed.

Have you ever really studied the lighting in restaurants? Possibly not, because in better restaurants the lighting is so subdued you're not conscious of it. Yet it is an important factor in creating the atmosphere the management desires. It can range from the bright, cheerful lighting of the quick lunch places to unobtrusive lights in a restaurant that encourages leisurely and gracious dining. Here the lighting will frequently combine mellow contrasts, subtle downlights, and diffuse illumination from coves, valances, and soffits. Downlighting is particularly effective in catching the sparkle of silver, crystal, and china. Ideally a table should be lighted from several directions for a natural, flattering look to both people and food. Dimmer controls are strongly recommended.

Perhaps you have no clearly defined dining area, but must eat and entertain in a corner or ell of your living room. You might borrow the idea of a New York lighting designer. Although he claims to dislike theatrical effects in residential lighting, you may think the way he lights his dining area—consisting of a big wooden buffet table against a wall of his living room—rather dramatic. Above the table are a series of recessed downlights which, at small dinner parties, are dimmed during the cocktail hour. When dinner is served, the lighting level is turned up to cast a rosy glow on the food, guests, and a brilliant tapestry hanging on the wall behind the table. Later, when the last morsel is gone, the table will again recede into dimness. Living-room lights are adjusted for the guests' mood, and sometimes lazy dancing patterns of color float across the ceiling. One way to achieve this is to conceal a rotating projector with colored plastic discs behind a cove near the ceiling.

If the dining area opens directly from the living room, the lighting in both must be blended and co-ordinated. In any room where the family or guests sit around a table, the light on the table itself is of prime importance. This can be accomplished by downlighting from recessed spotlights or by a fixture hung directly over the table.

While dining-room chandeliers provide some light, they are essentially decorative and should be supplemented by other sources of light—possibly from a valance, a soffit, or a wall bracket. The type of chandelier you select will, of course, depend on your furnishings. Among those appropriate for a dining room are brass fixtures with globular lamps, wrought-iron candelabra, crystal chandeliers, and pewter reproductions. Whatever your mood—Mediterranean, English country, formal French, Early American—you can easily complement it.

If your furnishings are contemporary and your dining area is small, you might prefer a group of pendant lights, adjusted at varying heights, or a pulley fixture that can be lifted or lowered and is mounted on a traverse track to slide across the ceiling. This type of fixture is particularly desirable if the dining table must double as a study or work table.

To achieve dramatic effects in a formal dining room, remember the technique of wall washing (especially if you have a mural or a collection of art) and use recessed spots or concealed strips to highlight a collection of heirloom china or a niche filled with crystal. And don't forget that while many people love the romantic glow created by candlelight (real or electrified), others like to see the food they are eating. You may be able to appease both by bathing the tabletop in soft light from two adjustable shutter pinpoint spots.

Actually there's no limit to the effects you can create. In one home tiny pinpoints of light embedded in the ceiling were controlled to suggest twinkling stars. For an alfresco atmosphere, plants and feathery trees (real or artificial) can be silhouetted against a luminous panel. In one house a luminous wall was made of cutout plywood with shirred white sheer fabric stretched on the back and backlighted by yellow, blue, and pink fluorescent tubes. These combine to give a white light of depth and distance.

ACCESSORIES

Dining-room accessories fall into three categories—wall ornaments, bibelots for windowed cabinets or open shelves, plus any serving pieces on display such as tea or coffee services. These accessories are extremely important and should be chosen with great care and taste as they are attention getters and in many ways the strongest statement of personal knowledge and decorating skill which you make in the dining room or in any room of the home. Sometimes a whole room is built around a treasured accessory or accessories such as one fabulous painting or a collection of exquisite china. The entire color scheme and style of the room could be inspired by the accessory, and

Contemporary dining rooms can be both streamlined and comfortable. Tufted velvet dining chairs offer the ultimate in decorative luxury and comfort and promise to extend the dinner hour far beyond dessert and coffee. Blue silk covers walls, printed velvet makes the draperies and cylindrical cornice. Large serving-storage cabinet is on opposite wall. Parsons dining table has burl graining.

ETHAN ALLEN, INC.

Last-minute dining without the aid of servants is executed with finesse in dining room set up for a buffet dinner. Table, with leaves dropped, is set up in advance, leaving space for individual arrangement of chairs and snack tables. Dry sink also performs as a buffet table. Striking window treatment is composed of shirred curtains stretched within white frames and a pair of tall plaid fabric covered screens.

Set aside an area for dining within the larger living room. Here the separation is given visual definition by the insertion of a contrasting circle of carpet within the deeper colored carpeting that is installed wall-to-wall. Informal rattan dining table and chairs provide an unexpected contrast to the crushed velvet covers of a sofa and chairs. Victorian tapestry creates a backdrop for dining arrangement.

ANSO® NYLON CARPET FIBER BY ALLIED CHEMICAL CORPORATION

Mirror adds luster and elegance; it also fools the eye—a wonderful idea for this moderate-sized dining area. Formal fruitwood table with marquetry top is teamed with Louis XVI chairs in a distressed white painted finish, embellished by plain and patterned velvet upholstery. Rosewood frames filled with white shutters compose an unusual window design. Parquet floor is bleached white.

Some of the distinctive, avant garde furniture designs now available offer a solution to dining with grace in a limited area. Glass-topped table with tubular steel base can take six chairs. Intriguing steel-framed chairs are practical with removable covers that snap off. Oak and glass wall unit has adjustable shelves, serviceable at mealtimes.

CELAN

Black and white plus one bold color—in this case brilliant green—is a foolproof color recipe for a dramatic look in the dining room. Here the color theme is generated by the oversized paisley patterned fabric which covers walls and drapes entryway to small sitting alcove. Sleek, streamlined style of table and chairs is counterpointed by rich wood finish of traditional serving cabinet.

See-through furniture seems to take up less space than the solid-looking conventional designs. Eight-sided Plexiglas table accomplishes this for dining corner of a living room. Decorative bentwood and cane chairs provide a contrast of style and material. White wicker console table under boldly abstract construction functions as an informal serving table or buffet.

MONSANTO TEXTILES COMPANY

The mood and style of a tropical house are captured by this handsome floating two-deck dining and sitting room. Pale paneling and earth tones are relieved by sharp blue and gold accents. Glass-top extension table has two barrel-shaped dining chairs. African artifacts complete the mood.

the placement and choice of furniture would be made with the intention of best displaying an outstanding collection. Here, too, one can create a more sophisticated look by selecting accessories that contrast with the style of the room such as using antiques and period reproductions in a modern setting or amusing glass and Plexiglas cubes and paperweights in a traditional room. One wonderful tip—a change in accessories can give your room a face lift, a completely fresh and new look, without actually changing furniture arrangement or buying any new furniture. So if you want a different effect in your dining room, yet want to or have to keep the furniture you own, invest in some new paintings or a collection of pewter or delft or take out the silver and crystal you may be keeping under wraps and display them.

DINING FOYERS

When no separate dining alcove or area exists, and when the living room is small, the entrance foyer can be utilized as a place for dining. The challenge of decorating such a foyer is to make it look primarily like an impressive entry and to play down its dining-room role, except at mealtimes. This means providing a dining table that takes up little space when not in use. Perhaps the best choice here would be a drop-leaf table or a console that opens up into a table. Both of these would stand unobtrusively against a main wall of the area. They could be made into decorative focal points by the placement of a few accessories such as a handsome bowl filled with flowers, a cluster of candlesticks, a collection of figurines. Above the table you can hang a beautifully framed mirror or make an interesting wall arrangement with a juxtaposition of prints, carvings, and other wall hangings. This would also be a great place to hang a pair of sconces for their decorative value and to shed light upon the dining area. Background design is all important in the planning of the dining foyer. This usually dark and windowless place must be transformed into a bright and lively spot if one wants to dine within a sparkling atmosphere.

Here's the place for a sensational, though expensive, wallpaper. You don't need much of it, so it won't be that large an outlay. A wallpaper whose design is worked out in a bright, bold color against a pale background will tend to enlarge the room because the softer color will stand in a separate dimension behind the bolder one. Wall coverings with a glossy texture that reflect light are ideal for such an

Tented gazebo effect creates the illusion of a formal dining room in an apartment foyer. Embroidered top of skirted table repeats the fabric used on armoire doors. Tent is made from a simple carpentry frame, draped inside and out to conceal the lumber. Shag carpeting is nylon tweed.

area as they add sparkle and depth. Verticals and horizontals can be accentuated or minimized by stripes and geometrics—an effective ploy for low ceilings or small, cramped areas. So too are mirrors— paving one complete wall with mirror adds glitter and visually multiplies the available space. If the table is placed against the mirrored wall, the whole arrangement is provided with a spectacular "view." Another way to give the area a view is to paper the largest wall with a mural that is strongly three-dimensional. One often assumes that a small-scaled paper is the most suitable choice for a small area; however, sometimes for dramatic effect an overscaled design can create a dazzling backdrop as well as a feeling of greater space. We would suggest a highly decorative and easily maintained floor for a dining foyer and would recommend the absence of any rug or soft floor covering. Vinyl, marble, heavily waxed wood floors add a gleaming look and contribute to the feeling of space as well as to the mobility of furniture arrangement when the room is set up for dining.

Dining chairs can be placed at either side of the table, extra chairs may be part of the permanent living-room plan. Another possibility is the use of folding or stacked chairs, which can be easily stored in a closet when not in use.

DINING ALCOVES

When a dining alcove or ell adjoins a living room, it must of course be planned in relationship to the main living area. This includes choice of color scheme, floor covering, wall paint or covering, and style of furniture. The area must be designed as a continuation of the living room yet have a separate identity. If the dining ell has an area rug, the design of the rug can be similar to that of the living-room carpet in feeling and coloration, yet distinct and different. One wall could be papered in a print that repeats the fabric used on two living-room chairs. If predominantly wood furniture is used in the living room (as tables and cabinets), then perhaps a glass or lacquered table should be chosen to give the dining area its own mood and change of pace. The dining ell can be partially divided from the major living area by means of a room divider or screen or by an archway constructed of plywood and painted the color of the walls or covered with fabric. The basic consideration for furniture placement in such an area would be traffic patterns, especially if the area opens to the kitchen as well as to the living room. It therefore makes sense, in such cases, to select a compact, yet expansible, table that can be opened up to extend into the living room for large dinner parties. Try not to crowd the dining area with storage cabinets. When placing a break-front or a china cabinet, the total layout of the entire area (including the living room) should be considered. Perhaps a large storage piece could be included as part of the living area floor plan, leaving the dining alcove free of any cabinetry.

LIVING-DINING ROOMS

Most of us would like to have some separate area of the home marked off for dining, even it if is only a small alcove or foyer. When none exists, the living room must of necessity serve both for dining and living and the design and decoration of the entire room must be planned accordingly. There are several ways to establish a dining area in a living room. The first, and most obvious, way is to mark off part of the living room, usually that area nearest to the kitchen, as the dining section and to furnish this area with dining table, chairs, and dining storage pieces. Often a sofa facing a fireplace at right angles to the wall will be the line of demarcation between dining and living. In the long, narrow living room that builders favor so much for new high-rise apartments, it is often effective to identify the two areas with a free-standing piece of furniture or room divider or a beaded curtain, a screen, floor-to-ceiling panel, or cluster of potted plants. A second way to arrange a living-dining room is to use for the dining table a piece of furniture that functions in other ways outside of mealtime. For example, a large writing table, a standing game table, a skirted table, or even a large cocktail table can all serve for dining, though positioned as an integral part of the living-room decoration. A cluster of four T-square end tables, scattered strategically around the room, can be bunched together for dining. Folding tables can be whipped out of storage for an instant dining area, or you can include decorative stands that hold folding tray tables for individual service. There are also those wonderful Scandinavian tables that are very shallow yet open up to seat a large number of guests. A teacart can also be harnessed for intimate dining for two—the entire meal can be served on and from this handy piece of furniture. And don't overlook a bar as a dining surface in disguise or even the handsome hunt table one would use in a traditional English setting.

CHAPTER SIXTEEN

THE KITCHEN

THE KITCHEN, unlike other rooms, is largely a matter of surface coating to strike the decorative note you prefer. To be sure, there are a few structural considerations and resultant choices you must make and these should be taken up now. For example, if you want an Early American kitchen with a fireplace, the chimney must be part of your architectural plan. Moldings and doors must be specified that blend with the theme. There are six-panel doors for the Colonial look, flush doors for the contemporary, arched-panel units for French Provincial, three-panel for Early American, etc., all stock units to be found at your local lumberyard. The same for cornice moldings and door-frame moldings. Of course, there's no need to be slavish about a theme. If you want sliding patio windows leading from an Early American kitchen to the terrace, have them, but use the kind with snap-in grilles that will add to the small-paned look that is authentic for the period. And the doors can be framed inside and out with the correct moldings.

How to Set the Background

The elements that go to make up the background of the kitchen—which is essentially its decoration—include floor, walls, windows, cabinets, and counters. Here we'll show how flooring materials, paint, wallpaper, and so on can provide you with attractive and practical ways to plan or alter your kitchen's decor. We'll build from the floor up. In this room above all others you want practicality, namely a floor that won't show soil, will be long-wearing, and can be easily damp-mopped clean. You also want a floor that's safe, that's not so slick that you have to watch your step as you go through the intricate footwork that food preparation often entails. You also want a resilient surface, or enough resiliency to avoid weary feet, because you are apt to be on them most of the time you're in this room.

So you have these choices: vinyl, vinyl-asbestos and rubber tile, sheet vinyl, asphalt tile or embossed linoleum; the last two being the least expensive and the least long-wearing. There is wood, provided that it is stained and then given a urethane finish or some plastic finish that makes it more or less impermeable. There is ceramic tile including quarry tile, but if you worry about resiliency you'll want to be sure that it is installed over wood or plywood. The same goes for marble, flagstone, or old brick, all of which are better installed directly over a concrete slab, creating a dense, hard, unyielding surface. The same goes for terrazzo, a most practical material used a lot in Florida, California, and other warm climates because it adds to coolness. All of these masonry floor materials are totally practical, too, so if you want to use one of them, one solution is to place a rubber section or piece of carpet in the most frequently used section, usually the sink and the path from sink to cooktop. Last and newest in the floor-covering roster is carpet which comes in special, easy-care and soil-resistant fibers and finishes which make it practical and comfortable even when installed over a concrete slab. This kind of so-called indoor-outdoor carpet is relatively inexpensive, good-wearing, and comes in attractive colors and patterns.

For a streamlined kitchen, the following are good choices because they blend with the contemporary look: in masonry, terrazzo, marble, and ceramic tile, preferably in light space-stretching tones, and ceramic tile. Sheet vinyl, vinyl-asbestos, and solid vinyl tile come in colors and patterns that are suitable. Patterns should be small or indistinct, like the vinyls which simulate marble or other masonry, and colors in any floor for a contemporary room are better in light space-stretching tones. For the provincial look, the picture changes, for here dark tones and distinct patterns are required. In masonry, quarry tile, either square, hexagonal, or in a modified fleur-de-lis, trefoil or quartrefoil pattern is good. The other-than-square design is especially helpful in setting the French Provincial look. Old brick is marvelous for any provincial effect, laid in stacked bond or herringbone pattern; it is especially suitable for the Early American or country kitchen. Any of the sheet vinyls, vinyl tiles, and embossed inlaid linoleums that simulate brick or ceramic-tile patterns are excellent. The kitchens of old usually had rough pine or oak flooring and these can be

Kitchen décor can be as interesting as any in the home, as proved by a sleek, contemporary room which features bamboo-patterned vinyl wall covering for ceiling and valance for a white, vinyl-impregnated window shade which was given a matching bamboo border in acrylic paint.

simulated today with random oak plank, pegged and stained dark, or random pine treated similarly. To get an authentic look with new pine boards, one designer we know has them installed first and gets a distressed look by having all the workmen tramp over them during construction. Then they are swept clean, stained, finished in urethane, and lightly waxed. The Spanish or Mediterranean look, for example, is essentially a provincial look with some stylistic motifs added, so any of the preceding would be suitable. The motifs are important and there are a good many designs in vinyl and linoleum taken from authentic Spanish-tile patterns.

IDEAS FOR WALL TREATMENT

Walls are another main contributor to decor as well as practicality. A washable surface is a must, so semigloss or high gloss paint, plastic-surfaced wallpaper or other covering, plastic-finished hardboard or plywood paneling or ceramic tile are the recommended materials. Contemporary treatment calls for painted plaster or gypsum board; neutral, light-toned, mildly textured wall covering like simulated grass cloth; ceramic tile, again in light tones and usually only to the above-counter height with painted plaster above. A fully tiled wall is good-looking though expensive. For the traditional room, French country, Early American, Colonial, or Mediterranean, there are documentary wallpapers which come surface-treated or can be treated for easy cleaning. The better wallpaper houses have a wide selection taken from old papers and fabrics; they often have matching fabric, in fact, so that you can blend walls and kitchen curtains. Such a documentary is a sure way to a true look. Wood-paneled walls, either individual tongued-and-grooved boards of pine, or plywood grooved to look random can be used. Plywood comes in many surfaces, so that you can have pecky cypress, birch, oak, rosewood, and other rare woods besides pine. They come in pastel-toned finishes and most are treated for damp-cleaning. A great look for the country kitchen is with barn siding and and the real thing makes a handsome kitchen, although plywood and laminate panels simulating it give a good effect, too. There are wallpapers that simulate brick and wood and, of course, hardboard comes in almost any simulated finish you can think of.

CEILING

The ceiling is part of the background also and for the contemporary room the choice is often a luminous ceiling with light sources behind sheets of translucent plastic, held in place in a metal grid. There are many systems of this kind on the market which are easy to install. The traditional room relies heavily on the counterpoint of white against stained wood. A plaster or gypsum board ceiling with structural or decorative beams makes a good ceiling for the country kitchen. A black wrought-iron chandelier played against it is a dramatic accent. The provincial look can be furthered by an all-papered ceiling or with patterned paper in a documentary design installed between beams.

A brightly tiled bay window in the kitchen is a pleasant location for the dining area. Here, the peninsula also sets apart a small home office area. The division doesn't break up the sense of space: Black and white ceramic tile floor and dark painted cabinets relate all the areas visually.

WINDOWS

The kitchen with a view is one of the most inviting, but even without a view openness is important to keep you from a feeling of confinement, since so much time is spent there. If the kitchen is one with the family room or breakfast area, it will enjoy an airiness through their windows. For over the sink or any counter, the glider window is recommended over the double-hung one, because it is easier to operate. Roll-out casements are easier, too, since they open with one-hand turn of a crank. Whichever kind of window you use, choose a design with open expanses of glass for the contemporary scheme and small-paned units for the traditional. There are even diamond-shaped panes for the Cotswold or cottage look which can add to the country kitchen. A Dutch door is a good idea for the service entrance, be-

The L-shape in traditional guise: shuttered and ruffle-valanced window is the location of sink and dishwasher; the electric console range with double ovens and the refrigerator are on the adjacent wall. Ceramic tile counter and splash are practical with stain-proof group.

The L-shaped arrangement is ideal for the large kitchen which is part of an informal living area. Here, strongly-grained wood cabinets run almost to ceiling height, in a geometric design that blends with the quarry tile floor. Note abundance of down-light over all work surfaces.

cause it adds a rustic touch and also permits light and egress. Here again, you have a choice of oblong or diamond panes. They come in ponderosa pine and in stock panel door sizes.

For control of light, you can use window shades, traverse curtains, cafes, or shutters. Shades can be laminated in fabric to blend with wallpaper and the fabric can be prefinished for wiping clean. Louvered shutters are a good choice for the country kitchen as they can be stained (special walnut is a good stain to use for a provincial look; just apply with a brush and leave without wiping; it looks antique and has a fruitwood appearance on pine). Curtains in the kitchen proper should be the same as in a family room, or any other room, onto which it opens. This gives decorative continuity, so important in making space seems larger. For example, if you have a bank of high windows over the sink in cafe curtains, use the same fabric as traverse floor-to-ceiling draperies for sliding glass family-room doors that open onto a terrace. For the sleek, modern kitchen with sliding glass doors, vertical window shades are effective, floor to ceiling.

CABINETS AND COUNTERS AS PART OF DECOR

Cabinet fronts are the main help to set the period style in a kitchen. If you use manufactured cabinets, the brochures in color will give you ideas for decorating your type of kitchen. They will also help you choose the right cabinet for the period you want. Suffice it to say here that arched-panel doors are better suited to the Mediterranean and French Provincial looks; square-panel doors for the Colonial or Early American country look; grooved-plank doors are effective in the Early American room. The plainer the better is the word for the contemporary kitchen; flush doors and simple hardware and as blond a finish as possible are the order of the day here. As far as painted cabinets are concerned, they are another sure way of establishing the correct period look. (You must remember, however, that if the existing cabinets were factory-made, they likely have a baked-on finish which you will be sacrificing if you paint over it.) There are certain colors which denote certain periods (Williamsburg green for Colonial, for example; antique French blue for provincial; barn red for Early American, etc.). Using a color closely identified with the style of your choice will help, also, in your choice of counter laminate, ceramic tile, or other work surfaces. There are many patterns in both plastic and ceramic that are authentic to traditional periods. Study

One great advantage of the corridor is that it provides great cabinet space. Here, base and wall cabinets line both walls plus an end area where double ovens are located. Avocado carpet blends with appliances; cabinets are bright pink, laminate counters pumpkin. Sink is avocado.

these before making a choice. The contemporary kitchen can use cabinets in bold colors and in several different colors, using them in large blocks. For example, use one bank at the sink, in bright blue; base cabinets of an island in bright yellow; those of the cooktop in red. Wall cabinets, then, would repeat these colors in white counters, white cabinets, white walls, a case of surface treatment following function; clinical white for food preparation. For the natural wood look in the modern idiom, chopping-block counters are impressive. Reversible panels for cabinet doors will permit a decorative touch to tie in with the rest of your theme. Certain appliances—dishwasher and refrigerator—often permit decorative fronts to be applied in frames that come with the units or as frame kits which can be ordered. These provide areas for traditional pattern or contemporary color blocks. If you want the wood look, you can have it in the same finish to match your cabinets by using the frame kits on dishwasher and refrigerator. A few ranges offer this feature, too.

The "Keeping Room" Kitchen

A favorite kitchen look is the old American country kitchen. It is an attempt to return to the "keeping room" of our Early American days where people sat at the fireside or snacked at an informal table while the cook worked and talked to her family and guests. It was the heart of the house, literally, because that was where it was always warm and the tempting scent of cooking prevailed. The ingredients of the room are a big, wood-burning fireplace, a comfortable, chintzy sitting area nearby, preferably with a rocker, a table and chairs always set up for dinner or games, the warmth of natural wood and patterned fabric, the personal accessories—a quilt on the sofa for an afternoon nap, a homespun tablecloth, prints, paintings, and maps lovingly chosen, a chime clock on the mantel with a pair of brass candlesticks, large, gleaming, and impressive. The hearth is broad and of old brick, with black-iron fire tools at one side and big andirons of black iron with brass finials. Maybe the whole fireplace wall is brick with the hearth running full-room width, providing a ledge for logs, a butter churn, and some of the kitchen implements of yesteryear.

Fortunately for us, it is possible to create this nostalgia and bypass the heavy chore that meal preparation was in those days. Our new, compact equipment and cabinets can give full service and take only one corner ell of the big room. With appliances in copper color, walnut-stained cabinets and chopping-block counters, the food-preparation center blends so unobtrusively that the mood is not in the least weakened. With a documentary chintz, gleaming dark floors of wood, or vinyl which simulates it, rough antique beams overhead, or some of the new foamed-plastic variety, one tenth the weight but so authentic-looking it is difficult to tell real from simulated, you can re-create the room of olden days in terms of current materials.

COLOR IN THE KITCHEN

No chapter on decoration would be complete without a discussion about color. It is one of the most basic and yet least expensive tools you have to work with in the planning of any room. We have already touched on the colors that help to establish the various period themes. The important fact to remember here is that the same color schemes apply to a Colonial kitchen as to a Colonial living room. Also remember that you have at your disposal an enormous range of color in the components you will use. The only limited color palette is in the major appliances themselves and fortunately the standard line of the major manufacturers includes at least one color suitable for each period style. The colors common to almost all lines are copper, yellow, avocado, and a shade of wheat gold, plus the noncolor white which can be worked successfully into almost any scheme. In fact, white is often a good choice, because appliances must be lived with a long time and it is easy to change colors around them in walls, curtains, and decorative accessories. In addition, leading manufacturers have more dramatic colors—red, blue, and black, another noncolor—but these are usually not part of the full line and, unfortunately, not always in the top of the line, the units with the most prized features. So if you want red or black, you may have to do without an automatic ice maker or a double-oven console range. It is best to inquire what the various colors come in before you get your heart set on a scheme, otherwise you will be disappointed. Also, keep in mind that colorful accessories—towels, pot holders, canister sets, pictures, posters, the whole range of "removables"—can go a long way toward creating a different look and making the kitchen a more pleasant place to work in.

The living kitchen is the rule nowadays and it deserves the same

ELKAY MANUFACTURING

The Early American look was found for a compact U-kitchen through the use of grooved oak cabinets with H-hinges, pressure-applied Delft paper "tile" and antique brick cooking niche. Kitchen carpet simulates the braided rug of bygone days, box beams, the open ceiling joists of the old-fashioned country kitchen.

Kitchen proximity to other rooms must be handled carefully. Here, a corridor kitchen in full view of the living room repeats its provincial idiom. Cabinets, coppertone appliances and carpet restate the brown tone of living-room walls and flooring. Wood beams, arched cabinet and tile-like wallpaper add to the traditional air.

GENERAL ELECTRIC COMPANY

Two versions of a cathedral ceilinged kitchen reveal how surface decoration can give different effects. A slightly oriental ambience is created with a system of reversible door panels, some with a bamboo motif, others, plain red. Wicker chairs and honeycomb light fixtures are part of the theme.

In this guise, the mood is contemporary with avocado appliances accented with yellow cabinet fronts in some cases, black in others with yellow and white whimsical fruit designs. A trellis wallpaper seems to make the room more intimate. Globe lights and chopping block top for the island are other "now" touches.

Today's kitchen equipment permits a choice of almost any decoration style. Here is a pretty blue, white and yellow scheme with
quarry tile as an accent on the floor. To locate sink near the window and also adjacent to pass-through-snack counter, a corner,
stainless steel unit was chosen.

Proving that today's kitchen can boast any decorative style, here is a French country room for cooking, complete with arch-front cabinets, iron and crystal chandelier, Louis XV desk chair and filagree wrought-iron dining group. Even the telephone is French and the floor of vinyl brick adds to the rusticity of fieldstone wall. Note black and white wallpaper and its reverse-color match for fabric chair seats.

Cabinets which dominate kitchen walls need not give the impression of a solid mass. It is interesting to jog the balance by mixing natural wood and painted units. In this contemporary design, red groove-front wall cabinets blend with, yet accent, the walnut ones. White pulls tie both together decoratively.

Blue and gold make for a striking kitchen, softened with the mellow patina of wood cabinets. Kitchen carpet, vividly patterned, picks up the tone of the counter laminate. Note the thru-wall air conditioner which blends with the cabinetry and louvered shutters of the same wood tone which can close off the dining room.

A good arrangement for the kitchen which shares space with a family room is an L-shape, with a peninsula defining a dining area. Similar cabinets tie the two areas together, as do wall color and wall-to-wall carpet. White porcelain sink with raised pylon for controls blends nicely with the counter laminate and recessed cooktop.

FRIGIDAIRE, DIVISION OF GENERAL MOTORS CORPORATION

Bright solution for a combination family room-kitchen in compact quarters is built around the color of appliances. Fronts of wall cabinets, counter laminate and panels of the sink island help decorative unity, punctuated with touches of red in patterned wallpaper, a folding door that closes off the laundry, and base cabinet fronts. Play area for tots is defined by change in flooring.

The country look includes painted shutters, floral wallpaper, brick-like vinyl tile floor and provincial cabinets in a rich fruitwood finish and arched, raised panel cabinet doors. Double-bowl stainless steel sink is in an angled jog, giving sense of separation to a china storage area near dining.

The Mediterranean look was interpreted here in arched amber glass windows at the sink counter, cabinets with arched panel doors and black iron chandelier. Over-40" span of triple-bowl stainless steel sink creates a broad clean-up center with dishwasher at left in wood front to blend with cabinets.

Compactness to the limit: an apartment kitchen-dining solution with full equipment plus a stacked washer and dryer in a 24" laundry center at extreme right. Carpet sweeps through both spaces, repeats color of appliances, drapery and upholstery for continuity. Corner sink is a space saver.

FRIGIDAIRE

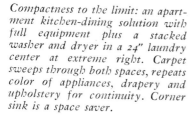

Lighting was carefully planned in this corridor kitchen which has a luminous ceiling over the range-oven and its work area. The sink, the most-used work center, is illuminated by day with a triple-bay window. Color was well handled: avocado of appliances, blue of trim are picked up in wallpaper.

TAPPAN

DEL-MAR CABINETS, DIVISION OF CHAMPION INTERNATIONAL.

The living look is seen in a kitchen design that utilizes appliance fronts as part of a closely matched decorative scheme. A bold paisley used for walls was employed to cover panels which come as part of frame kits for dishwasher, range and double-door refrigerator-freezer. The dark-stained, manufactured cabinets give the look of fine furniture.

Proving that the angular, squared-off kitchen design is not a must, here is a corridor arrangement with a curving wall on one side. White appliances, still the best-selling "non-color," look well in an oriental scheme with touches of red. Unusual idea: oven between walls, windows above and below.

GENERAL ELECTRIC COMPANY

colorful treatment as any other room. If it is part of the family room or some other informal sitting area, it is likely the most lived-in room in the house and families want to live colorfully. Also, the kitchen is an integral part of the home, and it should continue the house-wide interior theme; by so doing, it helps to make the whole house seem more spacious. Going from a Georgian living or dining room into a totally crisp, contemporary kitchen makes the whole house seem disjointed and keeps everyone from wanting to gather there. However, if the rest of the house is breathlessly contemporary, it seems perfectly logical and comfortable to find more of the same in the kitchen.

How to Use Pattern

Balance is the watchword here. There is so much going on in the kitchen with the appliances themselves, the many utensils and cabinets, all creating pattern, that this element must be used carefully. As we have seen, certain decorative styles will permit more pattern than others; in fact, some, like Early American, specifically require it. However, it is wise to hold it to certain areas. For example, if you want a busy documentary wallpaper-curtain ensemble, keep countertops and flooring subdued. Or, keep counter laminate in a solid color and the floor in a pattern of about the same scale as the wall covering. If the cabinets permit decorated fronts with reversible panels, then it may be best to keep walls, floor, and counters in a solid color that blends with the dominant color in the print of the cabinet door. Repeat the same pattern in the fabric for curtains, table mats, dish towels, and other accessories, if possible. If cabinets are in a boldly grained wood, keep to a subdued design in other elements. Don't overlook the ceiling as a source of pattern and color: In the small kitchen, papering exposed walls and ceiling in the same small pattern will help to make the room seem larger. But if you do this, choose pastel appliances in a tone found in the paper and keep counters a plain color and the floor fairly neutral. Or keep walls, cabinets, and appliances—the entire band around the room—subdued and use patterned ceiling and floor. In the contemporary kitchen, the cabinets and appliances will furnish blocks of pattern, and counters, floor, walls, and ceiling should be in white or a pastel. That way, pattern will result architecturally, a basic role in this style.

KITCHEN LIGHTING

The days of those stark white kitchens are gone and no one mourns them. Today's kitchens are taking on the look and activities of a family room. Lighting, naturally, has kept pace with these changes, and that dreary, white fixture in the center of the ceiling is now an antique—one without value. In planning your kitchen lighting, you must first decide on the activities that will go on in various areas.

How many areas do you actually have? The sink and dishwashing center is a major one, and the range another. How about a mixing or serving counter? Is there counter space for eating or a separate dining table? How much counter space needs to be lighted? What about lighting the interior of storage cabinets? Is your laundry center attached to the kitchen? Deciding on the areas that involve visual work is a major step in achieving good kitchen lighting.

General illumination for the kitchen is usually provided overhead in one of three ways. First, there are the fluorescent ceiling fixtures. Many are being dressed up with warm, wood trim to match cabinets.

A tiny kitchen was arranged in a workable U-shape with sink at the base under a window with a shade of floral cutouts taken from the wall covering. Refrigerator is at the right, hooded gas range-oven at the left. The peninsula helps to keep the cook out of the line of house traffic.

Even a circular fixture of pure white molded glass holding three 100-watt incandescent bulbs is set into a frame of genuine walnut veneer.

Then come the luminous ceiling panels or in some cases an entire ceiling can be luminous, 20-, 30-, and 40-watt warm white de luxe fluorescent tubes are concealed above white diffusing panels, marked off with wood grids or false beams. This gives a soft and flattering light. Since cabinets, counters, and appliances in a kitchen usually have a glossy surface reflecting light, some sort of diffusion is desirable. Sometimes it's possible to create a skylight effect with translucent panels and wood strips. It can be recessed in the ceiling or take the form of a v-shaped trough or an inverted v.

A third possibility is to light all four sides of a kitchen near the ceiling by installing valances over windows and cove lighting over cabinets. A family in Chicago did this after years of suffering with two ceiling globes and were amazed at the glare-free results.

However, they discovered they needed supplementary lighting in the work areas to eliminate sharp contrasts in the dark shadows found on counters beneath cabinets. To solve this problem they installed concealed strip lighting (fluorescent tubes) under all wall cabinets. This type of lighting is also recommended for hoods, whether they are small ones over a surface cooking unit or large ones over a central island.

To light such work areas as the sink, food-preparation center, or serving counter, you can install recessed downlights, or shielded reflector bulbs in the ceiling, or fluorescent tubes, recessed in a soffit behind a luminous panel. (Three 40-watt, four-foot tubes would give even light.) Beware of heat from unshielded reflector bulbs in any area where you are apt to stand for long periods of time.

The trend to the country look in kitchen decor, whether it's Mediterranean, English, French, or American, is extremely popular, and you may wish to select some hanging fixtures to accent certain areas. The chandeliers might resemble a wagon wheel, old-fashioned kerosene lamps on a wrought-iron base, or diffused globes on a brass base. Coach-style wall or suspended lanterns or a post lantern to mark the boundary between kitchen and dining area would also be appropriate for the country look.

If the setting is contemporary, you can install luminescent shoji wall panels for a purely decorative note and use a variety of airy, suspended bubble fixtures in a dining or desk area. Here again the ad-

In an apartment kitchen, space was found for a small dining counter near the window. The white laminate area was simply made by attaching to the window wall with angle irons and to an end storage wall, with a single leg supporting the rest. A wide window shade filters direct sunlight.

justable pull-down is particularly helpful in concentrating or dispersing the light. In such a lamp a minimum of 120 watts is recommended.

One handsome Mediterranean kitchen could have looked dark and gloomy since its cabinets are a deep walnut and its walls are covered with a rich red flocked paper. Even its sink is a brilliant red. However, three recessed 150-watt reflector bulbs over the cabinets and four in the sink area give the room a warm and pleasing glow.

A WORD OF CAUTION

If your home or apartment is rented, you should reconsider before undertaking such extensive redecorating ideas as replacing counters or flooring, painting walls or cabinets. With a short lease, it is wise not to do extreme things. For example, in an apartment the cost of removing dark paint or wallpaper put up several years previously could cost you your entire security deposit. Read the small print in your lease carefully.

If you own an apartment on a co-operative basis, consider yourself a homeowner when it comes to decorating. Also, if you have a long lease at low rent, it may be worth it to you to do considerable decorative remodeling. But it would be wise to come to an understanding with your landlord with an exchange of letters that will protect you against replacement when the lease is up. Armed with that, it is only a matter of how much you want to spend to create a whole new kitchen look, with paper, flooring, even new cabinets, lighting, and certain additional or replacement appliances.

CHAPTER SEVENTEEN

THE FAMILY ROOM

IN THE early 1950s, a new room began to be sketched in on the floor plans of single-family dwellings. Sometimes it was labeled the rumpus room, or quite commonly it was known as the playroom or recreation room. Gradually, as the '50s began to give increased study and attention to the interactions of the members of the family unit, the name of this room began to change. Eventually, rumpus room and other appellations that implied a "play" nature disappeared, and to give the room a slightly different focus, the term "family room" became favored—a designation that remains.

So many versions of what a family room is supposed to be have been proposed by experts in fields from architecture to sociology that the term really defies clear description. Generally speaking, it is considered a "second living room," but one that is less formal and more flexible than the primary living room. An added space for group living is especially desirable when there are several members of a family at different age levels. Children, teen-agers, and elderly people usually have needs and interests that differ from those of the middle-age group. To solve the problems that invariably arise when we attempt to bridge the generation gap, a home that provides two (or even more) family living areas is a decided aid. Basically, the auxiliary living area, i.e., the family room, should be a carefree place for all who use it. This is a room where there should be no worry about delicate fabrics or fragile furnishings. How to achieve a family room that delights the eyes, relaxes the body, and is kind to the pocketbook is one of the aims of this chapter.

You may not have given it much thought, but these days it is almost impossible to miss finding a family room in newer housing. House hunters who are seriously examining the residential market can't help but be familiar with this omnipresent room, whether they have been tramping in and out of model houses or leafing through home-furnishings magazines or studying plans in an architect's office. In older home-improvement projects, the family room, say builders, is the leading "add on" in refurbishing. To leave the family room off the drawing boards of plans of new houses would be tantamount to forgetting the kitchen.

The last word is an important one in relation to the family room. In a significant number of contemporary layouts, the family room is sketched in adjacent to, or at least conveniently near, the kitchen. It makes good sense and is in keeping with the nature of the room to have this area where you can make provisions for the serving of meals and refreshments. Also, when making plans for a new house, try to arrange it so that the family room is accessible to an outdoor area: patio, terrace, or garden.

RECLAIMING A FAMILY ROOM

Yet the house that is not planned for all its members' home activities and fruitful use of leisure really doesn't offer much more than a furnished motel suite. Children, especially, should be exposed to their father's tinkering with his power tools, their mother's painting, and grandmother's skill at needlepoint. The woman who fears her family will make a "mess" of the house is doing nothing to fan the flame of creativity and family fun. A laissez-faire family room where anyone can, figuratively, let down his hair, relax, and putter is a needed buoy for those too concerned about a house-with-everything-in-its-place. For them, space in the home for family functions is where you find it. Here are some other areas to which anyone may turn.

One of the favorite spots to "reclaim" is the basement. A drab cellar with bleak, cold walls and Rube Goldberg-like pipes and equipment can metamorphose into a play space for the family. A major consideration here should be the choice of materials. Basements suffer from lack of light, ease of access, and have temperatures that go from cold and clammy to just too hot. When creating a family room below ground level, look for floor coverings that are suitable for use below grade and wall treatments that will provide an attractive background yet have wearing qualities. Make special provisions for heat, air conditioning, and the control of humidity. Artificial lighting must supplement the little or none of the natural kind available.

In this well-planned house, the recreation room is located directly off the terrace. To provide convenient access to the outdoor pool-and-sunning area, two pairs of Andersen Perma-Shield vinyl-clad wood patio doors were installed. Note how the draperies were hung at the far side of each door so as to not interfere with the flow of traffic.

If the basement doesn't take to remodeling, take a look at the upper part of your house. Older buildings often have attics that can do more than act as catchalls for old trunks and out-of-season sporting equipment. With proper insulation, part of an attic can become a sewing room, carpentry room, or photographic darkroom. But be sure that the activities to be centered in it will not disturb those on the floor below. In finding the spot for your family room, do consider the bedrooms. In an old Victorian house, they may be too numerous for you. However, in a newer house, by doing some juggling, you may be able to turn one into general family use. One family we know made one bedroom of their four-bedroom house into a dormitory setup for their three young sons so that the third "child's room" could be used as an all-family recreation area.

Here are some other ideas for closing in an extra space. A young husband walled in the breezeway between house and garage; a second fellow, who enclosed a porch, created a handsome family room-dinette that overlooks the rear garden. In another case, after a family meeting, it was decided to do away with the separate dining room, and instead, use the space for a music-and-game room. In a wide upstairs hall, a family of adults lined the walls with bookshelves, dropped a chandelier over a round table, encircled it with four upholstered chairs, and called the result their family minilibrary. Going further afield, a small-car family decided that their garage could enclose both a car and a pool table. They covered the cement floor with an indoor-outdoor carpet that lets grease stains sponge off, painted the inner garage walls bright green, tacked up some inexpensive posters depicting auto rallies, moved in the pool table, and by plugging in an electric room heater, enjoyed billiards even in the middle of winter. (In warm weather, they keep the garage doors open for ventilation.)

Even if you have just signed the mortgage agreement on a brand-new house, the room labeled "family" on the builder's plans need not be restricted to just second living-room function because of its name. A home, to be a home, must be an active place, reflecting the ever-changing parade of interests and hobbies of its occupants, individually and as a unit. That's where the unique flexibility of function of the "family room-plus" comes in, and that's why its use defies clear-cut definition. To find places for all the things that reflect the activities of those who live in the house, the family room is fast shedding one purpose and is assuming a hyphenated name.

FAMILY ROOM-KITCHEN

So much for the family room that is. What about the older residence, a house which has not been expanded, one that was constructed at a time when the second living room was not common? In a house where the family room is not, space can still be allocated for group living. Some older homes, in fact, are naturals for the easy addition of family-oriented space. Take those houses with big kitchens, built in an earlier era when meal preparations went on in a large, spacious room and where, too, there might have been a pantry and breakfast nook. (Interestingly, the kitchen cycle has been completed. Big, old-fashioned kitchens disappeared, to be replaced by tiny, lablike things.

And now they are gone too, and the family-size kitchen has become popular once again.)

Large, out-of-date kitchens can be modernized to include the latest mechanical developments and still allow room for family activities. For those with tiny children, the family room-kitchen is ideal, as the mother can keep her eyes on her children as she goes about her meal preparations. When making an older kitchen into such a dual-purpose room, it is not difficult to childproof it from obvious dangers to toddlers. Look for a range with dials at the back where they can't be reached by inquisitive fingers, wall ovens placed where their doors can't be opened, base cabinets on which you can install locks.

Hard-surface flooring throughout the room will make it easy to maintain general cleanup and give quick attention to spilled water colors and such in the children's play area. Furniture should be of clean lines and functional, minus sharp edges and points. And do select fabrics of the easy-clean variety.

The family room-kitchen is welcomed, too, by those who fancy the more time-consuming types of gourmet cookery but still want to take part in the family fun. It's not very rewarding to be in a separate room stirring the sauce when your child tells that amusing story of what happened on his way home from school. If the family doesn't have small children and prefers the convenience-meal type of thing to coq au vin, the converted family room might be located in another part of the house. The old kitchen could be used then, for example, as a kitchen-laundry. Remember that when children approach teen age, they and the rest of the family will be happier if another area of the home can be salvaged for their activities, projects, and parties. It isn't much fun for teens to entertain their friends in a family room-kitchen (or anywhere else, as a matter of fact) where older members of the family can be breathing down their necks.

Family Room-Dining Area

Take the matter of the family room-dining area. As we mentioned before, a convenient location for the family room is cheek by jowl to the kitchen. Families who emphasize informality in their day-to-day lives like plans where the family room also joins up with a dining area. (This is true even in those cases where "serious" meals may be served in an ell of the living room.) For casual rooms such as these, stay away from the conventional dining-room furniture merchandised as

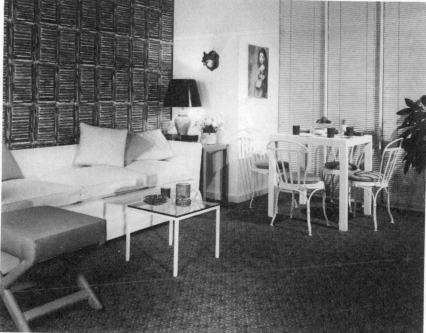

Practicality is a key word in the planning of any family room. Chosen for this heavy-traffic area was a printed carpet backed with latex foam rubber to reduce noise and clatter. Although the carpet won't fade, narrow-slatted Venetian blinds were installed to control sunlight and texturally complement the cane-patterned wallpaper.

a suite. You definitely do not need a table, dining chairs, buffet, china cabinet, and/or serving table. If you already own these and they are beginning to show signs of wear, be a bit ruthless. Keep the table and essential chairs, the buffet if it isn't too cumbersome for your family-room space, and sell or give away the rest.

If you own no dining furniture, that's just fine. Unfettered, you can try some imaginative tricks. Take the matter of a dining table. Who says you need a large rectangular table smack in the center of the room? This placement is too rigid for a family room, and, besides, the position of the table will make for awkward traffic if everyone must skirt it to get in and out of the room.

If you do need a big table, keep it out of the way; against a long wall or, if you have a view of a garden, in front of the windows. Or, if you are buying a new table, consider the choices which await you. There is no need to stick to wood. And there is no need to stick to that rectangular shape either. Today you can find tables topped in marble, slate, glass, Plexiglas, and a practical selection of fool-the-eye plastics that resemble "real" materials but are much easier to care for. In dimensions, there are rounds, ovals, boat shapes, and octagonals. Many sport self-storing leaves.

If yours is a small family, just two of you, you might consider a "disappearing" table. There is a model that folds up into a secretarylike unit; one that flips up against the wall with its "back" doubling as a mirror; and any number of sophisticated modular wall systems of which a dining table is an integral part. Shop around. Or you might like a 32 by 32-inch card table that opens to double its size at mealtime and has room to accommodate six without anyone's elbow sticking in anyone else's ribs. Better yet, you could get two such tables. Placed end to end, you will have a generous buffetlike space, should you press the family room into an informal party room. Or, for more frequent use, the adults can play bridge at one table; the kids, checkers at the other.

When considering chairs, remember that they do not have to match the table; indeed, your room might be more attractive if they don't, as dining areas tend to get quite "woody" in appearance. Chairs with painted frames or gaily covered seats will help relieve this look. A good idea for the young family is slipcovered seats for chairs. They can be easily reupholstered when a change in color or pattern is wanted. And as accidents do occur in a family with youngsters, frequent changes are sometimes necessary.

For nondining, a comfortable upholstered piece is needed. If the room is small, a short sofa will do nicely, supplemented by an upholstered chair, perhaps with ottoman. (The kind that opens so that you can stow away magazines and the past Sunday's newspapers is an added convenience.) Individual furniture items that are attractive in this setting include French bakery racks of metal (for potted plants and books), a grandfather's clock, old washstands, stacks of straw hampers (inexpensive and good for the storage of paper napkins and such), and that boon to the family room, the mobile serving cart.

China and silver can be stored in the kitchen, or seldom-used pieces, like turkey platters, can be housed in family-room built-ins of base cupboards topped by cabinets with metal mesh doors. (You can use these to partially hide hi-fi speakers and to display accessories like pewter mugs or a collection of copper pots.) Don't hesitate in using the excitement of color on walls, floors, and windows. Walls and windows take the decorating lead here. High-keyed colors and bold patterns will be effective and can be combined with one or more paneled walls or a wooden room dado. In an area where spills are common, a hard-surface flooring that is nonkitcheny in look or an easy-to-care-for indoor-outdoor carpeting would be good. The latter would be very effective if the room is off a patio where the same flooring (in an outdoor quality) could be continued out of doors.

Family Room-Music Center

When Congreve wrote "Music hath charms to soothe the savage breast," he did not have in mind the small boy practicing on his snare drums while his mother burns the roast. The family that loves music or is trying to instill an appreciation for it into the lives of its younger members has the perfect opportunity to capitalize on the advantages of a separate family room. Because music is frequently a passive interest rather than an active one, the family room that also acts as a music center need not play up easy maintenance. Here, attention to fidelity of sound is of the greatest importance.

If you are sound minded, pay careful attention to the materials used in this room. Here, wall-to-wall carpeting, thick and deep in pile, is not a luxury but a wise acoustical move. So are lined draperies of a closely woven fabric that can be drawn over the windows when necessary. To assure those not in the family room during practice sessions a modicum of privacy and peace, consider installing an acoustical building material over walls and ceiling. (Some of these products can cover your present surfaces.) Naturally, you won't locate the music center in an open-area part of the house, but in one that is separate and has a door that can be firmly closed.

Be sure to measure the dimensions of the room before making any major purchase. Armed with this information, you hopefully won't get carried away by a grand piano at an auction if there is no way to get it into the room, be it by door or window. If your music room is on other than the ground floor, the cost of hoisting a large instrument can be formidable. If you are stereo buffs, do check to make sure the size of the room will permit proper separation of speakers. Be sure, too, if you possess a valuable instrument—piano, harp, violin, or such —that the temperature and humidity controls for your music room are suitable.

Sometimes size dictates where you will place an instrument. In that

Music has charms to soothe the weary family. It's nice to have ample seating space when everyone sits back to listen in this home entertainment center. Cabinets of rosewood-tone vinyl veneer that resists stains and scratches hold the stereo, radio, television and what-have-you.

case, as with a piano, it becomes the focal point of your decor and you must arrange the furnishings to fit. But, if you are a hi-fi or tape fan, your interests need not dictate the physical arrangement of the room. Your equipment can be installed in a special cabinet that is treated as a piece of furniture, or you may prefer a system that conceals an entertainment center. A closet with bifold doors can be built into a wall, or your sound system can be part of a modular wall unit. In either case, easily operated doors can expose the components when they are wanted, conceal them when they are out of use. If your family is a group of listeners rather than performers, you will need a number of comfortable upholstered chairs, supplemented, perhaps, by some cushions for floor sitting. Seating should be planned for maximum flexibility. You will find, for example, that there are individual seating units that can be clipped together to form a handsome sofa or shifted into individual arrangements. There are even modern seats that lift completely out of their frames and can be placed on the floor for informal comfort. If you, or one or more of your family, receive personal joy and gratification from strumming the guitar or playing the zither or whatever, make sure that there is ample space for practice, room for music (if needed), sufficient light, and convenient outlets for any needed electric accessories.

Family Room-Game Room

A family room that functions as a miniature clubhouse should be completely removed from concerns about delicate fabrics or fragile furnishings or easy-to-harm surfaces. For this type of "fun room" choose the most near-to-indestructible materials that you can lay your hands on. Walls should be sheathed in a wood laminate or a washable vinyl or, at the very least, be painted with an acrylic or rubber-base paint that can survive periodic washings.

Your floor can be covered with a vinyl or vinyl-asbestos tile, if you are partial to hard-surface materials. Are the kids hopscotch fans? Then you might like big tiles in black and white. Do the teen-agers find shuffleboard fun? Shuffleboard insets, which can be bought ready-cut, can be installed when your floor is laid. If you are thinking about more conventional hard-surface flooring, remember that multicolors won't show heel marks and dirt. As pretty as a solid white or solid black floor might look in a magazine, these colors will show every scuff and soil mark.

If your family has its quota of young wrigglers who are on the floor most of the time, you might like the warmth and comfort of a foam-cushioned indoor-outdoor carpet. Many of these have a feltlike surface, come in solids and patterns, can be laid wall to wall, as with conventional carpeting, or put down in tiles. It's even easy for the amateur carpet layer to cut out inlays, big circles and such, and insert them in the carpeting. Those who have hobbies like golf will find that a miniature putting green made of a grasslike synthetic can be set in the family-room floor.

If the games your family indulges in mean that the furniture must often be shifted, make sure that it is not heavy in weight. Try to keep seating units on the smallish side too. A love seat is certainly easier to shove than a four-seat sofa; canvas director's chairs are more movable than heavy recliners.

For all of your upholstery, go easy care. This is the ideal place for a vinyl or other washable synthetic. If you must have a conventional fabric, slipcover your furniture in a sturdy duck or denim that can be tossed into the washing machine and then eased back over cushions with little or no ironing. Stretch nylon follows the same minimal-care principle. Incidentally, if you have little children, you might consider two sets of slipcovers, one for "on," the other for the wash. Games mean that a place will be needed to store equipment. Perforated hardboard panels on the walls can hold shelves and all kinds of hooks so that model airplanes, tennis rackets, and other equipment can be neatly hung up.

Or ready-made or unfinished cabinets and chests (or Salvation Army salvages) can be lined up on the perimeter of the room, away from the active mid-room area, and be used to hold game boards, checkers, and the like. Darts are not only fun as a family game, but the boards make an effective wall treatment, too. The darts themselves belong in your cabinets when out of use, of course.

Keep window treatments on the simple side. Shutters, colorful shades, or wash-and-hang cafe curtains avoid maintenance concerns.

Finally, double check to make sure all the materials in the room can "take it." Do the counters and tabletops resist heat, mars, and spots? Is wooden furniture painted so that you can wipe it off with a damp rag? Are there posters on the walls, instead of glass-covered pictures subject to breakage during an indoor ball game? Does the wall clock have a plastic face for the very same reason?

FAMILY ROOM-GUEST ROOM

There are so many exciting and decorative ways other than the studio couch to add sleeping space to the family room that we think you will want to consider them. It is well worth investing in a sofa that doubles as a bed. The obvious advantages of comfortable seating, as well as a napping place, are there. There are many variations on the sofa-bed theme, from little love seats to commodious queen-size sofa-beds. (For more information on convertible bedding see Chapter Twenty-three "The Apartment.") Sleeping place isn't the only requirement for this type of family room. Guests need places to put

Bright color—the red of plaid carpet, chair seats, chandelier and book bindings—ties a family-room scheme together and blends with the mellow wood of a cabinet system that gives the room architectural interest where none existed. Generous table surface is ideal for family snacks, games and the hobbies of both parents and children.

Early American flavor is attained with a wall section treated with rough-sawn pine boards, shuttered window treatment and adaptations of provincial pieces. Painted wood furniture blends nicely with natural grain of stained cabinet and small desk, a must for the well-appointed family room. Color combination of greeny gold and blue is a restful solution.

Ask a man what he appreciates in his study and he will probably say muted colors and natural-looking materials. The scheme here, a subtle blend of tones of toast, brown and gold and the use of rugged textures and effects are slated to win masculine approval. The deep wing chair was designed for comfort plus good looks while the Parsons table-desk is sturdy yet sleek.

A comfortable, big sofa is a must for the ideal family retreat. Here, an Early American high-backed design in a homespun plaid does double duty as a sleeper for the occasional overnight guest. Vibrant wall color is restated in braided rug and wall decor, accented with white and yellow.

SIMMONS HIDE-A-BED SOFA

CARPETING BY BARWICK, OF KODEL POLYESTER

A handsome and practical family room-music center encourages the talen: of the entire clan: those who practice and those who receive their pleasur: from listening. Carpeting swathes the walls and ceiling as well as the floo: acting as insulation which improves the room's acoustics while providing a ric: background for sleek modern furnishings.

An eclectic mix in the family room highlights a father's nautical interests. The color scheme is blue and green with off-white accents, mainly the contemporary fireside chairs. Wall unit stores family hobby supplies behind doors, displays favorite books and collections. Desk, open on two sides, is a convenient spot for snacks, too.

Multipurpose is the word for a room planned to satisfy the needs of family and guests. The basic functions of study, television watching and stereo enjoyment are supplemented by sofas providing sleep for two. The mood is quiet, with tones of rust and brown predominating in upholstery and wood pieces.

A mini-kitchen setup in the family room blends colorfully into the over-all decor, set off with vibrant blue ceiling beams. Vinyl brick flooring picks up the snack bar color, while sofa and armchairs extend the blue motif. Note bar stools that use the fabric and the tassel fringe of shades which pull down to hide decorative storage bays.

HICKORY
MANUFACTURERS

SIMMONS HIDE-A-BED SOFA

their gear, so a folding luggage stand that you stash away in the closet when out of use is a great asset. Consider, too, the campaign chest with drawers, a nice nonbedroom look for easy storage.

FAMILY ROOM-MINIKITCHEN

One of the newest transmutations of the family room is the family room-minikitchen. Obviously, this marriage is most suited to those home people whose family room is more than a hop, skip, and jump from the kitchen proper. It makes most sense for the auxiliary living room that is part of the basement or in a distant bedroom wing or snuggled up in the attic. This type of minikitchen is obviously not planned to produce the best meal anyone has ever tasted. It is an aid for snack preparation and an especial boon to the care and feeding of teen-agers. If there is an available sink, great. Build around it. If not, and you have to transport cold water, consider stowing away a couple of gallons of bottled water in a corner cabinet—there are still many pluses favoring this setup.

The kitcheny props needed are not expensive and are mostly of a plug-into-the-electrical-outlet nature. First and foremost, make sure that your wiring is adequate to carry powerful current consumers. Even a toaster can be a greater strain on your electric system than you may suspect. Probably the most popular additions will be the plug-in coffeepot or teakettle. Most of the supplies needed to brew these beverages—the coffee or tea, sugar, and a dry coffee cream substitute—don't require refrigeration. A separate shelf will do. But if your family does insist on "real cream" and juice that spurts from a genuine, not a plastic, lemon, a small refrigerator can be a wise investment.

Minimodels have been around for years and are favorite "extras" when decorating executive offices. Frequently of plastic but wood in tone, they have been promoted not so much for their milk-keeping properties, but to store ice cubes and keep mixers chilled so that when a drink is in order after the completion of a business deal, glasses and some of the potent stuff are all that are needed. This type of basic refrigerator is now so common and low in price that it can even be found in some dime stores. More sophisticated little refrigerators have generous freezer sections and magnetically controlled doors. There are even wheel-about models that have a freezer and door storage racks. One has a base like a bar cart and can be plugged in anywhere.

Bar cart or mobile servers are especially useful names in the vocabulary of someone furnishing a family room-kitchenette. Some of these are inexpensive metal trolleys, and others stand handsomely by, looking like innocent little cabinets until a buffet is needed. Then their tops swing open to double or triple the original space and a stainproof plastic surface is exposed. Usually, they boast drawers and glassware storage space too. Some of the more elaborate models have electric tops that keep hot food at serving temperature for hours, or wells for ice cubes.

For a semiserious cook, a two-burner electric cooktop can help would-be gourmets exercise their expertise. All kinds of other table-top gadgetry can find itself in the eating-oriented family room: chafing dish, fondue pot, electric corn popper, sandwich toaster, bun warmer, and those two essentials, the blender and the can opener, are just a few examples of specialty items. If one or more cooking devices are used, good ventilation becomes a must. A window exhaust fan such as is normally used in a kitchen is well worth considering, as is the type of room air conditioner that blows air out as well as in.

In a family room, serving addenda are most appropriate decoratively if they are made of easy-care, wood-finish laminate or enameled in a nonkitcheny hue. Pots, pans, and other necessaries can be filed away in base or wall cabinets. If a full-size table doesn't fit into the scheme of things, folding snack tables are a good bet. Disposables have risen so far above the old white-paper-napkins-and-plates look that the accessories chosen for eating and drinking can feast the eyes while you feast the stomach and then be tossed in the trash can. Besides paper, there are now many clear or colorful tumblers and plates in inexpensive plastic that are good candidates for family-room use.

Family Room-Hobby Room

The live-in seamstress is no more, and with space at a premium in the house, the separate sewing room has disappeared with her. But women still sew and follow as well a wealth of other hobbies and interests that they want to enjoy, not in isolation, but in physical closeness to other members of their family. And what better place for hobbies than the family room? If a woman favors sewing, the family room should provide adequate space for her machine. If it is an up-to-date model, to the uninitiated it will appear to be a good-looking chest or cabinet. If she chooses to use a portable machine, the home sewer must make sure she has a table of the right height and space for prolonged sessions of stitching. Too, there must be a place to cut out patterns without undue bending. Almost as essential as the sewing machine are an ironing board and iron and a place to store them when not in use.

A folding screen can be a practical and good-looking room accessory if you want to hide your ironing equipment. Screens come in many forms: wood, woven plastic, folding shutters, frames that can be filled with shirred fabric to match the window treatment, etc. Not only can a screen shield the unneeded pressing aids, it also can conceal a cabinet into which are filed patterns, threads, fabric, or works in progress. If sewing isn't a prime interest, another form of needlework probably is. Enjoying a renaissance in the midst of our computer age are all sorts of embroidery, needlepoint, and crewel work. Some attribute the popularity of these to an unconscious protest against automation, but whatever the reason, women of all ages are knitting and doing needlepoint in significantly growing numbers. Interestingly, their productions are directed toward the home, and we find pillows, chair seats, and, from the needles of the more ambitious, even rugs.

Another craft that is a natural for the family room is weaving. Obviously, a loom takes up a lot of room and is warranted here only when there is a greater need to be creative than to find a place to sit. The loom should be set up in an area where there is natural light, if at all possible. If weaving is your interest, take a cue from professional designers. Many of them consider their yarn supplies so attractive to look at that they keep them on open shelves set against their walls. You can do the same, adding color and convenience to the family room at the same time you are making a rug or throw that will later add to the home in another way.

If your hobby is a messier kind, such as pottery making, it is best carried on in a room that has a sink and a work area that can be closed off by sliding panels or louvered doors. Please don't be turned off by the gooey wetness of this hobby. Pottery can be an excellent activity for an entire family to follow, can be adapted to the needs of the very young as well as adults, and from the practical standpoint, can result in products that will enrich the home with an individual touch. The same advice applies, too, to drawing, painting, and sculpture. Here again, conceal the project when it is not being worked upon or the family room will reflect a psychological as well as visual lack of neatness.

The handyman in the family may want to locate his workroom in the family room. But because of the nature of the supplies needed and the space taken up by carpentry and such, we think it more advisable that the workroom be a separate entity.

There can be provisions for other hobbies in or near a family room. If there are home-movie buffs in your family, a miniature projection room is very nice indeed. All that is needed is a projector, screen (roll-up or hideaway nature is suggested), and black-out shades or curtains for the windows. A flexible seating arrangement is in order if there are to be several viewers; comfortable yet lightweight chairs, the kind that can be stacked in a closet, make a good investment. Cushions are an optional extra for long periods of sitting. The type of photographic gear is dictated by the budget and inclinations of the family. Growing in popularity in some sections of the country is the practice of renting commercial films, both of entertainment and educational nature. By its very nature a photographic darkroom must be separate from the family room.

Family Room-Laundry

Every household must make some provision for taking care of the family wash. In many families the automatic washer is considered as essential a piece of equipment as the kitchen stove. The dryer, too, is rapidly reaching the same status. Although the ironer is not felt to be nearly as essential, it too, is gradually leaving the luxury category. Sometimes the laundry center is planned as a part of a kitchen or bath. Traditionally, a favorite location for it has been the basement. But these days many homes have combination family/utility rooms and laundries on the main floor. Although the most desirable and convenient location for the home laundry has not as yet been determined by home economists and architects, and preferences vary with the individual homemaker, placement in a family-room setting should be seriously considered.

If decided upon, the laundry part of the combination must be planned and equipped efficiently. In addition to the major equipment chosen, a large table or counter for sorting soiled items and folding clean ones should be included. There must also be convenient cabinets for storing soaps, detergents, bleaches, and other supplies. In spite of all the miracle fabrics on the market, some ironing still exists in almost every home, but, happily, its burdens can be lightened. The generally cheerful and pleasant atmosphere of the family room is one of the prime reasons given for doing the ironing, if not the washing and drying, in this spot. The housewife can work in a relaxing setting and have the company of other people while she does her work or, at the very least, be entertained by the radio, television, or hi-fi.

While, for convenience, laundry equipment that is "out in the open" is the most usual, there is no reason why washer and dryer cannot be concealed behind louvered cabinets and rolled out into the room when needed. If desired, the practical part of the room can be hidden behind folding screens, or a ceiling track installed and an inexpensive folding door used to divide the room. For "lighter" division, a flexible screen of colored beads is pretty and has the advantage of letting air circulate freely throughout the entire room. When making an appliance color choice, if you opt for white, you are following the national preference. Although washers and dryers come in yellow, turquoise, coppertone, and other hues, white still leads, probably because of the housewife's association of it with cleanliness.

FAMILY ROOM-EXERCISE ROOM

Weight watching is just one segment of our current emphasis on health and physical fitness. Recognition of the importance of regular exercise for everyone from infant on up has led some people to incorporate space for physical activity into their family rooms. The man or woman who makes routine use of a supplementary exercise device, such as an Exercycle, can do his mock bicycle riding here and keep his equipment behind curtains or screens when it is out of use. Obviously, to practice this form of physical discipline when one is not alone requires a particular type of temperament. So, too, does weight lifting and some other forms of calisthenics.

Hard-surface flooring, covered by an exercise mat, makes a fine place to do push-ups, knee bends, headstands, and such. Whether it is jumping rope, rhythmic exercises to music, or some other type of physical training, the regimen has a much greater chance of success if it is turned into an all-family project. Obviously, certain activities, like ballet dancing, won't be pursued by everyone, but the family room makes a good place for practicing them too. In the case of dance, a mirror and a barre would be helpful. When designing a house in which the family room is to be near the bedroom wing, it is often possible to incorporate between these areas a sauna, another health-and-relaxation item which, like the outdoor swimming pool, is beginning to be favored by homeowners.

As you can see from the foregoing, today's family room is the most free-form room in the house. It can encompass all the activities of a given family in one space—TV, games, hobbies, simple relaxation while listening to music, and some of the less laborious chores such as laundry, ironing, and sewing. The combination of activities that your family requires will dictate its size and equipment, its furniture and accessories.

ARCHITECTURAL DETAILS

Because the family room, especially if it is part of an older home, may be located in an off-beat part of the house, such as the basement or an enclosed sun porch, it may seem to have more than its share of architectural problems. As with "difficult" windows, you simply have to face them, for they won't go away. But, unlike the window where you used camouflage, try to turn architectural defects into focal points. If you don't, the remedy can be expensive remodeling, something you want to avoid in the family room and den. If that down-in-the-cellar room has a maze of pipes meandering across the ceiling, scrape off any loose paint, cover the pipes with a coat of metal primer, and then paint them in bright colors, making them attention getters on purpose. Red, purple, and hot pink pipes in a room with pale pink walls carries a carnival-like gaiety and establishes the room's color scheme. Or perhaps the room has several uneven jogs. Paint the "impossible" little walls in contrast to the others. A clear grass green for the jogs, bright blue for the "good" walls, and a floor tiled in blue and green give you a fresh, cheerful setting. If you are stuck with a fuse box, you can hide that behind a poster. But why not decorate it in a Mondrian-like geometric of yellow, green, and blue?

Perhaps it's molding-framed panels in the study that offend you. If they are on rough-textured walls, you think they look 1920-ish. Well, left the way you've found them, they do indeed appear out of date. But why not give them a contemporary look? Paint the moldings a color taken from the wallpaper with which you fill in the panels and continue the background tone of the paper in your wall color. Or stain the moldings a walnut wood tone and insert a beige-, brown-, and black-checked fabric in the panels. Use the same fabric to up-

A fireplace, a built-in advantage for any room, stars in this cozy den. The walls, upholstered to match the plaid of the lounge chair, pick up the red of the fire. For relaxation, there is a tuxedo sofa as well as the chair. For homework, a desk is an integral part of Early American bunching units.

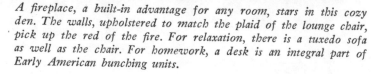

holster your sofa, cover a chair, or as draperies. If you have a staircase in the room, you have a built-in asset rather than a problem. The space under it, reached through sliding doors, can make a wonderful catchall for awkward equipment such as skis and camping gear. And, if you wish, you can even hinge each stair so that you can stow away in it small items like gardening tools that are out of season.

Some fortunate folk have rooms with fireplaces. They are wonderful for warmth, real and psychological; practical for indoor corn popping or midwinter marshmallow roasting. If you have a fireplace, do make it the focal spot of the room. Arrange sofa and chairs so that they turn toward the hearth. If you don't have a built-in fireplace, take a look at the many free-standing ones now on the market. Although most are of modern design, some reproduce the old-fashioned black metal stove that our great-grandparents used for warmth and cheer. When shopping for one of these devices, make sure the model you choose is properly vented for your room.

Some people complain not of architectural difficulties, but that they must decorate a room with no distinction at all. Boxlike modern rooms need extra features. There are now lightweight plastic beams which come in several wood finishes which can crisscross a ceiling or go down a wall Tudor-fashion. After you've cut them to size with a sharp knife, they are applied with a special adhesive. Or you can "brick" or "fieldstone" or otherwise cover a plain wall with a natural-looking material. Some bricks are the real McCoy—sliverlike sections which adhere to a special backing and are put up like wall tiles. Other products are made of fiber glass. Not only do they look like structural elements, they even have a cool "hand."

CHAPTER EIGHTEEN

THE STUDY

YEARS AGO, before the family room was invented, larger homes boasted a library which might or might not have a few books, but was primarily an informal living area which could be used in a relaxed way, apart from the parlor or living room which was always kept in pristine condition. In the 1930s and '40s, and to this day, this area was known more widely as a "den." Today, where this room still prevails, it is known as the study and is not to be confused with the family room, although both spaces share many attributes. Both are for informality apart from the formal living room; both are more or less off limits to guests; both are decorated in a casual way. The difference is that the study is essentially that: it is a kind of home office, a reading room, an area for quiet pursuits where a book or magazine can be enjoyed in solitude, a place where phonograph records can be played, a spot for writing a letter or taking a nap during an afternoon.

First of all, it is a relatively small room, not nearly so large as the family room or the living room. It is a hideaway and that usually implies modest dimensions. So furniture requirements are not great. There should be a desk with its chair, a lounge chair or two, and a small sofa, with at least one lamp table flanking it and a coffee table nearby. If it must double in brass, as it were, the sofa can be a dual purpose sofa-bed to sleep a guest in a pinch. In that case, there might be a small chest of drawers. If it has a fireplace, the arrangement is simple with lounge chairs on the window wall, sofa on the opposite wall, so that both can enjoy the fireplace at one end of the room. At the other, the desk can be positioned, with a window at the left of one seated at the desk for good natural light.

As for colors, this is a good place for a dark, though not somber, scheme. There is something about dark colors—particularly brown and the earth tones—that makes for quiet study, solitude, and contemplation. If any of this palette is included in the house-wide color plan, seize on it and build a scheme for the study around it. If not, use one or two of the accent colors of your over-all plan and extend them. This room is a good place for a monochromatic scheme, one muted color used for walls, ceiling, drapery, carpet, enlivened with a few well-chosen accent colors in throw pillows, decorative prints, lamp shades.

Again, like the family room, this one must never say "no," so it is important to choose upholstery coverings that are rugged. Tweedy fabrics are good, also leather for a man's retreat, a rough linen chintz for a woman's. Vinyls are too slick-looking for the most part to be suitable. Nubby fabrics for sofa and chairs might be in different tones of the same basic color. Draw draperies are a good choice for window treatment, because they impart the sense of envelopment that is important here. They should be lined and closed tight for naps and evening fastness. For a contemporary scheme, louvered shutters are a good choice. The room background is ideally wood paneling, but a wallpaper simulating wood grain or fabric applied to the walls can be most effective. Wallpaper in a geometric pattern, but not a floral or a busy design, is good. The important thing to remember when choosing wallpaper or fabric for a backdrop is that it not be distracting. If you're there to read or write a letter, you don't want to be drawn to some intricate pattern that disturbs you.

If you're doing a traditional scheme, an Oriental rug in quiet shades is perfect. In a contemporary scheme, a magnificent new Moroccan design in muted earth colors would serve. Wall-to-wall carpet is excellent, because, again, it imparts a sense of enclosure and quiet. A small Oriental or Moroccan thrown over it at the fireplace is a nice touch. If you have good wood floors and want to show them, don't show much. You don't want a click-clack as you walk about, so buy a good-size area rug. Hard-surface vinyl, marble, tile, etc. are not ideal choices because of their cold and noise factors.

This is another place for quite personal accessories. Photographs which always look out of place in a formal living room are delightful here, in silver frames on the desk, matted and framed in a wall grouping, or scattered on some of the small tables and on the mantel. Personal trophies, collections, and other memorabilia find their right home in the study. Desk accessories are important: a book of addresses and telephone numbers, a leather folder for current letters, bills and important papers, a functional table lamp, a holder for pencils and pens. For smokers, a big, fire-safe ashtray. If intimate entertaining is done here, a cellarette with liquors and glasses is a must, also a wet bar and an ice maker.

When it comes to illumination, a soft cove of light makes excellent background lighting. For specific lighting, you'll want the desk lamp, as mentioned, and suitable light for reading or sewing for the sofa and each of the chairs. An illuminated wall cabinet to display a collection of favorite china, trophies, or hobbies makes good background lighting, too. If you have good paintings on walls, ceiling spots are a must if they can be arranged, because they will pinpoint the paintings but keep the rest of the room in whatever degree of light you wish. You can enjoy the art in an otherwise darkened room, which makes for great repose.

Last but not least, books can form the background of the room and, displayed in their shelves with soft light playing over the leather bindings, they will lend great character to the room. A built-in shelf at each side of a fireplace makes for symmetry; cabinets below the shelves are good storage. If you want to conceal a bar or a personal wall safe, there are fake bindings sold by the foot which look for all the world like real leather books and can be hinged for access to what is behind. And for the book motif, without many volumes, don't forget the many wallpapers that have a bookshelf design. They're in muted colorings and make an effective background for a study.

A final word. The study is not the most popular room in the hierarchy of today's home, but it can be a most useful one. If you have an extra bedroom and don't know what to do with it, let this be a plea to consider a study. It will pay dividends in peace of mind, in quiet hours alone and apart, and in service to guests if you plan it as a dual-purpose space.

CHAPTER NINETEEN

THE MASTER BEDROOM

THE BEDROOM, for whomever it is designed, is the most personal room in the house. This is especially true of the master bedroom which should be an enjoyable retreat for husband and wife, a place to be alone together. This setting can have many shapes: It can be strictly a bedroom, or a bedroom that includes a sitting area, or separate rooms joined by dressing-bath facilities. It can double in the daytime as a home office, a reading room, a sewing center, or just be an adult refuge. There are as many ways to arrange these surroundings as there are personal living patterns. You may dream of a nostalgic setting with a canopied bed or have in mind silver foil on the wall and a furry spread. In a master bedroom, you have the chance to indulge your private whims, have your favorite things around you, choose colors that become you and do things for your well-being. Since the room (or rooms) should reflect the individuals, we will not attempt precise decorating formulas, but rather offer choices that you can adapt to your own space, budget, and life style.

The Practical Aspects

Before we get to appearance, which will differ with the individuals, let's dwell on functional needs, common to all. It takes careful planning to dovetail the practical elements and make the room work well for you. No amount of surface decoration will compensate for a disorganized room. So, let's examine what a bedroom is really for. To start with the obvious, it is a room for a bed and sleeping. You will want to choose a bed (or beds) to suit you and your husband and aim for a comfortable environment to help you get to sleep and stay that way. A bedroom is for storage of the myriad items of male and female apparel, in a variety of shapes and sizes, in and out of season. Efficient arrangement encourages neatness and preserves clothes. Ease of access preserves dispositions. A bedroom is for traffic during the daily routines of washing, dressing, and grooming.

A bedroom is for intimacy and any refinement that aids compatibility is a worthy investment. Color, beauty, lighting, and comfort are important here, plus an assurance of privacy. A bedroom can offer fringe benefits as desired: perhaps a lounge chair for a daytime pause, television, a desk for quiet correspondence, cupboards for hobby projects, health and exercise equipment, a minirefrigerator bar for late snacks, whatever completes your private life.

If a bedroom supplies all of these needs smoothly, it is a pretty good room, only awaiting the personal stamp of your decoration. Its appearance will evolve as you work out each step of planning along with us. Through your selection of furniture, fabrics, colors, and little touches, you are expressing yourself and making the room individually yours. If you let the way you *feel* about a selection guide you, rather than following imposed taste, it will be even more yours. If you are unsure, decorating guidelines can help you find a general direction.

You may already have a visual goal in mind, but you'd do better to keep your mind open at first. Explore new design thinking and possibilities in furnishings and arrangement. Since this will be your private world, you can shape it any way you like.

Start Your Plan with the Bed

First, decide whether you will want one or two beds and what size suits you and your partner best. It is a statistical fact that we are taller and heavier than our grandparents. When some of us outgrew the dimensions of the standard bed, the queen and king size were invented. As more long-limbed people discovered the comfort of ample space for sleeping, the larger sizes became standard. Blanket and sheet manufacturers now provide the extra sizes as regular items. In fact, the trend today is toward phasing out the standard double or "full" bed at fifty-four inches wide and establishing the queen size at sixty inches as the standard for two. Half of the current full bed, or twenty-seven inches, is only equivalent to the width of a baby's crib.

However, no individual is a statistic and there is still a good percentage of medium-sized people around. If a standard double bed provides sufficient sleeping space for two, there is no need to go to a larger size, particularly if it would crowd a small room. Besides, the bedding for a standard double costs less than for larger sizes. For the most width in a single unit, there is the king-size bed at seventy-six inches.

The twin bed, thirty-nine inches wide, provides separate sleeping comfort, as well as individual choice in the firmness of mattress and number of blankets. The beds can be placed apart or joined with a single headboard. Joined twins are two inches wider than a king-size bed. The twin also is expanding. A leading mail-order house offers a "super-twin," forty-eight inches wide. This approximates the width of the old three-quarter bed, which is being discontinued as such. So, if you have trouble finding a new three-quarter bed, try for the extra-wide twin. The dimensions mentioned have all been widths. Standard lengths for full and twin beds are seventy-five inches; queen- and king-size beds are eighty inches long, as are X-long doubles and twins. Beyond that, there are superlong sizes for basketball players and Texans. These are chiefly custom-made. Bedding is available to fit the standard sizes.

MAKE A ROOM PLAN

Because it is the largest element in a bedroom, the bed is placed first. Before you set your heart on a particular type of bed or beds, you will have to face the facts of space. Will your chosen bed fit into your room? Will it still leave room for other necessary bedroom functions? Now is the time to draw a plan to scale. This will tell you what types of beds you can consider realistically and whether there is still space for, say, a wide double dresser as well. On no account, however, stint on your physical comfort; have your bed large enough.

Make the room plan first on graph paper, quarter-inch scale. Measure the length and width of your room, marking the position of doors and windows and any other architectural breaks. Do this carefully, as the difference of a few inches may determine whether you can have a double or a queen-size bed. On contrasting paper, scale the beds you are considering and cut them out. Try the beds on the plan in different locations. The dimensions given on the bed-size chart are for box springs and mattresses. If a conventional bed with head- and footboard is considered, add six inches to the length; for a headboard only, add three or more inches, depending upon the style. Check whether access to your bedroom, space on the stairs and in the hall will permit the moving in of a king-size bed, if that is your choice. In cramped quarters, an alternative is to use twin box springs for the foundation and a foam top mattress in king size. The foam is more bendable than the inner-spring type and can go around corners.

For quick reference without a plan, here are some rough size estimates. A double bed flanked by two night tables takes about eight and a half feet of wall space; and twin beds with one table between them, the same. A queen-size bed with two tables takes nine feet, and a king (or joined twins) about ten and a half feet with two tables. Note that a king-size bed is almost square.

Consider the bed placement along with other needs in the room: access to storage, easy traffic patterns for dressing, and space for leisure activities. Its primary test placement, however, will reveal how much space there is available for other pieces. If the room is small, you might need to think "vertically" about clothes storage, choosing a tall chest instead of a wide dresser. It may seem, what with all the doors to the bath, closets, and entry, plus windows, that there is only one place the bed will go. Here are a few placements, some standard, some unusual.

Placement of a Double, Queen- or King-size Bed

1. Give the bed major billing right in the center of a long wall. Dramatize it with a canopy or decorative treatment behind it. In such a layout, the bed serves nicely to separate the dressing actions of partners, allowing room on each side for individual night tables and areas for clothes storage and grooming.

2. Place the double bed off center on a long wall. This allows space at the larger end of the room for another major furniture grouping, such as easy chairs and a television set, or a game or coffee table, as you please. To save space, omit one night table and use another piece, a dresser or desk to hold the bedside lamp. There is no need for symmetry in arrangement. Asymmetry can be in balance.

3. If the room is long and narrow, try the bed centered on the short wall farthest from the doorway. This position accommodates a room divider or draperies to further insulate the sleeping area. The near end of the room is left free as a dressing, sitting, or work area.

4. A little off-beat, but a solution to save space in a narrow room: Place the long side of a double bed against the wall, like a superdivan. Use a mattress combination the long way against a king-size headboard; it will fit. Or make a backdrop of drapery. Add bolsters or oversize pillows.

5. Treating the bed as an island, placed right in the center of the room. The bed can be a box bed with built-in counters, aimed for this purpose; or it can be a box spring and mattress on legs, served by low tables. Or the head can be placed against the covered rear side of a dresser or low chest. A circular bed, naturally, is also free-standing. One practical advantage of this arrangement is that the walls are free for storage.

6. If the room seems impossibly broken up by windows, don't give up. A bed is not usually located under a window because of the possibility of drafts and too much light. But, given a tight opening (or one made so by weatherstripping or storm windows) and ample draperies with snug shades, the bed can be comfortable. If the window presents a bad view, it can be permanently shielded. And a window with its architectural interest and drapery can provide a backdrop for the bed. If the window is narrower than the bed, equalize the sizes by draping the window to the bed width.

Placement of Twin Beds

1. One arrangement places a shared night table, or low dresser, or small desk between two twins. Though standard, this takes major space in the center of the room and doesn't make the most of the versatility possible with twin beds. Twins can be located almost anywhere in the room and often help to solve an irregular plan.

2. Twin beds, of course, can be pushed together, in which case they roughly equal the width of a king-size bed and are treated the same in planning. They can share a common headboard, stand solid, or be mounted on swing-out frames for easy making.

3. Twins can be placed parallel along opposite walls, thus freeing the center of the room for easy chairs around a fireplace, perhaps, or for just plain running room, or for making a small room seem larger. This plan allows the sense of privacy desired by some without going as far as a separate room. A room divider, such as drapery, would enhance this privacy. The arrangement is ideal for a shared children's room.

An exotic look is in order for the master bedroom since it is the most personal haven in the home. A startling background color combines with a sharp paisley design in fabric and area rug. Note how fabric is used to upholster bed and chest, how folding screens in wall color stack unobtrusively.

WALLCOVERING INDUSTRY BUREAU (IMPERIAL)

A small sitting area at the windows is a nicety for husband and wife to take a cup of morning coffee or play a game of cards. Brown and white unify this master bedroom, in a geometric spread in counterpoint with a paisley print for three-bay window shades, the area below sill, even a small Parsons table.

WINDOW SHADE MANUFACTURERS ASSOCIATION

An ensemble of matching fabric and wallpaper in a documentary floral pattern helps to add authenticity to a Colonial bedroom. Fabric restates the background in small ways—throw pillow for the armchair, dust ruffle for the bed. Note how the accent color, yellow, is used in a stool seat, an accessory, even in house plants on white painted corner stand.

The tradition-minded couple would
love this Early American bedroom.
The mellow look of pine is seen
not only in antique furniture, but
also in cornice and dado. Blue and
white china high on the magnificent cupboard shows how accessories can be used to interpret
color scheme.

The master suite can be coordinated, pattern and colorwise, from upholstery,
linen and bedside bouquet to towels and wallpaper in the adjoining bath.
Canopy and back panel of the twin beds were made from extra sheets. Careful shopping discovered the wallpaper of similar color and pattern.

BEDSPREAD BY BATES FABRICS, INC.

Headboard for a double bed was designed of 2 inch by 2 inch lumber and a yard of the same fabric as table skirt and fringed spread. White is a crisp accent in this master hideaway—in area rug that sets off the bed, in Parsons writing table, even the French telephone.

A warm and restful look pervades this bedroom, featuring a breakfast table and chairs and a dressing area. Old barn beams add architectural interest and negate the need for a headboard for the bed.

CARPET OF CRESLAN BY PATCRAFT

4. Another space-saving plan places the twin beds at right angles along the wall, separated and served by a square table in the corner. In a guest room used only occasionally for sleeping, one bed can be slid partially under the tabletop and space is conserved during the day. Turn the beds into divans by adding bolsters and you have a sitting room. This scheme also works for the one-room apartment, which must be a living room by day and a bedroom by night.

THE DECORATION PLAN

Up to now, we've been dealing with the physical layout of the room so that you can operate in it with ease. Now we come to decoration, the visible overlay that by your choice in furnishings, style, and color makes the room individually yours. More than any other room in the house, the master bedroom should reflect your desires. It is a background for the oneness you have together and is a very private world. Its design can be absolutely as you like it. The room should be conceived to weather a range of emotions, to serve times of fond affection, but equally important, to soothe when nerves are on edge. A comfortable and eye-pleasing bedroom is a pacifier. Since eye pleasing is so personal a matter, we pose no decorating rules, merely offer guidelines to help you through your decorating choices.

If you are starting from scratch and are new at decoration, you might play a "like-don't like" game with your spouse: testing your reactions to various style ideas. Cross off those that draw a negative reaction from either of you. Perhaps you can agree enthusiastically on one. Review the previous sections on style, color, and pattern, and develop your "game."

CHOICES IN BEDS

Time was that the choice of a bed was a simple matter. One chose twins or a double in the style of the bedroom "set." "His" and "Hers" dressers and night tables came with it and everything matched. A bed with head and foot was delivered to hold up the mattresses and all one had to do was make up the bed, (sheets were white, naturally), put clothes away, add a lamp or two, and the room was in service. Such ready furnishings may still be the ideal solution for some if, on careful analysis, a complete bedroom group serves the needs of storage and living and room plan. But, more often than not, today's house offers some built-in storage; selected single pieces serve needs and tastes more precisely; there is an urge for more imagination to personalize the room.

Breaking away from the norm most completely is the bed which can be anything that two people want, given the function of comfort. A bed can be a simple box spring and mattress with an attractive spread for a contemporary room. Or it can be canopied, fully or partially, in both traditional or contemporary style, with or without a four-poster bed. There is such a revival of interest in canopies that we have a special section later on how to achieve them. Or the bed can be unusual: an imposing antique like a carriage bed or a Victorian brass bed (be sure the size of an old bed will fit you), or a contemporary structure of molded plastic. There are modern box beds that surround the mattress with counter space; there are electric beds that adjust to different comfort positions for back and knees at the touch of a switch. Review also what furniture manufacturers have to offer in beds that accentuate styling themes. There are many pleasant surprises.

In any case, start with the proper underpinnings for the box springs. You can buy a metal frame in all standard sizes that will support a regular box spring, provide legs, and contain hardware for attachment to a headboard, if desired. There are swing-out frames for joined twins to facilitate bedmaking. Or you can purchase the spring fitted with legs. Six are best for long-lasting support. Box springs aimed for standing on the floor and possible attachment to headboards have specially fortified frames. Do not attempt to attach legs to a regular mattress intended for resting on bed rails. Support it with a metal frame, or build your own box frame out of wood.

HEADBOARDS AND BACKDROPS

Headboards plus a mattress combination are the ideal solution for many for reasons of space, economy, or the chance for unusual design. A headboard can be an elaborate affair or merely suggested. For a king-size bed, a headboard with center height will help to balance the width.

Most manufacturers of bedroom furniture offer a headboard to match the rest of their line, so you can be consistent in style if you choose. Even if your other furniture has no special style, the headboard can set a theme. Selections range across the whole field of design. Traditional wood patterns include the fiddleback, gallery, ladderback, pediment, cornice. There are contemporary designs in cane, metal, clear plastic, rattan, and other materials. Or the headboard can be upholstered. It might be a magnificent tufted structure with an ornate silhouette or a functional padded vinyl backrest with twin sections that adjust to the desired slant. Some headboards offer extra services around the bed. A familiar low-cost unit is the bookcase headboard, helpful when space is lacking for night tables, or a simple covered box with a flat counter would serve a similar purpose. There are also headboards that span beyond the bed and provide the functions of night tables on each side. The design effect of a headboard might partake more of architecture than furniture. For novelty, weathered shutters have been used effectively, also carved doors (placed sideways), iron gates, shingles, simulated brick and stone. These materials are not meant to be leaned against. Wedge pillows or bolsters provide the buffer.

Instead of a headboard, you might use a decorative panel to dramatize the bed. This could be of plywood paneling with a fine wood veneer: one four-foot-wide piece with a four-inch border would frame a double bed. Or a panel can be simulated with molding that frames fabric or wall covering of the same pattern as the spread. Or just glue on fabric in a panel and border it with self-stick trim repeated elsewhere. The panel can be canopy height, between six and seven feet, or to the ceiling if the room is low. Over a king-size bed, twin panels help to break up the width. Or, for greater softness, drape the bedhead wall with fabric, hung on a curtain rod. You might top off the folds with a swag gathered up at each corner. Or for a wide bed, create twin swags by drawing the fabric through a center loop and gathering it up at the sides. Use a print behind the bed and a matching solid for the swag, or vice versa. Or combine two prints.

Dressing the Bed

Since the bed or beds form an enormous expanse, they must be treated carefully or they will overpower the other decoration in the room. Pattern must be balanced carefully: A bold pattern for such a tremendous expanse can be justified only if other elements in the bedroom scheme are plain colored or if the room is quite large. The same rule goes for heavily textured bed covering—furs, thick string rugs, and the like.

The traditional company garb for a bed is the floor-length spread in a decorative fabric. This can be a simple unseamed type that drapes over the surface or the more formal fitted spread with welting that rims the top edges. There are many versions, some tailored with pinch pleats easing the corners, some with gathered folds. The welting can be of the same fabric, suggested to underplay an oversized bed; or it can be in a contrasting color or design, such as moss fringe. This calls attention to the bed, makes a double, say, or a twin look larger. In the same way, two stripes (ribbon or trim) running lengthwise on a spread about twelve to eighteen inches from the edges will slim down a queen- or king-sized bed. A full spread, with its unbroken line from the top edges to the floor, adds height to the bed and in a rich fabric can look elegant. In general, a fitted spread costs more than the unseamed type, but the final price depends upon the fabric chosen and the details of trimming.

A spread, merely for "show," off limits for husband and children, is out of date. You can have an opulent look in a modern fabric that is wrinkle-resistant, soil-repelling, easily washable, and permits daytime stretching out. Still, no matter how practical the fabric, the sheer bulk of a floor-length spread discourages the effort to take it off and put it back on, particularly with the larger beds. Too often, it is reserved just for company while the daily appearance of the bed suffers.

The answer to this is the popular smaller seamless throw or coverlet. Its partner is the dust ruffle which protects and conceals the box spring, so the lower part of the bed is always dressed, even when in use. A throw ends just below the top mattress, overlapping the dust ruffle, and this combination fully dresses mattresses on legs. With a box bed that conceals the bottom mattress, the dust ruffle is not needed; do give the box springs a zippered cover, though. Since throws are smaller, they are easier to handle than a full spread when folding or making the bed or washing, and they can be removed easily for a nap, if desired. In a do-work-yourself house, the throw-ruffle treatment provides the easiest bed to make or get into.

The idea of throws has stimulated imagination in bed dressing. All sorts of fabric and designs are suitable and can echo your decorating theme. Patchwork patterns reflect the nostalgic beginnings of throws. An antique quilt is a treasure; if you have one, strengthen it with backing for continued use. Or find a patchwork print. Or make your own patchwork quilt and brag about it. Designs are available in neddlework centers, or invent your own.

The Canopied Bed—Variations

If you really want to give your bed decorating importance and the sleeper a sense of shelter, consider a canopy or canopy "look." The current revival of interest in canopies has produced a wide choice in beds, both traditional and contemporary in design, both budget and high priced, and unlimited homemade variations. Basically, a canopy bed has four posts of equal height, from six to seven feet, carrying a frame or tester. This may be flat or curved, as in some Colonial designs. Over the frame goes a hood or canopy of fabric, finished with a valance. The full treatment calls for lengths of drapery covering each post, which by inference could be drawn to close completely, as in early castles. There are also handsome tester beds with wooden canopies that are used as they are, without drapery.

Given a four-poster and its own frame, you can clothe it fully for a lavish, cozy effect. In a small room, this might be overpowering. For a lighter feeling, omit the draperies at the foot and just use the hood, valance, and draperies at the head posts. Or for even more restraint, good with twin beds, omit the hood and draperies and just rim the top frame with a valance.

The bed can be tailored with solid-color fabric and pinch pleats on the valance or frilly with a floral print and ruffles. Or be individual with your own handicraft: Crochet a hood and valance or make a hood of string tightly wrapped close together across and around the frame. Or simply stretch a lovely fabric from the foot end of the frame to the head end and down behind the headboard, in soft pleated or gathered folds.

The most expensive way to a full canopy is to purchase a bed with frame and have the hood and draperies custom-made in a fabric of your choice. This is fine, if you are long on cash and short on the time or skill to make your own. Easier on the pocketbook are readymade canopies, available with matching spreads and window draperies, a help in co-ordinating the whole room. But actually, making your own canopy doesn't require great sewing skill and can yield great pride of accomplishment. In fact, armed with verve and imagination and sometimes a staple gun, you can take off in countless directions. For some designs, all you need is paint or glue. Here are a few ideas for achieving the canopy look.

Lacking a four-poster, you can create the illusion of one by erecting four posts, joined and braced at the top by a frame. Use four-by-fours or poles to the usual height of a canopy. Drape any of the ways suggested. Or omit the yardage, and merely suggest an enclosure. Cover the posts and frame with fabric, glued on with white glue; or sand and lacquer the wood. The shape becomes a modern object, defining space.

Broaden the usability of your bedroom by including an arrangement for dining. In elegant bedroom a round table skirted in beige velvet and paired with white bamboo chairs can also serve for letter writing and paper work. Room has serene white, rose and beige color scheme.

INTERIOR BY EVELYN LEROY, N.S.I.D.

A canopy is best used in a tall room, where there can be space above it. In a low-ceilinged room, you can carry the posts and frame all the way to the ceiling and anchor them there. Put a wood or fabric valance around the top, and lo, a canopy. You might cover the wood valance (posts, too) with self-stick vinyl or shiny foil or mirrored squares and call the job complete. Or continue with draperies at each post and maybe a top gathered underneath like a harem tent. Or you can really simplify matters. Forget the posts and frame and just hang draperies from ceiling rods mounted at right angles directly above the four bed corners. Gather the draperies at bed level with tasseled silk rope or matching tiebacks. Or hang strands of beads the same way.

Perhaps all that is needed in a small room is a canopy effect over the headboard. Install a box valance (which might also contain strip lighting), glue on fabric or wall covering, or paint it, maybe add a self-stick trimming; hang draperies down each side. When choosing a canopy fabric, relate it to other fabrics on the bed or in a room. It might match the spread or dust ruffle or draperies or upholstered chair. Often, a meaningful print is selected, one that you like and that carries out the room's theme. You might also combine prints; one lining the bed draperies and matching the spread, the other facing out and echoing the bed draperies.

SELECTING FURNITURE

If you have no bedroom furniture at all, a matched set in your chosen style can be an instant solution, often at a money-saving price. But a full set is no bargain if it doesn't quite fit your requirements or if you must buy more furniture than you need. A better alternative is to select single pieces that suit exactly, even though the price per item is slightly more. Sometimes a good buying pattern is to start with minimum basic pieces and add to them as the budget allows. If this is your plan, be sure the design you choose is "open stock," so you can find compatible furniture later. Ask about a possible time limit.

If you favor wood tones, you'll find ample in the popular walnut and traditional maple. Teak and mahogany are expensive favorites, birch and oak are less in cost. Returning on the market after two decades are blond woods. Woods can be mixed in a room, light tones with dark, but make the mix look purposeful: Have at least two pieces in the secondary tone. This freedom enables you to combine furniture you have, what you inherit, and some you find at a tag sale.

Don't forget the possibilities of painted pieces, lacquered shiny or antiqued. There is handsome stenciled furniture to buy, or again, you can custom-stencil your own with ready patterns or with a motif from your chosen fabric. Stenciling is easy when done with a spray.

To store the most in a minimum space, choose the units for combining into a compact wall. While the idea of flush bases and matching depths is usually identified with contemporary style, you can have units in traditional furniture. The wood finishes, contours, and hardware carry out the design feeling of Colonial, eighteenth century, and other styling. Such open stock matchable units have an advantage if you are just starting a home in, say, a temporary apart-

For the contemporary master bedroom, an interesting solution was found in spring mattresses atop a platform made of plywood and painted to blend with other woodwork. Mattresses are covered in the same small cotton print used for wall covering and for draperies with wood rings on a wood rod. The effect becomes an almost totally upholstered look.

ment. They can be added to, recombined, and given new uses when you expand later. A dresser doubles as the base to a china closet, a desk can become a vanity, and so on, suiting the piece to the circumstance.

The Bedroom Background

Walls, ceiling, floor, and window expanses can be decorated to your most exotic color preference. As we mentioned earlier, the master bedroom is the one space where you can depart from a house-wide color theme if you want to since it should reflect your most personal color preference. Chances are, however, that you have used a house-wide theme with colors that you like so that continuing one or all of these in the bedroom will work no hardship. You might consider using a deeper, richer tone of one of the colors if you want more drama; if you want greater serenity, choose a lighter, airier tone. This, of course, refers to the painted wall. If you want wallpaper, choose a small pattern for greater serenity, a bolder one for drama; the same rule of light and dark applies to the colors in the paper. Some people associate dark somber hues with slumber and if you do, you can paint or paper walls and ceiling accordingly, creating a true cavern effect.

Another solution for walls is to hang fabric. This creates an amazing aural effect that is conducive to slumber and repose. The absorbent fabric sound-deadens the room and the acoustics are somewhat like those in a recording studio. A wall of heavy drapery can give much the same effect. For a total sense of enclosure, you can also fabric-cover the ceiling or create a tentlike effect. Otherwise, paint the ceiling a somewhat darker shade of the wall color, if walls are fairly light. That will tend to bring the ceiling down, visually, and give greater intimacy.

Flooring

Wall-to-wall carpet in the bedroom does more than decorate. It provides warmth, softness underfoot, and absorbs sounds. Visually, it enlarges the room and unites the various furniture elements. If full carpeting is not advisable for you currently, then at least have a room-size rug. Or treat yourself to thick bedside rugs, maybe furry-type ones, which go over carpet, too. You may want an area rug to isolate a sitting or dressing area. Locate it so it doesn't present a tripping problem in the dark or in a busy traffic lane. The question of a plain or patterned carpet is related to the total scene. You might emphasize a beautiful pattern on the floor by choosing drapery and bed fabrics in related solid colors. Or use a solid color in the carpet to hold together lively pattern elsewhere.

Window Treatment

Windows are especially important in the bedroom where the control of light and air is critical. You will want light for daytime activities, but will want to shut it out for lazy mornings, afternoon naps, and in case of illness. You will want air both by day and night, so be sure to choose a treatment that can be manipulated easily to let in air. Window shades are available in a room-darkening material that looks the same as the translucent shade but blocks out sunlight. They can be laminated in a fabric to blend with your color and pattern scheme or are available in solid colors. There are also Venetian blinds designed for the bedroom. These close with a tight overlap to prevent light streaks, and for even greater darkness, some have channels at the sides and bottom to mask any light leaks at these spots. When it comes to traverse draperies, you can make them more effective against glare with an opaque lining.

If you decide on draperies, you can underplay the windows in a small room by using plain fabric in a color that matches the wall paint or patterned fabric that matches the wallpaper. If you wish to give a small window greater visual importance, hang the draperies well beyond the side frames and hang a deep valance above them. Other fabric solutions include cafe curtains and Roman shades. Your choice of window treatment will depend a great deal on whether you have a view to conceal or enjoy, the nearness or lack of neighbors, and how much insulation you need to black out noise and extreme temperatures. The presence of an air conditioner and its placement will also affect your choice of treatment. If you live in an area where air conditioning is required all or part of the year, you must find a window solution that permits air passage along with light control. One solution is the use of movable shutters which can be closed for light transmission, opened for air.

LIGHT IN THE BEDROOM

Although the bedroom presumably is for sleeping (and so would require no special lighting), it does lend itself to several other activities—dressing, grooming, reading, studying, and occasional writing. The decor of the bedroom is usually designed to make it a restful place, and its lighting should also be unobtrusive yet functional.

Except in many apartments, the central ceiling fixture has been eliminated from most bedrooms. For over-all lighting you can rely on valances or wall brackets. If a ceiling fixture is used it should hug the ceiling and be decorative, even gemlike and delicate. A purely masculine bedroom could take a simple, contemporary fixture, designed on crisp lines.

Placement of a large bed is often a problem in the master suite. Here, the window wall was the only possible location and, to prevent drafts and to give that wall a unified look, a series of hinged panels was created, covered in the same small-patterned fabric as the rest of the background. For decorative counterpoint, a large, daisy-like print was used for the spread.

Obviously, the two areas in the bedroom that need the best lighting for visual work are the bed itself for reading and writing and the bureau or dressing table where a man and woman may perform some grooming chores. In either case it is necessary for a person to see well, without strain. How can you achieve functional lighting for these areas, while at the same time not distract from the room's decor?

If the bed or beds are to be shared by two people, two separate reading lights or one that offers built-in flexibility should be used.

Bed and Bedding Sizes

TYPE	BEDS, MATTRESSES, FITTED SHEETS, (PRESHRUNK)	FLAT SHEETS	BLANKETS	BEDSPREADS
Twin	39"x75"	72"x104" (no iron) 72"x108" (cotton)	66"x90"	Standard Twin: 82"x112"
Long Twin	39"x80"	72"x115" (no iron) 72"x120" (cotton)	66"x108"	X-long Twin
Wide Twin (or) Three-fourths	48"x75"	Rare: use standard double.	Standard Double	Standard Double
Full or Double	54"x75"	81"x104" (no iron) 80"x108" (cotton)	80"x90"	Standard Double: 96"x112"
Queen	60"x80"	90"x115" (no iron) 90"x120" (cotton)	90"x108"	X-long Double
Calif. King	72"x84"	108"x115" (no iron) 108"x120" (cotton)	90"x108"	120"x120"*
King	76"x80"	108"x115" (no iron) 108"x120" (cotton)	90"x108"	120"x120"*

The above sizes are the most-used standards. Mattress sizes may vary with the manufacturer, may be one inch narrower.

* For spreads in large sizes, measure the individual bed; take the width of the mattress plus twice the length of the drop.

The lights can be mounted on the wall focusing directly on the person reading, and individually adjustable, or they could be separate lamps standing on the bedside tables. They could take the form of a built-in strip in or above the headboard, or a wall bracket that sheds light both upward and downward. For the latter, two separate tubes and switches are advisable. A modern replacement for a bedside lamp is the hanging pendant with tinted, textured globe. To read, however, you would need supplemental light from a strip over the headboard.

Although chandeliers may lend an air of opulence to a master bedroom, they are seldom practical. Wall-mounted crystal lamps or Colonial-styled globes with hobnail glass may be placed on either side of a mirror or flank a bed or pair of beds. Gaslight-type fixtures have also been adapted to lend charm to a boudoir. Central or wall fixtures should have dimmer controls.

While a pair of small standing lamps on the bureau or dressing table will give satisfactory light for adjusting a man's tie or studying the effect of a lady's jewelry, they do not provide good lighting for more careful grooming. If you do not have a separate dressing-room area or adequate bathroom lighting for shaving and make-up, you will need a portable make-up mirror surrounded by theatrical-type bulbs.

CHAPTER TWENTY

THE CHILD'S ROOM

THE VERY basis of a child's room is change and the key to decorating it is to realize that it should change every year. Decorating a child's room is no ordinary project, because it should reflect your child, not you. It should be the room he or she dreams of, not the room that you dreamed of. You see, a child's room is more than just another room. A child's room is a laboratory as well as a place to eat and sleep and study. It's his living room, the place where he'll spend most of his waking hours. It's where he'll learn about life, as well as about books, where he'll develop his interests, make his friendships, discover the world. Much as every child is different, so every child's room is different. Every child, whatever age, gives lots of clues as to the kind of room he wants, the kind of room he's happiest in. So read on to find the perfect room for your individual child.

Most experts suggest that you redecorate, or at least re-evaluate your children's room four times before they go off on their own. You will want to decorate a nursery for their infancy, then a short time later for their preschool years. Once school starts, their needs change once again and when they enter their teens, their interests, indeed, their whole life style changes drastically. Experts also say that little girls need attractive furnishings and little boys don't. Don't believe a word of it! Some little boys are very interested in their rooms, some little girls couldn't care less. Some children take an interest in their rooms when they're two or three. Some teen-age girls never do. These are just the norms for children's rooms, and so much depends on your individual child. Make adjustments for your own baby, and thank goodness that your child is different!

INFANCY

These are the needs for a nursery: crib, chest, light, table and chair for mother. Nice to have: bottle warmer, Bathinette, refrigerator.

Baby isn't at all interested in color and design. He's interested in sleeping and eating. He needs air and light and plenty of room to grow. The frilly nursery is what *you* think a nursery should be. Many a baby has slept in the proverbial trunk, with no permanent damage done, either physically or psychologically. A place to sleep is all he needs. The absolute must for a nursery is an environment in which you can control air and light. Baby's comfort is paramount. The optionals are things that are designed for your convenience. To control light in the room, have Venetian blinds or shades, plus curtains, so baby will be able to sleep during the daylight hours. Because baby's eyes are very sensitive and are attracted to light, don't allow unshaded bulbs within his range of vision. The ceiling light (which he will be looking at as he lies in his crib or bassinet) should have a reflector shield. As for air, a screen is helpful and really necessary if baby is sharing your room. It will protect him from drafts as well as control the amount of light his crib receives. It also has the psychological value of cutting down the amount of space around him so he won't feel lost in a large area. The other needs for infancy are optional. Of course it's much easier to change diapers and give baby a bath in the same room as his crib. But in reality, he can be carried to another area of the home. The same applies to a chair and table in the nursery. That's your pleasure. How nice to feed him next to the crib and think pleasant thoughts of what he'll grow up to be! To save on your footsteps, it would be lovely to arrange to have a hot plate near the baby's crib so the bottles can be warmed while you rest nearby. And a small refrigerator, too?

PRESCHOOL

These are the needs for the two-to-six-year-olds: crib-to-bed, chest, table and chairs, pin-up light over bed, light over table and chairs, wall display area, shelves for storage, clothes storage chest or closet. Truly two to six are the wonder years. This is the age of the greatest growth, the greatest adventure. In these formative years, your child learns about color and form and shape. He is curious about the world around him and his room is the field for discovery. A relaxed mother will share this great discovery through his eyes. A tense mother will just think he is "getting into things" and "messing up everything." Be a sharing mother by decorating his room for his size and his interests and by remembering that it will be a long time before he learns the virtues of neatness and cleanliness.

Primarily, and most important, remember that he is only a few feet tall. What the room looks like and how it functions below your waist is much more vital to your child than what's above the area his tiny hands can reach. And remember, secondly, that this is a great learning period for both muscles and mind. Arranging for development of both is a function of decorating a room. Muscles are developed by grasping, running, jumping. Even putting things away on open shelves (that are the right height!) is a way of co-ordinating hand muscles. And running little automobiles and trucks for endless hours over the floor develops proper co-ordination, too. Toys, of course, are the great awakeners of the mind, as well as ways of developing muscle groups. You and your child will learn his capabilities from his toys, so give plenty of room for their storage.

The third point to keep in mind for the two-to-six age is that a child changes and changes quickly within these years. Furnishings should be flexible and adaptable to his growth, should be able to change as he changes. If you have a son, you'll find that he'll need a lot more storage space than a girl. The miscellany that boys accumulate, it's been found, is almost double that of girls. He'll also need more floor space to play with erector sets or wrestle with friends. So if there's a choice of rooms, by all means give your son the larger one, whatever his age. And, by the way, expect it to be the messier, scruffier one, too.

As for the furniture itself, it should "grow" with the child. The table is most important. It should be large, with a hard surface that will take plenty of knocks, since this is a "laboratory" for junior's activities. With all the "furniture-in-parts" stores, it will be possible to replace the legs with longer ones as your child shoots up in height. Ditto the chairs. The number of chairs depends on how social your child is. Four or six kids may be trooping into his room every day. On the other hand, if your youngster is a loner, you won't have to stock up on small chairs for his visitors.

At some time during this period, usually at the start of nursery school, your little one will be ready to leave the crib and get a regular bed. There isn't any need to get a junior or youth bed first, but that

Teens with tiny rooms might consider the airy chic of wicker furniture. The light scale makes it ideal for bed/sitting rooms. This small room becomes a real den with the wildlife running riot on the walls and floor as well. The brilliant color combination of marigold yellow and shocking pink, as well as the wallpaper design, cuts the apparent size of the room and adds to the intimacy, but desk top and accessories in stark white cool down the heat of the jungle!

Built-ins can achieve a feminine as well as a practical look. This room for a very-loved little girl provides room for a visiting sleep-over guest via a trundle bed, plus plenty of space for putting away toys in the floor-to-ceiling unit. Note that the gay design is carried out in the easy-care, easy-to-apply hard-surface flooring.

Built-in modular units, similar to the types used in dens and living rooms, are a practical measure in rooms for both boys and girls. Units with and without drawers, counter surfaces and shelves are all available. Here the walnut arrangement goes well with the wood flooring while the bold plaid bedspread, shade and curtains give proper balance to the heavy scale of the storage pieces.

Thank heavens for little girls, and thank heavens for handy mothers! This lucky child has ceiling, walls and window shades made of an adhesive-backed fabric that is coordinated with her curtains and bedspread. The curtain treatment is duplicated in a small canopy that creates a niche for the bed. Colorful cubes on wheels can be rolled about for seating, are useful for storage, too.

Attic rooms are often delegated to the very young. This attic solves two problems: slanted walls and a room that is shared by children of different sexes. A gay, plaid fabric (pink for her, yellow for him) gives lightness and joy to a room that gets little sunlight. Sheeting fabric is applied to the walls as well as the sew-it-yourself dust ruffle and dressing-table skirt that is incorporated into the storage unit.

An Early American home need not call for traditional furnishings, as this shared bedroom dramatically proves. The floor is left unfinished and many of the beams are left in their natural state, although the clapboard wall is painted white. Red, white and blue, a recent, as well as an "early" American color scheme, has great appeal for girls as well as for boys.

Every inch counts in a bedroom that's shared by two young ladies. In this case, large quantities of white were used to make the room seem larger than it is. The other way to achieve space was by making floor-to-ceiling room dividers function as night tables with open and closed storage as well. To add freshness, the same fabric from the bedspread was run up the wall just behind the bed, as well as on the comfortable rocker.

Three in a room is as difficult to do as the Mexican hat trick! Start with a triple-decker bed and stick to simple, easy-to-clean furnishings like this tubular steel group with plastic surfaces. Make sure to select a color scheme (such as avocado green and blue) that is easy for lots of people (or at least three) to live with for a long time to come.

French Provincial is high on the list of favorites for teens. With today's small bedrooms, a little ingenuity is often needed to accommodate all the necessary furniture. This formal young lady chose a matching headboard, night table and petite desk. Then, instead of a cumbersome bureau, she hung shelves on chains for storage space. To keep the modern feeling, she selected up-to-date artwork and accessories plus an orange and pink color combination.

A boys' room should be able to take the rough and tumble of its active inhabitants with their varied interests. This shared room has a large round table and a commodious countertop in a plastic laminate that gives heavy usage with light care. Pegboard wall holds baskets for desk equipment and knickknacks, and provides a record of changing interests. Window treatment does not detract from wall arrangements.

WINDOW SHADE MANUFACTURERS ASSOCIATION

A handy mother can create a French Country bedroom for her youngster by investing time rather than money. Basic ingredients are a sewing machine and candy-striped sheets. The sheets are on the walls, curtains, laminated window shade and sewing-machine-quilted bedspread. To carry out the European look, moldings at the ceiling, floor and window frame were painted a deep color.

A shared bedroom can express two very distinct personalities. Bed on either end with a storage/divider right down the center creates two completely individual settings, even down to the carpet. Storage areas under both the bed plus drawers in divider give ample space. Note that the boy's side has a desk, while the pre-school toddler insisted on a miniature dressing table just like mommy's.

CRESLAN ACRYLIC FIBER

Bunk beds are often the answer in a family with a very social child. What's more they're fun, as well as functional. These beds can stack or be used separately. Ditto the cube tables which can be put together to form a large work surface or provide individual seating units. Fire-engine red carpet in a synthetic, ease-care fiber sparks the setting and takes daily punishment from its energetic master with no change.

This is the kind of room that needs lots of little chairs because its owner's friends will surely want to visit. Bright, bold colors, especially in the wallpaper, make it a sure winner with children. And parents (especially mothers) will like the gay collection of boxes that keeps the mess prettily out of sight. Note that all the furniture is close to the ground, within a child's easy reach.

depends on your child. Some youngsters love to feel grownup in a bed just like Daddy's or Mama's. Others simply feel lost in a big bed and need the youth bed as an intermediate transition.

During this age period, you will probably move the chair and table for your own use out of the room to provide space for the shelves and chest that will store toys and games and books. Keep all these storage items low so your child can reach for whatever he wants without calling you, or climbing on chairs to open drawers.

With this in mind, you might consider the dual-purpose sleeping unit known as the storage bed. This has a mattress and bolsters covered, day-bed fashion, with good-looking upholstery fabric, while underneath is a generous pull-out drawer for toys, or pillows and blankets.

Another important change in the room for this age is in the wall treatment. Whether you select paint or paper or plastic laminate, one of the walls should be a "learning" wall. Make it cork, make it pegboard, or make it just wooden strips. But make a wall that can adapt to a child's artwork or to pictures that will stimulate his interest. This learning wall should change weekly or monthly. The wall will build his ego and encourage his interest in different subjects.

SCHOOL YEARS

These are the needs for school years: twin bed, closet for clothes, storage, bookcase, and chest for clothes, book and game storage, desk, lamp and chair for study, comfortable chair and lamp for reading, lamp next to bed. The ages of six to twelve witness still another change in the life of your child and your child's room. The days of "all play" are gone, and part of his time will be spent in school. When he's home, part of his home time will be spent in homework. The need for durable, resilient flooring is still important, but you'll find that the wide, open space in the middle of the room is being encroached upon. There's the desk and the study chair, for one. Studying should be done in a pleasant atmosphere, and, if possible, away from the play area in the room. The chair itself should be a comfortable one, but not "too" comfortable since an upright position is the best for writing at a desk. Good lighting and a proper writing surface are, of course, important at this age.

This is also the time when your child will become quite social and have classmates in, especially over weekends when his life will begin to revolve around his school and school chums rather than his home and family. At some point, between the ages of six and twelve, your youngster is going to ask if "Johnny" (or "Jane") can sleep over. So you'll find that the wide, open spaces you've so carefully arranged will be diminished even further.

Along with the serious studying and the social needs, there are the growing hobbies. Storage needs become more particularized. Boys need space for keeping "collections," and girls for a suddenly enormous wardrobe. As a parent, you'll probably be fighting the problem of space!

TEEN YEARS

These are the needs for the teen years: twin bed plus one bed for overnight guest, desk, lamp and chair for study, chair and lamp for reading, storage space for clothes, schoolwork, games, radio, television, lamp for bedside reading. When does your youngster become a teen? Maybe ten, maybe eleven, maybe he'll be good enough to wait until he's thirteen! These days, most youngsters take on all the attributes of teens a bit younger. It's the stage between childhood and adulthood. The wise mother will gracefully step out of the picture at this period.

At this stage, girls will probably spend more time at home in their room (with friends and the door tightly closed, usually) than boys will. If they haven't campaigned for overnight guests before, expect it now—in spades! Also expect new demands for storage space for phonograph and records, TV, radio and all those new clothes which are so important. Almost all girls take an interest in what their rooms look like in this period. Let them decide for themselves. Be sure that they have the basics, desk, lamp, chair, good bed, but beyond that, let them make their own decisions. Many teens think ahead toward marriage and letting your formerly little girl make purchases that she can use in later years is not an unwise one. Well-designed furniture and lamps and storage pieces can make the transition very easily from a teen bedroom to a future living room.

For bedding, you might consider the hi-risers or trundles—a second bed that rolls away under the first when not in use—which have become a common solution to space, or lack of space, problems. Like the familiar bunk bed, they've been enjoying particular popularity in children's and teen-agers' rooms where an overnight friend is a frequent occurrence.

As for boys, they will probably be more interested in borrowing the family car than in thinking about what their room looks like. At some time the whole world becomes his "living room" and his bedroom is simply a place to hang his hat and baseball bat as well as to go to sleep. As with girls, the important role mother plays is to make sure the basics are provided. How the basics are arranged and decorated is usually of no interest to a grown-up son, and mother shouldn't be concerned as to how the room looks.

How to Buy Furniture

"Don't buy for the future" might be the byword in purchasing furniture for a child's room. Years ago, every mother bought a matching crib, chifforobe and chest, then youth beds and double chests in the exact same design. The result was a large hole in the budget and a very boring room and a very bored child.

Today's smart shopper waits to observe her child's needs, waits to see if her family will be expanding or if her new home will be expanding. Gradually, she adds pieces—some new, some moved from other parts of the house, some bought secondhand and then refurbished to start a whole new life with a young, new owner. All furniture bought for children's rooms should be light in weight, easy to move around during cleaning, and easy to clean. All of these are important tests that furniture should pass to get winning marks from mother. To score with children, furniture should also be small in scale. When you go to a department or furniture store to shop for your baby's first furniture, don't let a salesman convince you to buy a set that "grows" with your child. Be practical. You don't know what "direction" your child will grow in. What a pity to have bought a pink-and-white set, complete with rampant bunnies and lambs, only to discover that your little girl is developing into a tomboy.

Another reason to avoid so-called baby or juvenile furniture is by recalling that all the children's rooms you've ever seen have been decorated by adults. Grandmothers (in particular) love French Provincial styling and canopy beds and they're usually chosen by decorators or first-time mamas. The wise mother knows that froufrou and chichi furniture means more work for her. (Of course as little girls become less little, they may very well decide to play Scarlett O'Hara. French Provincial styling is, in fact, one of the most popular, according to teen surveys.)

Here are some shopping tips to keep in mind when looking for furniture for children's rooms:

Buying well-advertised, brand names usually means quality. These manufacturers stand behind their products, should you have questions about performance.

Shopping in a reputable store is equally important. Salesmen should be able to give you information about how the furniture is made as well as how much it costs.

Shop in more than just the baby and juvenile furniture sections of a store. Those are the places where you'll find the matched sets that look as though they have stood in the same place for years. Look in the closet department and bath shops for small, quilted-fabric chests of drawers. Also try the regular furniture departments. Many companies, aware of the needs of apartment living, manufacture small-scale chests, headboards, night tables, etc. that are just the right size for pint-sized people.

Shop at sale time. Most department stores hold furniture sales in February and August. At that time they dispose of their floor samples, the pieces that have been on display for six months. The scratches and mars that these pieces have acquired shouldn't make any difference as your youngster will be adding many more of his own.

Don't be afraid to ask questions. Even though the purchase you plan to make is a small one, speak up. If a salesman doesn't know the answer, be persistent. The catalogue from the manufacturer is probably sitting on the desk right in his office, with the answer to your question in it.

Examine hangtags carefully. Hangtags usually delineate the "hidden" qualities of furniture that you can't see—special finishes, special inside features that will be meaningful to you as a housekeeping mother.

Ask about delivery dates. The furniture industry is, alas, notoriously poor about shipments. Sometimes delivery is promised for three months and then the postponements start. Of course, baby can be kept in a drawer, but . . .

What to Look for in Furniture

Along with styling, you'll be looking for construction features that are particularly applicable to children's rooms. These are the most important ones: Look for dust panels. These are individual pieces of wood or plasterboard separating each drawer to keep the stored items clean. Without dust panels, objects fall from one drawer to another, thoroughly gumming up the works. If you're economizing on a chest of drawers, do make sure that there is a dust panel at the bottom of the lowest drawer, even if no others are used throughout. The bottom panel will keep dust and dirt from seeping into clean clothes and diapers.

Check the drawer joints where the sides are attached to the front and the back. Dovetailed joints are the best kind, but lock-joint construction is also sound. If only glue is used, this is a sign of inexpensive manufacturing technique.

Does the furniture fit firmly on the floor? Furniture for your bedroom or living room or dining area will never get the roughhousing that kids' rooms will. Rock the furniture back and forth. It should be easy to move, yet steady on its feet.

Are there corner blocks holding the chair, chest, or table legs in place? End and corner blocks, preferably notched and screwed into place, are used where rigidity is very important. It's an added plus in children's rooms where furniture should be durable and hard to tip over.

Although the basic construction of furniture is wood, the finishes very often are not. These are some of the finishes you'll find readily available:

Plastic Finishes. These are the modern miracles that make being a mother a joy instead of drudgery. Many plastic finishes are placed over the wood. They're transparent and yet they perform many services. Finishes can resist stains and scuff. These finishes do not affect the look of the wood.

Painted Finishes. Mothers still love the clean, fresh look of white enamel furniture in baby's rooms. No doubt the enamel, baked on, is easy to clean but its chippability is a disadvantage. For teens, lacquer-painted finishes are very much in vogue and are excellent do-it-yourself projects.

Plastic Laminates. Many plastic laminates have been designed to imitate wood finishes exactly and are used on tables and chests in traditional styles. In the area of modern furniture, plastic laminates come into their own. They appear in brilliant colors for tabletops and chests. Because furniture for tots and teens gets such hard use, laminates are an excellent choice.

Along with wood chests and tables that are topped with plastic laminates, it's possible to buy pieces that are completely made of this plastic. Parsons tables and cube tables are the great favorites, especially with teens, because of their brilliant colors. Now acrylic plastics have been made into both tables and cubes. Fashion-conscious teens love the see-through look, but mothers will probably dislike the rather high price tag and the ease of scratching. Plastic furniture is also available for seating. Not too long ago it was necessary to bone up on coils and stuffings before you went to buy a chair. Now, shopping for rugged seating is a breeze.

Though fiber glass has been available for several decades, it has only recently made its mark in furniture. Originally plastic chairs were available in only limited color combinations. Now the palette has broadened. Several versions have won the Good Design Award. They should win your comfort award, too. The chairs are easy to stack, easy to move, easy to wipe off. Junior sizes are available for the little members of your family, while social teens will want to buy them in stacks.

Another form of plastic chair, the blow-up vinyl, created a stir when it was introduced on the market a few years ago. Young people find blow-up chairs fun, and why not! Like plastic chairs, the inflatables come in large and small sizes. Tip: Don't let yourself be talked into a blow-up chair as a place to study. They're meant for lounging only, as the chair back doesn't give proper back support. The newest form of plastic is also molded. The technical name is thermoplastic and it appears in ultramodern styling. Mostly globular and sinuous in shape, these plastic seats are usually upholstered in gay vinyls. Still fairly expensive for all but the most pampered child, they give a cheerful portent of things to come.

The plastics industry has changed the whole upholstery world. Thanks to latex and polyurethane foam, furniture can come in marvelous shapes. Flexible and bendable, foam can be smoothly fitted to achieve slim-lined couches and chairs. Often, latex foam (more resilient and longer lasting than synthetic foam) is used for seat cushions, while the polyurethane covers arms and back. When the foam is covered with vinyl upholstery it's particularly suited to the needs of children and teens.

Vinyls have shoved nature's fibers aside. Although many designers deplore the fact that vinyls imitate leather and suede, many of them can't tell the difference between the two. So forget your memories of plastic-topped chairs in cheap dinette sets before you shop for a chair or couch for your child's room. The vinyls today are chic and high styled. As a matter of fact, many are so chic that they're available only through the interior design department of stores. The best vinyls are called "expanded" or "supported" which indicates that the plastic is laminated to a backing for stability. These elegant fabrics will not crack, can be wiped clean with a damp rag, and are well-nigh indestructible. In other words, a "must" for the younger generation.

If you can't find a vinyl fabric that suits your decorating needs, do ask about the new soil-retardant finishes. Many furniture manufacturers do not put hangtags on their product to indicate that the cover has been treated. But a salesman can look this up for you. You can even have the fabric treated if it ordinarily isn't.

These finishes are another test-tube story. Called a fluorochemical, the finish is a chemical shield which is odorless and invisible. You can't even tell by touching the fabric that it has been treated. This chemical shield keeps water-borne and oil stains on the surface of the fabric, and they will be completely removed if they are blotted up quickly. As an added plus, the shield keeps soot and soil on the surface of the fabric, ready to be vacuumed up. But these finishes, which do withstand dry cleaning, are not as mudproof, dessertproof, and sootproof as vinyls. They're probably better for more well-mannered teens than for high-spirited tots.

THE WALLS

In children's rooms, wall coverings are, indeed, wonderful. If you're a magazine clipper-outer, you've probably automatically chosen those with wallpapered walls. That's no surprise since decorators have a fondness for florals in girls' rooms and stripes and plaids in boys' rooms. As a matter of fact, you may very well have the wallpaper picked out already. It's usually the first thing that mothers do. But this is one area where you should exercise a little restraint. The most important point in choosing a wall treatment is not pattern but practicality. Most children, in case you didn't know, find walls an excellent medium for expressing their individual artistic talents. Surely there's hardly a mother who didn't go into her children's room at some point to find the walls covered with crayonwork or perhaps lipstick creations. So please be practical. And along with practicality, remember that a child lives in his room almost twenty-four hours a day. You probably have a whole series of rooms you can move to—the kitchen, bedroom, and living room. And if you are stuck in a one-room apartment, you probably spend only your evenings and weekends there. In short, you could get tired of a wallpaper with a pizzazz pattern if you had to live with it for a concentrated period of time the way a child does.

Basically there are three different ways you can cover walls:

Paint. This is the most inexpensive and simplest way of finishing walls. Use a rubber- (latex) or plastic-base paint. These new paints are easy to apply, dry quickly, and have little or no odor while drying. What's most important, you can touch up a wall or paint a bookcase or toy box the same color months later. You can also wash the walls when accidents happen. Latex and plastic paints leave a dull finish.

Although semigloss and gloss paints leave the kind of shine that's very "in" with decorators these days, they are difficult to apply smoothly. Many professional painters will show their temperamental side when asked to use gloss or semigloss paint for anything but woodwork. Alas, these two finishes cannot be touched up without showing, a distinct disadvantage when a child's room is in mind.

Should you choose an oil-base paint, you'll find that the finish is shinier and more interesting and that the paint can be scrubbed harder than the rubber- or plastic-base paint can. It is, however, almost impossible to match touch-ups and the colors darken if the paint is on the wall for any length of time.

Wall coverings. Once upon a time there was just wallpaper. And now the industry has changed its name to wall coverings. And rightly so. It's not just paper that's pasted up on walls. There's also vinyl. These papers have a thin coating of vinyl which makes them easy to scrub with detergent and water, hence ideal for children's rooms.

You may find that wall coverings are more expensive than you'd imagined. Then do a combination of wall covering and paint. This is the great compromise for children's rooms. If you (or your teen) have your heart set on a strong, vivid pattern such as a plaid, stripe, or busy floral, put it up on one wall and then paint the others. In that way, if your child tires of the pattern there's only one wall to redecorate.

As you go through wallpaper books, you'll find that the companies have been way ahead of you. Most richly patterned papers have "companion" papers with them. These usually pick one color in the design which then becomes the solid to use on the other three walls.

Most companion papers are textured grass cloth or burlap. Using these companion papers will ensure a perfect color match to the patterned wall, which is not a sure thing when you choose to paint.

Wall coverings have designs that will fit every pocketbook and every child or teen mood. An allover textured pattern like grass cloth, bamboo, brick, or stone will camouflage irregularities in the wall, as well as fingerprints and grime. As you probably know, a large design in bright colors will draw attention to a wall and make a room seem smaller. A wall covering with a faint texture in a light color will make a room seem larger.

A word about prepasted papers. Usually prepasted papers are considered mainly for kitchens and bathrooms, but they belong in children's rooms, too. The manufacturers' directions are very accurate and putting up the paper is just as simple as it sounds. No messy buckets of paste are required, and you needn't even buy a tray. Most people use the bathtub to soak the paper. What you will need is the old do-it-yourself stand-by: patience.

Paneling. Until very recently, the word "paneling" brought "wood" to mind. But no more, thanks to the explosive plastic industry. The same material, plastic laminates, that covers your counters in the kitchen can cover your children's walls. Plastic laminates now come in bold, bright colors as well as soft ones with dull finishes. There are also textural patterns and small miniprints. Although plastic laminates are more expensive than either paint or wallpaper to install, their maintenance is nil. You might consider a chair rail around the room with paneling below and wallpaper or paint above. The paneling will take all the hard knocks the most raucous child can give.

Other Wall Treatments. In children's rooms, walls can be useful as well as decorative. Areas of slate can be used as big blackboards for creative expression. Shiny laminated plastics can be crayoned and easily cleaned. Perforated hardboard permits endless pin-ups of toys, cutouts, alphabet letters. Cork will accept endless tacked and pinned drawings, magazine clippings, greeting cards—all the colorful things that delight and also instruct small children.

FLOORING

You should know a little about both hard (resilient) and soft (carpeting) surfaces for a child's room, no matter what the age. Babies need a soft surface for crawling and to prevent drafts, while they need a hard surface for walking and proper use of toys. The hard-surface flooring shouldn't, by the way, be heavily waxed, or else toddlers who are just learning to walk will be taking unnecessary spills. As for the rug in the child's room or nursery, it should be a washable one. Accidents of all sorts can happen, and a rug that can be popped into the washing machine is wise. As for teens, they too need the combination of hard- and soft-surface flooring. For a while, you will probably even wonder why you bothered buying chairs, when your teen-ager and friends will spend all their time sitting on the floor.

What Kind of Carpet to Buy

You needn't concern yourself with what type of construction is used in the manufacture of carpet today. Over 90 per cent of all carpets made in this country are tufted and that's likely what you're looking at. There is great variety in texture, but for the child's room, two types are recommended. Twist carpets don't show traffic and give rugged performance. However, you may find it in limited availability and in few colors. Loops are a good choice for areas that get lots of wear. Like twists they show no traffic patterns. Some of the new "fat" loops have an interesting hand-crafted look which may be just right for your child's room. The tight loops may seem less unusual, but they're easy to care for. Shag is the newest texture and comes with short yarns, long yarns, fat yarns, and skinny yarns. Many colors can be combined. So from the color standpoint, shag is interesting for the small-fry room. However, while the shag may hide dirt, it is not too practical for spills and all the mess that is bound to accumulate in this area of the home. When it comes to fibers, nylon is a good choice because it is abrasion resistant and offers outstanding service in areas that get a lot of wear. Olefin is good too because of its good abrasion and soil resistance. Polyester fibers have good abrasion and crush resistance and are easily cleaned.

What to Look for in Resilient Flooring

There isn't much doubt that the most successful and prettiest children's rooms have resilient flooring of one type or another—vinyl, cushioned vinyl, (with a thin layer of foam), or linoleum.

They add a bright, light look that children love. These flooring materials come in such a great abundance that it's possible to find a design that is bright, cheerful, and doesn't show dirt. There are patterns imitating slate, terrazzo, Spanish tiling, wood, marble chips, spatter designs, and small geometrics. There is also a brilliant array of solid colors which have great impact. The solids do, however, show dirt more quickly than the patterns.

Shop around from one dealer to another, because you'll find variations in price. And when you do ask about price, remember that resilient flooring prices are usually quoted in square feet, rather than in the square yard the way carpeting is priced. Multiply the square-foot price by nine to get a comparison between hard- and soft-floor coverings. Resilient flooring, which comes in both tiles and in sheets, is very often a do-it-yourself project for the man in the house. When you're figuring the costs on installation, don't forget the underlay, glue, and tools you'll need.

Some resilient floorings must be put down permanently, while others come in sheets and are, in effect, room-sized area rugs. If you rent, you will probably have to seek permission from the landlord to cement the flooring. And you may have to pay to have the flooring removed when you've removed yourself to different premises. Unlike carpeting, some resilient flooring needs special subflooring for proper installation.

There isn't anything wrong with wood flooring, except that it isn't colorful. If wood floors are in bad shape they can be refinished. A do-it-yourselfer can rent or borrow a sander to restore floors to good condition. They can even be restained to a tone other than the conventional dirty yellow brown. A dark floor, sparked with a fluffy area rug, is an excellent compromise. There are now special wood sealers that eliminate the deadly chore of waxing floors frequently. After a wood floor is sealed, it needs as little care as any other resilient flooring. (A detailed discussion of flooring is found in Chapter Nine.)

WINDOW TREATMENT

There is a great variety of pattern and color in ready-mades. Many of them are very suitable for children's rooms. Fabrics with bold patterns, like wallpaper, attract the eye and make a room seem smaller. Fabrics that are the same color as the wall will make a room seem larger than it is. This is a good treatment for an awkwardly placed window, as the drapery or curtain will simply block out the window when it is pulled.

LIGHTING

General illumination for children's rooms should be bright and cheerful, rather than the romantic, low lights for living room or bedroom. Cove lighting is a good choice, with the tubing shielded to direct light upward to the ceiling. It need not be expensive and is desirable for a child's area. When it comes to specific lighting, choose wall- or ceiling-hung lamps for children's rooms. This eliminates the problem of active children knocking over lamps and tripping on electric cords. There should be a fixture over a child's worktable or study area. The fixture should take between 150 and 200 watts for reading or studying. A ceiling-hung fixture that can be pulled down to the proper height is ideal for youngsters' worktables. But, again, make sure that the fixture does not have bulbs which cast their rays right down on the table. A fixture that takes three or four bulbs under its diffuser is far better than several independent pendants, no matter how attractive they appear. Wall-hung fixtures with swinging arms are just as good as ceiling-hung lighting fixtures.

When your child starts school he will be old enough for a study lamp. Pole lamps, goosenecks, bullets, high-intensity, and cylindrical lamps, believe it or not, are all inadvisable. A lamp with a large shade (and it could be a floor lamp with a swinging arm) is infinitely better to avoid eyestrain. Once again, the lamp should have a refracting bowl under the bulb. A fluorescent light, over a desk, is just as suitable, providing the bulb is shielded the way it is in cove lighting. The work surface or desk, by the way, should be light in color and nonglossy which, in illuminating terms, means nonreflective. If the desk top is wood, place a decorative blotter in a pale shade on the surface. With the invention of the ballpoint pen, blotters are no longer necessary for ink; they are useful for "blotting" up glare.

COLOR SCHEMES

Children have definite color preferences and it is advisable to cater to them, rather than deciding on colors *you* like or that follow a predetermined scheme in the rest of the house. Expose the child to different colors and watch reactions, then put colors together with him or her, perhaps using colorful blocks. In decorating children's rooms, you can automatically rule out a lot of soft, muted color combinations. No one really knows how the whole idea of baby pink and baby blue for nurseries started. Perhaps in the eighteenth century, because those are very eighteenth-century colors. They are also colors that adults think that children like. Children don't. Children like cheerful, sunny, bright, happy, zingy, bouncy, bold, energetic colors. And they should have them. The kind of colors we adults would put in a bathroom or a kitchen belong in a child's room. It's a well-known fact that colors affect mood, and children instinctively pick the warm happy colors. So avoid the pale pinks and blues and also avoid the neutrals. Rooms that are decorated in the now-fashionable "natural look" with slate and charcoal gray, cocoa and coffee brown have no child appeal. What we consider sophisticated they consider merely "blah."

Color schemes that use a lot of white are most effective for children's rooms. What about a red, white, and blue room for a boy? Red and white spatter flooring with a bright blue area rug. Then a minipatterned wallpaper on two walls in red, white, and blue with the other two in white. A bright blue corduroy bedspread with matching cafe curtains. Furniture will be modern in either dark wood tones or all white. And you have a room that will last from two to teens. What about a girl's room? A yellow, gold, and white modern floral print on the bedspread with matching wallpaper on the wall behind. Off-white flooring with a marigold area rug in a pouffy fiber. The other walls are white but the shutters at the window and the closet and entry door are painted a brilliant enamel yellow. A white window shade is trimmed in orange, which is the color of the ornate wicker chair and table. Headboard and chests are white, too.

PATTERN

One of the easiest ways to choose a color scheme is by picking a pattern and plucking the colors from it to dress the entire room. There are area rugs, sheet designs, wallpapers, and even plastic furniture with bold graphics. But go slow. Remember that your child (whatever the age) will be living in his or her bedroom for twice as many hours as you do in yours, so proceed with care. The current rage of two or three patterns in a room is beautiful in a photograph, but you'd get tired of it and your child will tire even more quickly.

Now, that doesn't mean that you can't use that zebra-striped rug or that floral bedspread. What it does mean is: Keep a tight rein on your enthusiasm and your child's, and limit the amount of patterned furnishings to those that are fairly inexpensive and easy to replace. Thus, do buy that zingy, washable area rug in polka dots, put up one wall of awning-striped paper, indulge in an op art bedspread. But don't upholster a chair or sleep sofa in an "active" pattern, or paper all four walls with a design that would keep even a sleepyhead up all night.

OTHER CONSIDERATIONS

Texture. This is the feel of the materials within the room, and they can range from the slickness of leather to the roughness of tweed. Most rooms have a combination of both and you've probably combined both without knowing it. Children tend to like the extremes— the slickness of leather and glass and the warmth and softness of fur. Paint or wallpaper, furniture surfaces, and a resilient flooring give the slicks to a room. A pouffy area rug and a chenille bedspread give the softness. Just be wary of erring on the side of too many slicks. A room with a patent-leather bedspread, no rug, and shutters at the window will look barren and uninviting.

Form. Everything you put in a room has shape or form. Most will be basically squares and rectangles. Squares give a feeling of regularity while rectangular shapes in furniture are most active and more interesting. Circles, via tables or lamps or bowls, also appear in most rooms. A combination of circles, rectangles, and squares will complement each other. A room of all circular pieces makes us feel uneasy since our eye doesn't have a place to rest, while a room that is made up of furniture that is all square is boring. The combination of furnishings that is created from squares, circles, and rectangles is most pleasing to the eye.

Traffic patterns. Allow enough space to open drawers in chests, closet doors, trundle beds. Easy access makes for easy living.

Activity areas. This is a very sober way of saying you should save footsteps. In other words, the crib in baby's room should be near the door so you don't have to cross the room to answer a cry or change a diaper. Likewise, in your teen's room, the radio and phonograph and

TV should be in one spot, away from the study area of desk and lamp and chair. If possible, the chest for storing clothes and the closet should be adjacent to each other. A full-length mirror and the dressing table should be nearby, too.

CHAPTER TWENTY-ONE

THE BATH

WHEN IT COMES to decoration the bath is the home's pampered darling. Such a wealth of decoration components has been developed especially for the bath that it makes bath decor an exciting adventure. Any color scheme in the rainbow is permissible. And there is no limitation in the range of materials to be considered: In addition to old favorites like ceramic tile, we now have all the plastic and plastic-surfaced products, carpet in its many fibers, and even natural wood, its beauty made safe from water and steam with special transparent coatings. Manufacturers have helped with a wide selection of ensembles—towels to wallpaper to curtains, making decoration relatively foolproof.

Where to begin in the project? A color scheme is basic. If you already have white fixtures, your choice is fairly wide; if you have colored fixtures, you must work around them. Since the space is usually small, it is important not to work with too many colors. A two-color plan—say, blue and white—with one accent color, red or yellow, for example. With white fixtures, you would then color your large expanses in blue, while yellow or red would provide contrast in towels, picture frames, an area rug. One good way to a scheme is to choose a wall covering—plastic coated, of course, for steam resistance—with a built-in color scheme, taking from its pattern the colors of all your other components. Another approach is with the ensemble mentioned above. There are so many sources of inspiration for a color scheme: A favorite painting or print you want to hang in the bath; patterned ceramic tile (if it is already installed or if you plan to include it); a favorite flower; or any of the color helps you might use in scheming a living room or bedroom. The key to successful bath decoration today is to approach it as you would approach any room in the home.

Yellow fixtures set the theme for a sunny bath, right, accented in red and white. Laminate counter is white, tiled tub niche the same. Features: a wall-hung toilet, easy to clean under, and a boldly scaled slab lavatory in vitreous china.

The bath with its own private terrace is part of the popular living look. Yellow fixtures set the theme, underscored by gold wall-to-wall carpet, upholstered stool and counter laminate. Patterned laminate in rust and gold on white was used for shower compartment, part of tub niche and most walls. One accent wall uses wood grain laminate of cabinets. Note towels as part of color scheme.

Cabinet manufacturers now include a wide line of "lavanities," units designed for the counter wash basin. Above, a broad counter spans three provincially-styled cabinets in a fruitwood finish and handsome brass hardware in the country manner.

From the same line, three units in contemporary style are bunched to create nearly a whole cabineted wall with twin basins, twin mirrors. Marble counter, tortoise shell wallpaper, and striking suspended chandelier add to the present-day look.

Choice of materials for bath décor is broad. Above is an unusual room done almost entirely in plastic. The back wall, tub enclosure doors and privacy panel for the toilet are acrylic. Walls, touch-latch cabinets and countertop are a laminate.

Several decorative materials combine at right. Wall is covered in vinyl-surfaced paper; wainscot is ceramic tile; lavatory has a marble top, vitreous china basin with a Greek key design in gold. Fittings are gold-plated, trimmed in malachite.

The carpet in the bath, above, repeats a motif of greenery established in the small courtyard. Highlights are colorful fixtures, twin lavatories in a custom island, a bidet and the low toilet silhouette. Contour tub is semi-sunken, adding to the sybaritic air.

Luxurious master bath, left, has a stall shower and a tub. Shower receptor is a new design which permits custom-tiled floor to match walls and floors. Glass panels and anodized brass trim are accents in the attractive blue and gold scheme.

If you are beginning a new bath, ponder carefully your choice of fixture color; you will be living with it for a long time. Be sure it is a color you and your family like and one you can work with decoratively. Luckily, today's fixture colors are fairly safe: pink, yellow, blue, beige, gray, and various shades of green including avocado. A few manufacturers offer black and maroon, but they can be tricky to decorate with and you may tire of them, so careful thought should go into their selection. Of the standard ones, gray and pink require the most deliberation: gray can be somber, especially in a room that isn't sunny, while pink has frilly connotations men are not always comfortable with. At least one manufacturer offers a line of lavatories in

ELJER

In the design of the compartmented bath, the sliding pocket is a great space-saver, eliminating door swings. Here the sliding door to the toilet compartment is surfaced in the same trellis design as a divider which gives the tub area a sense of compartmentation. Note wall-hung toilet, self-rimming lavatories which rest atop counter.

vivid colors, so if you want one fixture as a bright accent, this is a possibility. Standard gray, for example, can be sparked with emerald green or bright red in a counter washbasin.

Color co-ordination with adjacent rooms is important. In the small home especially, you will gain a greater sense of space if you let the bath continue a house-wide color theme. Going from a bedroom hall in beige and blue into a bath with beige fixtures and blue tile can afford a pleasant continuity. Especially important is decorating the master bedroom and its bath in tandem: You can find the same colors and patterns co-ordinated with sheets, towels, bedspreads, shower curtains, and window drapery. Tying the elements of decoration together is the mark of the well-decorated bath or whole house. And some of the country's leading color stylists and designers are working with manufacturers to provide ensembles that are not only stylish but also offer almost certain success.

THE DESIGN THEME

Second to your colors, an over-all stylistic idea is important in decorating the bath. As in any room, a period should be established, and it should be one that is consonant with the rest of the house. If your house is French Provincial, it is not necessary to go to streamlined contemporary in the baths simply because they are mechanical rooms. Every component of the bath except the fixtures themselves comes in almost any period style and the fixtures can be chosen in a color appropriate to the period you want. If the look is to be traditional, walls can be paneled and lavatory cabinet can be designed accordingly. Choose floor and wall materials that go with the period: For example, quarry tile in terra cotta color for floor and counters, a documentary print for curtains and matching vinyl-surfaced wallpaper and light fixtures in an eighteenth-century design will provide a traditional look. For a contemporary bath, sleek, light-colored surfaces, a streamlined lavatory cabinet, marble or white vinyl floor, and vivid accent colors in towels and paintings, wall-to-wall counter mirror, and a luminous, plastic ceiling will give a striking effect.

Other themes can be established with wall covering: a tropical look, a flower garden, a circus motif for a child's bath. The so-called terrace bath with sliding glass doors leading to a private outdoor sunning patio sets its own outdoor theme with plants inside and out for

This terrace bath features not only a private sun-bathing court accessible via double glass doors near the receptor tub-shower but also a repetition of the same natural materials indoors as out: plants, fieldstone. Wall-hung toilet is compartmented, giving the rest of the room a living look with wood floors and area rug.

relationship of the spaces. There can be a greenhouse bath where potted plants set the stage or a gallery bath in which paintings, carefully illuminated, create the effect. Possibilities are as unlimited as your imagination, tempered with practicality and the dictates of space.

DECORATIVE MATERIALS

When it comes to surface materials for the bath, there is almost no limit to choice. Of course, practicality being a must, it is important that materials be easy to wipe clean, steam- and moisture-resistant.

In this ceramic-tiled bathroom, with its generous use of mirrors, a husband can perform his stand-up shaving chore, while a wife can conveniently apply make-up in a comfortable, seated position. The toilet is compartmented and ceiling lighting is soft and diffused.

Ceramic tile has always been an ideal material for the bath precisely because of these properties. It comes in many colors and patterns and in various shapes to form an over-all pattern of itself. A skidproof crystalline glaze is the best surface for flooring; high gloss units can be used for walls. Either variety is suitable for countertops. Quarry tile, a form of ceramic, is excellent for all bath surfaces; it comes in the classic terra cotta and other colors, in hexagonal, trefoil, fleur-de-lis, and other designs. On walls, ceramic tile is applied with mastic over plaster or gypsum board, either to ceiling or chair-rail height, depending on the look you want to achieve. On the floor it is put down in concrete over metal lath or over plywood with waterproof mastic. The grout between tiles comes in an acid-resistant state that will not discolor (an old bugaboo solved several years ago); grout can also be integrally colored to blend with the tiles.

Other masonry materials for the bath include marble, travertine, slate, stone, and terrazzo. Marble, always rich and handsome in the bath, now comes in squares or rectangles about half an inch thick, and is relatively inexpensive, permitting its use in less costly installations than was formerly the case. A marble slab makes a handsome lavatory counter. Slate is excellent for floors and counters, not as well suited to walls. Stone makes a rugged floor and can be used for tub and shower walls. Brick, being porous, is suitable for flooring, but not good for walls where water splashes in abundance. Terrazzo is made by pouring a slurry of marble chips and concrete into squares defined by metal strips, then polishing when hard to the sheen of marble. It is an excellent flooring material and also good for stall shower bases and even sunken tubs.

Other possibilities for flooring include vinyl, vinyl asbestos, and asphalt tile in nine-inch and twelve-inch squares, embossed linoleum, and other sheet materials including vinyl which is available with a cushioned back for underfoot comfort. With all of these types of flooring, colors and patterns are available to blend with any period of decoration. For example, you can simulate delft tiles in vinyl squares, or add the look of Spanish tile in lineoleum. By using tiles with colorful feature-stripping, a striking effect can be achieved. Your floor-covering store or flooring contractor can show you color and pattern samples or you can write to manufacturers whose ads you see in magazines for color cards and brochures.

Carpet has been used in baths extensively for about ten years. There are certain obvious problems, the main one being cleanability in toilet and lavatory areas where spillage is unavoidable. New finishes and fibers that are impervious to stain have helped. The new indoor-outdoor carpets are excellent for the bath because of their special moisture-resistant properties. There is no denying that carpet is pleasant in an area where bare feet are the rule rather than the exception. One good solution is to have toilet and lavatory hung on the wall so that the carpet can be taken up easily and cleaned. It is an economical solution where building codes permit it to be installed right over plywood subfloor.

There are many choices for your walls. Gypsum board or plaster, painted in semigloss, is your least expensive solution and is adequate for all surfaces except shower walls. Wall coverings should be vinyl

The beauty of wood is now as practical as it is attractive in the bath. Here, a wall of California redwood continues outdoors to form a secluded sunning patio. Sunken tub is made of ceramic tile in a concave, circle design with an irregular apron of smooth, square tiles on three sides. Textured wall-to-wall carpet goes right to the sliding patio doors.

surfaced for the bath. This creates no limitation in choice, because elaborately flocked and other textured designs are now available in vinyl finish. These materials, of course, are not suitable for showers or tub walls where showers are used. Laminated hardboard panels with a baked-on plastic coating which come in patterns that simulate wood grain, marble, and other natural finishes are good choices for walls. They are usually found in sixteen-inch-wide panels which are tongue and groove, with top and bottom held in a metal grid. Panels are applied with mastic over gypsum or other wallboard. High-pressure laminates most often seen as counter surfacing are also good for paneling and can be used in tub and shower installations. Again there are many choices in color and pattern.

The Jacobean English style, again popular in interior design, is included in a compartmented bath which separates toilet and bidet in a rear area closed when desired with hinged panels. The outer compartment, accessible from the master bedroom, has twin lavatories and tub incorporated in a cabineted and paneled room with the dark, woody look of a library.

Wood, specially treated, is completely practical for bath walls and floor. It is now finished and sealed to retain its beautiful grain and tone. Plywood panels, similarly sealed and back-sealed, are easy to install in 4- by 8-foot sheets that can be nailed right to stud framing. California redwood which is highly resistant to water makes a beautiful, practical bath material for walls and ceiling. Rough-sawn western red cedar and cypress paneling are also suitable.

The "Living" Look

A relatively new concept in bath decoration is the "living" bath, one which looks first like a living area of the home and second like the functional room that it is. Intrinsic to the idea is the concept of compartmentation, in which at least the toilet is located in a separate cubicle and often the tub, too. Although there is now at least one toilet on the market which closes to look like a bench and can pass as furniture, cabinetry was the first step toward the living look some years ago. Once the lavatory didn't have to show its underpinnings and pipes, the clinical appearance could go. By recessing the washbasin, you could create something which looked like a piece of furniture and, with the help of moldings and hardware, in any period style preferred, from Early American to Louis XV. Manufacturers of kitchen cabinets quickly saw the possibilities and most of them now have a full line of vanitories in their full line of styles, wood finishes, and sizes to accommodate one or two washbasins. Finishes range from pale birch to dark oak, with fruitwood a popular choice between.

The living bath can include comfortable chairs, a desk, even a sofa. It becomes a kind of retreat or pampering room where hobbies and personal pursuits can be accommodated in private. Obviously, it requires large space for full possibilities, although it can be included in the smaller home where a third, small bedroom or study is sacrificed in favor of this interestingly compartmented space.

BATHROOM LIGHTING

Like the kitchen, the bathroom's light must be primarily utilitarian. A man shaving wants to see that he really has removed all traces of his five o'clock shadow, and a woman needs good visibility when she studies her make-up in the bathroom mirror. This does not mean to imply that the lighting must be dull and ugly—a message that some builders of middle-income apartments, unfortunately, have not yet received.

Most home builders are now alert to the fact that people want good lighting in their bathrooms but want it to be as attractive as possible. Even moderately priced new homes are being given the luxury treatment—from the colors, tiles, and equipment used to the sources of light. Bathrooms, perhaps more than any other single room in our homes, seem to reflect our affluent society.

One of the easiest ways to achieve decorative yet good general lighting is to install a luminous ceiling. If the bath is small, it will tend to make the room look larger. If it's spacious, the ceiling can cover one section—perhaps over the stall shower or as a luminous soffit over

Compartmentation permits simultaneous, private use of a bath with the toilet in a separate cubicle which can be closed off with hinged panels. Tub is in a second compartment. Twin lavatories are set into a laminate which blends with plastic-surfaced hardboard wall paneling with a soft wood grain.

the built-in vanity or countertop lavatory. De luxe fluorescent lamps, warm white for evening make-up and cool white for daytime, or a mixture of both, create a pleasing effect.

Although the trend in elegant bathrooms is for wall-to-wall mirrors, along with wall-to-wall carpeting, plenty of bathrooms still have only a single mirror over the washbowl. How to light it? The least desirable way (and one found frequently in older homes and apartments) is with a single wall fixture over the mirror. This puts shadows around the eyes, on the sides of the face, under the chin, and across the neck.

In order to erase those bothersome shadows, the light obviously must come from more than one direction. There are several possible solutions. A couple who bought an older home in New England, expecting to modernize it, decided to try lighting the mirror from both sides and above, and they hit on one of the most effective ways. They removed that glaring bulbous "eye" over the bowl and mirror, installed fluorescent strips on either side of the mirror and a modern grilled fixture on the ceiling directly overhead.

Framing three or four sides of a mirror with light is another approach. This can be done in a fairly straightforward fashion with strips of light or more theatrically with small frosted bulbs set in flowery brackets. Among the decorative fixtures used to flank mirrors are coach lamps for Early American decor, round Victorian lamps, or white glass pendants for a contemporary look.

In the area of a vanity or a dressing room adjoining a bathroom, there's almost no limit to the opulence of lighting fixtures, particularly those designed to flank a mirror. For instance, to add sparkle you can get heavy, faceted glass gems set in gold strips and concealing small bulbs. You can even have a matching gold ceiling fixture with the same type of faceted gem lights. Or your strip lights can take on a Florentine air with frosted glass shells holding theatrical bulbs. If the lights are to be concealed, you can shield them with textured glass strips sparkling like square-cut diamonds, or patterned crystal with baroque motifs of rich gold. The baths of ancient Rome had nothing on today's plush pads, and lighting makes a valuable contribution to this lavish look.

Easy Decorating Ideas

Here are a few ideas for sprucing up a bath, little changes that go a long way toward giving you a new, fresh look.

1. A framed valance over the tub, a panel of your drapery fabric, can be attached to a rectangular piece of plywood, wall-to-wall over the tub. Painted or dark-stained ponderosa pine molding found at the lumberyard can be mitered and nailed around to frame it. Shower curtain or side panels of drapery can be installed on the back of this valance.

2. In the small bath, the ceiling papered the same as walls will add interest and give a feeling of increased space.

3. An antique mirror over the lavatory counter will help set a period look. It can be hinged over an existing medicine cabinet.

4. The lavatory counter, continued with the same laminate in a narrower width across the tank of a toilet, will provide greater set-down space and minimize the toilet. Make certain the counter is high enough from the tank to permit the removal of the lid for service.

SHERLE WAGNER FITTINGS; MICHAEL GREER, DESIGNER

The bath now takes its place among the home's best decorated rooms. Treillage adds an outdoor look to an indoor room, heightened with trompe l'oeil vista panels on one wall and the ceiling. Highlight is a hand-carved onyx shell with fluted column and gold-plated faucet set.

5. A painted tray which blends with the decor can be used atop the toilet tank to hold decorative bottles and accessories, helping to bring that fixture into the bath scheme.

6. A chandelier can help greatly to establish period style.

7. A grouping of pictures, wood carvings, or small sculptures can add interest to the bath.

8. A luminous ceiling can lower a too-high bath and provide shadow-free diffused illumination for less money than you might think. You can get flat or corrugated plastic panels in a light aluminum framework and the system will hide a multitude of unsightly pipes, beams, etc.

9. Louvered shutters at a bath window are attractive, give privacy, yet permit control of light and air.

The Early American theme of bathroom here—which is decorated in red, white, and blue—is accented by the carriage lamps, eagle motif on the lavatories, and the soldiers on the countertop.

AMERICAN OLEAN TILE COMPANY

10. A shower panel at one or both ends of the tub can be made to match drapery fabric. An actual pull-across, working shower curtain of clear plastic is then installed on a separate rod behind.

11. Choose soap, facial tissue, and toilet tissue as part of your basic color scheme. Tissues also come in patterns that blend with various period themes.

12. Pretty bottles with water colored by vegetable dye in various hues can accent or blend with your color scheme and add a decorative touch on a lavatory counter or window.

13. A tub or shower door in a pattern that blends with your scheme, can add to the over-all effect.

14. An Oriental or other unusual area rug will help create the living look.

15. A washbasin recessed into an antique chest adds a touch of elegance to a bath or powder room and presents few plumbing or carpentry problems.

16. For a traditional bath, carriage lamps can be used as side lighting fixtures next to the mirror.

17. Use a special, beautiful, cut-glass or other water tumbler at the lavatory.

18. A small bouquet on the lavatory counter or atop the toilet adds a fresh, bright touch.

19. An old tub can be encased in wood or other material to give a whole new look to a bath. Be sure the plumber is in on the act to forestall service problems.

20. Mirror can be used in the tub enclosure to seemingly increase space.

CHAPTER TWENTY-TWO

MAKE ROOM FOR GUESTS

FEW FAMILIES TODAY have the luxury of space required to set aside a special room or rooms for guests. The usual rule is one family member doubling up and turning over his or her bed for the duration. Another prevalent guest solution is convertible bedding in another area of the house—the study or family room equipped with a sofa-bed. Let's take up these and other possibilities.

If you can set aside a bedroom or bedroom and bath for guests, here are a few decorating pointers. First, use a warm, welcoming color scheme and avoid bizarre colors; some people are not only turned off by purple or shocking pink, they also become actively ill when confronted with these colors. A combination of muted tones of your house-wide color scheme, if you prefer, is usually a good choice. By all means include twin beds; many visitors, though married many years, are not accustomed to sleeping together. Avoid frilliness in the bed and window treatments, keeping to a more tailored look. That way both men and women will feel more at ease.

For window treatments, no matter which type you choose—shutters, window shades, drapery—make sure that they close tight and give a darkened room both night and day. Guests like a change of pace when away from home and that often means sleeping late and many people can't abide a wink of light. For flooring, carpet or a thick area rug is a good idea, because the guest should be pampered and what is more pleasant than stepping onto a warm, comfortable rug when you may have forgotten your bedroom slippers? As for accessories, include plenty of ashtrays and by all means twin bedside tables with good reading lamps. What a joy it is to be able to get at that book you haven't had time to read and to be able to read late into the night. If you have a spare TV set, it's not a bad idea to include one here: The guest may be longing to watch a special program that coincides with his visit. And in this light, don't forget an idle-hour bookshelf; finding an interesting book can be a joy when you're on a holiday. And be sure to include an accurate alarm clock.

A guest room, to be a truly successful part of a home, should also be easy to care for. In an age of miracle materials and goofproof furniture finishes, there's absolutely no reason why the guest room can't be relatively maintenance-free. Think about this factor when you buy furnishings. Will the curtains take an occasional dunking and then drip dry wrinkle-free? Will the bedspread survive frequent sitting and shed dirt, spots, and stains? Will the desk and dresser tops resist scratches, cigarette burns, and moisture rings? And the rug or carpeting—is it durable and perhaps patterned or deep enough in color to hide footstep soil and soot? You may pay a little more for built-in protection, but the benefits to you as hostess and homemaker are well worth the price.

Furniture for the Guest Room

Furniture for the guest room should be comfortable and multipurpose functional. Your choice will depend on a number of things. For example, for what other activities is the room or area intended? Assume for the moment that your guest room is an extra bedroom, used infrequently by family, in reserve for guests. This is the ideal situation. Number one requisite, as was mentioned previously, is a comfortable bed. (*The subject of mattresses and box springs has been thoroughly covered in Chapter Nineteen, "The Master Bedroom."*)

You're usually wise to avoid buying the conventional bedroom "set"—the matching bed, bedside tables or cabinets, double or triple dresser, depending on your own particular taste. That may be the quickest and simplest way to furnish the room, but it's far from the most interesting or even the economically best. To begin with, abandon the idea that everything has to match. A certain degree of individuality is missing in a room where every piece of furniture carries the same motif. The effect is too often static, even boring.

Next to the bed, you'll want to provide some sort of desk-high cabinet or table—to hold reading lamp, book, midnight snack, and spectacles. Again, this could be the conventional type designed for bedside service, and if you have one, by all means use it. Parsons or T-square tables, too, have universal appeal and are compatible with nearly every decorating mood imaginable. Once a "custom" item, Parsons tables (named after the founder of Parsons School of Design, incidentally) are available today in virtually every size and color and at mass-produced prices. A desk-sized one placed at bedside means both lamp and table can do double duty—the table serving as both desk and night stand, the lamp benefiting both areas. The Parsons table is a natural way to add color and textural accent to a room. A shiny, lacquered finished in a bright color is a delightful contrast to other wood-finished pieces.

Another prospect for bedside service is the French étagère—an open-shelf unit for bric-a-brac restored to propriety by a number of American furniture manufacturers. These tall, stately pieces look more chic used in pairs—perhaps flanking either end of a day bed positioned lengthwise against the wall, for example. Not only do they lend utilitarian function, but architectural interest to the room as well. Similarly, bookcases, bookcase headboards, wall-hung shelves—all can be placed adjacent to the bed to hold a sundry of nighttime needs.

Still another guest-room must is some type of drawers. These, too, come in a vast variety of sizes and shapes and styles. There's no reason why a long and low dresser can't also serve as a bedside cabinet if so situated. But if floor space is in short supply, you'll do better to stick to a tall and narrow bureau. The French semainier, which literally means a seven-drawer chest, has been translated by American makers into a tall, thin bureau with drawers sized just right for lingerie, jewelry, scarves, and accessories. Because it takes up minimum floor space, it's often the perfect choice for that minute dressing area or generous walk-in closet where a wee bit wider bureau just wouldn't fit.

The armoire is another recently revived case piece deserving of applause. Usually designed to stow clothing, some now come fitted to house TVs, stereo systems, and refreshment centers instead. An armoire differs from a conventional chest of drawers in that it's usually larger and has doors, behind which may be shelves, drawers, or a rod for hanging things. Its impressive size lends an aura of authority to any room it graces, along with a wealth of organized storage space.

Not an absolute must, but certainly nice to have is a writing table or desk for the guest—some small (but not too small) surface adequately equipped for penning a postcard, recording an expense, making a note. This can be a standard writing desk or a clever improvisation. For want of the former, you might create legroom and headroom in a bookcase by merely removing a shelf or two above and below a desk-height shelf—thus creating a desk. Then, too, there are little wall-hung units with drop-down writing surfaces that are relatively inexpensive and simple to bracket to the wall anywhere. Many bookcase units have optional drop-leaf desk components. There are also dressing-table desks to choose from. Or you might furnish a small table and pair of chairs to double as desk and breakfasting place. The desk chair might be of the upright ladderback variety to which you've added a plumpy seat cushion or of a newer, perhaps plastic, swivel type. In addition to a desk chair, your guests will appreciate a comfortable place to relax—an upholstered piece such as a small sofa, a chaise longue or lounge chair with ottoman to put up the feet. A table and reading lamp should be close at hand—possibly shared between chair and bed.

"Making" Guest Rooms Throughout the House

Even if your house can't accommodate a bedroom just for guests, don't give up. With a little ingenuity, guest space can be plotted in almost any room of the house and convertible bedding can be the solution. We've seen Murphy beds pop out of such unexpected places as kitchen cabinets and dining-room buffets, suspended beds drop down from walls in basement recreation rooms and attics, living-room sofas and chairs—even hassocks—turn into beds at the flick of the wrist, day beds and studio couches in sewing rooms and utility areas for seating by day, sleeping by night. Children's rooms should ideally have room for at least one more—a sister or brother or an overnight friend—on an upper bunk, in a trundle, on a cushioned window seat, or a spare twin.

Granted, the finest quality bedding money can buy may not be quite as important in a guest spot as it is in your own bedroom, but one night's sleep on an old broken-down mattress can give its unfortunate occupant a backache for weeks. With that in mind, it's advisable to furnish the best guest bedding your budget will allow. Good bedding should be thought of as an investment anyway—necessary to well-being and good health. And, of course, there's always the possibility of the extra bed being pressed into more or less regular service by an addition to the family—perhaps another child, an aging parent, a foreign-exchange student, a live-in housekeeper.

"Found" space in an empty garage loft was turned into an efficiency apartment. Ideal for occasional use by a guest, frequent use by the family, the multipurpose room features a sit-and-sleep day-bed arrangement that incorporates two single beds. Bolsters along the back hide pillows and extra blankets. Lattice work forms a unique wall.

In these days of shrinking space and an increasingly mobile society, chances are your choice of guest bedding will be of the dual-purpose variety—serving as something else by day only to reveal its secret as a sleeper after dark. (Of course, standard bedding can be handsomely bolstered and covered to create the look of a couch or day bed.)

Not long ago, a decision to buy dual-purpose sleep equipment meant settling for second-rate fashion or no fashion at all. The uphol-

An "instant" guest room is created by a Murphy bed. Gaily patterned sheets shirred on a curtain rod effect a distinctive and practical headboard. A convenient shelf overhead stores extra bedding while a wicker trunk-table hoards bath towels and bed linens.

stery and styling choice in convertible sofas were slim. The alternative was a drab, utilitarian-looking studio couch or a jackknife-type, drop-back sofa that provided occupants—both daytime and nighttime—with something far less than comfort.

Happily, the situation today is greatly improved. Your problem presently is one of choice, not lack of it. In recent years, many well-known upholstery manufacturers have added convertible sofas to their lines (often with a choice of chairs, love seats, and stationary sofas in matching or co-ordinated styles and fabrics). Many bedding manufacturers have also. You can expect to find the same fashionable styling on a convertible sofa today that's available on conventional types. In fact, engineering advances now make possible the same luxurious deep-seated comfort you expect of standard styles. You can no longer count on sight or sitting to disclose the sofa's innermost secret —whether or not it hides a bed. (*For detailed information on convertible bedding, see Chapter Twenty-three, "The Apartment."*)

A family room and study are probably the most logical and popular places to put up company. Since they're bound to include seating space of some kind, it might as well be a bed in disguise. Happily, these areas are also apt to include chests, cabinet or other storage units, as well-convenient stashing spots for the guest's own clothing during a stay and such guest-room accouterments as bed linens, blankets, pillows, and towels.

Lacking both family room and study, with finesse, the living room or dining room can be furnished to sleep a guest. It's a bit trickier to convince the visitor, but if you provide for the basic necessities, he'll soon forget it's anything but a room for a guest. You may be fortunate enough to have a home with an unfinished basement or attic with guest-room potential. Or perhaps you have space over a garage that would be worth-while finishing off for the pleasure of both family and company. If your home presents you with a choice when it comes to the location of the guest place, base your decision on common sense. The quietest part of the house is obviously the best. No one wants to wrestle with the noise of street traffic throughout the night. Nor does one want to be awakened by a whiny child or barking dog. Even such small sounds as the motor of a refrigerator or the tick of a clock can become insurmountable annoyances when you're trying to fall asleep in a strange place. If at all possible, situate the guest room far from the hustle and bustle of traffic, both of family and the street outside.

THE GUEST BATH

The guest bath is ideally private and immediately adjacent to the guest room. Unfortunately, few modern homes and apartments cater to such luxury. More often we must make the best of a shared bath situation. If this is the case, then make the best of it. At the very least, you should allot a special space—shelf, clothes hook, oversized towel rack—for the guest's personal belongings. The family member or members with whom the bath must be shared should give first consideration to the guest—spending minimum time there, keeping his own things picked up, and cleaning up after himself and the guest, if necessary.

But even more important than appearance in the bath is function. Certain necessities are basic fare and should be provided whether the bath is shared or separate unto the guest. One prime requisite is a good mirror, adequately illuminated at either side and overhead. If you can arrange a second one opposite, strategically placed to bring the back of the head into view, so much the better (one of those three-panel mirrors in which the center panel is stationary, and the sides adjustable like "wings"). In addition to the lights around the mirror, the bath should have general illumination as well, preferably in the form of a center-ceiling fixture. The shower stall or tub shower is another key area for a light overhead for safety's sake, if for no other reason. There's nothing quite so distressing, however, as closing oneself up into darkness, then trying to see when one emerges clean.

The bath should be equipped with tub and shower—the latter with an adjustable shower head. Some like the exhilaration of a prickly needle-fine spray; others prefer giant, gentler droplets. It should also be adjustable direction-wise—to avoid wetting down a fresh hairdo.

Hooks on the wall or back of the door are absolutely indispensable. How exasperating it is to get undressed only to find there's no place to hang anything. Hooks may be anything from the simple and functional wrought-iron variety from the hardware store to elaborate decorative ones that serve the same purpose. Or you might substitute an interesting bentwood hatrack, or a curlicue wicker one, or a thrift-shop find such as one of those old oaken hatracks that graced turn-of-the-century vestibules. If space permits, consider a standing hatrack, perhaps given a face lift with a bright coat of paint. Hang-ups can be interesting.

Shelf space for the guests' belongings—his shaving equipment, her cosmetics—is another necessity. I'm all for shelves in the bath everywhere—on the wall, over the john, behind the door, anyplace you can fit them in. They come in handy for stacking extra towels, displaying a sundry of bath concoctions, caching a small book collection.

Towel bars should be ample in width and in plentiful supply. If your bath is deficient in this category, add a standing rack or an extension-pole towel tree. Guest towels—hand and bath—and facecloths should be supersize and extra-absorbent. And don't forget the shower cap for female visitors. When it comes to the shower or tub, make sure you provide a full-size bath bar of soap or even a soap on a rope. Those tiny guest delicacies may be all right for the upstairs powder room, but they're hardly satisfactory for actual bathing. It's thoughtful to offer a guest both a deodorant bar and a gentler facial bar of some sort.

A wastebasket is also on the must list, large enough in size so you're not afraid to toss something into it. And, of course, an ample supply of facial tissue and extra toilet paper almost goes without saying.

One other essential on my guest-bath list is a well-stocked medicine chest. Whether necessity or nicety may be debatable, but to avoid being summoned at an unlikely hour of the night or forcing the unfortunate guest to endure discomfort, it's well worth having there. By "well-stocked" I mean it should contain the simplest of remedies: aspirin, Alka-Seltzer, milk of magnesia, iodine, or antiseptic ointment for minor cuts and burns, cotton and Band-Aids. It should also include such things as extra toothbrushes, tooth paste and mouthwash, nail file, clipper, emery boards, shaving equipment, razor blades, depilatory, spray deodorant, hand lotion, cleansing cream, shampoo, clean combs and brushes, a small scissors, and adhesive tape.

These are the little extras that say you care enough—that instill you as a memorable hostess in the eyes of the guest. Such small favors as providing a place to sit—other than the obvious one—to apply make-up, comb hair, or merely to dry feet. Supplying an extra set of towels and facecloths is also a thoughtful gesture so that one set will always be dry and ready for use. For true luxury in the European tradition, you might furnish the guest with a bath "sheet" or a terry robe that he can literally wrap himself up in.

Soakers and tub sitters will appreciate a backrest or little inflatable pillow plus reading material close at hand. One guest bath I had the pleasure of visiting had a little tubside table—actually a folding bed tray with a terry toweling cover—on which were placed a selection of digest-size magazines, bubbling bath oil, an apothecary jar full of soap, a box of cigarettes, and an ashtray! Also nice to have close at hand are nail and bath brushes. Other subtleties for the bath beautiful might include a selection of fragrant concoctions—bath oil or foaming bubble bath (eliminates bathtub ring, by the way), after-bath astringent, dusting talc, body lotions for her, burly after-shave potions and spicy cologne for him—with a little sign imprinted "Please use."

Almost any visiting female, in residence more than a day or two, will have at least one hand wash of stockings and lingerie. Have a good cold-water soap on hand and a supply of little clip-type stocking hangers, plus a small drying rack of some kind. Guests, both male and female, will appreciate a bottle of cleaning fluid, a shoeshine cloth and polishes, and a good clothesbrush stashed away for their use somewhere.

As for decoratives in the bath, guests like to see pictures on the wall—prints, oil paintings, favorite snapshots in frames, or even children's art under glass. One clever couple mounted a pair of round jigsaw puzzles, framed them with ribbon trim, and hung them on the wall. Plants always introduce a special freshness to the bath and actually thrive in such steamy surroundings. And what could be a more pleasant finale than a bouquet of freshly cut flowers.

PRIVACY

The establishment of privacy need not be a complicated matter. The separate guest room unto itself, of course, presents no problem. But don't overlook the shared bath situation where it exists. It's only courteous to relegate family members to a second bathroom when possible, or in any instance, to let the guest go first. And the door of both bath and bedroom should be lockable from the inside.

Where the guest room is actually a portion of another room, the creative challenge is somewhat greater. However, the solution can often be a decorative as well as a functional one. For example, you might improvise some kind of room divider. It could be a free-standing bookcase unit that breaks the room into areas somewhat permanently—particularly effective in ell-shaped rooms—servicing both areas with display and storage space. Or you might incorporate one of a variety of sliding or folding doors that can be summoned into use whenever the occasion demands. Shoji screens or floating fabric panels that slide on floor and ceiling tracks suggest a certain tranquillity, can be relatively inexpensive, and are especially appropriate in modern interiors. If you're at all inventive, you'll probably dream up many more original treatments. Imagine the decorative impact of a series of ceiling-hung shades in color or pattern that pull down between enameled two by fours wedged between floor and ceiling to physically separate space.

Perhaps the simplest solution of all is an ordinary folding screen with an extraordinary look of some kind. A screen can be translucent

*A long-term visitor will delight in a bedroom that's self-sufficient—
or nearly so. This bedroom is outfitted for a miscellany of daytime
activities with its drop-down desk, snack table, reading chair, and
storage space everywhere. Rough textured white paneling provides
a refreshing background for the colorful room.*

or opaque, fabric covered or wallpapered, lacquered brightly or composed of common louvered doors that you've cleverly hinged together. It can be treated unobtrusively as an extension of the wall by
which it stands, or outstandingly to make an aesthetic statement of its
own. Its supreme versatility lies in its very portability. It might stand
muster against a wall, behind a sofa or chair by day, adding architectural interest, only to come out in the night to screen off a portion
of the room as a guest area.

All the comforts of a home away from home are wrapped up in this living-family room. Handsome paneling sets the stage and a translucent screen provides privacy for the guest. The sleep-inducing component is the love seat that converts to a single bed featuring a lift-up headrest for reading. In addition to the essentials, all the little extras are here—the bouquet of fresh flowers, the telephone, the dish of candy, the television set, the books selected with the guest's interest in mind.

A room is inadequate as a guest place if it lacks sufficient stashing space. There must first of all be some place to open a suitcase—one of those handy fold-away luggage racks, a desk top, tabletop or low bureau surface you've cleared of clutter. Next needed, of course, is space to hang—preferably a closet devoid of out-of-season clothes and well equipped with an assemblage of wooden or padded hangers —almost anything but those flimsy wire kind that come free from the dry cleaners. Suitcase-crushed clothes need breathing space if wrinkles are to fall out. Clothes hooks are also handy for caddying hats, handbags, belts, and the like. And a few special hangers for trousers and skirts will be greatly appreciated.

Lacking a closet in your guest abode? Improvise one. Summon the ubiquitous screen into use and position it in such a fashion so as to enclose a corner of the room. Hang a hatrack or an arrangement of hooks behind, furnish with an ample quantity of hangers, and you've a makeshift closet that will serve splendidly, forming a dressing area to boot, if you've judiciously placed a bureau there too. For supplementary hang-up space (but usually less attractive), those over-the-door racks will ease the squeeze in a pinch.

Drawer space is also a must for any guest spending more than one night. Empty at least one or two completely and invite your guest to use them. The amount of stowing space necessary to provide varies, of course, with the guest's anticipated length of stay. Better to overestimate than to create guest-room chaos by forcing the visitor to live out of his suitcase.

Surface space is important, too. Your guest needs a place to empty the contents of her handbag or his pockets, a place to spread out make-up and grooming paraphernalia. Hopefully you've provided a good light source and mirror immediately adjacent. The surface might be the top of a bureau, table, or desk, a vacant bookshelf, a built-in counter of a vanity chest. The better you anticipate storage needs, the less clutter you bestow upon your guest. And don't forget to provide some out-of-the-way spot for suitcase storage.

PART FOUR

Special Decoration

CHAPTER TWENTY-THREE

THE APARTMENT

THE DECORATION of the apartment is approached in the same manner as the single-family dwelling: in color planning, choice of style, furniture arrangement, etc. The only difference is that the planning must be stricter, especially if the apartment is small. Color continuity is most important in this case, because it will make the apartment seem and function as a larger entity. The eye will flow easily through the various rooms, precluding any feeling of decorative claustrophobia. The very small or one-room apartment is obviously a special matter and we will take up its decoration in detail. As you study this section, remember that many of the same principles apply to the decor of the three-, four-, five-room, or larger apartment.

To most people, the thought of living, dining, and sleeping in one room comfortably, to say nothing of brightly and imaginatively, seems remote. And yet hundreds of thousands of people do so with pleasure and style, as proved by the prevalence of this small unit in the new apartment buildings which jut into the skylines of our large cities. The incidence of bachelor and career-girl living and the budget-mindedness of newlyweds and retirees makes the one-room apartment loom large in living patterns today and in years to come. One-room living has a special appeal to these groups, perhaps because it presents the always fascinating challenge of trying to do much with little. This has a special appeal to those with a high degree of organization: The necessity of including as many of today's comforts as possible in small space poses an intriguing problem and the organized mind knows that with careful space planning, clever decoration, imaginative choice of furniture and its arrangement, it is possible to solve the problem and create a setting for amazingly expansive living. Besides all this, there is a magic about all apartment living, the lure of

A neat way to define apartment areas and still permit some light and ventilation is with a series of louvered ponderosa-pine shutters from the local lumberyard, hinged together and hung from a ceiling track. Here they define a dining area; they could work just as easily to demarcate a sleeping area in an apartment.

making a bright, personal world in the heart of the city, of creating by oneself a warm, inviting place to come to, where the crushing problems and pace of the metropolis can be shut out. And curiously, this magic seems to increase as the size of the apartment diminishes.

REPLANNING YOUR SPACE

Once you have chosen your one-room apartment, selected the paint, and measured each separate space, you are ready to start planning. If

A large single room was partially divided to form a study-dining area near the entrance by attaching two, 4-foot by 8-foot plywood panels to floor and ceiling. Holes were drilled into the concrete ceiling, then filled with plugs into which angle irons were screwed. At the base, a wood strip was nailed to the parquet and the plywood toe-nailed into it. Astragal moldings from the lumberyard decorated the panels which were then painted.

On the other side, the panels show their one good face; in this case, oak finished with a walnut stain. From a 4-foot by 4-foot piece of the same plywood, stained similarly, a corner lamp table was made, into which one of the single lounges rolls.

the management has given you a printed floor plan, you can work right on it, penciling lightly so that you can erase as you get other ideas. Or you can make measurements and draw the rooms on graph paper from the stationery store (quarter-inch scale is easiest, so that each square represents one foot). The ultimate aim in the small apartment is to get as much visual and living variety as possible. Each area should be planned so that you have a feeling of being in a separate space, and yet all must be planned together for over-all visual harmony. It is difficult, but it can be done.

First of all, if the entrance door opens right into the main room, you may want to create the sense of a foyer for privacy, which can be done with a folding screen or some kind of baffle. Most new buildings are a standard eight feet high, so one or two panels of 4-foot by 8-foot plywood can be used. One interesting approach is to have two panels cut to provide four 2-foot by 8-foot sections which can be joined with butterfly or two-way hinges and either painted to blend or contrast with walls or wallpaper. For an investment under forty dollars, you can have something good-looking which can be moved and always be used somewhere in a future home. (See Figure A.)

Next, you can concentrate on your large—or at least your only large—room. Just because it includes four walls, it doesn't have to be a single space. There are ways to partition areas according to function and to give privacy and variety. If the kitchen is off the part of the space closest to the entrance, as is usually the case, you can take, say, eight feet and form a dining foyer by installing plywood panels coming out from each side wall, with a space in the middle leading to a sleeping-living area or extending only from one wall, creating a passage to the rest of the space at one side. By positioning the panels cleverly, you can also create privacy from the entrance door. (See Figure B.) If light is a problem and you don't want to create a dark foyer, you can use translucent plastic panels, framed in wood like Japanese shojis (they can even slide to go all the way across the space); or another idea is to use old paneled doors, which can often be bought from demolition contractors for as little as a dollar apiece. By hinging them or adding plywood to top or bottom to get floor-to-ceiling height, you can create a handsome partition for little money. It can be painted, or, if you are very ambitious, the doors can be stripped of paint to the natural wood and stained, to accent the rest of your decorative scheme.

Depending on the location of windows, it may be possible to parti-

A standard arrangement with two windows and limited space yields a world of livability in one room. The provincial-style sofa opens to a double bed; Parsons table serves for desk or dining. Big use of one pattern makes space seem larger.

A variation on the same basic arrangement shows how a focal point can be created with a long, low table, an important picture and flanking lamps. Seating pieces then fall naturally at each side, the day-bed at the window doubling for slumber.

"SCOTCHGARD" FABRIC PROTECTOR AND KODEL POLYESTER

Again, a way to create a decorative catalyst for the long wall. Two Parsons tables end to end nest mobile ottomen. Clever window treatment masks radiator, air conditioner and awkward ceiling beam; corner screens mask jutting posts.

Here's a clever idea for an unexpected bonus in the small apartment, a niche. It becomes sleeping area by night, sitting area by day. Single mattress sits on platform carpeted same as floor. Thai-like wallpaper covers niche and window panels.

There is new furniture designed expressly for one-room living. A Victorian house-turned-apartments complements its streamlined and colorful crispness. Wall unit includes a desk, hi-fi, record storage and a folding single bed in the left bay.

For the mini-garden unit, a compact grouping of love seats, comfortable in tufted latex foam rubber, one of which opens to a bed. Benches in the same upholstery serve for extra seating or snack dining. Garden is clay-potted philodendron.

Dining at the window takes on flair with seats for metal outdoor chairs in room's two colors. Sofa bed is set apart with shutter wallpaper in the same green. End wall treatment hides a jumble of windows as well as heating-cooling: narrow Venetian blinds fall in bays demarcated by 1"×3" strips of lumber, painted white.

Pass-through to a mini-kitchen (in first apartment shown) became a snack bar with a counter in a white laminate. A Roman shade in a fabric to match plaid wallpaper drops down for formal moments. Note storage unit made of filagree hardboard and lumber. It holds hi-fi, TV and miscellany, has open shelves to display treasures.

SIMMONS HIDE-A-BED SOFA

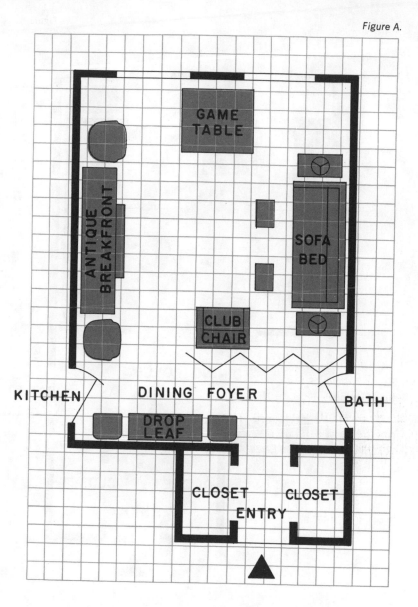

tion to form two completely separate rooms. This is often feasible in a corner apartment with windows on two walls. If the apartment is a two and a half with an ell that has a window, it is an easy matter to close this off as a separate sleeping room; the ell can be a private study. Here you will have to include one hinged panel for access. You can even frame in a regular door or merely hinge one 4-foot by

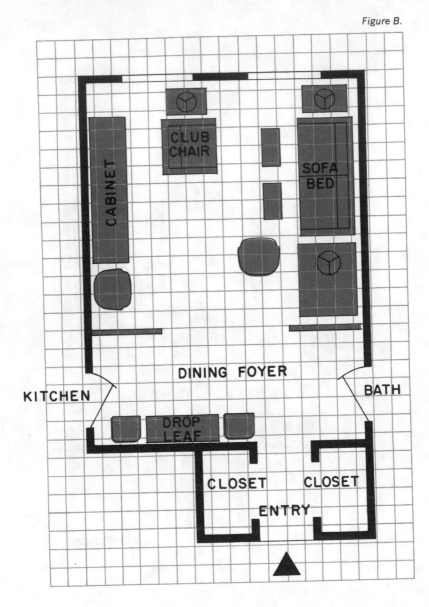

8-foot plywood panel to open. A ceiling track for drapery or narrow, hinged panels can also be used clear across the opening, with panels accordion-folding to one side as you need access.

Incidentally, speaking of plywood, remember that there are many grades and several sizes. The least expensive is the common fir plywood, which has a heavy, rather ordinary grain. This is quite satis-

Figure C.

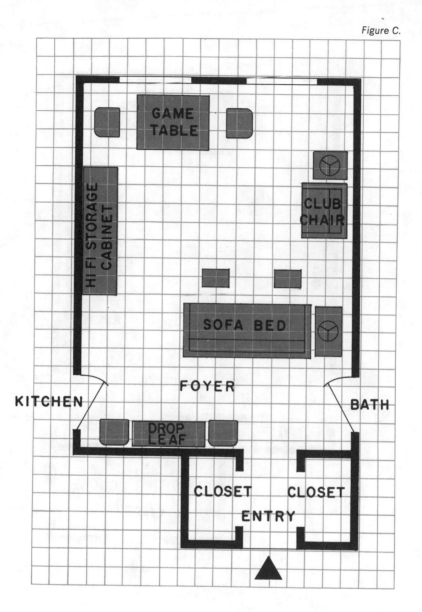

factory if you are planning to paint or paper it. Be sure to pick out your panels at the lumberyard, if possible. Be sure to get at least one good side free of knots and indentations and two good ones, if the screen or paneling is to be exposed on both sides. For better appearance, choose one of the many other wood finishes—oak, birch, even teak, and rosewood, if you prefer. And again, if the panels are to be

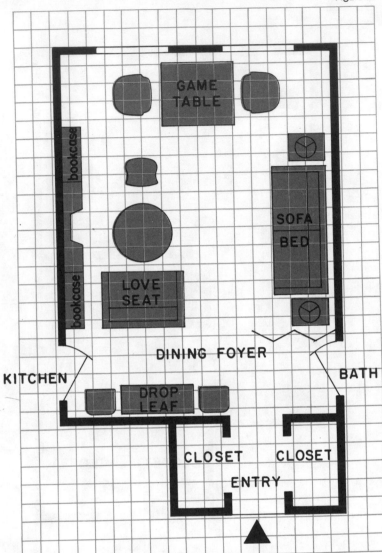

seen on both sides, specify two-faced panels. While you are at the lumberyard, study the variety of stock ponderosa pine moldings that are available. They can be used across the top of a partition to hide disparities, fillers, etc., and can be stained or painted to blend. Molding can also be used at the base and can be chosen to blend with the usual clamshell molding used in most new buildings as baseboard. If you don't do the project yourself, specify to the carpenter what you want or go with him to the lumberyard to choose the items. He'll be amazed and pleased that you know something about it, and it will help to arrive at a meeting of the minds. Nothing is more discouraging than being "surprised" by what a carpenter does.

Decoration to Make Space Seem Larger

There is a place for sprawling, bulky furniture, but it is certainly not in the one-room apartment. Nothing will make your room "work" more easily than small-scaled pieces of furniture. Fortunately, there is an abundance of furniture on the market today especially designed for apartment living, and it comes in many period styles and many price ranges. The traditionally styled pieces have been adapted for the eight-foot ceiling and reduced wall space so artfully that little of the charm of the period is lost. So shop wisely and carefully. Ask your furniture dealer to let you see complete manufacturers' catalogues rather than settle for what is on the floor. Most often, the dealer will have to order from the manufacturer anyway, with a six- to eight-week delivery, so you might just as well have what you want.

Convertible Bedding

Obviously, the first consideration is the type of bedding. If you have a sleeping ell and choose to use it as such, you can have a box spring and mattress set and a conventional sofa in the living room. Following are several possibilities.

The most popular choice remains the dual-purpose sofa or convertible sofa-bed. The major manufacturers offer dozens of styles and upholstery choices and many sizes. There is a chair-and-a-half size that offers a thirty-three-inch single-bed size; full-scale sofas that open to standard fifty-four-inch-wide double beds and extra-large, sectional sofa styles that open to queen and even king size, sixty inches and seventy-two inches respectively. There are also sectional designs in matching or co-ordinated styles and fabrics with one unit remaining as a sofa, while another opens as either a single or double bed; there are twin love-seat arrangements that open to create twin beds; and corner sectionals, one of which opens to a bed.

The convertible continues in greatest popularity because great

This hi-riser bed with trundle below little reveals its double life, covered in a damask-patterned, tailored cover and with heavy bolsters to create comfortable sofa backrest. A wall of paintings adds character and the visual variety so important in one-room living.

strides have been made to assure its foolproof appearance as a sofa by day. The bulky units of yesteryear have been redesigned to present slim backs; the metal mechanism, which must be sturdy, has been made as light as necessary strength permits; the telltale opening between seat pillows at the rear of the couch has been done away with in the best-designed models. Good styling is the order of the day with units available in standard Lawson designs, Early American wings and high-back wings, French country, Italian, Spanish, and good, clean-lined contemporary. In fact, today it is safe to say one can find a sofa-bed in almost any style available in the conventional sofa.

Prices are higher than for a comparable sofa, because of the expensive steel mechanism hidden within. It is important not to buy on price alone. There is no such thing as bargain bedding when it must perform comfortably at night and stylishly by day for years. So don't skimp on a convertible. And be sure to specify that you want the premium innerspring mattress; it costs extra but is well worth it. The mattress that comes with the sofa-bed is not always the best and won't stand up.

Following are some guidelines for purchasing convertible sofas:

Give the sofa the sit test. It should provide the same comfort you'd expect of a stationary sofa. Check "gaposis" between seat cushions at the rear, as mentioned before.

Test the open-and-close mechanism; with a "lift" you can easily manage (it varies from twenty to fifty pounds, so compare at the store).

Notice construction details. In quality convertibles the frame is reinforced to prevent wobbles, front legs are capped to save carpet wear, corners are rounded so as not to snag sheets. Preferred, also, is a convertible that opens up to standard bed height—certainly a boon to bedmaking.

Ask about upholstery. The choice is virtually limitless, but you'll be wise to investigate fabrics made from the new nonabsorbent, stain-repellent fibers, or fabrics that have been treated with a soil-and-stain-resistant finish such as Scotchgard or Zepel. Most fabrics can be so treated, if they have not been already; this protection is well worth the extra cost.

Notice cushion construction. Spring construction is heavier than polyfoam and Dacron—a consideration, since you will have to lug cushions every night when making up the bed.

When it comes to proper scale, there are two basic kinds of convertible sofas, one in which you sleep at right angles to the back, the other where you sleep parallel. The former is easier to make and pleasant for reading in bed, since its back acts as a headboard, but it obviously takes more floor space when opened (allow at least eight feet for it to open without disturbing free-standing pieces). The parallel arrangement takes a foot to eighteen inches less space and when closed has a slimmer look, because the back can be designed more compactly. However, it necessitates buying a long unit, since the bed must provide at least a seventy-four-inch length, and it opens in some models with a slight depression between the two parallel widths. The necessary length of this parallel style may preclude its use in the one-room apartment, depending on furniture arrangement. Scale by day is the important consideration, since traffic circulation is not a factor during sleeping hours, and here, choice is determined as with a conventional sofa and will be taken up under scale in relation to over-all furniture arrangement.

Another possibility for dual-purpose bedding is to buy a thirty- or thirty-three-inch mattress and box springs on legs, the so-called "Hollywood" bed, and use a tailored cover with bolsters and pillows. Or you can use a hi-riser or trundle bed, with the same arrangement, only doubled, with a separate mattress and springs which can be pulled out from under the upper unit and up to form either a double bed or two singles.

There are also attractive day beds on the market. They differ from standard twins in that the head- and footboard are usually of equal height so as to look like arms of a sofa when the bed is positioned lengthwise against the wall. Here, too, bolsters or supersized pillows covered to match the coverlet or upholstery are often used to line the wall and when removed they permit the unit to be made up as a regular thirty-three-inch bed. Day beds are available in French Provincial, Spanish, Italian, and contemporary designs, with a choice of suitable upholstery in each case. The beds are sometimes narrower in width than standard twins so as to provide a more comfortable depth for sitting. One arrangement enjoying current vogue is a pair of day beds placed at right angles to one another, bridged by a square corner table between. The end of one day bed slips under the table by day, not only to conserve valuable floor space, but to create a pleasant conversational area as well with tabletop surface for a lamp, books, bouquet, even a snack, if you wish. Both furniture and bedding manufacturers alike are offering these functional three-piece units.

A hangover from the Danish modern craze is the wood-frame sofa with slab-type foam cushion that can double as a mattress by night. Still being produced by many furniture makers, these sofas are usually considerably lower in price than fully upholstered convertible sofas—for reasons that are obvious.

The studio couch which has a pull-out second single bed is an old stand-by. This economical and forever-popular item is available upholstered in "tickings" so bright and colorful as to make spreads and coverlets passé, certainly unnecessary. Some have optional wood or upholstered backs or arms, giving them true day-bed status. Others come equipped with the usual wall-leaning bolsters or oversized pillows.

There is also the Murphy bed which folds into the wall or into a specially designed, stylish cabinet. Within, standard mattresses, from twin to double bed dimensions, can rest on several types of springs, flat-ribbon to coil. It is also quite possible to make one yourself by having an armoire designed and hinging a slab or plywood with a foam-rubber mattress on top. When the armoire doors are opened, the slab and mattress can be dropped forward to rest on a bench or pair of wood stools at the front. This type of wall-enclosed unit is a good choice, because it permits a fully made-up mattress to be lowered, saving work each night.

An interesting idea for the apartment is the "bed loft." It is built in the sleeping ell and is essentially a wood platform which supports a foam-rubber or innerspring mattress, usually fifty-four-inch width. The sleeping surface is raised up, permitting drawer storage space in the wood frame below, much in the manner of a sea captain's bed. A carpenter can easily construct it to the size of an ell with doors or drawers for much-needed storage, and, of course, it can be moved out when you leave and would make a useful piece of furniture for a child's room in a later house. It is important to choose your mattress first and let the carpenter work around its size.

Another storage-bed idea has a lounge unit with mattress and bolsters covered, day-bed fashion, with good-looking upholstery fabric, while underneath there is a generous pull-out drawer of the same size as the bed. This is a great way to hide pillows and blankets, plus extra sheets and a throw.

For sleeping space for an occasional visitor, you might consider a fold-away "rollaway" or a chair bed. The latter is an upholstered piece, sometimes with the same or similar quality bedding found in the more expensive full-size convertible sofas, which opens to accommodate a single sleeper. A less-expensive but also useful piece is the ottoman. It, too, opens to meet the needs of a guest and is a pleasing accent piece when not in nocturnal use. Both units offer narrow, confined sleeping, not recommended for every night, year in and year out.

OTHER FURNITURE POSSIBILITIES

Once you have made a decision about the bed, other choices follow—table and chairs, desk, upholstered pieces, coffee tables, and accessory furniture. Fortunately, there is a great deal of dual-purpose furniture available that can be used in many ways. For example, there are hi-lo tables that can serve as coffee tables at their low fourteen- or sixteen-inch height and then be raised to twenty-nine or thirty inches for dining, bridge, or desk work. Some are designed with drop leaves which can be raised for greater dining surface. Since you may be opening your sofa-bed each night, or arranging some kind of bedding, and since the coffee table is apt to be in front of it, you want a piece of furniture that is easy to move aside. If you cannot find a hi-lo table on casters, you can have a carpenter install casters on it or even do it yourself. The hardware store will have some kind of suitable rollers. If you plan a permanent dining group, then choose two small coffee tables, rather than one large one. Many feel this is a better arrangement in any case, because for buffet entertaining, it permits separate little tables for guests' plates.

Another good choice, especially if you have a dining foyer, is the console table which extends for dining. It can easily be moved from the wall for dinner parties, and extra leaves permit seating as many as eight. (Leaves may be stored in a high rack in a nearby closet.) It is always pleasant to dine near a window and a good solution is a compact, round dining table located at a window with four small-scaled side chairs around it at all times—for games or desk work. A table thirty-six inches in diameter with two twelve-inch leaves is a good choice. Other dining possibilities include a wall-hung, drop-down shelf, which you can have made from plywood and a patterned laminate—a wood grain or a design that blends with your decor—which when raised can be braced with legs or hinged struts (concealed when it is folded to the wall). When folded flush to the wall, it will give the appearance of a painting or decorative wall plaque.

Apartments almost never have enough storage. One striking antique serves as the decorative focal point and also holds a wealth of miscellaneous storage including bed linens for the sofa-bed on the opposite wall. The window treatment is ingenious: a woven wood shade drops to floor, hiding heating and air conditioning, but admitting light and air. Traverse drapery can close completely when required, matches damask of dining table and sofa.

The small breakfront which opens to a desk gives a place to display bric-a-brac and also a useful writing and work center when needed. It is a good idea to have one fine piece of furniture as a focal point of decoration and such a piece is a good investment for a future home. Remember, as you choose your furniture, that you will not always be in such confined quarters and select with an eye to a future house or larger apartment. The small-scaled dining and other pieces would be excellent for a future family or recreation room in a suburban house, while the breakfront desk would be useful and attractive in a bedroom or study.

As you plan your furniture, keep in mind that you are probably working with a rather narrow twelve-foot width, so shop for wall-hugging pieces. If you have a sleeping ell and can have a conventional sofa and chair grouping in the living-dining area—your "main" room —the slimmest, simplest sofa is the best choice, with a pair of light, easily moved armchairs. Reproduction French chairs with wood arms and upholstered backs and seats are suitable, being open and light-scaled, comfortable, and stylish. Such chairs can be moved to a dining table as host chairs, too. When it comes to upholstery, choose light colors (they always make a room look larger) and avoid large-scaled, bizarre prints which have a tendency to close in on you. However, we will go into the matter of color in a later section.

FURNITURE ARRANGEMENT

After proper scale of furniture, its arrangement ranks next in importance. In small space, traffic flow is basic, so pieces must be placed to make space both look and work larger than it is. A second consideration, often overlooked, is that furniture can be arranged for variety, that is to give an impression to the one who lives in a small space that there are many different areas, to make a one-room apartment seem as though it had several rooms. In effect you can create a living area, dining area, TV-library area, and a sleeping area all in one room. A third consideration is convenience: pieces should be located for ease of serving, for an orderly relationship to kitchen and bath—sleep furniture near bath, dining furniture near kitchen.

Since this is a section of the book better illustrated by diagrams than by words, there are accompanying sketches to show viable arrangements in average-sized space. It is, of course, impossible to anticipate every size of room and every arrangement of doors, windows, and other architectural details. However, in each of the three above-named considerations in furniture arrangement, there are some guide-posts. The first basic is to use as few pieces as are absolutely necessary. Packing many pieces into relatively small space is never a good idea, and in the one-room apartment, it can be fatal. The room will function poorly and look cluttered. For circulation, the rule is, keep pieces out of the center of the room. If your room is especially large

A focal point can be manufactured where required by adding a false fireplace. This one, a French Provincial style, helps to set the decorative theme of a small flat as well. Moldings, a graceful curve to match the mantel design, were applied to the flush entrance door; bricklike wallpaper, tole chandelier, and figured carpet add to the theme. Dining table and side chairs in Louis XV style move to side wall when not in use.

and you want to use a sofa broadside to create a passageway to the kitchen or bath or to demarcate a foyer where none exists, it is possible. (See Figure C.) Ordinarily, however, you will be happier placing all furniture along walls and leaving an open, central space, especially if, to get to the bath or a sleeping ell, you must cross the main area.

If the room itself suggests a focal point around which furniture can be arranged, you have a great boon. A fireplace, an especially large window with a view, a built-in book wall—all can be "grouped around," as it were, to make an inviting arrangement. If you aren't so lucky, you can create a focal point with a magnificent piece of furniture—a cabinet, credenza, or breakfront, or with a low, long shelf

and an arrangement of prints, plaques, and paintings on the wall
above. (See Figure A.) One large, fine painting or piece of sculpture
alone can form a focal point. You can achieve the effect of a fireplace
with a handsome mantel. Some people dislike this kind of dissimula-
tion, but many fine designers consider it quite permissible to use anything which gives a characterless space some distinction.

However, if you build around a fireplace, cabinet, or whatever, it
isn't wise to flank it with a sofa on one side and a pair of armchairs on
the other, as might be done in a regular living room, unless the space
is exceptionally wide. For example, with the fireplace on one long
side wall, if the room is only twelve or fourteen feet in width, a sofa

*In the main sitting area of this apartment, a sofa-bed little reveals its dual
function along a picture wall decorated as the focal point of the room. A
pair of French country armchairs and a deep sprawly lounge chair and
ottoman form a comfortable conversation grouping. Danish modern dining
group with four chairs is at the window, near the kitchen entrance.*

would jut too far into the room and impede traffic. Better to use an armchair on either side of the focal point, or a love seat on one side, a table and armchair opposite. Then place the sofa on the opposite wall, facing the fireplace. There will be space to pass through and space to open the sofa to a bed, if such is the sleeping arrangement.

In the one-room apartment, the windows are usually at the far end of the room. These can, with clever drapery or other window treatment, become the focal point to decorate around. Since you are working with the deeper room measurement, you can use a sofa and a pair of chairs with a coffee table between, without cutting into traffic flow. (See Figure B.) However, if the bed must open for sleeping, use light, easily moved chairs and table. Another pleasant solution is to use the area near the window as a location for dining. There is something about dining with a view that is stimulating, and even if the view is negligible, the light seems to aid the appetite. If the kitchen is at the other end of the one room, serving may entail a few extra steps, but it is worth it. Should kitchen access be nearby, it is the only logical place. As mentioned earlier, dining furniture should be a permanent grouping which can be used for letter writing, games, or hobbies at other times, and for these pursuits, the light from the windows is helpful.

To illustrate several of our points, Figure D shows a dining-game group on the window wall, a sofa-bed with end tables on one adjacent wall, and a false fireplace with flanking bookcases and a love seat-chair group on the other. This keeps the center aisle of the space open at all times except when the sofa-bed is pulled out; it also affords great variety in living with one area for lounging, another for sleeping, another for dining; one area gives the look of a library. In fact, the whole scene gives the impression of being part of a larger home. This is the distillation of what the one-room apartment should do: it should look like part of a complete house.

Arrangement of pieces in auxiliary areas such as the foyer or sleeping ell is relatively simple, since space is usually tight. If the foyer is minuscule, there may be room for a small chair or bench plus a narrow console with a mirror above. If it is large, it is most often intended to double as a dining area. In that case the answer, as mentioned previously, is a console that opens for dining, again the narrower the better. Remember, this is the area of entrance into the apartment, and anything that either crowds it or makes it look crowded is undesirable. The standard sleeping ell has barely enough space for a three-quarter bed and a night table with a lamp. If it is equipped as a study, there would be space for a desk and chair, and perhaps a small table or file case. The walls themselves will dictate the arrangement. If you partition the opening, you will gain another wall which will facilitate the arrangement. If you have a window, and most ells do, try to locate the desk so that the light comes over your left shoulder as you work.

WALL COLORS AND BACKGROUND TREATMENTS

When it comes to wall treatments, we are once again up to space-stretching tricks. The general rule in small space is to paint everything the same color. This will give continuity plus a sense of greater area than exists as one proceeds from foyer to living-sleeping area, ell, bath, and kitchen. The use of any color for walls and ceilings can do wonders, but light colors are usually easier to live with than dark, and they do seem to make things look bigger. Dark colors give a cavernous look, to be sure, and they are dramatic, perhaps too dramatic for most homemakers to want to live with day in and day out. It also helps to remember that color can do wonders to seemingly change the proportions of rooms. For example, a long, narrow room is "widened" by painting one long wall and one end wall a darker color than the other two walls, or a noticeably darker shade of the same color. Accent wallpaper or paneling that is darker in tone than the paint of the opposite wall tends to help extend the painted wall visually.

An especially low ceiling seems higher when painted a much lighter color than walls, while a too-high one is "lowered" by a darker color. For some unknown reason, either a dark or light floor seems to work equally well spacewise. The eye automatically goes to the floor and for that reason it is wise to have the same floor treatment in all areas so that the eye is not "stopped" as it travels from one part of the apartment to another. Of course, separate kitchen and bath with doors can be a different tone and material, for practicality.

Special wall treatments can be attractive and useful in your decorative sleight of hand. One wall of figured paper makes a striking accent and, properly located, can serve as a foil to other walls and seemingly stretch them. Since you will not be buying much paper, it is well to buy expensively: a distinctive pattern and coloration should be used or the accent will be wasted. Look at the flock papers and damask designs and be sure it is part of your general color scheme used throughout the apartment. Be mindful, too, that if you install paper you run the risk of being billed by the landlord for removal when you move, unless you find that the next tenant likes the paper and wants to keep it. Another source of wall variety is with modular panels of printed hardboard and various grains of plywood. These come in 4-foot by 8-foot and 4-foot by 10-foot sheets and can be nailed to furring strips (thin, latticelike wood) which are nailed to the plaster wall. The panels can come down and travel with you when you move; furring strips can be easily removed, and the nail holes spackled and touched up with some of the original paint, so the landlord cannot hold you liable for damage.

Some of these new printed hardboard panels are exciting-looking and simulate damask fabric, wood grain of every imaginable kind, and many other patterns and textures. Your local lumberyard can show you color brochures and actual samples. Some have special finishing nails to blend with the color of the panels. Another way that you can take it with you is with fabric stretched on the wall. Simply remove the cornice molding at the ceiling, if there is any, tack the fabric up tight to the ceiling and as low to the baseboard as possible. Use double-faced masking tape for the seams, after turning under or trimming the selvage. Then replace the cornice or add a simple ponderosa pine molding from the lumberyard to finish it off at the top. Fabric gives a wonderful look and "feel" to a room and can be easily taken down and reused in some way in a future home.

Decorative Tricks

There are other ways to "extend" room dimensions than with color. One is with trompe l'oeil, which, translated from the French means "to fool the eye." A good device is scenic wallpaper that presents a perspective. There are many scenes to choose from at the better wallpaper stores. You can find a southern plantation, a Mediterranean seascape, an architectural panorama of ancient Rome, or present-day New York. These are apt to be expensive, so it is wise to mount them on wallboard for later removal. A wall of mirrors does wonders to make a room look wider. One clever idea is to buy many small mirrors at the dime store and install them with mirror-topped rosettes, which you can buy at a glass store. These can be inserted into the wall at the four corners, each one holding four mirrors in place at one point. Since in a large expanse, true mirror images are not important, the inexpensiveness of the units will not be apparent. If you want fidelity, buy a good plate-glass mirror. Again, it can be taken down when you move, although this usually requires a glazier to do with safety. If there is a good view from windows at the end of an apartment, a mirror along the adjacent wall can double its impact and permit you to enjoy the view without being directly in front of it.

An outdoor or garden look also has the ability to make small space more airy through association, simply by making the viewer feel he is out of doors. Brick wallpaper helps; light blue ceiling and white walls add to the effect; there are also trellis designs and scenics in wallpaper which give the feeling of being on a terrace. White or the classic Pompeian green outdoor iron furniture is suitable, and some of the better lines are substantial enough to serve well as indoor furniture. In fact, a few groups are now made with wood tabletops, expansible to seat many guests. Chair seats in a bright flowered chintz to blend with other upholstery, accessories chosen for an outdoor look, and a bower of real plants can combine to do wonders. This is an excellent way to really open up small space, provided that you like the garden look. A nice bonus is that the furniture can move to the terrace of an eventual house in the suburbs or country.

WINDOW IDEAS

Window treatment comes into play importantly even though the number of openings may be limited. Here is the place to plan as simple a treatment as possible, if only not to take up precious floor space. The general rule with windows is to decorate them to permit their main functions of admitting light and air. All too often the designer, amateur or professional, sets up an elaborate second window over the existing one, with heavy drapery, lambrequin, or other devices that bring the window out into the room. This is especially wrong in the one-room apartment where every inch counts. Chances are that if you decorate to let the window perform its function, the treatment will be successful.

To plan a treatment, study your windows. Is there one single expanse, as is often found in new buildings, or are there two or more standard double-hung units? Is there an air conditioner and, if so, is it in the window or a through-wall installation underneath? Is there a bulky radiator under the window which must be reckoned with?

What exposure does the window offer? Cold north light, warm morning east, late-afternoon west, or sunny south? If there is more than one window, are they uniform in scale, with an even line presented by frames, top and bottom? What standard equipment does the landlord provide—Venetian blinds, window shades, or nothing? Once you have analyzed what you have to work with, you can go ahead.

Too often, the amateur decorator thinks only of drapery as window treatment when many other more suitable ideas are available to her. For example, if you want to give an airy effect with the outdoor look, louvered shutters are an excellent solution. The shutters—and you can find them in many sizes, unfinished, at the local lumberyard —can be hinged together and fitted into the frame of the window. They take up no floor space, can be opened or closed according to needs for light and air, and can be painted or stained for any desired decorative effect. Shutters are a workable answer to the window air conditioner, since a bit of carpentry can detail a hinged panel that can be opened for access to the control panel, yet remain closed for appearance sake, whether or not the unit is in use, since cooled air can come through the louvers.

Window shades are another space-making solution, since they too fit into window frames. Shades are available in a variety of patterns and colors and, of course, can be laminated with your own fabric to match colors and patterns used elsewhere in the room. They can be hung conventionally or reverse roll with the cylindrical roller concealed from view. They come translucent and opaque, permitting degrees of brightness during daylight or total darkness, day or night. The window shade is also helpful camouflage for air conditioners, either in the window or through the wall below the window. With the latter installation, you can create a design with a series of shades, some of which pull down to the floor to hide the unit. And don't forget, shades can be arranged to pull from the floor up or across the window expanse, with the cylinder attached to the side frame.

The standard Venetian blind is so well known as to need no description. Usually it must be used with some kind of softening drapery, although an effective contemporary look can be achieved with the blinds exposed. With the latter arrangement, it is interesting to create a design with blocks of different colors in a Mondrian-like effect. Vertical Venetian blinds are more interesting than the horizontal installation and they can be used floor to ceiling across an en-

Contemporary drama in tight quarters was created with dark walls and floor, light window treatment, rug, and white canvas British officers chairs. The cover for sofa-bed and ottoman, a nod at tradition, acts as softener to the scheme. Note crisply striped window shades and dining table made of bamboo "A's" and glass top.

tire expanse, covering air conditioner and radiator and making many individual windows look like one. They give the contemporary architectural look par excellence and control illumination for interesting effects.

Other solutions include Roman shades, Austrian blinds, simple plywood panels which can be painted, wallpapered, or fabric-covered to blend with decor, cafe curtains, or regular French-pleated curtains running to the top of the window frame. All of these are space savers, since they occupy only window depth. Floor-length drapery has the advantages of creating cozy warmth and covering a multitude of architectural oddities, since it can traverse to form an entire expanse at night while by day floor-length, sheer glass curtains are revealed underneath. However, they tend to look heavy and confining, especially if a fabric with a dark color and bold pattern is used. This can be an advantage if the room is particularly long and rather narrow, provided the windows are at the far end. Drapery then appears to bring the narrow end wall forward and to make it seem wider. If drapery is used, by all means hang it floor to ceiling so that an entire wall is treated architecturally. Skimpy draperies which run only to the height of the window frame as a narrow column concealing the side frame tend to chop up the room visually. If you do not want the expense of wall-to-wall fabric, at least use two full end panels, butted to the wall on each side and running to the ceiling.

Steam and hot water radiators may present other problems at the window wall. Again, an architectural solution is the best design. If the radiator is long, a good idea is to create a wood case, extended on the sides to run from one side wall to the other. Grille or cane can be used to cover openings which release convected air into the room. The extension beyond the radiator width creates a ledge across the top, plus useful if shallow cabinets at each side. Drapery can then be tailored to run from the ceiling to the top of the ledge. This ledge can also be made wider than the radiator requires, providing an interesting location for books, bibelots, and, if the height is right, for table lamps to illuminate sofa and chairs. The width must be calculated, however, in relation to the depth of the room; it is important not to take up any more floor space than necessary unless it pulls its weight in usefulness and convenience.

FLOOR TREATMENT

When it comes to floors, the usual fare in apartments is oak strip or oak block for the main area, ceramic tile in the bath, and asphalt or vinyl tile in the kitchen. If the building is new and you rent before the wood floors are finished, you may have a choice of light or dark. Most building managements will finish the oak the standard blond way, in the mistaken belief that most people prefer it and that it is "safe." Actually, dark floors are considered by discriminating apartment dwellers not only more attractive as a background for furniture and other decor, but also more space-extending and more practical. So if you can control the initial finish, specify a medium-dark walnut with a liquid urethane coating, topped with a coat or two of paste wax, machine-buffed. That will give you a floor that will hold up attractively with routine care.

If you are faced with an already-blond-finished oak floor, it can be sanded and refinished. Sanding is not the easiest and most pleasant task, but you can do it yourself with a rented sander and an auxiliary edger for scraping baseboard and other hard-to-reach areas. One space 12 feet by 22 feet can be done in an afternoon. You would use rough sandpaper for the first cut, followed by one going-over with medium, and a final cut with fine paper. If you have strips of oak or other wood, follow up and down the length of the boards; do not cut across. If it is oak block with the units laid with grain at right angles to each other, you can go up and down lengthwise or across the width of the room. Vacuum the sawdust thoroughly, then wipe off the residue with a soft clean cloth before applying the stain. A sealer-type stain is best. To get the tone you want, try mixing small parts of medium and dark walnut. You can test it in a closet or some area that will not be seen. Then use a wide brush or a roller devised for floor work. With most stains you have to wipe off, let dry for a day, and apply a second coat, wiping off again. Don't apply the stain too liberally, forming puddles; you will get an uneven look. Wipe a section at a time promptly, since stain is a penetrating product and works quickly. The liquid urethane is a plastic sealer, transparent and hard-wearing. Apply it according to directions and let it dry thoroughly before using the paste wax. You can usually rent an electric buffer at the same place you rent the sander.

Whatever you do, have the same finish throughout all the open areas—entrance hall, foyer, and main room, plus sleeping ell if you have one. However, if the ell is partitioned off so that it functions as a separate room, it can be finished differently, since it will not be seen as the eye sweeps the apartment on entering. If the ell is arranged for sleeping, wall-to-wall carpet is pleasant underfoot and might even continue into the bath. Since space is small, this is not an expensive treatment.

Carpeting for the main room is another matter. It can be costly, and although you can take the carpet with you when you move, it seldom if ever fits another space. However, a piece 12 feet or 15 feet by 22 feet or so is a general size that can be trimmed and bound relatively inexpensively to serve as an area carpet in another home. It can be cut to give two 9-foot by 12-foot pieces, which are always useful, so you may decide it is a good investment. It is certainly easier than having floors scraped and refinished. If you decide on carpet, keep it a light, neutral shade that will blend with your color scheme. In fact, if your walls are light gray or beige, carpet in the same tone will make the place seem quite large. Such a neutral color will prove to be more useful in a later home, also.

If you want the streamlined look of vinyl tile and one of the many decorative effects it makes possible, there are ways to install it so that you can remove it when you leave. Vinyl tile is expensive, and this is usually a consideration, plus the fact that there may be the danger of having to pay for its removal if it is semipermanently installed. And remember that with today's mastic, it has to be literally dug up off the floor for removal, which is costly. An alternative is to put down heavy kraft paper over the wood floor with double-faced mastic tape, using the tape along the borders and joints only. Then the tile can be installed with regular cement over the paper. When it comes time to move, the tile will come up fairly easily, and chances are it can be used again. In small areas—foyers, kitchens, baths, entranceways—vinyl tiles can be put down individually with double-faced mastic tape. Foot pressure and gravity will assure a tight bond. A large space like the main living area may not respond to this type of installation, and, in addition, it is a time-consuming and tedious chore which you probably would have to do yourself, since a professional tile installer would not want to take the time to put each tile down on tape. If you decide on this method, be sure to buy twelve-inch-square tiles rather than nine-inch, since there will be less taping involved.

Various patterns of vinyl can help seemingly extend space. Alternating light and dark tiles laid on the diagonal like a checkerboard can lead the eye beyond room dimensions. Other pattern possibilities are limitless. If you create a highly patterned design, however, keep other elements in the room plain—drapery, upholstery, etc.—to avoid a too-busy look that will seem confining. Usually the best solution with tile is the same as with carpet, a light neutral or white (if you don't mind the maintenance problem white always brings).

If you retain the existing wood floor or put down tile, you will also want area rugs. Choose them as an integral part of your color and pattern scheme, whether they be Orientals, plain broadloom, the new textured Moroccan, Spanish, or other accent rugs. Area rugs can be more helpful in the one-room apartment to define various areas. For example, you can demarcate a sitting area of sofa, a pair of chairs, and a coffee table with one rug, a dining area with another, a TV corner with a third. A foyer that opens directly into a living room can be made to seem like an entity with a rug. If your floors are slick wood, be sure to put down rubber underlayment to guard against slipping. If several area rugs are used, they should relate to one another color and patternwise, or you will create a hodgepodge that looks cluttered. Also, do not change styles of rugs: If you want Orientals, use all Orientals and preferably the same kind—Hamadan, Souruk, or whatever. You can't mix Moroccan, American Indian, and Oriental. It can be interesting to use rugs of the same style and pattern, but in different colorations that are part of your color plan. That way, you get variety and demarcation but also design harmony.

LIGHTING

Standard apartment illumination is meager and uninspiring—inexpensive and unattractive ceiling fixtures in foyer, kitchen, and bath, plus the legally required minimum of base plugs and wall outlets. To gain drama in the foyer or living area if it has a ceiling fixture, invest in a handsome chandelier, take down the existing fixtures and put them away for replacement when you leave, and install your own. An electrician can do this for you at nominal cost. An elegant crystal and iron or brass ceiling fixture will go a long way toward creating an interesting entrance into the apartment and one in the living area will make it gain importance as a substantial home rather than a temporary shelter. Proper scale is vital with a chandelier: a too-small one looks puny and a too-large one overpowering. A twelve- or fifteen-foot-wide room can take a fixture three feet in diameter nicely and perhaps even forty inches. It is better to overscale slightly than the opposite. Be sure to select one, however, that doesn't drop too far into the room; you'll want at least eighty inches of clearance from the floor. So if you have the standard eight-and-a-half-foot ceiling height, you'll need a broad, shallow fixture. There are some handsome ones in Colonial Williamsburg style with shallow, sweeping branches for candle-like bulbs. Study the catalogues in the electrical shop in your neighborhood and look for one with a depth of twenty inches or so.

There isn't too much that can be done in the bath unless you want to replace the chandelier there too. There is most always a fluorescent fixture of some kind for mirror illumination. Unfortunately, it is usually over the mirror, which is the worst kind for grooming, since it is so unflattering. You can buy plug-in fluorescents to flank each side of the mirror, which is the preferable kind of light. If you are in an older building with a too-high bath ceiling, a simple and relatively inexpensive way to gain intimacy and good light at the same time is with a dropped luminous ceiling. A fluorescent fixture with two or three tubes can be installed in the existing outlet; then a metal strip is fastened around the room at the height you desire. Into this a metal grid fits which holds panels of translucent plastic, either flat or corrugated. This goes a long way toward modernizing a bath and is worth the money, if you have a long lease. The same treatment is excellent in the older kitchen, providing shadow-free illumination that is so restful while meals are being prepared.

In the kitchen, a must are under-cabinet fluorescent strips. If they are not already there, you can buy plug-in units—the same kind used vertically to flank the bath mirror can be installed horizontally under cabinets to give marvelous work light where you need it. In a new building where ceilings are not high, the insignificant ceiling fixture can be replaced or given new interest with whimsical paper covers such as the Japanese ones which simulate Tiffany stained-glass globes. The regular Oriental paper lantern can be fastened around the fixture, too, to give a pleasant and strong white light. Incidentally, use a bulb of good wattage, at least 150, to keep the kitchen from being a dungeon.

Color Scheming

We have already touched on the importance of establishing a light, neutral color background throughout the entire apartment for visual continuity and to make over-all space seem more pervasive. At the time that may have seemed, in addition, the route to dullness. Now, however, we are ready to extend the color plan to dispel any hint of monotony or lack of originality. The rule in a sound color plan is to have one basic hue and two or at most three accents. For example, if your background is a French gray for walls, woodwork, doors, etc., you could warm it up with red and yellow plus touches of black. Against one long, gray wall, your convertible sofa-bed might be upholstered in a solid red. A print fabric in the same red and yellow on a white or light gray ground could be found for draperies and seat pads for a pair of wood-framed, open armchairs. Use sofa pillows in yellow and black, black lamp bases with yellow shades, yellow ceramic ashtrays. For parties, yellow roses or chrysanthemums would add sparkle. To continue the theme into the auxiliary spaces, gray bath walls would be relieved with a yellow shower curtain, red bath towels, mat, and rug, while bright yellow and red cookware would personalize a kitchen with walls and cabinets in the same gray.

A compact kitchen that closes into the wall makes possible a combination sitting-dining-sleeping-cooking area. A four-foot unit wtih oven, refrigerator, sink, and cooktop is flanked with a dishwasher and a base cabinet in the same provincial style as the line of wall cabinets above. An electronic air purifier handles steam and cooking odors. Stock ponderosa-pine doors, eighteen inches wide and with four panels, are eight feet tall.

As you can see, the objective is to create an aura of comfortable relaxation, punched up with a balanced counterpoint of bright tones which work well together. Other good combinations—white walls with blue and green, plus accents of yellow, pale yellow walls combined with orange and green, or beige (not the usual landlord's buff, but a soft, warm champagne tone) with chocolate brown and touches of white and black. And speaking of background color, be on hand when the painters are starting to do your walls. For a small tip, they will often enliven the color you have selected from the landlord's offerings; make it a bit warmer or slant it to a shade of gray, beige, or whatever that is more to your liking. If the white that is offered is more an old-fashioned ivory (often the case), get the painter to bring it closer to a dead white.

While the landlord's offerings may seem terribly limited, actually this can be a help by giving you a springboard from which to choose other colors. Of course, if you can afford to bypass what the landlord provides, the sky is the limit. Sometimes the landlord will pay the painters to apply a different color, if you supply the paint. The situation is different in each instance, but we are primarily talking about the large, fairly new apartment buildings, and in this case, it may all be fairly cut and dried, with the super having to follow a prescribed course. In any event, it pays to get the super on your side at the outset, and a tip of ten dollars or so may pay dividends in personalized treatment, not only when it comes to paint colors, but all along the line.

Once you have chosen the background color, you will logically ask, "How do I translate this into a complete scheme?" There are any number of attractive schemes around you at all times if you know how to look for them: A print fabric or wallpaper you like will offer a compatible grouping of hues; a favorite painting, a bouquet, a bowl of fruit or vegetables; color photographs in decorating magazines, the brochures of manufacturers, room settings in color films or TV, model rooms in department stores—all are sound ways to a group of colors you can live with happily. Be sure, too, that you really enjoy the color combination before you start buying to implement it, because if you accessorize closely with bath towels, table linens, lamps, throw pillows, and all the rest, you are making a sizable investment in things you'll have to live with a long time, both in this apartment and in some future home.

In this light, remember that for most people the one-room apartment is the beginning rather than the end of the line in homemaking. Whatever you choose will likely be part of a later house or larger apartment. If you choose a color scheme you like and carry it out carefully, the chances are that the components can go into an eventual family room, living room, or study almost "as is," so that you will have one well-co-ordinated room to start with in a future home. For that reason, it may pay to spend more rather than less, to buy good value that will endure in a succession of homes. Then too, one-room living as an adventurous beginning should reflect a lighthearted and casual approach to homemaking. For that reason, it is well to choose colors and an over-all look that is not too self-conscious or crushingly formal. A fresh, bright, airy scheme of jewel colors will serve better than a contrived and intricate blend of exotic hues. No matter what you do to the apartment, it is still finite; no guest will be fooled into thinking otherwise. By all means plan it to look as though it might be part of a larger home but not of a mansion. If you get too elegant, you may make living complicated by trying to function smoothly in small space with furniture and colors that might be pleasant in the sitting room of a house where you spend an hour a day at most.

CHAPTER TWENTY-FOUR

STORAGE

IT HAS BEEN SAID that storage is like money; you never have enough. Few houses and almost no apartments have adequate storage and so it becomes necessary to invent it. There are ways this can be done attractively, designed to be an integral part of a decorating plan without necessarily revealing the primary purpose of storing possessions. You can choose between two kinds of storage items: pieces of furniture to buy or projects to build. Let's go through the house room by room and see what is available.

For the Living Room

•Look for a wall-hung shelf, console height, to run nearly the full length of a wall. These frequently have handsome pulls to indicate the storage drawers. There is room under the storage shelf to slide a number of mobile seating stools. While this shelf is distributed across the country, should you not find something just like it in your city, look for two slim drawers exactly alike, and, using wall brackets underneath, put them up side by side.

Look also for triple-duty cubes cushioned for seating and made with a lift-off top to store not too large items such as games, records, and paperbacks. Third duty occurs when the softly padded top reverses to become a firm, neatly outlined checkerboard game table.

Free-standing wall systems in many varieties form a generous portion of the do-it-yourself type of furniture available in kits. One example is this: three bookcase storage units, the center unit equipped with a bar shelf with open space underneath. Here you can store items such as a sewing work basket, a covered toy box, or a small

One wonderful solution as to "where to put what" and still have easy access to items stored is the free-standing wall storage system shown here. It takes only a small amount of floor space and offers unlimited storage variety. Units rearrange easily. Can be placed back to back to form an island or shifted from one area to another to accommodate new storage needs. Handsome enough for any room.

storage trunk to hold extra napkins, candles, and flower holders. Units on either side of the center are bookcase storage shelves with the exception of the lower area of each which is a closed cabinet with sliding doors for easy access.

Storage cart for a wheel-easy serving of refreshments anywhere about the home. When closed, it looks like a rectangular chest. To open, the tabletop splits apart in the center, two ends flip back and out to the side to make two serving areas, while the front half of the chest tips downward to form a tray. Storage inside is for china, glass, beverage bottles, napkins, and anything else needed for instant serving in any room. This cart is distributed nationally; however, if you do not find one exactly as described here, there are many fine adaptations which would serve you equally well.

Campaign chests in satiny woods and finishes all hold a great deal of storage; many move anywhere on wheels. All could function anywhere in any room. In front of a sofa the chest could serve as a cocktail table. In another space with a foam-rubber cushion added it could become an extra seat.

Ottomans come in many shapes, sizes, and materials. Some roll on casters anywhere you wish, and some have top cushions that lift off to store any unbreakable item that clutters a room. Others have spacious bases with room enough for toss pillows or furry toys.

Today's apartments and new homes are usually shells, with little or no architectural interest and very limited storage space. Wall systems can come to the rescue, satisfying both needs at once. This corner of a contemporary living room is completely furnished with ready-to-assemble pieces. Wall units, desk, chairs, bunching tables, even the latter-day version of the old grandfather's clock can be put together by the owner.

JS/PERMANEER

Wall storage systems can put years of cumulative living smack up against the wall, while freeing great chunks of living-room space. Easily attached arrangements of shelves, cabinets, or desks are available to suit almost any space, any storage need, and any budget.

These include:

a) Slotted wall panels to receive brackets for shelves.

b) Slotted metal strips that attach to the wall with screws (both "a" and "b" can be removed with a screwdriver when you want to move).

c) Slotted free-standing suspension poles that reach from floor to ceiling. The poles are held in place by pressure rather than by screws or nails.

Brackets attach at any width you wish; shelves come in different lengths, and, once a system is installed, at any time you wish you can change a shelf to a higher or lower position, or remove it altogether to add wall-hung furniture components such as cabinets, open-out desks, or table panels. (More details on this type of storage in Chapter Twenty-five, "People on the Move.")

• Stereo storage can come in a long, table-height double cabinet with music in the left section (cabinet), while the right section has a lift top that uncovers a plastic mixing service for bar duty. Double doors below open to disclose shelves for china, glass, and napkins with a tall space reserved for beverage bottles.

Storage on Your Own

If you would like to initiate a storage project on your own such as putting up wooden shelves, it's a good idea to check your lumberyard dealer. He will cut shelves to your specifications if you wish, will help you with sizes of shelves, doors, cabinets, drawers, the type of wall strips needed if you plan to use them, and the brackets.

You might find space under a window to build a low storage cabinet. Check with a carpenter or handyman to see if the idea is practical in your particular home, and get his price for the job. If you put shelves in the cabinet you can use a portion of it for storing magazines, extra ashtrays, candles, and vases. Save some room for a wine rack if you care to. (Be certain it is not near a radiator as wine should be stored at room temperature.) Use the top of the table-height cabinet surface as an extra serving space when entertaining.

In an empty corner you might use a screen to hide whatever you wish to store there. To make a screen, hinge two, three, or four panel doors together. Stain or paint them, or cover with a colorful fabric. It's a good place to store the sewing machine, vacuum cleaner, or those tall flower vases so difficult to fit in anywhere.

In a small space anything that will hold storage counts. If you have an old trunk or foot locker that is the right size for a bench seat, coffee table, or end table, dress it up with a cover of colorful, washable vinyl, or self-sticking washable wallpaper. It will be great for storing cocktail accessories, blankets, linens, and all those extra ashtrays you need for special occasions. To use it as a seat, cut a slab of latex foam rubber to fit the top area and cover it with a color that fits your room scheme.

Note: If a foot locker is scarce in your home, buy a strong cardboard one for a few dollars. To keep the cardboard from buckling, use a spray adhesive before you cover it with washable wallpaper or fabric.

A job for your favorite handyman could be a wall-length box-type platform, seat high, made out of plywood with three or four sliding door panels for inserting such things as logs for the fireplace, books you can't bear to part with, and stacks of magazines you think you will find time to read. Paint the platform the color of the wall; add slim square seat pads made of foam rubber, and decorate this storage-seating area with brightly colored toss pillows.

If crewelwork or any kind of hand stitchery relaxes you, and you wish to have a neatly organized sewing-storage kit beside one of your favorite chairs in the living room (in addition to similar provisions for sewing in the laundry, bedroom, and porch areas), there's a portable sewing caddy on the market with space provided for scissors, a special compartment for buttons, tape measure, needles and such, along with spindles to hold spools of thread and a tray for pincushions. The caddy has a revolving base to make things easy to find, plus a carrying handle.

FAMILY ROOM

You may be one of the thousands trying to make every room work seven days a week and do double and triple duties. If so, you will appreciate the rather dizzying manipulations of various wall storage systems, the hidden assets in a series of modular wall units (both types briefly mentioned in the previous section), plus other multifunction-

Clever cover for built-ins. Here a handsome print in mustard, green, and tangerine has been laminated to window shades, and all clutter stashed behind. Two shades control light at windows, others act as pull-down doors for these attractive storage closets that line entire wall. Train board, which folds up against wall, is covered in dark green sailcloth; flip-down exercise board (same fabric), and seat cushions in red. Carpet is mustard.

ing storage-angled furniture designed to make every room do more in less space. Wall storage systems will:

a) Provide a place for television, stereo, records, radio, hobby collections, art objects, books, and magazines—all the things you want in a family room to enjoy your leisure time.

b) Display a neatly paneled door behind which stands a full-length single bed ready for use by an overnight guest. There is storage room also for linens and blankets.

c) Present a cabinet door which drops down to reveal a writing desk with neatly pigeonholed slots and drawers to store all the essentials of a miniature home office. This will be appreciated by junior members of the family as well as adults. And it can create a denlike working atmosphere when it's time to pay monthly bills.

Other storage-oriented furniture ready to do many tricks in a many-purposed room includes:

Distinctive setting for a home office uses modern, easy-care materials. Storage areas and furniture surfaces of formica all wipe clean with a damp cloth. Doors (to left of window wall) conceal more storage and are covered with a washable wallcovering flocked with an acrylic fiber. Carpeting and pleated Roman shade are made to shed soil and retain beautiful color.

The "any-room" armoire. If the word "armoire" brings to your mind a highly polished, beautiful piece of furniture (in a rather formal way) that was usually in the bedroom—and usually was used only for clothing—that is yesterday's armoire. Today's designs in armoires cover a wide range in both looks and storage uses. Whether it is handsomely carved or is a casual, cabinet-type piece of furniture, it will go into any room and is made to take care of clothing plus just about anything else.

Placed in a family room, an armoire with adjustable shelves will make room for an entertainment center of television, stereo, radio, and records. Some have a lower cabinet space ready to house a small refrigerator, with the top surface of the cabinet roomy enough to hold a small electric stove, a coffeepot, cups, and saucers—everything for instant snacking.

Another type is a wide wall cabinet that has the looks of an attractive armoire but is actually a Murphy bed and cabinet—all in one unit, with storage shelves and plenty of space for bedding.

Collectible cubes. A practical storage plan for apartment renters, military personnel, and all who move often is a collection of panels and "connectors" designed to form a storage cube. Storage material arrives flat in a kit. From a fifteen-inch panel and a notched connector, you build your own open-faced storage cube. Kits hold enough panels to make either six, four, or three cubes, and you buy according to your needs. If you have forty-five inches of wall space, you can notch together and connect three cubes in a row horizontally, and top with three more. For corner storage tower, stack them up using three or four cubes.

Made with a washable finish in white, black, or flame, the cubes are sturdy enough to house hi-fi equipment, a record collection, or a well-stocked bar in the family room (or anywhere else). They could also hold china, glassware, and serving pieces, or guest towels and soaps. A child might like his own corner tower to hold his toys.

Chest-table. This has lots of storage, rolls around easily on casters, and looks like a conventional table-high cube when closed. It has a two-way flip to its top, which swivels out to form a square table for dining, holding hot dishes, or acting as a buffet. A single door on left holds big storage items, while five graduated drawers on right hold more of anything. A handy "mover" to load up with food in the kitchen and roll into any area about the home.

This serviceable storage roll around is so marvelously handy it is produced in a variety of designs and materials, which are also great storage holders and movers. Look for them if you do not find the one described here in your city.

All-in-one cocktail table. This storage idea which operates on a lazy Susan swivel has six sides. Doors on three sides hide adjustable shelves to store cocktail party needs, or to hold books and magazines in an upright position.

Magazine storage. Very exciting, very revolutionary changes are being made in items for magazine storage with the thought of using little space, being practical, and still adding good looks to any area. Two rather dramatic but very useful types are listed below. You'll be sure to find something similar in your local stores, if not the two suggested here, to beat the magazine clutter:

a) A see-through end table with four open shelves building up a small tower of over a hundred magazines in a flat, see-at-a-glance position.

b) An end table that is a slim fourteen-inch-wide ribbon of plastic formed all in one piece without sides. It swoops forward to form a tabletop, then downward to shape a generous magazine and newspaper holder, then (still the same one-piece plastic) loops upward and down again to form the second and front side of the table.

To Create Space

Use a few square feet of space in one corner of the family room (or living room) to build a work corner. Use plywood to make a counter shelf, extending it three or four feet in both directions (from the corner). Make it longer if you have space. Add a small drawer on the left side and reserve undershelf space for a pull-up chair. Build more drawers, perhaps three or four on the right side. Cover this new work-and-storage area with a durable, stain-resistant, and washable fabric-backed vinyl. This could be in the same pattern as your wall covering on the wall or one that blends with it.

You now have a perfect place for tinkering with a hobby such as film splicing, sorting stamps, mending china, writing, or doing the family mending.

If there are avid readers in the family along with avid hobbyists, one way to give them both privacy in the family room is to separate them by a wall storage unit. Put the books, writing desk, and all things pertaining to quiet meditation on the "readers'" side, and store the games-participation equipment on the other side of the storage divider.

Storage shelves about eight inches wide, built to form a niche from floor to ceiling on both sides of a window, could be painted to match the window shades, creating an attractive frame for the window, in addition to adding storage space. Books could go on the upper shelves, while china and glassware would be more convenient if placed on the middle shelves; any other articles on the lower regions.

This same idea is suitable in a dining room, where you might wish to add a slim door to cover the storage shelves in order to store all types of dining necessities, many of which are not display items.

In your favorite sewing area—whether it is the family room, laundry area, or an enclosed back porch—on the wall behind your own home-office desk you might put up perforated hardboard to hang up the things you need to mend or just sew buttons on. The "hang-ups" might include an orderly sewing chest with as many as twenty-four small see-through plastic drawers cased in a steel frame that takes up approximately a foot of space. (Some chests are smaller.) Drawers will hold various-sized spools of thread, needles, thimbles, pins, and other items that usually aren't where you want them. And there are adjustable dividers in each small drawer to take care of size variations.

DINING ROOM

New marvels in dining storage in the way of furniture pieces are making it easier and pleasanter to dine even in a small space, with all the essentials close by. It is even possible to find a whole dining room on wheels, where one compact cabinet opens out to produce shelves, an extendible table, plus all the other aids for dining graciously.

With so many new and minisize, table-high, roll-around refrigerators, low and movable storage chests, and serving carts with storage added, it's now an easy thing to dine casually almost anywhere in the house. Minispace dining comes from a wall-hung system that brings along its own storage while it creates a regular dining area. It includes:

a) Closed storage cabinets, table high, for linens, china, serving pieces, and casseroles. Top surface area creates an extra space for serving.

b) Table shelf pops out when needed for dining, then smoothly telescopes back.

c) Open shelves above the storage cabinets hold any additional dining needs plus flowers or figurines.

Roll-a-round buffet will do double service. It provides a whole chest of storage space divided into various-sized drawers, plus an open shelf at the bottom. Drawers are spaced to hold china, crystal, and linens, while the open shelf will store larger items such as casseroles, vases, or bottles. In addition, the formica-covered top of the buffet flips backward to give extra serving space.

Double-unit wall-hung storage, table height, with a luminous band of light running through center of twin cabinets. Convenient height gives sideboard service for buffet dining, plus generous storage drawers to hold linens and other dining needs.

If you have a closet near the dining room, you can easily create a place for storing table linens in this way: On one side of the closet put in "slide-out" shelves made out of one-fourth-inch-thick hardboard at least twenty-four inches wide. Space the shelves from the floor to the ceiling. Here put tablecloths, place mats, and napkins. Because the linens are sharing this closet with a space for other storage, it's a simple project to cover the shelves by attaching a window shade to the ceiling. Measure your space before you order the shade so it will cover the full ceiling-to-floor space.

In your server or sideboard near, or in, the dining room, use wooden rollers on which to roll some of your larger dining cloths to keep them wrinkle free. Some servers come equipped with these rollers, but if yours does not have them they are available in department stores in almost any required size.

To create storage space in a large dining room, one complete wall could harbor storage items on narrow, built-in shelves concealed behind beautifully paneled doors. Each door can open easily to a specific storage section, such as one for bulky table pads, a stand-up space for trays, tureens, coffeepots, and all the other space-consuming dining needs. And, as you open a door, everything is seen at a glance.

Doors are available at your lumber dealer's, and you can get them in styles to harmonize with the design and architecture of your interior. Wooden doors can be painted to match your room's decorating scheme.

For the homemaker with only a small space reserved for dining, just a few shelves are easy to put up, using brackets to hold them. Shelves will take care of extra serving pieces and won't look utilitarian when intermingled with decorative objects such as framed prints, paintings, ceramic art, or flowers.

Just one extra serving counter can be of tremendous help when entertaining. At other times use it as a storage shelf. The shelf can be made of inexpensive, unfinished lumber or plywood. Before installing it, wrap the bare shelf with decorative, stain-resistant, fabric-backed, vinyl wall covering. Try to find a covering that blends with or matches your wall. When not in use as a storage-serving counter, use it to display a small, distinctive lamp or a candelabrum.

When checking into the advantages of some of the wall-hung furniture storage systems, remember that these units can be arranged in ways other than just straight against a wall or straight out from a wall. They will turn corners. For example, in separating a living room from a dining area in an ell-shaped room, the suspended shelves and cabinets can be made to flow around a corner to give the living-room side storage for hi-fi components and books, while the dining side has plenty of space for all dining requirements.

FOYER

It's easy to create a traffic jam when the space in an entranceway is at an absolute minimum, the furniture is too big, and guests arrive all at one time. Well-designed storage pieces that are slender and wall hugging are available. Here are just a few from a rather extensive collection:

Miniature obelisk high-riser cabinet is obelisk shaped with wood back and shelves to hold precious curios that might otherwise be lost to sight when scattered around the living room. Storage drawer at the bottom will assist in the purge on clutter, and the entire floor space used is about thirteen inches of wall space with approximately seven inches extending into the room.

Miniature wall storage system is a simple, narrow version of the many wall storage systems. Shelves are slender and not too deep, while cabinets below for hiding storage are carefully designed not to protrude into the traffic lane.

Grandfather clock is tall and imperious with a lower cabinet tall enough to hold such storage as extra long candles, umbrellas, and tall flower vases.

Closet armoire is slender, nearly six feet tall, with cane-paneled doors. Just right for guests' wraps in a narrow entranceway. Lower drawer will hold checkerboard, bridge cards, and score pads.

This area is an ideal space for a long, slim platform chest built with a lift-up top to store rain hats, boots, and extra umbrellas. When painted and seat pads added, it could serve for both seating and storage.

KITCHEN

Look for the following in your local department or specialty store:

Swing-a-round storage is found in a tall kitchen cabinet with shelves that rotate around 360 degrees to make use of every bit of storage space and to bring it into view easily. More storage space is available from door shelves on the inside of the cabinet door.

Cookware storage that takes little space is possible in a slim étagère not more than a foot wide at its base, with shelves tapering slightly as they go upward. Eight shelves will hold some of today's brightly colored cookware and free kitchen cabinets of their bulk.

Storage shelves that form a storage unit on the back of a full-size kitchen cabinet door come with as many as five to ten shelves. Another door hides the contents of the shelves. (Practical for the bathroom's inside door and on the inside of closet doors.)

An ideal storage arrangement would be to have each major appliance, such as the range and refrigerator, teamed with its own cabinet storage, plus a work top where small equipment and staple food items that are used together could be stored together.

Design Your Own Kitchen Storage

If you haven't used pegboard as a handy hang-up for kitchen utensils (and many other items), look for it in panels that are punched to receive hooks and hanging hardware. Your lumber dealer will provide you with the size of metal or plastic accessories needed to fit the type of perforated hardboard you are going to use. Hang the kitchen utensils you use everyday on the wall right in front of you. It gets them off the work surface, saves you time in locating them when needed, and it saves storage space in the cabinets.

When new cabinets are necessary but not in the budget, put up slim wooden shelves in any wall space around the kitchen that is free. Often there is about a foot or more of free space between the refrigerator and the enclosing wall. Shelves could run from the floor to the ceiling and would store innumerable canned foods and packaged items.

Another place to use pegboard is inside the broom closet. Measure the width and height of the closet, then ask your lumber dealer to cut a strip of pegboard to fit. Be certain to ask for the right hooks to hang up dry mops, dustpans, brooms, and anything else that clutters up a closet when it isn't hung up.

In many rented apartments, the space below the sink is for storage but does not have shelves. Ask your lumber dealer about slide-out shelves that you can install yourself. This will eliminate a lot of bending and searching, and you will be more likely to make full use of the space at the back of the cabinet.

Every kitchen needs a desk near the active area for planning menus, phoning the grocer, reading new recipes, or just sitting for a second cup of coffee or tea. If you have only three feet of wall space, you could install a desk-high, wall-hung shelf that includes a drawer, then add several shelves above it for more storage. It is possible now to buy shelves "flat" in a kit, and packed in with the shelves are brackets, nails, and whatever the manufacturer provides for his particular shelves.

Corner work-height cabinets in the kitchen are marvelous, but it is often difficult to reach way back in the shelf. For little money, a manufacturer of rubber-made items makes handy, slide-out shelves so that not one bit of storage space is wasted. The same firm makes round lazy Susan-type revolving trays. These go anywhere, in the cabinet or on top, and are fine whirl-arounders for spices or small cans of foods that often get lost in the back of a cabinet shelf.

To keep fragile cocktail snacks from crushing, leave them in their see-through bags and hang them on a peg under the upper cabinets (above the work surface) or under a side shelf. Most have a hole in the sealed top part of the bag so they will hang easily.

Bedrooms

Bedrooms in addition to sleeping use have become a place to read, write, watch television, and listen to music. Aside from the highly unusual beds designed for the '70s, much of the multipurpose furnishings for the bedroom could go in other "living room" areas.

Storage stashers are showing up in many places:

• Space-aged bed with a storage wall behind it and a push button in its side. You push to start up a number of gadgets on the wall behind the bed such as television, stereo, tape recorder, and a movie projector geared to focus on the opposite wall. Added to its other tricks, the bed can rise at the foot or head, and even revolve.

• Double-storage bookcase, tall, free-standing, with six shelves in each of the double bookcases which have hinged cases on either side. Storage unit holds books, fruit, flowers, or ceramic art. It serves also to form a screen from the sitting-dressing area of the bedroom. Moves easily.

• Minispace armoire slightly over two feet wide, nearly six feet tall and engineered to hold lots of everything. Beginning at the bottom, three spacious drawers end about desk height, then double doors shoot upward to conceal sliver-thin storage drawers plus several well-arranged shelves.

• "Island bed" which stands free from all four walls on a platform, with the reverse side of its headboard housing six spacious drawers for storage. There is more storage space under the bed's padded platform in the form of two generous-sized drawers.

• Ninety-eight-inch circular bed that conceals in its (circular) headboard the bed pillows, alarm clock, and radio.

• Cool cabinet on wheels that holds up a small refrigerator that looks like a square chest. Cart shelf below the refrigerator provides space for open storage of china, glassware, casserole dishes, coffeepot, or any other needs for late night snacking.

• Headboard storage which includes a series of low shelves to serve as a night table and a bookcase, thereby freeing the floor of these two items. It also has a closed cabinet to store bed linens.

• Wall storage units, ideal for small bedrooms, that combine to get all the room furniture on one wall with the exception of the bed and an armchair. A tall wardrobe, dressing table, storage chests, and shelves are all a part of the wall storage unit.

• Hidden entertainment cabinet, tall and slender with storage space for television and hi-fi. More space is left over on one side for clothing, books, and decorative objects.

• Double-decker magazine rack that stores books on two decks, while magazines and newspapers have the end space on two sides on both upper and lower decks. Said to hold at least fifty books and the same number of magazines or newspapers, it rolls easily with your favorite bedtime reading.

• Wall-hung desk, actually a shelf with a spacious drawer that would give good, practical service when attached sill high in front of a window. Designed to hold writing materials, sewing equipment, and cosmetics.

• Under-bed storage, an extra long and slim aluminum box to hold blankets and bed linens. The same type of storage box is available in see-through plastic.

Other Storage Ideas

If your bedroom happens to have a deep windowsill and it isn't doing anything to help with your storage dilemma, use it to hold some of the things you refuse to part with, such as minichests in all colors and sizes (from three to four inches on up) which can hold pins, buttons, picture hooks, and other oddments. Intersperse the tiny chests with indoor potted plants, books, and statuary.

One ingenious interior designer used this idea to create wall storage (which could be used in most any room). Built-ins below the windowsill consisted of white chests alternating with radiators and a large white table which camouflaged the air conditioner behind it. In this way the designer coped with heat and cooling systems while adding a ready-made desk, dining and storage areas—all of which were set off by dramatic window shades in a bold, abstract design.

Even if you aren't a handy do-it-yourselfer, you can put up shelves that are "self-adhering." Screws and nails are not needed, and when you buy a "unit" of shelves, the package includes plaques and brackets. There might be just enough room between two windows in your bedroom where shelves would hold attractively framed photographs, a clock, and books.

You'll find seating that's easily moved in one of those strong woven willow "baskets" that actually are trunks. They are especially strong, and a seat pad is easily made by cutting an oblong piece of foam rubber to fit the top and covering it with an easy-care fabric. Inside this gem, store anything lightweight that needs hiding.

BATHROOM

You can be a pampered sybarite in your own home with a lavish array of personal comforts in the new retreat from daily pressures—the bathroom. Designers of bathroom equipment and decorative accessories have made this room's furnishings both functional and flexible, yet with all the conveniences of an elaborately outfitted home spa. Luxuries include a sunken bathing pool (the size of a tub), fold-down manicure shelves, pedicure seats, a sauna, massage table, and provisions for indoor sun bathing. Some very practical innovations are wall-hung toilets and wall-hung lavatories which make undercleaning easier; twin basins in the same cabinet to serve two people at the same time and give double storage space in cabinets below; plus trim, ceiling-high wall units that combine closed cabinets with open shelves.

If your concern at the moment is not a new bathroom but the need to know how to store the influx of bath, beauty, and cleaning products now cluttering up your old one, here are some suggestions which can be used to de-clutter.

Totem-pole cabinets. These are used for the space that might be wasted on the wall behind the toilet tank. Small vanity cabinets with sliding doors are hung almost ceiling high on adjustable brass suction poles. These can be used to store the extra grooming supplies. Lower cabinets on the totem pole can store the most-used items such as soap and tissues. Poles are available to fit the area from toilet tank to ceiling or from floor to ceiling.

"Close-by" storage. Two suggestions for keeping bath towels within easy grabbing reach are:

a) A four-tiered towel rack which can be hung up by over-the-door brackets. Designed for the standard flush door.

b) A wall-hung series of Lucite shelves. Put up close to the lavatory, they will show off the pretty colors in toweling from counter to ceiling.

Mirror mates. Slim cabinets that extend just a few inches from the wall are available to hang on both sides of the usual mirror-covered cabinet above the lavatory. This should take care of everyone's small items that clutter and impede progress while dressing.

Door storage. Slim, full-length door cabinets attached to the back of your bathroom door. Shelves from the bottom of the door on up will store all of your hidables when the cabinet door closes. (Also usable

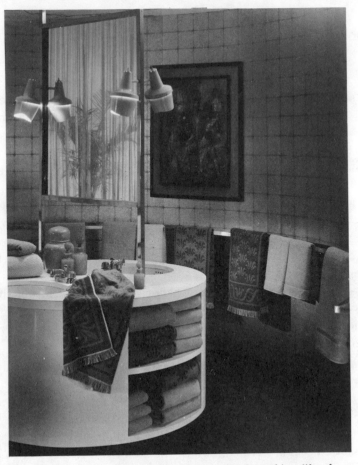

To make you feel rich and pampered, there's nothing like the softness of a deeply-piled bath towel. Storing this luxurious item within easy reach is solved here by using the space below an oval-shaped cabinet with twin basins, and by hanging it on a curved rung going around the bathroom. The beautiful colors of the various towels make a delightful picture.

for storage when placed on the inside of kitchen or closet doors.)

Bench-type storage chest. A double-use chest that looks like a seafaring trunk has shelves to store extra bath supplies. Made of plastic-finished hardboard, it can be kept near the tub for seating.

Quick access storage. Oval-shaped sink with an oval-shaped cabinet underneath gives ready access to bath necessities including bath towels.

Fool-the-eye storage hampers: a) Hamper with a cushioned top acts like a bath seat, looks like a suitcase, and is great for storage. It's chair-seat high and can also be borrowed as a vanity stool.

b) Desk-high hamper looks as if it were made of shutters (but isn't), has generous top surface for cosmetics, a top drawer for general storage, and a tilt-out front for storing laundry.

For Do-It-Yourselfers

If you are fortunate in having a good-sized bathroom, use one end of it to add a boudoir setting. In the section for unpainted furniture in a department or specialty store, find a vanity shelf with one drawer that fits your wall space. Cover the shelf with something that will withstand steam and heat, such as a vinyl wall covering. Add a mirror above it, and use the surface of the shelf to display all your pretty perfume bottles, while the uglies can go inside the drawer.

Because you look for every bit of storage space anywhere and everywhere in the bathroom, check the area just above the lavatory and under the mirror of the medicine cabinet. There may be room for a slim shelf to hold soap, an attractive holder for tubed supplies (to keep them organized in one place), plus a tissue box.

Investigate the space on the wall high above your tub (assuming that your shower is separate from the tub). There may be room for several small, built-in cabinets for storing extra supplies of grooming needs.

In some of the older types of rented apartments, the bath lavatory often has an open space beneath it. To give this area a finished look and to create extra storage space, add a softly gathered skirt made of an easy-care fabric to enclose the plumbing fixtures. Fasten or stick the skirt to the lower edge of the basin with washable, double-faced tape—the kind you find at sewing accessory counters in department stores.

To store an extra supply of towels away from the easily accessible area but still "there," hang them just under the ceiling on any wall space available—on slim, plastic rods hung in parallel lines. By using an array of brightly colored towels, you can add a big splash of color to the room.

Before shopping for anything such as wood to make a cabinet, be sure to measure the exact space you have available.

Whatever you plan to buy for the bath, make certain it will withstand heat and moisture. For instance, if you wish to cover a slim, floor-to-ceiling shelf arrangement, use a vinyl-coated window shade which is treated to withstand bathroom temperatures.

CHAPTER TWENTY-FIVE

PEOPLE ON THE MOVE

WHO IS ON THE GO? Almost everyone, it seems. Why? For a number of reasons. Most often mentioned is a change dictated by one's employer or the inducements of a new job in a distant city. Or there may be a longing to escape the pressures of city life for the pleasures of the suburbs; or, conversely, the desire for the stimulation of urbanity by those whose children have left "the nest." Or take the needs of the senior citizens. They may find that retirement dictates a more compact home which is easy to maintain. Perhaps it is one located where the climate is more benign than where they have been housekeeping. No matter why they move, "people on the move" all have something in common. They must make similar decisions, avoid the same pitfalls, and juggle the challenges of decorating new homes. They wonder if it pays to move old furniture to new surroundings; if they face the prospect of picking up and packing several times, they need to learn how to choose furnishings which offer maximum flexibility.

PLANNING FLEXIBLE DECORATION

Preplanning to take your place, decoratively speaking, as a member of the current generation of mobile American families is advisable, and means adopting a positive attitude toward furnishing from the very beginning. Don't fall victim to a "we'll just have to make do" philosophy because you can't see ahead to what will await you in the future. Frankly, this head-in-the-sand approach has little validity at a time in the evolution of the furniture industry when the primary stress is on function. True, if you know for certain that you will be moving often, you have to be a bit more purposeful and practical and less casual in your basic choice of furnishings. But there is much within the reach of those in this category who have more flair than finance. And there is no one who couldn't benefit from the guidelines being set forth here, even if they move only once in a lifetime.

Now is as good a time as any to take stock of your present furnishings. When doing so, remember that the average American family will move five times during the husband's working years and perhaps once again at retirement time. So, although you may not yet have experienced your first shift of address, you may soon have to, and then perhaps have to again and again.

Avoid Oversize Pieces

As you look around your rooms, evaluate your existing furnishings for flexibility. If you are thinking of making additional purchases or any time that you do, even if no move is in sight, avoid making impulse buys and be guided by a plan for the mobile family. In the interest of potential future relocations especially avoid choosing:

grand pianos	large glass- or marble-topped tables
nine-foot sofas	custom-made lambrequins
one-piece breakfronts	banquet-size dining tables
oversized dressers	suites of furniture
king-sized beds	furniture with painted finishes likely to chip
wall-to-wall carpet	
bookcases with glass doors	breakable accessories
supersize mirrors	

If you have ever moved and have had to make special arrangements, or pay extra to move furniture which had to be mounted on top of the elevator instead of inside it, or if your moving men were slowed down by stairs and turns, or if you, as a do-it-yourself mover, had to stand large pieces on end to manipulate them, you will think twice about transporting oversized pieces of furniture ever again. If you have never had any of these unfortunate experiences, plan now to avoid them.

If you are particularly fond of the decorative look of oversized furniture, try to think of alternative ways to achieve the same effect. For instance, if you love the look of a nine-foot sofa, you might consider buying a two- or three-piece sofa that fits together and then disassembles, rather than a cumbersome nine-foot-long one. You will be especially pleased that you've done this when you move into a house with rooms of different sizes and shapes, where the dimensions of such a large one-piece item may make its inclusion totally impracticable. Other substitutes for these awkward pieces will be discussed in the forthcoming sections.

Transitional Furnishings

Virtually all major furniture companies, budget to high-priced, proudly offer good, clean-cut pieces that are transitional in design. You may not know this word, transitional, as it is a fairly recent entry to the home-furnishings vocabulary. Basically, it refers to those styles which are neither line-for-line copies of period pieces nor moving-to-the-moon modern. They are particularly useful for people on the move. Happily too, transitional or, as they are sometimes called, eclectic furnishings combine the best of two worlds. They use the most advanced technological achievements—laminated constructions and marproof surfaces, for example—and blend them with borrowed, but simplified, design idioms of the past. Most professionals in design feel that transitional furnishings form the backbone of the most exciting rooms around. If you wish, you can do your entire home in a style which, so to speak, does the mixing for you.

But too much of anything can become a bore. So you will find transitional furniture most rewarding if you use it to set a consistent background and then choose another style that is compatible, but interestingly different, to work as an accent. Transitional basics can be complemented by Early American, Oriental, Provincial, the formal forms of France and England, and even glass-and-steel modern and, remarkably, any one of the combinations will make an arresting mix.

Standard Modules

Next, you should seek out units that come in standard modules so that they can be combined in a variety of attractive ways. For the most part, these units are case goods, thirty or thirty-six inches wide. These widths were decided upon by the manufacturers because they are calculated to fit most architectural space available. There are also a few seating units of this type, so don't overlook them. Standard modules come in all finishes and can be co-ordinated into any design period, historical or contemporary.

These are furnishings that are designed for "stacking" or "bunching." The former means that the additions are meant to be combined vertically, as in a hutch with which you top a buffet base. Pieces that bunch are grouped horizontally. An example would be low tables that stand next to each other and resemble a single long piece. These items can of course be used alone. Buy good pieces that amass to some functional purpose such as a wall for the storage of linens and entertainment needs, plus the display of books. Later on, or in different surroundings, these versatile pieces can separate into a room divider, chests to flank a sofa, a home bar, etc.

Don't think in terms of separately furnishing the living room, bedroom, or dining room. Place your emphasis on versatility. And just because you already own a piece or two of furniture from a collection that was labeled "bedroom" doesn't mean that it has to stay there and only there. Put your dollars down now on pieces that are so flexible, so useful that they can star in one room today and be equally attractive and practical in another later on. More and more pieces are currently being designed for all-through-the-house use. Shop for these and forget about pieces which don't adapt.

Your living-room chest can be used in the foyer tomorrow. A thirty-two-inch square table which opens up to a festive board at which six can dine can be closed and shifted into the family room as a game table in a later setting. A desk is a suitable piece for a living room, family room, bedroom and, in this era where we are looking for more than mealtime use of the dining room, there too.

Fortunately for you, we have escaped from that monotonous period when all furniture came in sets. We know one woman whose mother used to boast of her "complete" twenty-four-piece bedroom set. It included everything from a wardrobe to dressing-table stool and gave her no room to express her individuality.

Her daughter moves in another cycle. Wooden transitional pieces can now be effectively combined with brightly lacquered or antique-finished units, with Plexiglas and shiny chrome, with hammered brass and clear glass. So, if in spite of all your careful planning when you move you find you must add another piece or two, there is no rule which says it must match your other possessions.

FREE-STANDING SYSTEMS

These systems are impermanent solutions which, fortunately, look as pleasing, if skillfully assembled, as permanent bookshelves and cabinets. There are many types of temporary wall systems. Although many are wall hung, a significant number have the free-standing flexibility that is even more beneficial to people on the move.

Budget Types. The least expensive consist of metal tension poles which come in several heights to accommodate varying ceiling-to-floor dimensions, and brackets or loops which form the skeleton on which to build a shelf-and-cabinet system. Found now most often in wood-grained metal or inexpensive chipcore components (supports must be strong metal, of course) this garden variety of space saver and room shaper can be found in almost any hardware store. You can install it yourself, have it put up by a neighborhood handyman or the man of your own house. Although perfectly functional, these budget types won't win any prizes for outstanding design and are really more suitable for a family or recreation room than an "on-show" living room unless you are just starting to collect your household needs.

Stacking Units. The next step up, both from the standpoint of finance and aesthetics, is stacking units. In finished versions, you'll find these in conventional furniture stores. Three of the most popular design motifs here are the Colonial look, sleek unadorned modern, and the most recent edition, Mediterranean. Stacking units often start off with a plinth base that hugs the floor. On it you stack, building-block fashion, a row (or two or three) of cabinets and, perhaps, a desk or bar or bookshelf unit. You'll find that louvered sliding doors are common on the cabinets. When you stack, take care that you don't build too high or you may be creating a safety hazard. Be sure that the stacking pieces are braced one to another. Some models come with pegs for this purpose. If they don't, use inexpensive metal brackets and bolts. If the backs of the pieces are unfinished, you can dress them up with a stick-on vinyl material, wallpaper, glued-on fabric, or cork tiles. (The latter are very nice for creating a giant bulletin board from which you can hang an arrangement of posters or other art works.) In one informal setting we recently saw the "wrong" side of the stacking units covered with rustic straw place mats. They made a colorful, texturally interesting, and very inexpensive treatment. Finally, you can arrange two sets of stacking units back to back for the ultimate in storage.

Do-it-yourself people can head for the unpainted-furniture shops which have sprung up from coast to coast to seek out unpainted wooden versions of the stacking pieces. Among the newest versions of these creations are multipurpose cubes which come in pine or birch. These are based on a module that is fifteen inches tall, fifteen inches deep, and fifteen inches or thirty inches wide. You buy the cubes singly, according to your needs, and then mix, match, and stack them to your own desires. Among the cube versions, you will find ones that are backless and open, others with backs, rectangulars, cubes with shelves, sliding doors, and double drawers. There are desk bars too.

De Luxe Types. Other and most expensive versions of the storage alternatives are modular components made of fine cabinet woods. Hung on room walls when space saving rather than room division is paramount, these designs can also be found in free-standing systems. Using supporting rods or poles, the most ultra of these types add a screw or two at either ceiling or floor for added stability. (These can easily be disengaged when you move on. They seldom leave damage at which a landlord can point, nor are they considered by owners as built-ins which must be left behind by tenants.) Even more elaborate (and costly too) are variations in which shelves, cabinets, and chests seem to "float" on concealed fittings which go into a wall divider that is of ceiling height and which, to the uninitiated observer it is, indeed, a real wall instead of a partition. Made in sections, the wall that isn't can be knocked down when you are on the move once again. This type of system, usually a European import, comes in exotic woods such as rosewood or teak, and in walnut and oak too. In a very modern mode, free-standing systems are now coming from countries such as Italy, Germany, and Switzerland in colorful plastic blocks as well as clear acrylics. New, too, on the market is a system of colorful storage drawers, from very shallow to very deep. These can be stacked anyway you desire, even back to back or in ell formations. The drawers, in a vinyl finish, come in orange or white with mat-finish chrome pulls.

The Growth of Components. Over the past decade, we have seen the variety of components in free-standing systems go from simple bookshelves and hi-fi cabinets, desks, and tables to very sophisticated versions which are almost miniature apartments. These, which once again are of European origin, are very popular abroad in countries such as Germany and Holland where closets have traditionally never been a standard part of residential construction. One of the most exciting systems to come here of late is a very sophisticated plan which is in a go-with-everything white polyester finish in a design stripped of all unnecessary curves and lines. Exterior hardware, too, is kept to a functional minimum. The shopper has the option of choosing, in addition to the expected cabinets and cupboard, fold-down beds, flip-up tables, bookshelves that pivot to reveal a bed on the reverse side, and wardrobes with niches for everything from shoes to hats. There are even "his" and "hers" wardrobes outfitted for the convenience of each sex.

Although the do-it-yourselfer won't find this kind of system ready for him to build as yet, nor the plastic ones either, who knows what the future may hold? Meanwhile, he can find modular components, more highly styled and costly than the unpainted wooden kind, in specialized stores which cater to furniture you can build yourself. These are establishments where fine cabinet woods, which either the customer or the shop will oil-finish, are sold rather than soft woods which must be paint-finished. Components are sold by mail order as well as in retail shops. In one of these stores we recently checked out the variety available in free-standing systems. Cabinets, two feet, two and one-half feet, and three feet wide, came in rosewood, walnut, and teak. In addition to the usual storage, record, hi-fi, and bar cabinets, there were minichests, two or three drawers high, which could be set on the bookshelves that are part of all the systems. Other handy single drawers were designed to be screwed under shelves or inside cabinets. The variety of metal poles was amazing. You would have to decide among brass or pewter finishes, aluminum in brassed, silvered, or bronzed looks, or good old black or white.

PORTABLE CLOSETS

Ever know anyone with enough closets? It's taken what seems forever, but furniture manufacturers recognize, at long last, that people sometimes need more room for coats and hats and dresses and suits than for the storage of silver tea sets. As you have just read, closets are being added to the components of storage systems. Even the unpainted-furniture folk are coming up with models that you won't be ashamed to show off at home. There are heavy-duty units with solid panel or louver doors that come with pole and shelf for storage. Good for people who move are piggy-back wardrobes in which the base, a not-too-tall size on convenient casters, can be topped by a companion that's two feet high. Storage closets, provided with adjustable shelves, will hold all kinds of athletic gear, luggage, and, yes, that silver tea set. One maker of wallboard is even offering do-it-yourself directions for constructing a wardrobe that you can take with you when you move. What a far cry from those cardboard closets in which Grandma used to store out-of-season clothing up in the attic!

PORTABLE BEDDING

There are many choices for those who may live in Mobile one year, Minneapolis the next. Some suggestions for bedding are the convertible sofa (suggested if the sofa-bed is to be used regularly); the Murphy fold-away bed, recessed by day in a cabinet; the trundle bed; the chair bed or ottoman; or even a storage bed (a lounge unit with a pull-out drawer underneath the bed). (For information on these and other sleeping units, refer to Chapter Twenty-three, "The Apartment.")

If you still have your heart set on king-size bedding despite these other choices, consider the following suggestion. Get a free-standing king-size headboard. Front it with two twin bed springs and mattresses that, when used on a special frame, lock into place at night, swing apart for easier bedmaking during the day. You will find such a solution makes particular sense for those who move and never know just how big a master bedroom their new quarters will have.

When it comes to springs and mattresses, do cater to your individual preferences. There is a "plus" among the features of latex foam and urethane mattresses we think you should consider, however. Unlike innersprings, the foam types bend and can get in and out of doorways with comparative ease.

STORAGE PIECES

This is another category of furniture that is particularly adaptable to budget-conscious Americans on the move. Choose storage pieces that can be shipped, packed with household goods and then serve as furniture. Let's talk a bit about trunks. You may not think that they are sufficiently glamorous to be stationed anywhere but in the basement or storage room. But in some parts of the country, trunks are quite a fad.

Antiques dealers are scouring the countryside for old trunks and even foot lockers. They go to sources such as auctions and house sales. Once they get the trunks (at a pittance, of course), they clean them out and paint or oil the exterior. Inside, they are painstakingly lined in fabrics such as chintz or calico or treated to a Victorian-type wallpaper. Completed, the trunks draw very fancy prices. You might try your own hand at trunk-ing. There is no need to limit yourself to using old trunks, of course. What is commonly called the Hong Kong trunk is also handy to have. Made of wicker with brassbound corners and hardware, it comes in many sizes and can lend lots of charm to a bedroom, family room, child's room, or even a wide hall.

Other good traveling companions for you are toy chests and cedar chests. When buying the former, be sure to get a well-made, sturdy model and it will be useful for years on end. We know of a toy chest which has been in constant use for eighteen years. (At present it holds records.) When the toy chest shows signs of wear, all you need do is to treat it to a coat of paint. As for cedar chests, they have sentimental value as "hope chests" as well as being practical for storage of linens.

You might even think about those fiber glass storage chests which you find in the dime store that are designed to hold out-of-season clothing, extra blankets, and such. These usually come in an imitation wood grain in a buff background, although one manufacturer now has them in color with floral-print lids. But there is no reason why you can't cover one of the undistinguished boxes with adhesive-back vinyl and create an attractive chest-table that is sturdy enough to hold a lamp and ashtray while, under its lid, you keep seldom-used stuff such as water colors and brushes from a seldom-pursued hobby.

We've even seen some "interim" desks made in a similar way. (The chests are stronger than you may think and have a life expectancy of a year or so.) One serviceable desk was made of pedestals that were really triple stacks of cardboard file cabinets (sometimes called "transfer files") topped by a wooden slab. The whole unit was covered, once again, with that versatile self-stick vinyl material, this time in a high-gloss black for the files and a jumbo black-and-white houndstooth for the top.

In another case where clothes hampers had been purchased outright, rather than rented from a moving company, new use was found for them in the new home. Two boxes were upended and became the bases for a dressing table. (The top in this case was a sheet of thick, clear glass.) The hampers were covered with a prepasted wallpaper that was used for one wall of the master bedroom and a very handsome over-all effect was the result.

Too, we've come across a make-do chest in a boy's room where six cardboard file cabinets were stacked together in double tiers. They were disguised with inexpensive cork tiles which came with a self-stick backing and each box then labeled, "Shirts," "Socks," etc., as a gentle nudge toward neatness in a twelve-year-old's retreat.

COLOR PLANNING

What discourages women probably more than any other aspect of a pack-up-and-go existence is that they can't plan an attractive color scheme for a series of homes. Nonsense! Don't let yourself fall into any mental traps about color. These days, the walls are apt to be white or a soft pastel. According to surveys by the paint people, these backgrounds predominate across the land.

Unless you happen to rent a house in an older neighborhood in which the occupants stayed with a scheme that prevailed around the time of World War II, it is doubtful if you will ever open the door on a room with dark hunter-green walls in a flat finish and shiny white enamel woodwork and trim. And in the unlikely event that this should happen to you, remember that color can be changed. All that most landlords require, should you decide that you simply cannot live with whatever they have provided in the way of a background, is that you restore the walls to their original condition when you move out. In these days, with the paint industry so co-operatively providing products that dry in a half hour, have no odor, cover previous paints in, at the most, two coats, and can be applied by the amateur with a roller, there simply is no excuse for you to live with a "shell" that doesn't appeal to you. Not only does paint completely change the aspect of a room, it too is about the least expensive tool you can use to make a transformation.

WINDOW TREATMENTS

It will be impossible to foresee what type and size of windows you may encounter in your next home, so you must wait. However, that doesn't mean you should discard the expensive living-room draperies.

Chances are they can be altered to fit somewhere in the next place and if you happen to be a skilled seamstress, you'll doubtless take the sewing machine along. Don't forget the window shades you can find at dime stores in the larger shopping centers. They are a quick, inexpensive way to privacy and clean, neat good looks.

FLOORING

For years, what-to-do-about-the-floors was an unsettling problem for those who didn't have a permanent home. The knowledge that they would be moving on in a year or two was a deterrent to budgeting a sizable sum for the floor.

Wall-to-Wall Carpet. Most likely, you will want some sort of rugs. If you like wall-to-wall carpeting, better face up to some facts. You will have to try to sell it to the next occupant when you move, someone who, chances are, won't like your choice of color or fiber or will notice the spot that you simply couldn't get off, or you, as we have already noted, will need to take it up when you leave. Theoretically, after you take the carpet up, or rather after a professional removes it (carpeting is tacked into place, you know), you can have it cleaned and shipped to your new place where it can be recut to the new dimensions of another room. Ah, but theory is not fact. In the majority of cases, carpeting simply doesn't work out a second time. Either it has faded somewhat because of the previous placement of furniture, shows wear in traffic paths, or is inadequate in size. If you absolutely have your heart set on wall-to-wall, look for an apartment or house in which it has already been installed. You will find that this is quite common in some areas. For example, carpeting is "standard" in many apartments in Southern California. Here, too, draperies often come with a home.

Room-size Rugs. All things considered, if you are a "carpet person" the best choice for you will be a rug. And the best size is still the adaptable old standard, the nine-by-twelve-footer. In a smallish room, it will cover most (or all) of the floor. In a larger one, it will become an important floor accent. Another idea is to buy two matching rugs, somewhat smaller. An 8 foot by 10 foot dimension is suggested. In some situations, where you have a big room, you can use them together. As an alternative, they can be separated. One might go in a bedroom, the other in a dining room. Remember that standard-size rugs can be turned to equalize wear. They are also easy to remove for a periodic professional cleaning.

Area Rugs. Area rugs, which are available in a variety of sizes from the tiny "fireside" dimension to the popular 3 feet by 5 feet and 6 feet by 9 feet, are also excellent choices for those who require flexibility. They let you expose lots of fine wood flooring. Or, if you do happen to rent a place already covered with carpeting, the area rug can appropriately be laid on top of it. In addition, area rugs can define areas of activity. You can place one in front of the sofa to delineate a conversation spot or use it to mark off the dining area or suggest a foyer. Because these rugs cover a more limited space, you can pick more ebullient colors and designs and, perhaps, deep-pile textures that wouldn't "work" in a room-size rug. Happily, you can discover attractive area rugs at relatively low cost, a boon if you are nearing the end of a home-furnishings budget. If you can afford it, you might buy a valuable old Oriental. If you tire of it on the floor, hang it on the wall.

ACCESSORIES

If you move around a lot, become a collector. Don't acquire a lot of trivia or junk, but establish a family hobby that fits in with your home life. Aside from art there are many accessories to take away the dull and impersonal look of a new home. Among useful accessories, there are small boxes and chests, candy jars, desk appointments, plates, and such. Decorative accessories, commonly called bibelots, are nice to have but annoying to pack and repack and ship halfway across the country. Of course, a few bibelots are nice, but not breakable Staffordshire dogs or seldom-used demitasse cups.

Collect, but please don't clutter. Clutter can be charming and individual, but it doesn't belong in your life style. Try to be selective in your accessories and learn how to compose them meaningfully. When you visit the better shops, take a look at how they display their accessories. Notice how often objects are grouped by category or size or color. A collection of paperweights enhances a corner of a desk, a curio cabinet holds pewter mugs, greenery goes on an étagère. Tabletop accessories in the living room can be charming. Small boxes, perhaps. Or sea shells you found at the beach supplemented by some that you bought. Or all your candlesticks arranged together.

When arranging accessories, think in terms of depth. Always place your larger, taller pieces toward the back, smaller ones to the front. Avoid the repetition of pairs. In a bookcase, for example, don't have, mixed with your books, a pair of candlesticks on one shelf, a pair of statues on another and a pair of vases on a third. Get as much variety into the arrangement of accessories as possible. You will soon find that there is no such thing as an ideal arrangement. The fun of having accessories is that you can put them into different combinations in different homes and work out new patterns and compositions.

CHAPTER TWENTY-SIX

THE VACATION HOME

ONE OF THE MOST EXCITING homemaking trends today is the wide-spread popularity of the vacation house. Variously referred to as the second home, the weekend home, or the leisure home, it was once the exclusive province of the rich in middle age or beyond. Now it encompasses almost all economic and age groups and, in fact, if it is identified with any group, it seems to be the young to whom a ski lodge or a beach house is a desired part of living. One of the most pleasant facets of the vacation life style is that it creates an opportunity for a carefree, colorful, light-hearted existence, and it should be planned as an escape from the pressures of status, convention, and routine that plague most homemakers in a workaday city life. The watchword in planning the decor of this kind of a home is low maintenance. Nobody wants to spend endless hours caring for a house when its very purpose is leisure. So as the interiors are planned, easy care must be considered first, every step of the way.

CHOICE OF BACKGROUND MATERIALS

Modular materials are a good choice for interior surfaces, and those which are prefinished cut down on maintenance. For walls, painted plaster is better in some areas than others; plaster is not the best in humid, ocean, or lakeside climates. However, plaster is usually painted and that means repainting. Better to choose a fabric-coated gypsum board with a tough, scrub-proof vinyl surface or to apply vinyl wall covering over regular gypsum board. Prefinished hardboard comes in a variety of finishes which simulate dozens of wood grains, plus colorful patterns and solid colors. All are plastic-finished, medium-density laminates which can be wiped down with a damp cloth and, except for the most soiled areas of the home like children's rooms, don't often need that. Plywood panels are now mostly prefinished for a damp-wipe surface and these offer the beauty of real wood in almost unlimited tones, natural and colored. These panels, ³⁄₁₆ inch to ½ inch thick, can be found at bargain prices, sometimes as low as three to four dollars for a 4-foot-by-8-foot sheet.

Ceilings are not subject to wear, so maintenance is not much of a factor here. However, prefinished materials such as those which come with the grid system of suspended ceiling, discussed previously, are an obvious choice, since they will not need future painting, only routine vacuuming. Acoustical ceiling tile is a good choice for recreation rooms and children's rooms, since noise is apt to occur there and if the vacation house is small, noise control is especially important. You can get acoustical tile which is stapled, tongue and groove, to a wood framework or to a subceiling of thin plywood, wallboard, or some other unfinished material. Or acoustical tile can be found as part of a suspended system.

FLOORING

The most vital area of the leisure home from the standpoint of both wear and maintenance is the floor. Holiday living invariably means a lot of coming and going, casual entertaining, and great indoor-outdoor traffic. At the beach this means abrasive sand will be tracked in, and at the mountains, lake, or country it means dirt and, in rainy weather, mud. Coco mats for foot wiping at each entrance door will be helpful and in the country, old-fashioned metal foot scrapers. But in the final analysis, the floor has to be able to take punishment and not demand endless vacuuming and polishing. At the beach, the best answer is a wood floor, either plank pine or oak or oak blocks. Oak-block flooring comes in nine-inch and twelve-inch squares, and is usually prefinished with liquid urethane or some tough coating applied at the factory. This will delay discoloration and surface damage, but in the end the sand will cause abrasion. Occasional paste wax buffing will help forestall abrasion and the block floor will look well for many years.

Plank floor, simply stained and given an initial liquid urethane coating will last a long time. When the urethane wears off, give the sur-

Minimum frills and attention to easy-care materials make this manufactured leisure home literally a breeze to live in. Prefinished oak block flooring is simply swept out; deck is left to weather, with rain running off between spaced boards; there are no moldings to catch dust. Metal-framed sliding glass doors provide complete indoor-outdoor access.

face another coat or just let the floor gradually assume a weathered look. Sweeping with a broom or vacuum will be all that is required. Composition flooring does not as a rule hold up under the abrasion of sand. Vinyl and vinyl-asbestos tiles will show scratch marks and become dull colored. Asphalt tile has the same problem. Rubber tile fares better because its surface is not as hard. Embossed linoleum is not a wise choice for sandy areas.

Composition tile and sheet flooring are fine for the dirt and mud locations. It's a good idea not to choose either very dark or light colors and solid patterns. An over-all patterned, neutral-colored sheet vinyl or vinyl-asphalt or vinyl-asbestos tile will show the least soil, and all can be damp mopped and waxed occasionally for good appearance. Carpet is not a sensible choice for areas subject to heavy traffic, either in sandy or muddy locations. It can be satisfactory in bedrooms where a snug feeling is pleasant. Carpet in the kitchen is not the best for the leisure home where bare, damp, and often wet feet are constant visitors. Carpet outdoors on deck and terraces, even of the new, specially developed, weather-resistant variety, is not recommended, because after heavy rains, it doesn't dry fast enough. A wood duckboard deck drains water off as it rains and when the sun comes out can be dry in an hour or less. Carpet remains soggy for a much longer time.

If you can afford brick, flagstone, or terrazzo, these materials are ideal for the vacation house, especially the beach house, because they never require more than vacuuming and always look wonderful. However, for modest budgets, your best bet is a simple, neutral-looking wood floor, enlivened with bright area rugs which can be shaken outdoors over beach or woods. If you try for the meticulously polished look that city floors have, you will make yourself a slave and also be disappointed in the results.

Wherever possible, use high-density laminates for set-down surfaces. Tabletops, counters in the kitchen, surfaces of built-ins, shower enclosure, windowsills, lavatory counters in the bath—all are candidates for the good looks and easy care of laminates, which require only water and occasionally soap and water to keep them shining. No other precautions are necessary except not cutting on them with knives or setting down hot pots in the kitchen. Properly installed, a laminate will provide endless years of beauty and service.

COLOR SCHEME

The color scheme should be planned throughout the house and in relation to the exterior colors, both of the house itself and the surrounding landscape. For example, if you have a beach house in driftwood gray siding, with bright blue doors and white trim, a good scheme would be a neutral beige or gray background color for the living and dining area, certainly, and perhaps for the master bedroom. Remember that at the beach, if you have large expanses of glass which you likely will, dead white will cause almost unbearable glare

The now and the then are part of the scene. Vacationers seem to want contemporary, open planning, big windows and easy-care floors, but they want the mellow warmth of the past, too. Here, a big, free-standing chimney of old brick with flagstone hearth, raised for easy fire-building, serves as a divider between living room and kitchen-dining area.

Views, everywhere possible, along with privacy are a basic part of the leisure home. Here, a shed roof was designed to create high, clerestory windows that give a sky and treetop view on one side of a living room which has a full wall of glass on the other. The whimsical framing element forms a ladder for a closer look at the sky if desired.

Wood is a perfect material for the beach; it weathers beautifully and is easy to tend. It also seems at home with the colors of sand and sky. Here, cedar walls and floor, inside and out, give a clean, scrubbed look, enlivened with a few antique accessories as accents. Furniture is simple: canvas chairs shrug off sand and moisture; table is raw wood.

Bright color and pattern are basic in the decor of the beach house, if only as contrast to the expanses of sand and sea. Fabrics and textured rug plus a few painted pieces of furniture, an abstract painting and whimsical accessories make this living room look like gaiety. Bright as they are, all surfaces, it is well to note, can be easily kept clean.

INTERIOR BY ANGELO DONGHIA
OF BURGE-DONGHIA, INC.

The A-frame has many advantages, one of which is that both the living-dining area on the lower floor and the upper sleeping balcony can enjoy the view. In this striking design, life is colorful: the lower deck is painted pumpkin, exposed framing purple, lower floor red, upper white. Textured rugs on both levels (they shake out in a trice) are a potpourri of hues.

A ski house should be a snuggery against the wintry blasts of snow and cold, and today, a window wall presents no problem. With insulating glass and excellent central heating systems available, it's possible to have open views and total comfort. Wall-to-wall carpet, pine paneling and other decorative elements add to the emotional impact of warmth.

MASONITE CORPORATION

Coordinated exterior decoration is especially important for the vacation house where a festive air is wanted indoors and out. Here grooved hardboard panels, painted a soft blue, are accented by white fascia and window trim. Red, blue and white accessories add verve. The deck is fir, stained driftwood gray and open-spaced for drainage.

Holiday living is compact and easy, with windows for enjoying the leafy view and a big deck for sunning. Walls paneled in wood-grained hardboard are easy to keep clean; the prefabricated fireplace is a bright decorative accent by day, a source of heat at night. Built-in sofa conceals a roll-out bed; wall storage system forms a decorative music center.

MASONITE CORPORATION

because of the reflection of the sun on sandy surroundings and on the water. A soft neutral will temper this. A sandy beige for walls and woodwork, on the other hand, will relate to the outdoors and at the same time soften the glare. Blue is a natural, picking up the water color as it does, and with this color already established at the front door, it is a pleasant choice for upholstered pieces in the living room and in draperies. Bright accents in the other primary colors, red and yellow, will give a lot of sparkle in lamps, decorative pillows, ash-trays, and all other finishing touches. An area rug in blue plus one or both of the accents will look fine over a dark-stained wood floor. Remember, the more continuity you keep throughout the house in color, the more livable the effect will be and the greater the sense of space. The latter factor is important in vacation living where the stern realities of the budget have likely dictated rather small rooms and not too many of them at that.

Conversely, when you plan the colors for a house in the mountains or the woods, you'll likely want white walls or some light, reflecting tone to offset the darkness of the forest around you. You may also want to reintroduce the green color which predominates outdoors and you can turn to orange, rust, and yellow for accent colors. These will enliven dark wood pieces and the rustic look that seems at home in the ski cabin or lodge. If you are using wood paneled walls, choose panels that are extremely light in tone or use plywood and paint it white. The mountain house often has quite high ceilings and big pat-terns are appropriate for drapery and upholstery fabrics. The point is that in the mountains you want a snugness in contrast to the over-powering vastness of the outdoors. At the beach where the terrain is more open and friendly, a light pervasive look has more emotional ap-peal.

THE IMPORTANCE OF SCALE

In line with the space problem, it is important to keep to small-scaled and light-looking pieces of furniture. And here, take this bit of ad-vice: Don't use the second home as a depository for all the castoffs of your mother-in-law or the furniture you have outgrown in your per-manent home but feel is too good to discard. I have visited many a delightful vacation house, which looked attractive on the outside. However, the minute you entered the front door the effect was lost

Ski cabin packs a lot of storage on one wall with a system of hung cabinets and shelves in adjustable wall tracks. Speakers are spaced for good stereo listening, with hi-fi controls in a sliding door cabinet below. Molded fiber glass furniture, fur rug, colorful prefabricated fireplace add to the comfortable "now" look, while wood adds familiar warmth.

because every old dreadnaught armchair, sofa, and dining group from the city house had been foisted on the leisure house, defeating the whole purpose of the place, namely, an escape from the problems of city living. Far better to make tables of packing crates covered in bright felt and buy simple white-framed director's chairs with cheerful canvas seats and backs and wait until you can afford what you want, at which time the folding armchairs can go out to the deck.

Scale, then, is a watchword in your choice of furniture. Two love seats (perhaps they turn into beds for extra guests) are preferable to one mammoth sofa. Two small, easily moved coffee tables look less crowded than one huge oblong. Keep lamps on the medium side and, please, don't follow the development cliché of putting one right in the middle of a big window. The vacation house is the place to depart from such unattractive conventions. Use several smallish area rugs rather than one big one, which would be difficult to shake out. Wherever possible, use dual-purpose furniture—narrow console tables that open to form dining tables, hi-lo coffee tables that raise to dining height, settles that flip their tops to become dining tables, chairs and even ottomans that open to sleeping cots, to name a few possibilities.

Texture is important in both the beach and mountain retreat. Glossy damasks and satins have no place in the vacation house; choose denims or sailcloth which come in cheerful colors and can be popped into the washer and dryer when they show soil. Nubby synthetic blends will hold up well on sofas and chairs and will look right; choose pieces that have fabrics with a preservative finish. Shag-type rugs that shake out are better than broadloom twists and close-woven floor coverings that must be vacuumed to remove sand and dirt.

TRADITIONAL OR CONTEMPORARY?

Choice of decorative style is an important decision. If your house is sleekly modern in its architecture, you'll want to stay with that style for the interior. However, you can also have a transitional mix. A few antique pieces of furniture—a handsome breakfront, an old cupboard —and antique accessories can lend great warmth and character. Today's most prevalent style is eclectic, a blend of elements, so have the things around you that you like, but keep the major pieces—sofas, tables, armchairs—contemporary. As mentioned before, contemporary seems right at the beach, but it's quite possible to do a charming Cape Cod seaside cottage and use almost all traditional furniture —either antiques, reproductions, or a blend—and cover the upholstered pieces in fabrics practical for the beach. The wood pieces don't have to have the somber, dark finishes often associated with traditional; a few painted pieces in bright colors are perfectly authentic and will give a gay air.

The mountain lodge, if in the rustic chalet style rather than the modern A-frame design, looks and works well with traditional decoration. Dark oak pieces combined with bright chintz fabrics, decorated pottery lamps in strong colors, and lots of flowered pillows will give an inviting feeling. And remember that floral fabrics come in stylized, contemporary patterns that bypass any dated look. A bold floral for a big, comfortable sofa in tufted club style will look won-

Mellow look of this combination bed-living room in a mountain cottage stems from pale knotty pine floors, antique brick chimney, dark stained beams, the texture of the fur throw over the lounge bed, and the casual mixture of the antique and the modern. Big window expanse was left uncurtained, protected by dense woods from neighboring houses.

derful. A nice touch, too, is an ample Welsh cupboard or some other type of open hutch, or a country cupboard with a collection of country ceramic plates—faience, Italian, or French reproductions—which will add sparkle to a whole wall and be useful, too. You can use the plates at meals. Set a color theme and stick to it in fabrics, pillows, even the dinnerware, and the rooms will look important and expensively done, even though the fabrics may be under two dollars a yard from a mill-end shop.

For the A-frame ski house, more families are turning to contemporary interior design, although the classic "A" is also a traditional roof form and will lend itself to familiar decor. For either style, it is important to keep an over-all, neutral background color. The A-frame is rather chopped up inside, what with gable window, balcony, exposed second-floor areas, and several doors below leading to rooms in the rear. A single color will help tie all these elements together. If you go the contemporary route, stay with solid blocks of color in upholstered pieces and keep the pattern to contemporary paintings, abstract area rugs (and there are some beauties being made today that look like paintings on the floor), and modern lamps and lighting fixtures. Keep in mind that you will have an enormous panoramic view of something through that big front window and you don't want to compete with nature's pattern. In fact, work with it in greens and earth colors for your over-all scheme.

Whatever else you do, make your vacation home reflect you and your family. This is the place for a display of your favorite hobbies—oil or water-color paintings, plants, boating prints, a collection of photographs if someone is a shutterbug. This will give a relaxed atmosphere and also provide everyone with a sense of participation; they'll feel that this house is really "theirs." However, it may take a bit of disciplining; you'll have a mass of clutter if everyone's hobby is in the act at once. Changing the exhibit on one pegboard wall is a good way to satisfy everyone and keep the hobbies a decorative asset.

WINDOW TREATMENT

The way you decorate windows will have a great bearing not only on the enjoyment of your house aesthetically, but also on your physical comfort. In the living areas, at least, you are apt to have large, scenic windows or at least one expanse looking out over beach, water, dis-

Irregular shape of a Long Island beach house makes for interesting interior spaces. Kitchen fits neatly in one arch-windowed bay, defined by grooved plywood paneling which sweeps across ceiling and down over wall. High clerestory window sports a colorful "flying" fish for a touch of whimsy; colors are repeated in canvas of director's chairs.

tant hills, or just into the native greenery. If the big window faces north, you can leave it completely open, as no direct sunlight will bother you. If you dislike the black void that appears at night, a few spotlights outdoors will give you a cheerful picture in the evening, summer and winter. However, more often, the view is apt to be in a different direction, subject to sunlight and you will need something to temper it. The best idea and easiest to operate is traverse drapery that can be pulled across with cords. Be sure this is floor to ceiling, so that it looks architectural, that is, like an integral part of the room rather than something tacked on. If the expanse is large, choose a light, translucent cloth—not an open weave necessarily but something that lets light through, so that you can cut off the strong sun in the afternoon and still have a glow in the room. Choose a light cotton or a synthetic which is easily washable and requires no ironing. You can have it partially dried in a machine and then hang it up to fall straight in final drying.

If you use the house in winter, you may want to add an insulating lining to the drapery, which at night will keep in heat stored during the day. This will cut down on the translucency, however. Some large windows—for example, the big gable expanse of the A-frame—may be difficult to fit with traverse drapery and you may have to settle for what is in essence a giant cafe curtain—a horizontal expanse with an open gable above. This will give privacy at night and can help somewhat to keep out the sun by day. Window shades are another good possibility for the vacation house because of their easy maintenance factor, and these often can be adapted to gable or other oddly shaped windows. For smaller windows, shades are an excellent choice and can be laminated in patterned fabric that blends with the other elements of decor. Shades are in a finish which can be damp wiped for easy cleaning. Other possibilities for small windows are cafe curtains, wood shutter panels, and Venetian blinds (the latter are not recommended where there is heavy dust, as they are not the easiest to vacuum or damp wipe clean).

By all means avoid the slightest fussy treatment. Elaborate swags, complicated Roman shades, lambrequins, vertical blinds, and other devices—as decorative as they may be—will only complicate living and defeat the purpose of the carefree home. The best rule to follow is to design a treatment which will afford privacy, temper the sunlight, while admitting air. The latter is especially important for the summer house, which is sought out often to escape the heat of the city. Many times, elaborate window treatments demand that room air conditioners be used, which seems foolish in the light of the fresh, cool country or sea air that is available; unless, of course, there are allergy or other health considerations which demand the use of filtered, controlled, cooled air.

CHAPTER TWENTY-SEVEN

EXTERIOR DECORATION

THE NEW ACCENT on outdoor living has brought with it a whole new emphasis on what can be called "exterior" as opposed to "interior" decor. The day when the choice in outdoor appointments was limited and furniture and accessories were a hodgepodge of styles, colors, and patterns is past. Today, the choice is enormous, in every component from metal furniture to portable barbecues to waterproof pillows. In fact, your selections may range as broadly as they do for interior decor, all of which leads to the question: What are the differences between the two? What considerations are there in choosing appointments for outdoor rooms?

First of all, there are practical considerations which do not hold in indoor rooms. Inside the house, decorating components—sofas, chairs, tables, pictures, etc.—remain in a fairly constant position, and, of course, they are sheltered from the elements. Outdoors, they must be taken up and stored for the most part, and this calls for stackable, folding, collapsible, and mobile furniture. Much of it must be easily moved in a hurry as storms approach, so it must be lightweight, too. What can remain in rain and storm must be specially prefinished accordingly. Metal furniture must be anodized, wood pieces, heavily varnished, fabrics rain- and mildew-resistant and, above all, as sunfast as possible.

From the aesthetic or decorative standpoint, components can be chosen much as are the ones for inside rooms. Again, it is basic to think in terms of outdoor floor, walls, and ceiling. There's no reason under the sun why, for example, the brick or clapboard of the house structure which forms the back wall of the terrace cannot display a painting, a lighting sconce, a piece of wall sculpture, or a series of prints, which can be put up only in good weather or can be framed or otherwise treated for weather resistance. The main thing to keep in mind is not to be hidebound in your thinking. By the same token, if you want an Oriental rug or shag carpet, have it and be prepared to take it up if rain threatens. Or choose the new indoor-outdoor carpet that can be left in the rain. (However, remember that it doesn't dry as fast as the surrounding wood deck or flagstone paving, so you may squish and squash in soggy discomfort for a while.)

Indoor-Outdoor Relationship

Rooms on either side of a glass wall should be decorated in tandem. It is visually disturbing to stand in a pastel French living room and look out at a terrace with breathlessly contemporary white chaises and tables, upholstery and umbrellas in strong, primary colors. The outdoor room should look and function as a continuation of inner space and, vice versa, the indoor room should appear related to the outdoor. (The latter is not quite as important, however, because during most of the day it is difficult to see through the glass into the darker interior.) Be that as it may, the entire house will seem more pleasant and also more spacious if there is an over-all scheme, so if, for example, your colors are blue and green with accents of yellow, it is an easy matter to find the same tones for the upholstery of outdoor furniture, either plain or patterned. And remember that patterns should be kept in the same genre: If you have a floral for the living-room sofa in a country house provincial theme, choose a floral for outdoors with the same general feeling, and if you can't find one, stick to solid colors outdoors.

Keep in mind also that the plainer outdoor elements are the better, since they will be competing with the pattern of nature—trees, sky, clouds, grass, flowers. In most cases, if you want harmony, solid colors and simple-line furniture are best. However, often a sophisticated scheme is desired as a deliberate contrast to nature and if this is the case, use stripes, intricate florals, and geometric patterns that act as strong foils. To paraphrase the old adage, you can either "lick 'em or join 'em" in exterior decoration. The accent scheme which makes a very definite distinction between natural and man-designed can be exciting, but again, it is only appropriate for a house which has the same sharp, sophisticated scheme indoors. Such a scheme employs colors that are exotic—black, very dark greens, purples, bitter greens, shocking pinks—providing the sharpest contrast.

When architect John Billings redesigned this turn-of-the-century house in Pittsburgh, he kept the front porch, but changed its entrance from the front to the side. Openings in the heavy brick were filled with iron filigree panels for lightness; floor was carpeted; light-colored Roman shades of translucent sailcloth give privacy with illumination. Door leading to the living room makes porch its outdoor counterpart.

Another consideration in any design plan is the location of the property. A beach house with its deck perched on a dune will demand a far different quality than an apartment terrace or a suburban house with a view of trees, shrubs, and flowers. Canvas director's chairs and sling cots that may look fine on a sundeck overlooking the ocean would seem out of place in a country setting. Conversely, quite formal terrace pieces would be stilted at the beach. Much of the mood to be established, designwise, depends on the degree of formality or informality associated with the geographical area in question. The life enjoyed in a ski cabin in Vermont will be highly casual and what outdoor activity is possible on the deck, at least in the ski season, will call for informal, even rustic simplicity. In summer, redwood furniture and simple patterns and fabrics will seem quite at home in the woodsy landscape.

Outdoor Furniture

Many different materials are used in the design and manufacture of furniture that must withstand exposure to the elements, to some degree or other. Wicker, rattan, peel cane, bamboo, and other tropical materials are not capable of much weather resistance, even though painted, varnished, prefinished in a plastic coating, or otherwise treated. These pieces, as attractive as many of them are, are better used on a porch or some sheltered space. If used on the deck or terrace, they should be brought under cover or draped against the rain, dew, and other moisture. The fanciful peacock chair that gave an exotic look to the porches of late Victorian times is still a favorite decorative accent. Antique wicker pieces are highly prized and priced today and are being used as much for solariums, garden rooms, and other indoor spaces as they are for sheltered patios and porches. There are many excellent reproductions of such old pieces being made in Hong Kong and imported—wicker elephant tables, canopied sofas, whimsical chairs, and all the rest. Rattan is being interpreted in beautiful designs, as elegant as any sophisticated, formal pieces for living room, as well as for garden rooms, lanais, or patios. Bamboo chaises longues, sofas, and chairs have received the same design attention.

Some types of wood furniture can be left outdoors to weather; for example, the redwood so-called Adirondack furniture, large, rather awkward pieces that were in vogue ten or fifteen years ago. These are

With the new outdoor carpet of ribbon-type polypropylene an outdoor room can be as comfortable underfoot as its indoor counterpart. Synthetic rubber backing eliminates need for underpadding and can be cemented to the deck surface or simply laid on. To contrast with the natural setting, flame red carpet was used, punctuated with white outdoor furniture.

still being made and they can be suitable for large decks of beach houses and ski cabins. Redwood, which is highly resistant to moisture, is now being used for much lighter scaled, better designed pieces, too. Some of it is folding; some employs metal as an auxiliary material. Redwood lumber, available at the local building materials dealer, can be made into simple benches, tables, etc., as a do-it-yourself project. Plans for such pieces are often available at the yard or can be found in handyman magazines. The long harvest table with sawbuck legs and long benches at each side is available at many garden centers and department stores and makes a useful dining group for outdoors.

Wood, usually oak, is also used for the famous director's chair, the folding armchair with canvas sling back and seat. The wood parts come either painted or heavily varnished and they will stand up outdoors to an extent. If you leave them out all the time, they may last a season or two in fairly respectable condition. Of course, if the frames hold up, you can buy canvas replacements for the seats, which simply slide into grooves in the two sides of the seat frame, and just loop over the two back spindles for the back. These are mail-order items in the home-service magazines or can be found in some department and specialty stores. They come in several colors, plus white and black.

Metal and plastic are the two best materials for outdoor use. Painted anodized aluminum is now being fashioned into beautiful, lightweight designs, which are often used as indoor furniture too, because of their attractiveness. The joints are specially welded to prevent collection of moisture and the frames are given an undercoating, then sprayed again in a color. Used with them are plastic strapping or vinyl cord; the former is sometimes used as the foundation for seat cushions. Wrought iron is also widely used and carefully joined and anodized against rust. It is worked in many different styles ranging from New Orleans filigree designs and Spanish scrollwork to severe contemporary. The chairs and sofas often have expanded metal seats as the platform for innerspring cushions. Tables have glass, plastic, fiber glass, or expanded metal tops, sometimes with a center hole for location of an umbrella. The furniture comes in many painted finishes and in a variety of upholstery choices. Be sure to look at the joints for water fastness and inquire about the finish. This type of furniture can stay outdoors during summer months for many seasons before any sign of rust. The best brands are guaranteed rustproof for a certain number of years. However, it is well to bring such pieces indoors for winter storage or cover them securely with plastic. Be careful about the kind of tabletop that is offered and make sure you get one that is shatterproof. It is also possible to use marble and other stone materials for the top rather than glass or plastic.

Make certain that upholstery has specially sealed seams to make entrance of water impossible under normal use. There are new methods of making seat and back cushions to ensure this. Vinyl fabrics are the best; specially treated canvas holds up, but not as well. For the interior fill of the cushions, there are a number of materials being used—Dacron, polyfoam, latex foam rubber—all synthetics, all resistant to moisture if any enters, all providing quite comfortable seating. In some of the more elaborate outdoor sofas and love seats, these are often used in conjunction with galvanized innersprings.

ACCESSORIES FOR OUTDOOR ROOMS

Just as with indoor decoration, you can co-ordinate in color, pattern, and style all your accessories from ashtrays to art objects. To be sure, there are special considerations once again. For example, it is wise to select ashtrays that are somewhat hooded so that ashes do not blow about. The stay-put tray is good, too; there are some fabric ones with sand or pebbles in a pouchlike design that are good table huggers. Plastic is good, if it is more or less unbreakable. Winds are going to come up, unexpectedly at times, so sturdy objects are good choices.

We have already mentioned the possibility of hanging paintings and other types of murals on outdoor walls. Sculpture is another art form that is especially suitable for deck or terrace. Pieces in stone or cast ceramic are quite beautiful and weatherproof; certain metal sculpture, if heavily painted, is attractive, especially for the contemporary deck or patio. Decorative urns are a correct touch for the traditional terrace and make ideal planters. These are available in antique marble, granite, or other stone; there are also newly cast ones of concrete that are reasonable and readily available. Wayside garden marts, once again, are good places to look. For antique garden pieces, auctions and antique shops in areas where there were once large estate gardens, which have been subdivided, are likely bets.

A theme will help in the choice of outdoor art. For example, if you have a blue, yellow, and white scheme in a traditional house, reproduction Della Robbia plaques on stucco or brick walls would be lovely. For the severely modern house, the terrace or deck wall is a likely place for a striking piece of wall sculpture, a contemporary

Screened potting shed doubles as a semioutdoor sitting room for a beach house. A rustic air is underscored with exposed wood shingles for walls, open ceiling beams, hanging pots, and wood flats filled with plants in simple clay pots. White furniture of expanded metal and bright pillows are accents.

The garden room provides year 'round enjoyment of house plants and a gracious setting for relaxing and informal entertaining. This room has been designed as an adjunct to the outer terrace and garden, but the potted plants on the shelf and in the low metal floor planter make it an indoor garden in its own right.

This charming brick-walled garden room has a flagstone floor and built-in planter, also of bricks, for plants. Some of the plants, such as the ivy which climbs up the wall, are permanent, but the owners rely on an array of flowering plants for seasonal display. At Christmas time, several pots of cyclamen provide cheering, long-lasting color.

The same garden room in spring. Color is provided by pots of primroses mixed with cyclamen. Additional color is added by forced branches of yellow forsythia. In fall, potted chrysanthemums are the main feature.

The jade plant (crassula), with its fleshy leaves and thick stems, looks like an exotic miniature tree. The plants can be pruned and trained to assume a variety of forms and shapes. Choose containers like the ones shown or select authentic Japanese bonsai pots for an oriental effect.

PHOTOGRAPHY BY ROCHE

An entrance hall echoes the flavor of a Spanish patio with its free use of potted plants. Red geraniums repeat the red color of the potted plants in the wall mural. Plants used in this fashion can be changed or rotated as necessary. At holiday time, red poinsettias or kalanchoë can be substituted for the red geraniums.

AMITICO DELFT AND KALEIDOSCOPE, VINYL TILE/KELVINATOR APPLIANCES

Kitchens are getting prettier all the time! They are usually well lighted and invite introduction of many kinds of house plants. Geraniums, shown here, can be a happy choice, but equally enjoyable can be African violets, small pots of cactus plants, and many herbs, like rosemary, parsley, basil, which are used in cooking.

An indoor garden complete with statuary dwells in this modern version of marble halls. The garden contains Easter lilies, tulips and hyacinths—which can be obtained from early winter to late spring from florists—and foliage plants, which are skillfully arranged to hide the plants' pots.

House plants have moved into the bathroom. The angular structure and tile pattern of this bath, which is naturally well lighted because of generous window space, benefits from contrast with cutleaf philodendron and drooping spider plant in the hanging pot.

As much garden as outdoor living area is this slightly raised deck of Douglas fir. The structure is simple—a large, square pad of 2 by 4s laid flat over a framework of joists with spaces left between them for rain runoff. Maintenance is kept at a minimum here by the easily swept deck, the plants in containers, the reliance on low-upkeep evergreens, and the ground beds, which are heavily mulched with pebbles to smother weeds and retain soil moisture.

sunburst or a free-form design in metal, planned to add to the color and pattern through weather exposure. The Mediterranean patio has a built-in scheme that can be interpreted with large alas, the huge vases copied from the vessels in which olive oil was once brought to the New World. These are now cast in terra cotta and make unusually scaled accessories. Large jars also come in glazed ceramic and in many wonderful colors. Remember, if you use them, to add of bit of kerosene if water collects; they can be good breeding places for mosquitoes and other insects.

Mosaic tile, used in many ways, is excellent outdoors. Special weather-resistant grout can be used. Wall plaques, panels that form baffles or screens, whole walls of the house can be decorated with mosaics. You can make geometric designs of your own ideas and can even execute them yourself with readily available tiles, by gluing them to hardboard with epoxy and filling in later with grout. Mosaic tabletops are useful and attractive outdoors. In fact, tile, being one of the oldest man-made products for outdoor use, is limited in its alfresco applications only by your imagination.

Not only can art objects be chosen to your scheme, but useful items, too. Towels for sun bathing, mats, big canvas pillows for lounging on the deck, folding small tables and stools, bar equipment, barbecues, and all the other requirements for full living out of doors. All are available in a rainbow of colors to select from and many have patterned elements to blend with your over-all look. For example, small tables come with laminated tops in a variety of patterns or solids. For sling stools and director's chairs with removable cloth panels, if you can't find a pattern and colors in ready-mades, buy canvas by the yard and stitch it over the slings that come with the units.

The Total Scheme

As you plan your outdoor-living world, remember to take all elements into consideration, just as you would with an interior room. Your floor may be a wood deck, weathered or new, flagstone paving, stone, brick, or concrete, and each one of these will help to dictate a color and pattern scheme. If it is wood, you have a natural expanse to play against, so you can be bold with bright colors and large patterns. If it is brick, which has so much pattern and a dominant color of its own, you are more limited: Big expanses of solid colors may be better for chaises and sofas. If it is stone or flagstone, you'll need fresh, light colors to play against the grayness; while if it is marble, your choices will have to be carefully formal in pattern and color.

Similarly, the walls of the house will play a part. White clapboard will allow a free choice; brick or stone a more limited one. The materials themselves and the design of the house, its windows and other ar-

A flowering dogwood has been trained in espalier fashion to make attractive tracery against the house wall. Dogwoods are amenable to many forms of training to suit the site and to restrain their growth. Pruning should be done in late spring. The Japanese holly, here used as a low, formal hedge on each side of the dogwood, is an equally versatile shrub.

chitectural features are important to consider. If your terrace has a wall with a bank of French windows leading into the living or dining room, they may dictate the beginning of a country, even rustic look in chintzy patterns and fresh colors. Very contemporary furniture in solids of primary colors wouldn't look nearly as well, but it would be perfect against an expanse of glass doors in a contemporary house. If part of your terrace is covered or you are decorating a porch, the ceiling must be taken into account. One way to jazz up an old porch is to paint its ceiling with bold stripes or a colorful stencil design or to cover it with gay fabric, draped like a tent or stretched and tacked flat. This will likely be the dominant note for the area, so you can play subtle color and pattern against it on the floor and wall, also in furniture and accessories. A trellis over the terrace dictates its pattern similarly, canvas awnings the same.

As you can see, the point is to play one element against another for visual contrast. Decorating the outdoor room is the same as doing an indoor: It is a subtle tapestry, an intricate weaving of pattern, color, scale, and, above all, the emotional associations that we all have with these elements. If it all sounds too pretentious and elaborate for doing a simple porch or patio, keep in mind that the aim is not to be stuffy, but to spend your money wisely, no matter how much or little, and to arrive at the most comfortable, pleasant, and good-looking scheme you can. Many people with nothing but money can make an otherwise lovely terrace quite ordinary just by failing to understand these principles.

CHAPTER TWENTY-EIGHT

HOUSE PLANTS

Rooms without any living plants often seem sterile and lacking in warmth. On the other hand, rooms containing house plants appear to be full of vitality and a sense of intimacy. The presence of plants, like people, gives meaning and animation to a room full of otherwise inanimate objects.

Decorating with house plants in many ways is the easiest part of interior decoration. While some plants will grow better or look better in some situations, there are no absolute rights and wrongs in their use to intimidate beginners.

House plants are suited to any type of architecture and any style of decor ranging from informal to formal. Today there is an array of different kinds of house plants for decorative purposes. There is much variation in the shape, size, texture, and color of leaves, and as it is the foliage of most plants that is the dominant decorative element, the designer has a wide selection of plants useful for their foliage effect alone. For a plant whose foliage is definitely frilly and which might be effective in a room largely Victorian in style, there is the Boston fern variety known as Fluffy Ruffles. For rooms furnished in Art Nouveau fashion, there are such house plants as the Hawaiian ti (*Cordyline terminalis*) and Cleopatra begonia, both with reddish-tinged leaves exotic enough to fit the rather excessively unreal world of Art Nouveau. Many of the tropical plants available universally today have big, bold leaves especially effective in modern interiors, where too many angles and starkly plain walls call for the visual relief of leafy shapes and textures.

There are many kinds of flowering house plants, too, although the importance of their flowers is generally less in the decorative scheme today than that of the leaves. For one thing, most flowering house plants are not ever-blooming, although the African violet (*Saint-paulia*) comes close to falling in this category, and there are others—certain orchids and the azalea—that have amazingly lengthy blooming periods. Yet, because of their varying seasons of bloom and sometimes short duration of bloom, flowering house plants can be all the more valuable in decorating interiors. They can be considered transient accents and used and enjoyed like a bouquet or flower arrangement—perhaps even to be discarded when their flowers have faded. Flowering house plants can become the stars of arrangements of more permanent plants and can be placed in prominent positions as they come into bloom. It is possible to light up rather somber winter windows around Christmas with colorful poinsettias and kalanchoe. The bright red flowers of both plants will show up even more against the greenery of nonflowering plants. A few cineraria plants in full bloom can be just as effective among foliage plants in late winter and around Easter.

And, of course, there are the same opportunities with flowering plants as with foliage plants to fit the plant to the style of the decor. The fuchsia belongs to a lush Victorian setting or to a sun porch or terrace with rattan furniture. There is the anthurium (both *Anthurium andraeanum* and *A. scherzerianum*) whose "patent-leather" flowers seem so suitable to the Art Nouveau period. Yet the anthurium, handsome in leaf and flower, is elegant enough for the most exquisitely formal furnishings. It would also look right in many modern rooms, which emphasizes again the versatility of house plants and how easy it is to decorate with them.

CHANCES OF SUCCESS WITH PLANTS

To use house plants decoratively, it is necessary to grow them. Yet even this process can be reduced to a simple, minimal routine, such as watering a pot when the soil is dry or keeping the plant out of cold drafts or, at the other extreme, not standing it next to a blazing fire in the fireplace or placing it on a hot radiator. Many plants will be perfectly happy with this common-sense treatment which any sensible person, without much or any previous gardening experience, can give.

The greatest success with house plants is achieved, though, when they are given at least a little tender, loving care and an effort is made to meet their special requirements. The majority of plants, many of them with the most decorative possibilities, have surprisingly few requirements, however, and even they are hardly in the class of hard-and-fast rules. The African violet is a good example of a plant which seems to respond well to various kinds of care.

Actually, much in modern living and architectural trends helps both the beginner and more experienced gardener to grow plants more successfully indoors. Most windows today are much larger than they used to be. Many living rooms, if they do not possess a generous-sized picture window, have floor-to-ceiling windows which let in more than enough light for most plants. Even apartment houses are being constructed with greater window space. For interiors where adequate light is still lacking, modern technology has helped by developing fluorescent lights which can be placed in various ways to supply the missing light or to supplement inadequate amounts of light.

Another aspect of modern living which helps in the growing of house plants is our increasing awareness of the need for adequate humidity indoors. Centrally heated homes can become too dry for the welfare of fine furniture and pianos and for the comfort of plants and people. When nothing can be done to increase humidity, a state of affairs especially prevalent in apartments, there are plants—succulents, cacti, and snake plant (*Sansevieria trifasciata*) are examples—which endure dry atmospheres, but the majority of plants perform best with ample humidity. There are various ways of providing the right amount of humidity in our homes. One of the easiest and most efficient is the incorporation of a humidifying device in the heating system. This practice, which is becoming more and more common, is another improvement in the indoor environment for house plants.

How to Choose Plants

The homemaker who sets out to look for new carpeting, for example, doesn't depart for the stores until she has given much conscious (and subconscious) consideration to her own likes and dislikes as well as to such factors as the shape of the room, the kind of light it receives, the furniture and ornaments it already contains, and future acquisitions she has in mind. She doesn't just decide, on a moment's notice, that an antique gold carpet is what she'll buy just because she likes the color. For the best result in decorating with house plants, do give some thought to the entire picture. Study the plant descriptions and illustrations and consider the space the plants are to occupy. Don't just choose a pink azalea because you like the color, without regard to the surroundings it should, ideally, complement.

For a large room, it's wise to choose large-scale plants, even small trees or medium-sized shrubs, that are adaptable to the light conditions. Do avoid the overfussy effect of too many small plants dotted around in large spaces. A small room that needs intimate touches might be overwhelmed by a fine big Norfolk Island pine standing in the corner, but it might be just the room for several favorite flowering plants (if light is ample) or for pots of African violets, Chinese evergreen, and baby's tears (*Helxine*), if light is poor. All three will do quite well under the light of ordinary table or reading lamps.

The low-ceilinged rooms typical of much modern construction have, even if they are large in floor space, a problem of proportion. This can be dealt with by choosing furniture that is mostly low and fairly small in scale; towering armoires and breakfronts are out, unfortunately for the possessors (or would-be possessors) of such pieces. However, small-scale furniture can sometimes give a monotonously low effect. When this happens, an accent plant chosen for its height and its silhouette (but not so tall that it crowds the ceiling) can break the "horizon," adding apparent height without being overpowering.

Old-fashioned high-ceilinged rooms that survive from a more spacious day can be a paradise for the indoor gardener if they have, or can be supplied with, enough light to permit the growth of a collection of really sizable specimens. In the instance of one city apartment that housed an enviably lush plant collection, the owners provided themselves with waterproof trays filled with pebbles upon which the tubs and pots stood. Such trays, which can be made to order at a sheet-metal shop, simplify housekeeping greatly. They catch any drips from watering and add to the humidity, too.

Color of foliage and flowers is to be considered in choosing your plants. A canny selection can result in spectacular effects. In a room containing mostly plain colors and surfaces, the paisley-like patterns of massed coleus can be stunning. Conversely, if the decorative scheme is one of many patterns and colors intermingled (currently very fashionable), even more color and pattern can be contributed to the riotous effect by the very same plants. In terms of brilliant color, the croton, a plant with heavy, waxy foliage, is to be recommended in spite of its being a generally difficult house plant for the North. If you consider crotons as visitors, to be discarded when drafts or temperature changes cause them to drop their leaves, they're worth having for their compact size—two feet or so—and their leaf colors of bright orange, red, brown, yellow, and green. While they're with you, try to give them high humidity, plenty of light, and a warm temperature.

Less brilliant than coleus and crotons are the plants in creamy shades, perhaps suitable for quieter rooms. In this group are some of the coleus varieties and variegated ivies. For a shimmering grape-purple touch, there is the Hawaiian ti plant, and an even more striking shade is seen in the purplish-red tradescantias. Brilliant reds and pinks flame in the leaves of coleus and certain begonias and in the flowers of some begonias and African violets, not to mention the perennially charming geraniums and pelargoniums. Shades of gold are found in golden pothos, variegated nephthytis, and variegated Chinese evergreen.

Using plants to their best advantage is a creative contribution to the decorating of a room and can eventually give more personal satisfaction than the selection of a lifeless sofa or chair. While all rooms do not necessarily require the presence of plants, there is hardly a part of a dwelling where they are likely to be out of place. Even basement space that would be otherwise wasted can be converted into a "garden room" or green retreat by installing shelves for plants and fluorescent lights. Such a room provides a good place for growing plants that can later be moved into other rooms for display.

SMALL PLANTS AS DECORATION

There are many ways to use smaller plants. Such use is determined by the degree of interest you have in plants. If you find the growing of African violets is becoming a hobby (and it often develops into one), you may want to purchase one of the many attractive plant stands that have been especially designed to show off these charming plants. A choice African violet in a low pot can make a delightful centerpiece on a dining-room table; or place one on a low coffee table so that the pattern of leaves and flowers can be viewed from above. African violets respond especially well to fluorescent lights, so from one to several plants can be grown under lights installed above one shelf of a bookcase. Books and house plants always make an attractive combination. The same is true of plants and paintings and statuary.

It is a good idea to keep several small foliage plants on hand for quick and temporary decorating effects. The plants can be heart-leaf philodendron, asparagus fern, table fern, or ivy and should be in small pots, about two and one-half to three inches in diameter. Three or four plants (still in their pots) can be grouped together in a large bowl to serve as a table centerpiece. (Colorful fruits—apples, oranges, a pineapple—can be added to the bowl.) One plant can be placed in a favorite piece of china or pewter to serve as a temporary decoration on an end table or bedside table in the guest room. If you have a glass-topped cocktail table, arrange several small plants beneath it in a tray on the floor for an indoor-garden effect.

For a sunny window that does not become too cold in winter, a parade of small pots of exotic-shaped cacti on the top of the lower sash or on a glass shelf (fastened to the molding so the window can be raised without disturbing the plants) can be entertaining. Cacti need very little water compared to most house plants, making them an excellent choice for those who want as little fuss with plants' needs as possible.

Larger plants of succulents and cacti, especially those with extreme shapes, make bold modern effects when from one to about three pots are used on a window with a wide ledge. Generally, cactus plants should be kept to themselves rather than being mixed with other plants.

Making an indoor window garden of plants can be one of the most personally satisfying ways to use house plants attractively. Several plants can be combined, or combine as many as will fit the space; again, the choice depends somewhat on the degree of interest you have in house plants. Taller plants can be placed at the side or close to the window. Lower plants and trailers are arranged in front. Vines like hoya, ivy, or creeping fig can be trained to frame all or part of a window by standing the pots at the rear and side, or by hanging the pots about halfway from the top of the window at the side, or by placing the pots in brackets fastened to the molding.

Shelves can be attached to most windows to increase the area for displaying plants. Most mail-order seed catalogues list metal adjustable shelves which will fit standard-size windows. Often the plants on the shelves offer a more attractive view than that outside the window.

Most window gardens contain a mixture of foliage plants with some flowering plants used as accents. The number of flowering plants you choose depends on the amount of sunshine the window receives. Such plants as amaryllis, azalea, freesia, veltheimia, begonia, and African violet will bloom in a window that gets a fews hours of sunshine, then good light the rest of the day; and of course you can buy plants like chrysanthemum, cyclamen, primrose, poinsettia, kalanchoe, and others in full bloom from a florist to add to the display.

Windows that receive no direct sunshine at all can be filled with foliage plants such as ferns, pick-a-back plant (*Tolmeia*), ivy, certain begonias, kangaroo vine, philodendron, and other tropical foliage plants if the temperature does not drop below 65 degrees F. at night. Even African violets may flower in northern exposure if the light is bright and not dimmed by close, high buildings.

The arrangement of a window garden can be improved by standing some pots on inverted pots or blocks. And generally you will want to turn the pots occasionally to enjoy the plants' best "faces," which usually develop toward the greatest amount of light.

OTHER INDOOR GARDENS

Many modern homes are being built with permanent indoor planters that are either raised or sunk below floor level, so that the plants in them appear to be growing from the ground. Most are rectangular in shape, but they can be round and only large enough to accommodate a single large plant. Temporary planters can be built of wood or metal or can be purchased. Some are made of plastic. They can be raised to waist level or rest on the floor. The depth of a planter should be about eight inches, even more for really large plants if plants are to grow directly in the planter. Two-tiered planters can be constructed: The top tier can derive its light from a window and the lower tier, a foot or so above the floor, can be lighted by fluorescent tubes installed above it on the bottom of the top tier.

An attractive bookshelf-planter combination can be made with a wall-hanging unit: The top shelves can be for books and a lower shelf, close to eye level, for plants. A fluorescent light fixture can be installed above the plant shelf and be camouflaged by a facing of wood. Other planters can be constructed to serve as room dividers or screens. Interesting effects can be obtained by painting them or covering them with some of the easy-to-apply materials like pressed cork or self-adhesive wall coverings.

All sorts of interesting miniature indoor gardens can be made in glass-enclosed containers. Terraria filled with small African violets, fittonia (a dainty creeper with precisely veined leaves), dwarf fig, baby's tears, or plants collected from the woods become a fascinating segment of the plant world. Equally intriguing to make and observe are bottle gardens, which can be made in apothecary jars, wine bottles, brandy snifters, or fish bowls. Once planted and enclosed, such glass gardens require a modicum of water only very occasionally. They should receive good light but not be allowed to bake in the sun. Other interesting minature gardens can be built in trays and low containers. Before making one of these, go to the library and observe how the Japanese make their tray gardens in one of the many books devoted to the subject. They are true works of art and bear no resemblance to the "dish gardens" found in florist shops.

About Containers

Pots and other containers for house plants can be important in the decorative picture and are another means whereby the homemaker can express personal taste and ingenuity. Plant groups at windows are so arranged that the pots are not evident, but elsewhere the container can be in as much of the spotlight as the plant itself. Containers should be in balance and harmony with the plants they hold as well as their surroundings. There is no problem today in finding suitable, handsome containers. Redwood tubs, soy tubs of bamboo and wood, oak tubs, and tubs of brass are all fine for large, treelike plants; the one you select depends on the rest of your decor. Clay pots of various shapes—especially those imported from Italy and Mexico—are still the best for the health of most plants. Antique and secondhand shops yield other containers, and there is no reason why you cannot use one of your own treasured antiques. Some antiques are more appreciated when put to a practical use. Plastic pots can be serviceable even if they are not always beautiful. Some of the colors used for plastic pots are improving. Any plastic container lacking drainage holes can have them punched in by inserting a red-hot ice pick or awl a few times in the bottom. Heat the pick by holding it over a stove burner for a few minutes.

Choose Your Plant

Plants to Grow in Water
      Paper-white Narcissus   English ivy
      Hyacinth   Chinese evergreen

Heart-leaf philodendron
German ivy
Sweet potato yam or vine

Umbrella plant
Wandering Jew

Fragrance in Foliage and Flowers

Paper-white Narcissus
Hyacinth
Freesia
Citrus
Gardenia
Scented-leaved geraniums
Rosemary

Jade plant
Star jasmine
Myrtle
Snake plant
Sweet olive
Wax plant

Plants for Cool Garden Rooms or Window Gardens

Gardenia
Camellia
Sweet olive
Freesia
Cyclamen
Ivy
Primrose
Oleander

Veltheimia
Norfolk Island pine
Geraniums
Azalea
Chrysanthemum
Podocarpus
Spring bulbs
Many orchids

Easy-to-Grow Plants

Philodendron
Jade plant
Chinese evergreen
Grape ivy
Kangaroo vine
Screw pine
Palm
Dracena

Cast-iron plant
India rubber plant
Cacti (for sun)
Snake plant
Nephthytis
Dumb cane
Monstera
Spider plant

Foliage Plants for Big, Bold Effects

Cast-iron plant	Dracena
Large-leaved philodendrons	Snake plant
Monstera	Umbrella tree (schefflera)
Fig plants	Umbrella plant (Cyperus)
Boston and other ferns	Fatshedera
Norfolk Island pine	Podocarpus
Large-leaved begonias	Screw pine
Palm	Fatsia
Dumb cane	

Plants with Variegated or Colored Foliage

Coleus	Tradescantia
Many begonias	Dumb cane
Variegated ivy	Nephthytis green gold
Wax plant	Variegated Chinese evergreen
Hawaiian ti	Snake plant
Dracena	Caladium
Variegated screw pine	Bromeliads
Golden pothos	Spider plant

Plants to Hang

Ivy geranium	Heart-leaf philodenron
Most scented-leaved geraniums	Most ferns
Kangaroo vine	Tradescantia
Pick-a-back plant	German ivy
English ivy	Fuchsia
Cleopatra begonia and others	Spider plant
Tradescantia (wandering Jew)	Strawberry geranium (or
Pothos	mother-of-thousands or
	strawberry begonia)

Plants to Train as Vines (usually need support)

Wax plant	Grape ivy

German ivy
Sweet potato yam or vine
English ivy
Dwarf fig

Kangaroo vine
Heart-leaf philodendron
Morning-glory (grow
  from seeds)

Plants for Sunny Windows

Cacti and succulents
Camellia
Azalea
Geraniums
Spring bulbs
Shrimp plant
Begonia
Star jasmine
Jade plant

Flowering maple
Crown of thorns
Chrysanthemum
Amaryllis
Paper-white narcissus
Hyacinth (in water)
Veltheimia
Herbs
Citrus

Plants for North Windows (and least-light areas)

Ferns
Monstera
Heart-leaf and other
  philodendrons
Cast-iron plant
Fatshedera
Grape ivy
Kangaroo vine
English ivy
India rubber plant

Chinese evergreen
Screw pine
Snake plant
Umbrella tree
Dumb cane
Nephthytis
Fittonia
Fatsia
Fiddle-leaf fig

Plants for East and West Windows (good light)

African violet
Gloxinia
Christmas cactus
Pick-a-back plant
Spider plant

Spathyphyllum
Peperomia
Coleus
Plus most of plants
  listed for sunny windows

CHAPTER TWENTY-NINE

MISCELLANEOUS AIDS

HERE AND THERE in previous chapters we have alluded to the fact that there are many free sources of decorating information available to most homemakers. Let's now analyze these in detail and see what the amateur decorator can reasonably expect to glean from them.

In most large cities there are one or more museums which present period rooms, authentic to the last detail in furniture and all the other components. There may not be a single room in the group which is in the style you prefer, but you can learn much from them. For example, you can see how the professional designer who put them together used colors and patterns for an over-all effect, how furniture was arranged, how paintings, bric-a-brac, and other accessories were distributed, how windows were treated. The Metropolitan Museum of Art in New York has seventeenth- and eighteenth-century French, English, and Italian rooms, plus the American Wing which includes dozens of complete room settings and vignettes, all with sound ideas. Perhaps a room suggests one idea you can use with a bit of adaptation and that leads to this important fact to remember as you view museum displays: Study a room not for a literal translation in your home, but as a springboard for your imagination. Use what you see as an exercise in design; try to see why the professional arranged the components as he did.

In some cities, Dayton, Ohio, for example, the local museum is itself an interesting old home which has been revamped for use as a museum. In this case the structure has architectural details, room arrangements, and other features that may offer ideas. A stairway treatment, a ceiling lighting fixture, the moldings and woodwork, the illumination of artworks—any of these may present possibilities for adaptation to your own rooms.

Remember, too, that there is a wealth of ideas for color schemes in the painting galleries of all museums. Famous artists usually had an infallible instinct for putting colors together and a painting can suggest a combination you never had thought of. Some museums sell prints of good quality of the paintings they show and these can be framed to lend special character to your own walls. Other meticulous reproductions of ancient artifacts are offered in museum shops and these make fine decorative accessories. Just don't go overboard and use too many of them or you'll run the risk of having your living room look like the museum shop.

And while we're on the subject of museums, the larger ones offer free lectures on certain subjects which may add to your storehouse of design information. Ask for a program of events; there may be a subject that intrigues you.

House Tours

The restoration of Colonial Williamsburg by John D. Rockefeller, Jr., in the 1920s did more to call attention to the value of old and historic homes and the necessity of their preservation than any other event in our design history. It also gave wealthy families the idea of turning over fine structures to the municipal, state, or federal government and reaping the tax benefits. With the help of local preservation groups and, often, the National Trust for Historic Preservation, such homes have been meticulously restored with authentic furniture and all components skillfully chosen and arranged by top professional designers. These old structures are especially helpful for the amateur decorator because they present a co-ordinated, house-wide design plan. As one travels through the rooms one can study the relationship of the color schemes, wall, floor, and window treatments and arrive at a better understanding of how to manipulate these elements in an over-all plan. As you travel around the United States on vacation, watch for signs and literature on such historic homes and take time to leave the beaten path to visit them.

In addition to single examples, some cities have annual tours of their best designed houses. Natchez, Mississippi, has a famous pilgrimage; New York; New Orleans; Key West, Florida; Litchfield, Connecticut; and scores of other cities in all parts of the country have civic groups which organize public tours of the most interesting local residences. Most often these homes have been restored and decorated by professionals, so again, you have an opportunity to see sound design principles at work. There are always hostesses on hand who can give you specific information on details of each room you visit, so if a fabric or an accessory interests you, you can often find out how to locate it for your own design scheme. There will be a tendency to rush you through these homes, but try to avoid this so that you can study the rooms in some detail. You may not like many of them; they may not be at all to your taste of present interest in terms of period style, but again, use them as an exercise. For example, a room or a house may not at first reveal its underlying color scheme. You may have to observe carefully to decide which are the three or four basic colors and which are the accents. You may see an alternate furniture arrangement and can compare its advantages or disadvantages to the one the designer chose to use. You may not like a certain patterned fabric, but the way it was balanced with other patterns can give you an idea.

MODEL ROOMS IN STORES

At the outset, a word of caution is necessary. You must remember as you view and study this type of room that it is a promotional display, deliberately designed to stimulate the sale of furniture and other decoration components. For that reason, the best of such model rooms may be completely unsuited to family living. The secret of gaining design tips from them is to scale the ideas down. In each case there is a basic idea the professional designer was trying to present—perhaps a contemporary statement on new lighting techniques, or a way of using a modern fabric pattern on antique upholstered furniture, or how a change in level in a high-ceilinged room can give it a whole new dimension. Once you have discovered the underlying concept, you can then put the design pieces together, as it were, and use or discard them according to your own taste and needs. As you study these rooms, remember that they are essentially a stage set with a missing wall, so that what furniture is used would be placed differently in an actual, four-walled room. Remember, too, that display illumination is far brighter than what would be desired in an inhabited room, that colors are apt to be either more intense or muted than those for comfortable living, that patterns may be overscaled and furniture too packed in.

In most department and furniture stores the designers who styled the room or rooms are on staff and should be available to discuss aspects of the design with you. If not too busy, they are usually pleased to hear pertinent questions that show they have hit the decorative mark and will be glad to tell why or how they did a certain thing in the plan. Remember, they are also interested in selling store merchandise, so don't be bashful about approaching them. And don't feel that you have to buy necessarily. If possible, it's best to view a collection of model rooms quite soon after they are opened to the public, simply because as time goes on, individual pieces of furniture may be sold off the floor and others substituted which are not exactly right, or rather not what the designer originally considered right.

HOME-SERVICE MAGAZINES

Today's newsstand is well stocked with decorating magazines, some monthly, others special issues that appear semiannually or quarterly. Some of these offer photographs and printed information of top quality; others are simply a patchwork of free photographs that an editor has received from various publicity sources which promote home-furnishings products. In some cases, the publicity pictures are of display rooms designed by top professionals and are full of excellent ideas. In others, they are badly conceived and photographed product puffery. Leaf through the magazine before buying it and notice the weight of the paper, the quality of the color printing and the general layout. If they seem flimsy and cheap, the chances are that the design ideas presented in the room settings are not the best either. Go to the quality magazines whose names have been a household word for many years; chances are they have the best and most exclusive material, rooms by the best professionals, and printed matter that is ideaful and sound.

If a photograph of a room setting appeals to you, study it and read the caption. It should tell you why a design treatment was used and give pointers that will be helpful in your own problems, even though the scheme may not be exactly what you want. In fact, it will almost never be. Many women keep a loose-leaf collection of such magazine pages they can refer to long after the issue itself has been discarded. Group the clipped pages under specific headings for easy reference— window treatments in one envelope or section, flooring ideas in another, color schemes in a third, and so on. Notice, too, that many of the special decorating issues have pages devoted to brochures on various subjects that are available for a nominal mailing cost. These are promotional pamphlets from manufacturers of decorating components and even though they are "selling" merchandise they often have a wealth of information and visual ideas from some of the best interior designers in the country. And if you are interested in buying a given component, you should find pertinent information on its construction and function that will help you to decide on one or another competitive product.

TELEVISION AND FILMS

As you view the ubiquitous tube or sit in a movie theater, don't get so involved in the plot that you fail to notice the room settings. A lot of careful thought on the part of skilled set designers goes into the backgrounds of the best TV programs and films, and with color presentations, the schemes are very closely thought out. In cases where historical accuracy is important, you can be sure that a lot of research went into the designs. The networks and film companies are sticklers for authenticity, because if mistakes are made, they are flooded with letters. So you can usually be sure of sound periodicity. Set designers usually know the market for new merchandise, so a new lamp or type of sofa or headboard presented is available on the market. Note the name of the set designer and write to him. He'll be flattered that you noticed and chances are you'll get a reply with a resource where you can find a given component.

PAINT, WALLPAPER, AND FABRIC SHOPS

These are other valuable sources of free information. The best paint stores feature racks of color chips of various paints they sell. When trying to decide on a color scheme, choose a dozen or more chips that interest you, take them home and juggle and compare until you have the three main colors and a few accents. Too often homemakers think of these free color samples merely in terms of a color for a wall or a single piece of furniture. To the amateur interior designer they offer far more.

Paint and department stores have wallpapers, too, and a patterned paper can suggest a color scheme. You can get free swatches of papers to take with you and mull over until you decide on a scheme. You can or cannot use the given paper in your room, but you can capitalize on a group of colors put together by a professional wallpaper designer who is a skilled color stylist. This gives you an almost foolproof scheme.

A fabric store is another gold mine of help. A group of swatches may be yours for the asking and, again, you can use the colors together with assurance that they are correct.

And in this light, don't forget the wealth of brochures and free samples available from home shows. Manufacturers set up displays specifically to present ideas and give information on their wares.

All in all, there is a world of ideas available to you at little or no cost. It's all in knowing how to use what is, essentially, an embarrassment of riches in home furnishings.

A FINAL WORD

IF YOU HAVE persevered through the foregoing pages, we hope that you have gained an insight, if not a rather thorough knowledge, of the basics of interior design. In any case, you have discovered a springboard into the exciting world of decoration and taken a first strong step as an amateur decorator. We have attempted here to outline the principles, so it is important to point out that the components of decor that are available in the market place change constantly so that you have an ever-widening range of choice in designs, materials, and treatments. The world of man-made fibers and plastics will expand tremendously as time goes on and, here again, they will bring new stimulus to your imagination. By using what you have gleaned in these pages along with new discoveries, you can add to the excitement of your environment.

All in all, the greatest satisfaction this book can bring is in helping you create a more stimulating and rewarding life style for you and your family. That is the true reward of a well-designed and decorated home—that it coalesces all the facets that make for a serene and productive life, that it becomes the center and end-all for happy times and purposeful pursuits. If our book has in any way contributed to this goal, we feel that we have hit the mark. With this thought we wish you a warm welcome into the adventure of decoration, perhaps the most enjoyable and certainly the most personal of creative endeavors.

INDEX